Emotional Development and Intellectual Disability

A guide to understanding emotional development and its implications

Jac de Bruijn, Jolanda Vonk,
Ad van den Broek and Brian Twint

Pavilion

Emotional Development and Intellectual Disability

A guide to understanding emotional development and its implications

Published by:
Pavilion Publishing and Media Ltd
Blue Sky Offices, 25 Cecil Pashley Way
Shoreham-by-Sea, West Sussex
BN43 5FF

Tel: 01273 434 943
Email: info@pavpub.com
Web: www.pavpub.com

Published 2021

A catalogue record for this book is available from the British Library.

English language version

ISBN: 978-1-914010-58-3

Pavilion Publishing and Media is a leading publisher of books, training materials and digital content in mental health, social care and allied fields. Pavilion and its imprints offer must-have knowledge and innovative learning solutions underpinned by sound research and professional values.

Editors: Jac de Bruijn, Jolanda Vonk, Ad van den Broek and Brian Twint.
Production editor: Louisa Robertson, Pavilion Publishing and Media Ltd
Cover design: Emma Dawe, Pavilion Publishing and Media Ltd
Page layout and typesetting: Phil Morash, Pavilion Publishing and Media Ltd
Printing: Severn

Contents

Preface

As an undergraduate I remember attending a seminar on 'The Mentally Retarded' and hearing this statement from a recognised scholar: 'No brain … no pain'. This statement has remained with me all these years because it reflects how many people historically have viewed people with intellectual disabilities as different and, because of their difference, as lacking the same hopes, dreams, frustrations and, yes, emotions as those who are 'normal'. Yet, in most of my conversations with individuals with intellectual disabilities, I have been (and still am) impressed by how normal their emotions are, given the situations they have experienced and the lack of opportunities they have had.

Given the above, as I read the introductory chapter of this manual and studied carefully the table of contents, it became clear to me that contributors to this text faced three challenges: first, how to conceptualise emotional behaviour; second, how to align that conceptualisation to emotional development and its assessment; and third, how to integrate and balance the qualities of emotional behaviour that are common to all people with the manifestation of emotional behaviour in people with intellectual disabilities. Addressing these three challenges is not an easy task, and I applaud the editors and contributors for acknowledging the key role that emotional behaviour plays in the lives of people with intellectual disabilities, and for sharing their current efforts to: (a) conceptualise the development of emotional behaviour in people with intellectual disabilities (part I), (b) describe the relation between emotional development research and practical situations (part II) and (c) discuss the assessment of emotional development and the application of this information to services and supports (part III).

In our efforts to understand emotional development and its expression in the lives of people with intellectual disabilities, I would like to propose that readers and users of this manual stand outside the box and ask themselves the following four 'what if' questions.

What if we view emotional development and behaviour in people with intellectual disabilities from a positive rather than a negative perspective?

Historically, there has been more attention paid to negative rather than positive emotions in people with intellectual disabilities. This emphasis on negativity reflects the historical focus on defects and pathology, rather than strengths, potential and capacities. Recently, the principles of positive psychology, the capacities approach to disability and the concept of quality of life have shifted the focus of research and practice to a focus on personal well-being, individual strengths, positive emotions and similarities in emotional experience. In reference to the last of these, there are strong similarities cross-culturally in the expression of happiness/enjoyment, sadness, anger, fear, surprise and disgust. These are generally viewed as normal emotions, which we have all seen expressed in people with intellectual disabilities across cultures, ages, genders, situations and degrees of functional limitation.

What if we view emotional development and behaviour as an adaptive behaviour?

As commonly defined, adaptive behaviour is the collection of conceptual, social and practical skills that have been learned and performed by people in their everyday lives. Furthermore, adaptive behaviour is (a) developmental and increases in complexity with age, (b) related to the expectations of age and demands of particular contexts, (c) assessed on the basis of the individual's typical performance and (d) assessed in reference to the community settings that are typical for age peers. By viewing emotional development and behaviour from an adaptive behaviour perspective, one can assess its direct and indirect influence on cognitive, social and practical skills, and use multiple teaching strategies and augmentative communication systems to assist in the performance of conceptual, social and practical adaptive skills. For example, teaching strategies and augmentative communication systems assist in learning or performing conceptual skills, such as effectively communicating thoughts and ideas; social skills, such as learning from experience; and practical skills, such as self-care and maintaining a safe environment.

What if we view emotional development and behaviour as a support need?

Viewing emotional development and behaviour as a support need is consistent with the current supports paradigm that posits that one can mitigate a person's disability by designing individualised interventions, services and supports based on understanding and addressing the individual's support needs. Viewing emotional development and behaviour from this perspective has two significant implications. First, it focuses on efforts to identify the supports that a person needs to participate more successfully in normal life activities, and, second, it emphasises a holistic approach to supports provision. This holistic approach encompasses systems of supports that are interconnected networks of resources and strategies that promote the development and interests of a person and enhance the individual's functioning and personal well-being. Effective systems of supports are characterised as (a) being person centred, comprehensive, co-ordinated and outcome oriented and (b) encompassing choice and personal autonomy, inclusive environments, generic supports and specialised supports.

What if we view emotional development and behaviour as a quality of life domain?

Emotional well-being is a widely recognised quality of life (QOL) domain. Our cross-cultural work in QOL has validated the universal nature of the emotional well-being domain and its enhancement through the application of support strategies based on principles and practices related to equity, empowerment, inclusion and self-determination. Viewing emotional development and behaviour as a core QOL domain also implies a focus on environmental and contextual enabling factors. These factors include living in safe, secure and predictable environments; promoting a sense of well-being; maximising capabilities and opportunities; and having the freedom to engage in major life activities.

There is a remaining question: is it possible to integrate all four of these 'what ifs' into an integrative conceptual model that provides the basis for theory development, application and research? It is worth considering. For example, in an integrative conceptual model, emotional development and behaviour are viewed from a positive perspective and considered an adaptive behaviour skill. As an adaptive behaviour skill, individualised systems of supports are provided to facilitate the individual's adaptation to and involvement in regular life activities. These supports incorporate support values and support facilitating conditions. As a core QOL domain, public policies and service delivery patterns focus on the QOL principles and environmental/contextual conditions that facilitate one's emotional well-being.

In conclusion, this manual's editors, advisory board members and contributors recognise and acknowledge the complexity of emotional development in people with intellectual disabilities. This complexity is due in part to the fact that emotionality has a cognitive/appraisal component, a physiological/subjective component and a behavioural/expressive component. Added to this complexity is the frequent co-occurrence of intellectual disabilities and mental disorders. Despite the challenges that this complexity creates, contributors to the manual believe that it is time for the field to embark on a scientific and sound approach to understanding the development and expression of emotionality in people with intellectual disabilities, and to develop those interventions, services and supports that enhance its appropriate and full expression. This manual is a significant contribution to that effort.

Robert L Schalock, PhD
December 2020

Editorial

Jac de Bruijn, Jolanda Vonk, Ad van den Broek and Brian Twint

This is in many ways a remarkable manual. In recent years there has been a marked increase in the attention paid around the world to emotional development in the care and support of people with intellectual disabilities. Anton Došen has played a pioneering role in this on a national and international level since the 1980s, not only by developing a theoretical model of basic emotional needs but also by drawing up an experiential scale that has offered a solution for professionals seeking to better understand their clients in all their developmental aspects. For decades, work is this area has focused only on assessing and recording the cognitive capacities or intellectual disabilities of clients. However, this ultimately did not meet the basic needs of the clients. Understanding the client nowadays also involves a focus on other aspects, including 'emotional development'. Understanding people's emotional development and resilience requires us to understand people's contexts or environments, and this applies especially to people with intellectual disabilities. Aware of the important role of emotional development, a number of enthusiastic professionals founded the Dutch National Network Emotional Development (LNEO), and recently further professionals working in care and research have formed international collaborations through the Network of Europeans on Emotional Development (NEED), a special interest group of the International Association for the Scientific Study of Intellectual and Developmental Disabilities (IASSIDD). It is their mission to promote professional research and practice in relation to emotional development. In 2015 some professionals in the Netherlands decided to jointly publish a manual on emotional development in people with intellectual disabilities. Colleagues in Berlin and Ghent co-operated in this first publication. It did not stop there. Research and practice activities intensified, and meetings took place. What you find in this manual is the result of this international collaboration. Thanks are primarily due to our colleagues who have contributed. They work every day in the conviction that exchanging experiences and research will lead to better understanding and support. We were guided by an international advisory board, so we would like to thank its members: Anton Došen, Angela Hassiotis, Mark Hudson, Filip Morisse and Tanja Sappok. We would like especially to thank our friends at Pavilion Publishing, who have been enthusiastic from the start, for making this endeavour a reality. We of course would also like to thank Robert Schalock for his valuable preface. Thanks to all of them, this has become a special manual.

Introduction

Jac de Bruijn, Jolanda Vonk, Ad van den Broek and Brian Twint

The attention currently paid to the emotional development of people with intellectual disabilities is only a recent phenomenon. The subject has only been at the centre of attention since the early 1980s. At that time, Anton Došen made an initial contribution on this theme in the field of the care for people with intellectual disabilities. Since then more attention has been paid to emotional development not only in this field but also more broadly. For example, there has been a steadily growing emphasis on social and emotional aspects in support, in schools and education and in mental health research, for instance in relation to stress and trauma. However, the importance of emotional development, especially for people with intellectual disabilities, remains socially and culturally underappreciated. This has to be addressed. A special focus on emotional development is necessary for a more balanced view of educational and support practices. The American educational expert Linda Darling-Hammond states: 'I have no doubt that the survival of the human species depends on at least cultivating social and emotional intelligence, as is the case for the development of technological knowledge and skills' (Durlak *et al.* 2015, p. xi).

Meanwhile the attention on emotional development has become an integral part of caring for people with intellectual disabilities. It is not only in the Dutch-speaking region that there are networks of interested people dealing with this theme, such as the Dutch National Network Emotional Development (LNEO) and the Belgian Steunpunt Expertise Netwerk - Schaal Emotionele Ontwikkeling SEN-SEO. On an international level there is an increasing attention on emotional development, for instance through the Network of Europeans on Emotional Development (NEED) group, a special interest group of the International Association for the Scientific Study of Intellectual and Developmental Disabilities (IASSIDD), and in Germany, Italy, Belgium and England researchers and practitioners are increasingly focusing on the relevance of emotional development for care and education.

From the moment Došen brought emotional development to our attention, we have seen various elaborations of this theme in the practice of caring for people with intellectual disabilities: for example, in the assessment of emotional development, in the attention paid to attachment and attachment problems, in the focus on stress and trauma, in the appreciation of the importance of emotions in the relationship between supervisor and client and in the recognition of the importance of the emotional functioning of the supervisors themselves.

Why is this important? Taking emotional development into account is not only a theoretical challenge. It is important because every human being is a whole person, with social, cognitive, moral, physiological and emotional characteristics. Emotional development should be a part of our approach to human beings and should be seen in connection to all other aspects. We cannot address one without the others. It is important to understand the aspect of emotional development if we are to understand one another, and this understanding should determine the way we support people with intellectual disabilities.

With this broadening of interest, there will be more discussion within the field of care for people with intellectual disabilities. More detail will be added to the content of emotional development in assessment and in support. In terms of scientific frameworks, several ways of looking at emotional development are already emerging, for example a personality model, a competence model and a functioning model. However, in these developments in the field of emotional development there is no consensus as to how to deal with this theme in practice. There are still professionals who, concerning a mature person with an intellectual disability, for example, will state: 'I treat her like a three-year-old.' People will recognise these sorts of statements from daily interactions with counsellors. They express a general consensus about people with intellectual disabilities. However, they also raise questions in relation to the client's development and life experience. Does age matter? In what way or in what sense?

In the current situation, possessing a certain degree of emotional development is not in itself an indication criterion for the right to receive care, despite the knowledge we have about the fact that the emotional development of the client is an important starting point in everyday practice. Only the cognitive level of the client, expressed in an IQ (intelligence quotient) score, is considered an indication for care. The limitations of this cognition-oriented approach have been sufficiently described (De Bruijn *et al.* 2014) but are not yet affirmed in actual practice. Looking at the extended descriptions of intellectual disabilities in the classifications of the *Diagnostic and Statistical Manual of Mental Disorders* (fifth edition) or the International Classification of Diseases (11th revision), developments in relation to emotional development seem more promising. These classifications reveal that social and emotional functioning aspects are increasingly as much of a focus as the degree of mental functioning. However, the aspect of emotional development is not (yet) visible in the international description of human functioning and intellectual disability. The fact that there is no consensus yet is not in itself a reason for concern; we are in the midst of a development in our knowledge.

Practice, concepts and theories require discussion, critical debate, reflection and research. We look at differences in views and perspectives with sympathy, and such differences are reflected in this book. A number of authors are guided by an approach focusing on a discrepancy between emotion and cognition (Došen's approach), while others do not share this view (Wijnroks and Ponsioen, for example). We also have authors who make their own specific choices about the approach to emotional development. Despite the existing diversity of opinions, the editors and contributing authors are convinced that it is important to chart the current state of affairs and present it to the field, so it becomes possible ultimately to see where improvements can be made in research and support and to assess the usefulness of the concept of emotional development itself. The manual is based on the idea of emotional development as a construct, a composition of important principles related to the use of the concept of emotional development. This concept becomes more reliable and meaningful when we enter into discussion with each other.

Reading guide

This manual provides an up-to-date overview of the most important thoughts, developments and methodical approaches in the field of the emotional development of people with intellectual disabilities. The manual contributes to a better understanding of emotional development for an important group of people in society, strengthens the scientific foundation of this field and provides insight into the most important developments. The manual consists of four parts.

The first part focuses on insights into the concept of 'emotional development' and its implications in relation to intellectual disability. In chapter 1, the editors describe the concept of emotional development itself. The multifaceted nature of the concept becomes clear by looking at it from different viewpoints. Approaching the concept of emotional development as a construct can be helpful in its application. In chapter 2, Anton Došen describes the neurobiological aspects of emotional development. Insight into these basic aspects partly determines the practical value of the concept of emotional development. Jolanda Vonk, in chapter 3, elaborates the different stages of emotional development, extending the stages developed by Došen with two further phases. A broader view is set out in chapter 4 by Albert Ponsioen, who describes the intense and inextricable connection between emotional development, social development and adaptation. In chapter 5, Lex Wijnroks outlines the relationship with cognitive development, including the neurological aspects described by Došen. He advocates a clearly different view and stresses a neurocognitive approach to emotional development.

In part two, a number of core themes of emotional development in relation to research and practical situations are discussed. One of these themes is attachment in people with a intellectual disability. In chapter 6, Paula Sterkenburg, Sandra

Zaal and Paula Dekkers-Verbon describe a healthy attachment relationship as a necessary condition for emotion regulation. In chapter 7, Tanja Sappok and Els Ronsse pay attention to the emotional development of adults with an autism spectrum disorder (ASD) and an intellectual disability. In particular, the combination of ASD and intellectual disability plays a negative role in emotional development. Sappok and Ronsse develop their own assessment approach. In chapter 8, Welmoed Visser-Korevaar and Jolanda Vonk describe the theme of sexual development in relation to emotional development in people with intellectual disabilities. Sexual development is directly related to emotional development, and knowledge of this is therefore indispensable for proper support and treatment. Tanja Sappok and Marco Bertelli discuss a common theme in the care of people with mental disabilities in chapter 9: the connection with psychological problems and mental health. Chapter 10, by Rita Erlewein, focuses on family and systemic approaches in relation to emotional development.

Part three of this manual deals with the practice of care, especially assessment and support. The first chapters focus on the Scale of Emotional Development (SED) and its variations, and the last three chapters on emotional development and support. Chapter 11 describes the assessment of emotional development in people with intellectual disabilities. Stijn Vandevelde and Angelique Peters describe not only the instruments but also the context and conditions for an adequate diagnostic approach to emotional development. The instruments mentioned in this chapter are discussed in more detail in the following chapters. Tanja Sappok and Marieke Conty describe the Scale of Emotional Development – Short (SED-S) in chapter 12, setting out the content of this scale and discussing its reliability and validity. Chapter 13, by Filip Morisse, Soetkin Roskam, Leen De Neve and Anton Došen, focuses more extensively on the Scale of Emotional Development – Revised^2 (SED-R^2) as a diagnostic assessment instrument. In chapter 14, Rachel de Groot combines the SED-R^2 with the 'colour profile' as a specific tool for supporting the process of estimating developmental levels. In chapter 15, Bren Hesper, Rachel de Groot, Robert Didden and Henk Nijman show that research and diagnostics are developing rapidly within a specific area of care: the SED and risk assessment for people with a mild intellectual disability in forensic settings.

Ad van den Broek makes a contribution to support in chapter 16, which provides a general introduction to support in relation to emotional development, based on Došen's developmental dynamic model. The next chapter, 17, emphasises the use by parents and caregivers of information and communication technology devices to help with the regulation of emotions. Paula Sterkenburg and Vernandi Dyzel make clear how important this is for social relationships. Erik De Belie and Nicole Vliegen outline in chapter 18 the consequences of disorganised attachment for the child and their context and elaborate on therapeutic interventions aimed at recovery. Part III closes with a contribution by Gerrit Vignero, in chapter 19. He offers a specific approach, 'the thread', that aims to help supervisors and parents to deal appropriately with socio-emotional development.

Finally, part four consists of two chapters. Chapter 20 provides an overview of this manual by the editors. We review the contributions and the current state of affairs. We also look ahead, tracing some lines of development we can identify for future theory and research. The last chapter, 21, turns to the members of the advisory board, who each provide a statement on the overall theme of emotional development and intellectual disability.

A note on the text

Specific attention needs to be paid to the use of core concepts in this manual. Should we use 'stage' or 'phase' for example? In this manual we generally use the term 'stage' to refer to a part of the developmental process, as in the work of Erikson (1994).

Another core issue concerns the way we use 'diagnosis' or 'assessment'. We prefer the latter. The main reason for this lies in the process of interpreting developmental stages. To assess the developmental stage, one can use diagnostic instruments. So diagnostics are a means used to pursue the goal of assessment. A scale like the SED does help to assess the developmental stage, but it does not provide a diagnostic classification of this stage.

Editors

Jac de Bruijn is an independent consultant for healthcare and society (www.youcare.site) with more than 30 years' of experience in healthcare, especially for people with a disability. He is a former member of the Board of Directors of Stichting Prisma and was previously head of treatment and mental health psychologist. He worked as a lecturer at the Erasmus Medical Center, to which he is now affiliated as a guest lecturer. He published several books together with others and is specialised in methods and interventions for people with intellectual disability. He is passionate about inclusion, inclusive research and ethics of care.

Jolanda Vonk studied educational science at the Free University of Amsterdam (VU, cum laude). She works as a senior behavioral scientist at ORO/Lore in the Netherlands. She has worked in the field of intellectual disability for more than 30 years as a healthcare psychologist, remedial educationalist, sexologist, supervisor and coach. Jolanda also works as a consultant for the Centre of Expertise and Consultation (CCE), a national organization in the Netherlands that is deployed on demand for complex problems of people with intellectual disability or mental health problems. For ten years she has provided training for post-graduate education and to organizations on emotional development, sexology and social interaction in the professional relationship. Jolanda has written several publications on emotional development. She is also a member of the Network of Europeans on Emotional Development (NEED, 2015), a Special Interest Group (SIG) of EAMHID.

Ad van den Broek worked as a healthcare psychologist in the care of people with intellectual disabilities. Today he works at FORTIOR, which he founded in 2006 and for which he is now responsible together with Catja van den Broek. His interest is mainly in emotional and personality development in the context of the developmental dynamic model, and in methods in the field of relationship, contact, communication and support.

Brian Twint studied social work at the Amsterdam University of Applied Sciences and after a period in youth services, has been working for years as a personal supervisor and project leader in the field of intellectual disability. Twint is the original designer of the 'Affectief Bewuste Benadering' (Affective Conscious Approach), initiator of the Expertise Centre in Intellectual Disability in the Netherlands, and author of several books about and for people with intellectual disabilities.

A number of editors and authors are members of EAMHID and its special interest group 'NEED', also members of IASSIDD, working in the field of ID, as well as in universities doing research on emotional development.

Advisory board

In co-operation with the publisher, Pavilion, we have been able to produce this international and unique book. In order to optimise its quality, we wished to ensure critical and constructive feedback on the ideas included and choices made. To this end an advisory board was set up. All its members have contributed to the field of intellectual disability and emotional development and have ongoing commitments to research and practice. The members of the advisory board were asked to review the manual's content, structure, completeness and consistency. They were also willing to contribute to a closing chapter.

Members of the advisory board

Anton Došen, extraordinary professor of psychiatric aspects of intellectual disability at Radboud University Nijmegen (Netherlands), psychiatrist. For more than 30 years, he has worked on the development of psychiatric diagnostics and the treatment of problem behaviour and psychiatric disorders in people with intellectual disabilities, with a special focus on emotional development. To this end, he developed a scale, the SED, which is now used in various countries. He also leads various postgraduate courses and national and international projects to promote mental health in people with intellectual disabilities.

Angela Hassiotis, professor of psychiatry of intellectual disability at University College London and specialist consultant psychiatrist at the Camden Learning Disability Service, with a broad focus on people with intellectual disabilities: studies of perpetrators with intellectual disabilities, epidemiological studies of older people with intellectual disabilities (with and without Down's syndrome), evaluation of psychological interventions for challenging behaviour and cognitive behaviour therapy for common mental disorders, the measurement of stigma and its impact on well-being.

Mark Hudson, clinical psychologist at Autism East Midlands and assistant professor at the University of Nottingham. Particular areas of interest are developmental and relationship-based approaches for people with intellectual disability and autism, emotional development, attachment and developmental trauma in mentally challenged youth, neurodevelopmental problems and youth in the healthcare system. In these areas, he works with families using video feedback and systemic family therapy approaches.

Filip Morisse, care manager in the Psychiatric Centre Dr Guislain in Ghent. He has more than 25 years of experience in psychiatry observing and treating adults with intellectual disabilities and is currently doing a PhD on the SED-R. In addition, he offers consultant training and services in Flanders and the Netherlands and has a leading role in the SEN-SEO project in Flanders.

Tanja Sappok, head of the Department for Psychiatry, Psychotherapy and Psychosomatic Disorders and Manager Autism at the Queen Elisabeth Hospital in Berlin. She is an advisor/consultant in neurology, psychiatry and psychotherapy and lecturer at Charité –Berlin University of Medicine. She is a founder of NEED. Her scientific areas of interest are ASD, emotional development and problem behaviour in people with intellectual disabilities.

We offer special thanks to the members for their advice during the creation of this manual and for their contributions. Their efforts will help to ensure that the manual will fulfil its purposes of disseminating knowledge and contributing to the practice of everyday care and support.

Authors

Marco O. Bertelli, psychiatrist and psychotherapist, Scientific Director of CREA (Research and Clinical Center), San Sebastiano Foundation, Misericordia di Firenze, Florence, Italy, President of SIDiN (Italian Society for Neurodevelopmental Disorders), Past President of WPA-SPID (World Psychiatric Association – Section Psychiatry of Intellectual Disability), and Past President of the EAMHID (European Association for Mental Health in Intellectual Disability). Marco is consultant, supervisor and teacher for various Universities and health service providers as well as national and international research centres. Author of around 200 publications related to psychopathology, quality of life and nosology of autism spectrum disorders and intellectual developmental disorders. In 2011 he received the Honorary Life Membership of the World Psychiatric Association, for the excellence of service.

Marieke Conty is clinical psychologist with a focus on autism, developmental psychology and challenging behaviour. Marieke works in a large foundation (v. Bodelschwingh Foundation Bethel, Germany) that provides humanitarian and professional aid to people in need of support and assistance. She is Senior Area Manager of several supported and assisted living facilities for people with autism and intellectual disabilities. Her work includes leading the clinical psychologists' team and a specialist autism team. Marieke feels that working with the developmental approach with people with intellectual disabilities and teaching staff about this approach, can help with improving mental health and wellbeing of persons with intellectual developmental disorders.

Paula Dekkers-Verbon works as a scientist-practitioner in the research group 'Social Relations and Attachment' for people with visual or visual and intellectual disabilities, a combined effort of Bartiméus (an expert organisation concerned with people with visual disabilities) and the Department of Clinical Child and Family Studies of the Faculty of Behavioural and Movement Sciences of the Vrije Universiteit Amsterdam in the Netherlands. With a background in medical clinical practice (as a medical intern) and in the care for people with intellectual disabilities (as a behavioural expert), she now connects practice and research. Another project she is working on concerns stereotype and challenging behaviour in young children with visual and intellectual disabilities. Her special interests lie in early childhood development, infant mental health and attachment.

Erik De Belie is a behavioural therapist in special education and a psychodynamic child therapist. He is also part-time lecturer/researcher at the University College Ghent. Erik has extensive clinical experience as a therapist working with people with intellectual disabilities and their networks (families and residential care workers). He is recognised as a supervisor by the Flemish Association for Psychodynamic Therapy. In recent years he has published on intellectual disability, attachment, parenting, mentalisation, trauma and emotional availability. Erik also gives training, coaching and supervision to various teams and organisations that care for people with intellectual disabilities and their networks.

Leen De Neve is coordinator of a mobile team at P.C. Dr. Guislain (Belgium), working for adults with intellectual disability and mental health problems. She also takes care of consulting, education and training for organizations. Within the SEN-SEO-project in Flanders, Leen is one of the key players with special interest on the translation of the concept of emotional development into daily support.

Robert Didden is health care psychologist and researcher at Trajectum, a (forensic) facility at Zwolle. He is also professor at Behavioural Science Institute of the Radboud University at Nijmegen, The Netherlands. His clinical and research interests include addiction, aggression, and trauma in individuals with mild intellectual disabilities. He also published several international books in the field of care, support and interventions for people with intellectual disabilities.

Vernandi Dyzel is a researcher at the Department of Clinical Child and Family Studies of the Faculty of Behavioural and Movement Sciences at the Vrije Universiteit Amsterdam, in the Netherlands. Her work in the 'Social Relations and Attachment, Bartiméus – Vrije Universiteit Amsterdam' lab focuses on therapy and prevention in the field of persons with an intellectual disability. She has a master's degree in clinical psychology and is a registered clinical psychologist in South Africa. As a clinical psychologist, Dyzel has worked at several mental health and medical institutions and has experience in working with people with various disabilities, as well as their families.

Rita Erlewein studied human medicine in Tübingen and Heidelberg. She is specialist in paediatrics and neuropediatrics in developmental neurology at the University of Tübingen for 20 years. In Switzerland she was trained in child psychiatry, and working since 2011 on the development of a special unit for children and adolescents with ID and challenging behaviour. Since 2018 Rita is member of the NEED group. Training in systemic therapy and trauma therapy with special emphasis on children and adolescent trauma therapy.

Rachel de Groot is Health care psychologist and psychotherapist in training. at Dimence, a healthcare facility in Zwolle. Specialized in MID, challenging behaviour and emotional development and creative developer of the SED colour profile, which is widely used in the Netherlands and Belgium.

Bren Hesper is behavioural scientist and trainer at Trajectum, a forensic facility (Netherlands). His special interests are risk assessment, risk management and methods for holistic diagnostics of patients with mild intellectual disabilities.

Henk Nijman was Professor of Forensic Psychology at the Radboud University in Nijmegen, The Netherlands, and senior researcher at the forensic psychiatric institute Fivoor, The Netherlands. He passed away in February 2021, after finishing his contribution but before this guide was published. He will be remember as a well-valued colleague in the field of forensic psychiatry and the care of people with intellectual disabilities.

Angelique Peters is remedial educationalist generalist (https://www.nvo.nl/english-information.aspx) with a long experience in working with people with intellectual disabilities. She works as a therapist in a psychiatric institution, supporting persons with mental health problems combined with hearing disabilities and as consultant for CCE (https://cce.nl/about-cce). She is also Head Tutor at RINO Zuid for the education for remedial educationalist generalist.

Albert Ponsioen is chairman of the Gaming & Training Foundation (www.gamingandtraining.nl). The main objective of this foundation is developing interventions for children with executive function problems. One of their main products is Braingame Brian, a computerised training program. Until his retirement in 2020, Albert was working as a clinical neuropsychologist in an outpatient mental health care centre in the Netherlands for children with psychiatric problem, and as a staff member of a national research centre for children with intellectual disabilities (www.kenniscentrumlvb.nl). Special interests include children and youngsters with mild intellectual disabilities (MID), neuropsychological assessment and interventions, single case experimental design studies (www.e-sced.nl).

Els Ronsse is psychologist and psychotherapist at PsySense, a group practice in Flanders, which works with people with developmental disorders. Els is responsible for diagnostics, coaching of families and support for adults with autism. She has been working with people with intellectual disabilities and / or autism for 25 years, in both outpatient and residential settings, both as a consultant and as a supervisor. In addition, she has training and education on autism and/or emotional development in Flanders and the Netherlands. Els is also chair of the SEN-SEO project in Flanders, which aims at the development of knowledge, dissemination and raising awareness about emotional development.

Soetkin Roskam master in Special Education at Ghent University, worked for 16 years as remedial educationalist in a service center for people with an intellectual disability, where she organized the implementation of the SED. Since 2014 Soetkin works as staff member for intake, training and support at Styrka, a multifunctional center for children with intellectual disabilities. Soetkin worked as an active member of the SEN-SED project (i.e. the preparation of the SED-R), and a few years later on the revision to the SED-R^2. Since 2012, she has provided basic training on emotional development, on the SED-R^2 and on the translation to daily practice.

Robert L. Schalock has participated in the Editorial Boards of a number of different journals, including the *American Journal on Mental Retardation* (now *American Journal on Intellectual and Developmental Disabilities*), *Journal on Intellectual and Developmental Disabilities*, and the *Journal of Intellectual Disability Research*. He has been Member and Chair of the Board of numerous associations and is a former President of the American Association on Mental Retardation. He is also a member of numerous Committees of the American Association on Intellectual and Developmental Disabilities. Schalock has published books and articles on personal and program outcomes, the supports paradigm, adaptive behaviour, clinical judgment, and quality of life. He also travels across the world consulting on human service issues.

Paula Sterkenburg has a chair by special appointment in 'Persons with a visual or visual and intellectual disability, social relations and ICT' at the Department of Clinical Child and Family Studies of the Faculty of Behavioural and Movement Sciences and the Amsterdam Public Health (APH) research centre of the Vrije Universiteit Amsterdam, in the Netherlands. She is a licensed psychologist/therapist and works at Bartiméus Department of Psychotherapy in Doorn. She has received many awards for the way in which she has built bridges between research and practice. She is author and co-author of several books and publishes articles on persons with intellectual disabilities concerning social relations and information and communication technology.

Stijn Vandevelde is an associate professor at the Department of Special Needs Education ("Orthopedagogiek") of Ghent University, Belgium. His research interests focus on support of persons (both adolescents and adults) in vulnerable situations and their social network, including persons with intellectual disabilities and co-occurring mental health problems, adolescents with emotional and behavioral problems and persons with addiction problems, amongst others. Much of his research is grounded in a strengths-based approach, focusing on abilities, rather than exclusively on problems. An overview of publications can be consulted at: https://biblio.ugent.be/person/F5E90A2C-F0ED-11E1-A9DE-61C894A0A6B4

Gerrit Vignero has a master's degree in special education (KU Leuven, 1986). He works as a supervisor in an institute for children with intellectual disorders in Leuven. He has completed additional courses on contextual therapy, developmental psychology, 'discovery awareness' (the Heijkoop method) and the SED (Anton Došen). He developed the 'thread' model and method and has more than 10 years of experience applying this in Flanders and the Netherlands. He provides courses on the method in high schools and provides training, supervision and InterVision. Contact: gerritvignero@gmail.com or www.gerritvignero.be.

Welmoed Visser-Korevaar is orthopedagogue NVO and sexologist, NVVS. She has been working as a private practitioner for orthopedagogic consultancy 'Welmoed' since 2005. Welmoed is specialized in sexology among people with an intellectual disability (ID), with ASD and in youth in residential youth care, both research and treatment. With her expertise she also works since 2005 as a consultant for the Center for Consultation and Expertise (CCE) in the Netherlands, which focuses on complex casuistic. Besides this Welmoed gives lectures and trainings in the field of sexology in combination with her other specializations and writes a 2 montly column in a magazine about sexology issues in the care for people with an ID. She is also the secretary of the Dutch scientific society for sexology (NVVS).

Nicole Vliegen is a child psychologist and psychotherapist, and Full Professor in the Research group Clinical Psychology at KU Leuven. She has extensive clinical and research expertise in the domain of the development and treatment of children with traumatic experiences. She heads a psychodynamic team at PraxisP, the practice center of the Faculty of Psychology and Educational Sciences at KU Leuven. In that position she leads a two-year training in Infant Mental Health as well as a four-year postgraduate training in psychodynamic child psychotherapy at KU Leuven. She is co-author of several internationally and nationally published peer reviewed papers, and has co-reviewed several books in her areas of expertise.

Lex Wijnroks is a developmental psychologist with a specific interest in developmental neuropsychology. He started in 1997 as an assistant professor at the University of Utrecht and became an associate professor in 2017. He provides education in the field of developmental psychology, neuropsychology, neuropsychological diagnostics and care for people with intellectual disabilities. His research area concerns the early development of cognition, emotion, perception and attention in typical and atypical populations. In his recent publications he highlights new neuroscientific insights and explains how these insights can contribute to more knowledge and understanding of the functioning of people with intellectual disabilities.

Sandra Zaal studied clinical pedagogy at the University of Amsterdam. She works as a licensed psychologist/therapist at Cordaan, where she helps children and young people who have intellectual disabilities and often have additional problems. She also works with parents with intellectual disabilities and their children. Furthermore, she has many years of experience as a licensed psychologist in special needs education for children with severe learning difficulties. In her work, Zaal likes to focus on emotional development, attachment and sexual development.

References

Bruijn, J de, Buntinx, W, & Twint, B (Eds) (2014) *Verstandelijke beperking: definitie en context.* Amsterdam: SWP.

Durlak, JA, Domitrovich, CE, Weissberg, RP & Gullotta, TP (Eds) (2015) *Handbook of Social and Emotional Learning: Research and practice.* New York/London: Guilford Press.

Erikson, EH (1994) *Identity: Youth and crisis.* London: WW Norton & Company.

Schalock, RL, Borthwick-Duffy, SA, Bradley, VJ, Buntinx, WHE, Coulter, DL, Craig, EMP, Yeager, MH (2010) *Intellectual Disability: Definition, classification, and systems of supports* (11th edition). Washington: AAIDD.

Part I
Theoretical frameworks

Chapter 1
Emotional development and intellectual disability: introduction to a dynamic concept

Jac de Bruijn, Jolanda Vonk, Ad van den Broek and Brian Twint

Summary

This chapter focuses on the concept of emotional development in relation to different approaches used in care and support. Starting from overall personal development, we look at what emotional development means in relation to intellectual disability. Within the practice of daily care and support and treatment, emotional development is a common, even dominant concept. At the same time, there is a lack of clarity about its meaning, both in theory and in practice. Questions are asked about the value of emotional development, its reliability and its relationship to other aspects of development. After looking at definitions of emotion and emotional development provided by existing theories, we outline a broader frame for thinking about the concepts. This frame includes different perspectives or 'lenses' through which emotional development can be viewed: philosophical and social visions, the international vision of the American Association on Intellectual and Developmental Disabilities (AAIDD) and the framework of quality of care of the Dutch Disability Care Association (*Vereniging Gehandicaptenzorg Nederland, VGN*). It turns out that looking through the lenses of developmental psychology, upbringing or education places different accents on emotional development. No final definition is provided; rather, emotional development is presented as a 'construct', a basis for further theorisation, research and use in daily practice.

1 Emotions and development: a clarification

In the practice of care and support, different questions arise about what we understand by emotional development in relation to intellectual disability. All people have feelings and emotions. Everyone feels 'moved' from time to time, and expressions of emotion dominate the internet and other means of communication. However, what people understand by emotions and feelings differs from person to person. The meaning they give to their emotion is related not only to the environment and the event that occurs but also to the history of the person in question. Emotions and the way in which we experience them therefore always have contexts and histories and always undergo certain developments. This is no different for people with intellectual disabilities. Emotional development is nowadays often a focus in care for people with intellectual disabilities. Care or support plans advise connecting as closely as possible to the emotional development of clients. Behavioural scientists emphasise, in addition to the importance of cognitive functioning, the importance of the emotional developmental stage in diagnostic research. It is therefore important to clarify the concept of emotional development.

There are four reasons for this clarification. First, emotional development itself is not easy to distinguish from other concepts in a person's developmental process. Even the concept of 'emotion' itself is used with different meanings, such as (a variation in) feelings, a certain set of basic emotions, affects (such as various moods) or specific behaviour that fits a certain inner experience. The term 'emotional development' is not used unambiguously either: it is described as a 'stage-related' process, an 'emotional functioning' or 'emotional competence(s) or skills', or it is distinguished from a term such as 'emotional intelligence'.

Second, the approach to emotional development as a separate aspect of development is not without its problems. Sometimes it is not mentioned at all as a developmental aspect on its own (Kohnstamm, 2009), and it is often difficult to ascertain how the various developmental aspects, such as cognitive, motor, sexual, moral, linguistic or social development and the development of conscience, are interrelated. Personality theories and developmental theories are based on an integral idea of human development. The place of a separate dimension such as emotional development is difficult to distinguish.

Third, the practical meaning of emotional development in the assessment and support of people with intellectual disabilities is still insufficiently clear. This manual discusses assessment and research instruments (e.g. the Scale of Emotional Development – Revised2 and the Scale of Emotional Development – Short; see part III) as having possible applications for research into emotional development.

What implications does knowledge of the emotional development of people with intellectual disabilities have for psychodiagnostics, treatment and support? How does this knowledge influence our thinking and actions?

Fourth, the (neuro)biological sciences have left their traces in this field. It is no longer about emotional development as such but about how the brain and body function. We increasingly come across the idea that 'we are our brain', not only because of the work of Swaab (2010) but especially because of the attention paid to neurobiological functions. A number of authors in this book also specifically address this issue. These are all good reasons to elaborate on the various meanings given to the concept of emotional development and to see whether a shared understanding can be discovered.

2 What does a term express?

There are two opposing tendencies in the use of terms. For example, there is a strong human need to define terms as clearly as possible. This provides a basis for unambiguous communication and thus makes it easier to exchange information with each other. This approach is based on the idea that a term has a more-or-less fixed meaning, both theoretically and practically. There is also an opposite tendency: to use less-fixed terms, to allow for more open, free and individual meanings. One gives a meaning to a term in one's own approach or from one's point of view, given within a specific context. This often leads to new or idiosyncratic and selective definitions. Before we discuss emotional development, we consider the concept or term 'emotion'. The term is derived from the Latin *movere*, which means 'to move'. This is expressed in its use: it is described as an impulse, a whim, a need, a certain psychobiological and physical reaction to a situation, or a mood. In everyday language, the emphasis is mainly on the behavioural component of emotions i.e. the visible expressions of emotions, such as sadness, anger, fear and joy. With his analytical approach, Frijda (2007, 2008) has laid a foundation for a broad, integrated view of emotions. He connects biological-physiological and (neuro) psychological knowledge with 'emotional phenomena'. Frijda makes a distinction between the ways emotions are expressed: in behaviour, in physical manifestations and in subjective perception. He places these phenomena of emotions in an information processing process that can be analysed. With this we can answer the following questions: (1) What is the cause of the emotion or the emotional phenomenon? (2) What is the importance of showing emotions? (3) How does emotion ultimately become visible? Frijda states that emotion as a concept is an independent psychological category: 'There is a mechanism or a set of mechanisms aimed at guaranteeing the satisfaction of interests,' and that mechanism, according to Frijda, is the emotion (Frijda, 2008, p. 493).

Starting from this analytical approach, Frijda describes the emotions that are the most elementary drivers of action (on an instinctive level): anger, joy, sadness, fear, surprise and disgust. These are generally seen as basic emotions. There is an important difference between these and emotions that are linked not to actions but to objects. In the latter category are not basic emotions but, for example, emotions like jealousy or contempt (Frijda, 2008, p. 85). Sentiments, too, often refer to objects and are not basic emotions, for example the sentimental value of heirlooms. Emotions are also not the same as feelings. There is a clear difference in meaning and experience between 'I am angry' and 'I feel angry.' The latter is a form of conscious anticipation of something that could happen, namely my becoming angry. Feelings are thus reflective in nature, while a basic emotion is directly and concretely presentable. The same is seen in an emotion like passion, in which the need to express the emotion may be intense. Moreover, the concept of feeling covers a broader range of experiences. So you can feel lonely, but loneliness is not an emotion. For Frijda, feelings are mainly 'process monitoring mechanisms'; they monitor all parts of the emotion process: from stimulus, or cause, to final reaction in basic emotions. Feelings thus have a regulating effect (Frijda, 2008, p. 266). That they can be distinguished from 'moods' becomes clear in the characterisation of a mood as 'an affective state of a relatively enduring nature, which is not provoked by an external event, survives a specific event or is disproportionately long or intense' (Frijda, 2008, p. 266). While feelings are of a more short-term nature, moods determine a state of mind over a longer period of time. Moreover, they have no apparent stimulus.

2.1 What is emotional development?

A simple description of the concept of emotional development would be 'learning to deal with emotions'. In practice, however, it does not turn out to be that simple. Starting from Frijda's analytical approach to the emotions, according to which certain basic emotions are the most important motives for action, we can ask whether and when emotional development takes place. Rita Kohnstamm does not explicitly mention emotional development as an area of personal development in her magnum opus (2009). She places emotionality within other developmental domains, particularly within social and conscience development. Children's development proceeds most smoothly when they feel emotionally connected to people around them. In this way, relational experiences such as attachment form the basis for the child's social development. Vonk and Hosmar (2009) focus on emotional development, in line with Anton Došen's developmental dynamic approach, and offer concrete advice for the care of people with intellectual disabilities. They describe emotional development as 'a dynamic process in which the basic primary emotions further develop and crystallize into a differentiated emotional life and thus make a major contribution to the formation of personality'

(Vonk & Hosmar, 2009, p. 24). Vugts-de Groot (2009, 2013) states that an approach to different categories of reality, without connecting them to their own developmental domain of emotions, is an excellent addition to development-oriented thinking and vice versa. Došen (2014) speaks of emotional development as the development of basic emotional needs: 'Satisfying these basic needs leads to a positive emotional state and to the psychosocial development of the child' (Došen, 2014, p. 75). This development is strongly anchored in biological components.

So there is some tension in the concept of emotional development and its use in theory and practice. Although Frijda speaks of emotion as a separate psychological category, primarily as an information process, there is no consensus about there being a distinct process of emotional development, let alone about it playing a determining role or being determined only by basic needs. In normal development, the general principle is that physiological, social, emotional and cognitive development continually influence and stimulate each other.

2.2 Emotional development and intellectual disability

Although there is no consensus on the concept of emotional development or its utility value, the concept is at the same time indispensable in caring for people with intellectual disabilities. But what can we say about emotional development in people with intellectual disabilities? Do emotions develop in the same way as in people without these disabilities? Is there a limited development, or a delayed development, or both? Are there gaps, irregularities or disturbances that distinguish their development from that of people with 'normal' emotional development, insofar as these two groups of people can be distinguished? What do differences between levels or stages of emotional development and levels of cognitive skill mean? In practice, much use is made of a 'discrepancy' between the two dimensions, in which, following Došen's thesis, the stage of emotional development will always be lower than the cognitive level. In this context, it is good to know that the concept of cognitive level itself is also under discussion in theory and practice (De Bruijn *et al.* 2014). It is also the case that attachment (chapter 6 in this manual), as a core aspect of emotional development, can equally determine cognitive development or the degree of intellectual disability. Furthermore, the emotional development of people with an autism spectrum disorder, and also those with non-congenital brain damage, is viewed or interpreted differently from the emotional development of those without these conditions. Moreover, within the spectrum of genetic syndromes, there is a diversity of emotional behaviours associated with phenotypic aspects. This is, for example, particularly noticeable in Cornelia de Lange syndrome.

It is clear that there are various differing theories and practices surrounding the concept of emotional development. The mind map (figure 1.1) provides a framework for understanding the broader context of these theories and practices. This mind map can serve as a tool to map out different views or perspectives. In this way it becomes clear that the perspective from which we look at emotional development can make a lot of difference to how we conceive of the concept. The mind map mentions different perspectives on emotional development.

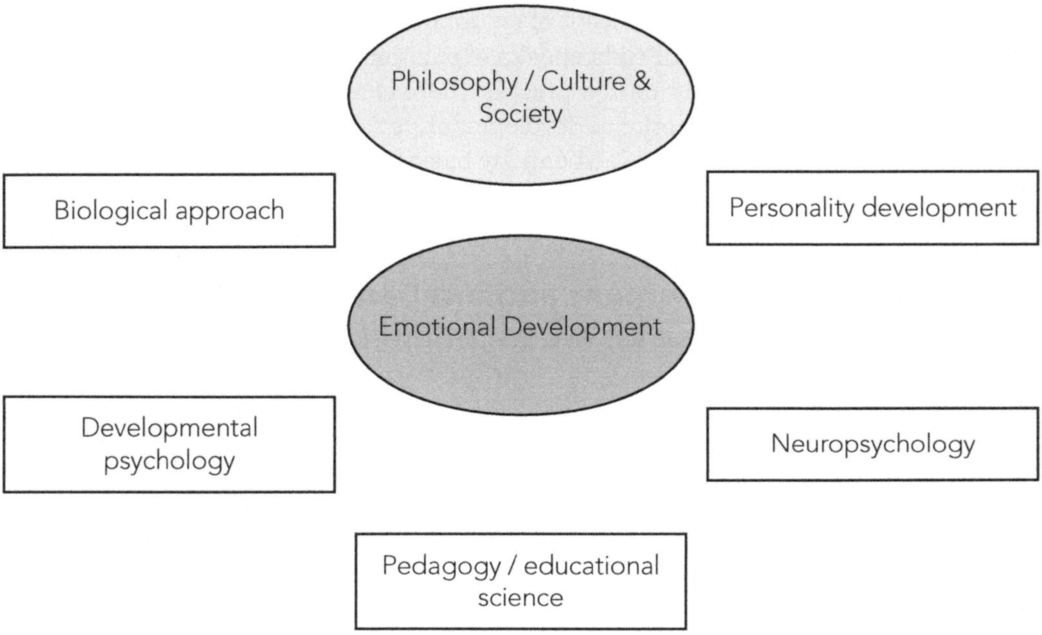

Figure 1.1 Emotional development in context

This chapter discusses three of the five perspectives on emotional development, excluding the biological and neuropsychological approaches. For these last two approaches we refer readers to chapters 2 and 5 of this manual. Wherever possible, emotional development is connected with intellectual disability in each perspective.

3 Emotional development from the point of view of philosophy, culture and society

Different cultures typify and experience emotions differently (Jadnanansing, 2010). Within the dialectic culture of Asian countries, experiencing a balance between emotions is of great importance. In Western countries, on the other hand, a typical dualistic experience and expression is dominant: you either have or show one emotion or the other. Differences between cultures can also be seen in the different facial expressions that people show when experiencing different emotions (Ekman, 2008). Within cultures there are also different views on the place, value and importance of emotions and emotional development. We see this reflected, for example, in the (philosophical-)cultural-social approach of Antonio Damasio, or the socio-economic angle of the capability approach of Martha Nussbaum and Amartya Sen. Damasio (2001, p. 67) accentuates the value of the emotional dimension as an aspect of the *condition humaine*, which differs within different cultures through its direct connection to the environment:

> *Our development and all our later experiences are permeated by emotions, and as a result, through conditioning almost all objects and situations in our experience are connected to the fundamental homeostatic regulation: reward and punishment, pleasure and pain, attraction and repulsion, personal advantage and personal disadvantage, and, inevitably, good (in the sense of life) and evil (in the sense of death). That is the natural 'condition humaine', whether we like it or not.* (Damasio, 2001, p. 67)

The capability-oriented approach, developed by the American philosopher Martha Nussbaum, focuses on human development in line with human rights. It starts with a very simple question: what can people really do and be? What real possibilities are open to them? This question may seem simple, but it is complex because the quality of a human life has to do with different elements, and the interrelationships between them need to be closely examined (Nussbaum, 2012, p. 10).

In order to do justice to the various elements of and mutual connections between quality of life and human existence, Nussbaum formulates 10 areas of life as 'areas of freedom' that are 'so essential that their removal would result in a life that does not correspond to human dignity' (Nussbaum, 2012, p. 55). Nussbaum regards the development of feelings as one of these 10 essential capabilities (possibilities):

> *Being able to be attached to things and people outside ourselves, to love those who love and care for us, to mourn in their absence; in general, to love, grieve and experience desire, gratitude and justified anger. Being able not to be inhibited in your emotional development by overwhelming worries and fears. To support this capability means to support forms of human relationships that can be shown to be essential to that development.* (Nussbaum, 2012, p. 58)

Beernink-Wissink (2015) shows that this approach is of value for the care of people with intellectual disabilities. She states that the emotional expressions of people with (severe) intellectual disabilities 'have something to say to us' and thus give meaning to existence (Beernink-Wissink, 2015, pp. 119–124). The aforementioned approaches are based on an inseparable connection between an emotion, the level of functioning, the related behaviour and the context in connection to well-being. In fact, the environment determines the way in which a limitation on each of these elements is visible or noticeable. It is therefore questionable to what extent the environment is capable of dealing adequately with people with disabilities, including with regard to their emotional development.

The AAIDD uses a working model to map the relationship to the context. It is intended as a support model, in which five aspects are integrally important for the implementation of the support. The five aspects are described as 'dimensions of human functioning'. It is striking that 'emotional functioning' is not mentioned as a separate dimension, nor is it part of the explanation. As such, it does not play a significant role within the model. Emotional development is seen in this model as a partial aspect of the various other dimensions.

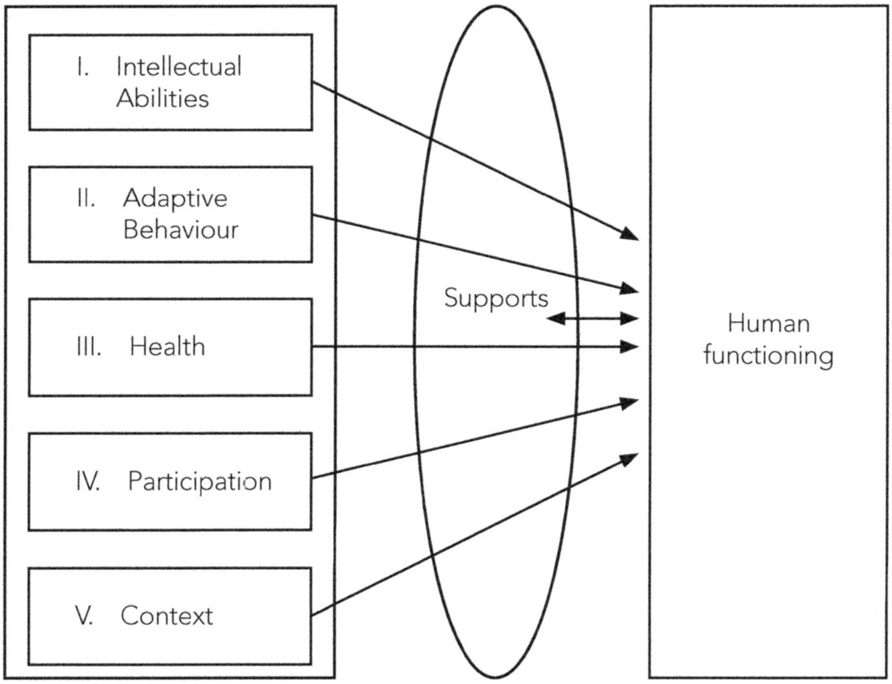

Figure 1.2 Conceptual framework of human functioning (AAIDD, 2010, p. 14)

Looking at the Dutch context and the VGN's quality framework, it is striking that the three pillars on which the framework is built do not pay any attention to emotional development in relation to intellectual disability. The three pillars consist of the following elements: pillar 1, quality data on the organisational level; pillar 2, quality data on the client level (pillar 2A) and concrete experience data on clients, but without the emotional aspect (pillar 2B); pillar 3, data on the relationship between client and professional.

So pillar 2B does not provide an inventory of aspects of emotional well-being, and pillar 3 lacks an unambiguous and well-founded interpretation of itself (VGN, 2007, 2013). The quality framework does refer to 'emotional security' (pillar 2) within freedom-restricting measures, but does not elaborate on this (see 2013, p. 30). In the quality of life framework, Schalock and Verdugo's eight domains are decisive for the quality of life (VGN, 2007, 2013). Emotional development cannot be discerned here, but is reflected in partial aspects within the various domains, such as experienced self-image, psychological well-being, relationships and the like. In order to get a better picture of emotional well-being, the capability-based approach (Nussbaum, 2012) would be a welcome alternative.

4 Emotional development from the perspective of personality development, developmental psychology, pedagogy and education

In addition to these broader approaches from the context of philosophy, culture and society, the importance of emotions and emotional development is also underlined in more human-scientific approaches to development. Each of these scientific approaches expresses a specific viewpoint.

4.1 Personality development and developmental psychology

In developmental and personality psychology we encounter different views of emotional development. For example, Sroufe developed a theory about the emotional development of children aged zero to four and a half years. He assumed that all emotions arise from three basic emotions that are already present at birth, namely pleasure, fear and frustration (Došen, 2014). For Greenspan, Wieder and Simons (2003), emotional development includes 'the changes in the world of the child's feelings and relationships' and cannot be separated from the child's motor, cognitive, social and language development. According to them, emotional development is a prerequisite for development in general. Greenspan developed a number of developmental milestones for this purpose, which Došen used in his personality theory. Došen's integrative personality approach is mentioned in several places in this manual. This underlines the impact of his view of emotional development on the care for people with intellectual disabilities. According to

Erikson (1981) psychosocial development takes place through emotional conflicts. During successive periods or stages of development, related to the stages in Piaget's cognitive theory, emotional conflicts have to be resolved in order to reach the next stage. Incidentally, this approach is not used in caring for people with intellectual disabilities. Developmental psychologists focusing on the child's earliest developmental stages emphasise the importance of the development of socio-emotional skills. After all, the degree of development of socio-emotional skills is regarded as an important predictor of, for example, levels of education and work, income and participation in criminal activities (Damon *et al.* 2015).

Attachment developmental psychology is particularly important in the attachment approach. Central to this is emotion regulation, which depends a sufficient amount of serotonin: too much serotonin in the brain increases irritability and impulsivity (Bruinsma & Loonen, 2006). According to this approach, emotion regulation is a matter of 'stress and balances'. Adequate support in case of stress and positive responsiveness (mirroring, which depends in part on mirror neurons, neurons that register the behaviour of others and lead to imitation) help to achieve emotional balance in vulnerable periods. This attachment provides a good basis for further development, and an inadequate attachment has negative consequences for emotional development. This makes the connection with an intellectual disability relevant: stress and fear may express themselves differently in the case of people with intellectual disabilities; these emotions sometimes last longer, and the response to them is delayed.

4.2 Education and teaching

In general, in education and teaching, emotional development is viewed through the lens of common developmental psychological approaches. In education and teaching, attention is paid mainly to the use of emotional development in a practical sense and its moral implications, but there is also a focus on the functional approach to emotional development and the concept of emotion as a competence. An example in education is the discrete emotions theory, according to which there is a basic set of emotions that manifest themselves differently during the stages of development. It is therefore important to recognise emotional development and to offer opportunities to manifest a specific set of emotions within each stage. This is about how emotions are handled in different stages (emotional competencies). In education and teaching, the connection between emotional and moral development is immediately clear. Anyone who deals with children and young people is explicitly confronted with the connection between emotional development and values and norms. Leeman and Wardekker (2004) criticise politics and society on a one-sided, moralistic view of upbringing and education and the lack of attention paid to emotional development in politics and society. Upbringing and education can develop moral competencies in children and adolescents by means of emotional 'guidance'. This more functionalistic approach to upbringing and education also becomes visible because the emphasis is placed on the utility value of emotions in social situations and the learning of appropriate emotional skills and competencies. A specific example of this is the increased interest in the concept of 'emotional intelligence' or the 'emotional quotient' (EQ). There are now many EQ tests with which you can discover how you function emotionally in certain situations. The utility value of EQ in relation to intellectual disability, however, is very limited.

Teaching emotional skills and competencies is not the same as handling 'emotional learning processes' well. In the Netherlands there is no equivalent of a standard work such as the *Handbook of Social and Emotional Learning* used in England (Durlak *et al.* 2015), but that does not mean that there is no attention paid to emotions within the development and learning process. This is made clear by the publication *Socio-emotional development in primary education: a continuous integral approach?* (Looman *et al.*). This integral approach is particularly important for appropriate education. The National Expertise Centre for Curriculum Development (SLO) has developed a separate socio-emotional learning programme for children with an obvious intellectual disability. This is a practical model that offers advice for daily activities. In this way, education is designed on the basis of what can be expected of the pupil at a certain age.

In this socio-emotional development learning programme for children with severe intellectual disabilities, socio-emotional development is divided into:

- self-confidence: promoting self-confidence and social resilience (self-image, self-conscious attitude)
- feelings, wishes and opinions: learning to deal with the feelings, wishes and opinions of yourself and others (positive and negative feelings, sexual feelings, role behaviour, prejudice and discrimination)
- social skills and relationships: developing social skills (working together, dealing with conflicts) and relationships (friendship, infatuation, love).

In the use of emotional skills and competencies we see a connection with emotional development as the acquisition of appropriate competencies. Hoekman, Miedema, Otten and Gielen (2007) adopt the definition proposed by Saarni, in which emotional development coincides with emotional competence, which is described as 'the ego's autonomous and deliberate action with regard to emotional events and situations'.

4.3 System theories

System theories can be mentioned as a specific perspective on emotions and context. They try to connect different approaches. System theories offer their own context for valuing emotions and emotional development and describe emotional components or aspects as parts of a whole (Savenije, Van Lawick and Reijmers, 2009). Thus, people's emotions never stand alone, and there is a connection with the social environment. On this view, emotions are more like indications of the extent to which relationships are functioning: think of aspects such as resilience, or relationships that are determined by emotions through non-verbal signals, loyalty and guilt. From this perspective, a proprietary system treatment based on attachment has been developed: emotionally focused therapy (EFT) (Wagenaar & Quené, 2008). Chapter 10 of this manual describes the relevance of a more family- and system-oriented approach.

5 Finally: a construct of emotional development

This chapter has sketched a multidimensional picture of emotional development. It is clear that for the time being there is no consensus on a definition. The concept of emotional development is therefore better seen as a 'construct' rather than a concept with one fixed meaning. A construct can be composed of a certain background and context, with a certain intention or function in relation to that context. This requires a careful description of what emotional development 'is'. Which aspects are conspicuously present within the diversity of meanings? Are there possible common denominators? How can we make the meaning of the construct 'emotional development' less ambiguous by drawing out the main aspects of the various characterisations on offer? For the definition of a construct we use the clues that Buntinx takes from Schalock and colleagues (De Bruijn, 2014, p. 20; Schalock *et al.* 2010). According to them, a construct must meet the following criteria:

1. The name of the construct serves to help us focus, or to pick something out and is therefore specific and unambiguous. Emotional development can be seen as a developmental aspect that can be distinguished from other constructs, but the question is whether it is unambiguous enough. At present, it is not clear that the construct is being used in such an unambiguous way when people refer to terms such as basic emotions and needs, emotional competencies and emotional functioning.
2. Unambiguous communication depends on the construct being used in an unambiguous way; it should therefore not be confused with other constructs.

This manual offers a first attempt at aligning different views of the construct of emotional development. In this way we may achieve unambiguous communication about a construct that is not yet completely unambiguous.

3. All parties involved in the field must be able to use the construct in the same way. Emotional development seems to be becoming more broadly accepted as an important and more usable aspect, but the current ambiguity reinforces the need for discussion about the construct.
4. The construct is a representation of the current state of knowledge and application. The use of emotional development in caring for people with intellectual disabilities dates from the mid-1980s and is therefore a fairly recent phenomenon. It is true that, thanks to Došen, the construct now has a more secure foundation, but work on the construct in relation to this field of care is still just beginning.
5. The name of the construct should be able to be used adequately within different circumstances, such as assessment, forms of support, policy and funding. When will this criterion have been sufficiently met? The diversity of views in this manual shows that it is often not met yet (although good first steps have been taken in this direction). We also see too much diversity in the way it is applied, and we see it inadequately used and not being given sufficient weight in, for example, indicative assessments.
6. When naming the construct, the 'emotional value' and/or related meanings evoked by the name of the concept must be taken into account. For example, we should seek to avoid one-sided, negative connotations when using the term 'emotional development'. By strongly emphasising emotional development and its relevance, the positive emotional value may be enhanced.

Ultimately, emotional development as a construct should meet these criteria, but currently it only meets them in part. Crucially, emotional development is accepted as an integral and distinguishable aspect of human development. As such it is important to recognise the fundamental role of emotional development in achieving full development. In the epilogue (chapter 20) an attempt is made to describe the construct in more detail on the basis of the developments that are outlined in this manual.

References

AAIDD (2010) *Intellectual Disability: Definition, classification, and systems of supports*. Washington, DC: American Association on Intellectual and Developmental Disabilities.

Beernink-Wissink, J (2015) *Floreren: Zoektocht naar goed leven voor mensen met een ernstige verstandelijke beperking en ernstige gedragsproblemen*. Delft: Eburon.

Bruijn, J de, Buntinx, W, & Twint, B (Eds) (2014) *Verstandelijke beperking: definitie en context*. Amsterdam: SWP.

Bruinsma, F & Loonen, AJM (2006) Neurobiologie van cognitie en emotionele motivatie. *Neuropraxis* **10** (3) 77–88.

Buntinx, W (2014) Inleiding. In: J de Bruijn, W Buntinx & B Twint (Eds) *Verstandelijke beperking: definitie en context* (pp17–38). Amsterdam: SWP.

Damasio, AR (2001) *Ik voel dus ik ben: Hoe gevoel en lichaam ons bewustzijn vormen*. Amsterdam: Wereldbibliotheek.

Damon EJ, Greenberg, M, & Crowley, M (2015) Early Social-Emotional Functioning and Public Health: The relationship between kindergarten social competence and future wellness. *American Journal of Public Health* 2015 e1 doi: 10.2105/AJPH.2015.302630.

Došen, A (2014) *Psychische stoornissen, probleemgedrag en verstandelijke beperking: Een integratieve benadering bij kinderen en volwassenen* (5th edition). Assen: Van Gorcum.

Durlak, JA, Domitrovich, CE, Weissberg, RP & Gullotta, TP (Eds) (2015) *Handbook of Social and Emotional Learning: Research and practice*. New York/London: Guilford Press.

Ekman, P (2008) *Gegrepen door emoties*. Amsterdam: Nieuwezijds.

Erikson, EH (1981) *Het kind en de samenleving* (9th edition). Utrecht/Antwerpen: Het Spectrum.

Frijda, N (2007) *De Wetten der Emoties*. Amsterdam: Bert Bakker.

Frijda, N (2008) *De Emoties*. Amsterdam: Bert Bakker.

Greenspan, SI, Wieder, S & Simons, R (2003) *Als uw kind speciale aandacht nodig heeft: Emotionele, sociale en intellectuele groei stimuleren*. Utrecht/ Antwerpen: Kosmos-Z&K.

Hoekman, J, Miedema, A, Otten, B & Gielen, J (2007) De constructie van een schaal voor de bepaling van het sociaal-emotioneel ontwikkelingsniveau: Achtergrond, opbouw en betrouwbaarheid van de esseon. *NTZ – Nederlands Tijdschrift voor de zorg aan mensen met verstandelijke beperkingen* **33** 215–232.

Jadnanansing, S (2010) *Oost-West, Goed-Slecht. Culturele verschillen in emotionele complexiteit* (bachelor's thesis). Amsterdam: UVA.

Kohnstamm, R (2009) *Kleine ontwikkelingspsychologie I: Het jonge kind* (6th edition). Houten: Bohn Stafleu van Loghum.

Leeman, Y & Wardekker, W.(2004) *Onderwijs met pedagogische kwaliteit*. Zwolle: Windesheim.

Looman, BLJ, Jager, M de, Tuk, B, Onrust, SA, Lammers, J, Spijkerman, M & Buijs, G (z.j.). *Sociaal-emotionele ontwikkeling in het primair onderwijs: Een doorlopende integrale aanpak?* Utrecht: Pharos/ Trimbos-instituut.

Nussbaum, M (2012) *Mogelijkheden scheppen: Een nieuwe benadering van de menselijke ontwikkeling*. Amsterdam: Ambo.

Savenije, A, Lawick, MJ van & Reijmers, ETM (Eds) (2009) *Handboek Systeemtherapie*. Utrecht: De Tijdstroom.

Schalock, RL, Borthwick-Duffy, SA, Bradley, VJ, Buntinx, WHE, Coulter, DL, Craig, EM & Yeager, MH (2010) *Intellectual Disability: Definition, classification, and systems of support – The 11th edition of the AAIDD definition manual*. Washington, DC: AAIDD.

National Expertise Centre for Curriculum Development SLO (z.j.). *Leerlijn sociaal emotionele ontwikkeling*. Enschede: SLO.

Swaab, D (2010) *Wij zijn ons brein: Van baarmoeder tot Alzheimer*. Amsterdam: Contact.

VGN (2007) *Visiedocument Kwaliteitskader Gehandicaptenzorg*. Utrecht: VGN.

VGN (2013) *Kwaliteitskader Gehandicaptenzorg: Visiedocument 2.0*. Utrecht: VGN.

Vonk, J & Hosmar, A (2009) *Emotionele ontwikkeling bij mensen met een beperking: Een denk- en handelingskader voor de praktijk*. Leuven: Acco.

Vugts-de Groot, B (2009) *Werken met ontwikkelingsleeftijden: Afstemmen op mensen met een verstandelijke beperking*. Barneveld: Nelissen.

Vugts-de Groot, B (2013) *Werken met ervaringsordening: Afstemmen op mensen met een (ernstige) verstandelijke beperking*. Amsterdam: Boom Nelissen.

Wagenaar, K & Quené, H (2008) Hechting en emoties: Emotionally focussed therapy. In: A Savenije, MJ van Lawick & ETM Reijmers (Eds) *Handboek Systeemtherapie* (pp347–354). Utrecht: De Tijdstroom.

Chapter 2 Neurobiological aspects of emotional development

Anton Došen

Summary

According to different investigators in the area of child development, the basic emotions with which a baby comes into the world (pleasure, fear, anger and social interest) arise as an expression of basic survival needs (nutrition, defence, reproduction and social contact), which are the product of the activity of neural systems spread over subcortical and cortical brain areas (Rutter, 1980; Izard & Harris, 1995; LeDoux, 2002; Damasio, 2010). The stimuli by which these systems are activated lead, in addition to emotions, to motivations that are responsible for behaviour. The emotional system and the cognitive system are two separate neural systems, which can develop independently to some degree (Izard *et al.*, 2006; LeDoux, 2002). Emotions initiate cognitive development, and together with cognitive development, they lead to social development. A discrepancy between emotional and cognitive development can leave someone vulnerable to behavioural and psychiatric disorders. Recognition of the level of emotional development offers a good insight into basic emotional needs, as well as into the reaction pattern and behavioural pattern of the person in question. Adapting the environment to the person's basic emotional needs is essential to supporting health and quality of life. With behavioural and psychiatric problems in people with intellectual disabilities, knowledge of the level of emotional development is important for the recognition of the mechanism of the problem, as well as for diagnosis and the formulation of a treatment plan.

1 Introduction

Before discussing the neurobiological aspects of emotional development in people with intellectual disabilities, for the sake of clarity, attention will first be paid to the neurobiological aspects of emotions in general.

Emotions are an essential part of human life. They play an essential role both in physical adaptation (internal homeostasis in the external environment) and in intrapersonal (sense of well-being) and interpersonal (adaptive social behaviour) psychological processes (LeDoux, 2002; Izard *et al.*, 2006). According to contemporary neuroscientists (LeDoux, 2002; Panksepp & Biven, 2012; Damasio, 2010), emotions can be defined as a function of basic survival needs that are activated by subcortical and cortical brain systems. In other words, primordial (basic) emotions arise as an expression of the basic survival needs (nutrition, defence, reproduction and social contact), which are the product of the activity of neural systems spread over subcortical and cortical areas (LeDoux, 2015). The stimuli by which these systems are activated lead, in addition to emotions, to motivations that are responsible for behaviour.

Emotions are part of the personality. The personality is defined as an emotional, cognitive and motivational whole that serves to adapt a person to the given circumstances (Harris, 1998; LeDoux, 2002; Sroufe *et al.*, 2005). The personality is seen as a result of the function of brain cell networks (biological substrate), psychosocial functions, life experiences and the individual style of responding to external circumstances. The personality is also referred to as an organisational system of obtained information through which the person develops a certain attitude and reaction style towards the outside world. Emotions play an essential role in this.

This chapter focuses on current views on the biology of emotions. It discusses the development of emotions and summarises our current understanding of the significance of emotional development in the care of people with intellectual disabilities.

2 The emergence of emotions

The emotions have been debated for centuries, leading to different theories of personality and different approaches to counselling. The best known are the psychoanalytic or psychodynamic-oriented approaches and the behavioural-cognitive approaches. In recent decades, a new, neuroscientific 'development perspective' has also attracted the attention of professionals. This developmental perspective studies the maturation of the brain in the context of the social experiences and living conditions of the person in question. The focus is on personality development and on processes that can lead to a psychologically healthy development (adaptation) or to behavioural problems and psychopathology (Cicchetti & Cohen, 2006). The developmental perspective is based on a number of new neurosciences, such as cognitive, affective and social neurosciences, and seeks support in molecular and cell neuroscience and theories of the development of 'self', attachment and mentalisation. An important topic within the development perspective is emotional development.

Kandel (2006) states: 'All mental processes are biological'. This means that emotions arise as a function of brain cells. While it was thought some time ago that the cells of the cerebral cortex (cortex) were responsible for the emotions, today there are researchers (Damasio, 2010; Panksepp & Biven, 2012) who claim that the primordial emotions arise primarily from the activity of lower (subcortical) brain areas such as the brainstem and hypothalamus. The so-called 'evolutionary perspective', which is based on the phylogenetic theory[1] of psychosocial development, also known as the 'triune brain' (MacLean, 1993), shares this point of view.

According to MacLean (1993), three brain parts can be distinguished in the phylogenetic development of humans (see figure 2.1), and these develop at different times during pregnancy. Each section serves to develop a specific function. The author speaks of the triune brain, a brain that is a unit of three parts, because it consists of a 'reptilian brain' (the brainstem), a brain of primitive mammals (the limbic system) and a human brain (the neocortex). The brainstem is said to be established as early as the 10th week of pregnancy, the limbic system develops after the fourth month of pregnancy, and the cerebral cortex is established after the sixth month of pregnancy and largely develops after birth. The brainstem provides physiological functions, but also two basic states of the individual – excitation (excitement) and relaxation – and reflexive responses to stimuli.

The limbic system is responsible for the emergence of the universal primordial basic emotions: pleasure, fear, anger and social interest (social attractiveness). The maturation of the cerebral cortex after birth creates the opportunity for cognitive development. This cognitive development leads to the differentiation of the basic emotions, which leads to social development (socially adapted behaviour).

1 The phylogenetic theory describes how a certain group of organisms (e.g. humans) developed during evolution.

Triune brain

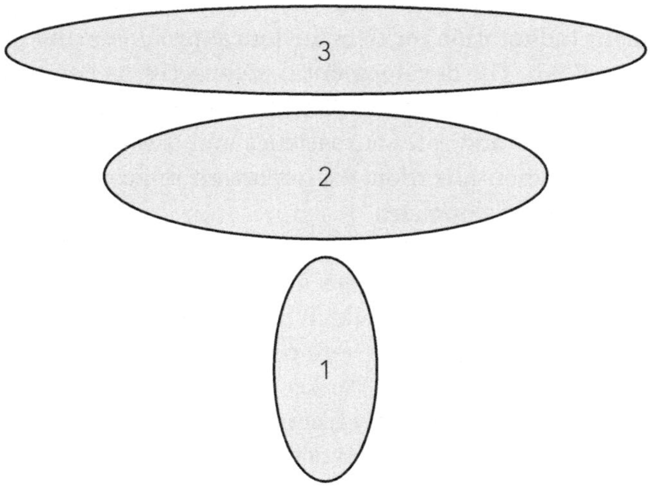

1. Brainstem: 10 weeks
   Primary emotions: stimulation, relaxation
2. Limbic system: four to five months
   Basic emotions: pleasure, fear, anger, positive social emotions
3. Cortex: six to seven months
   Emotions and cognition

Figure 2.1: The evolution theory of the triune brain (MacLean, 1993) (source: Došen, 2014)

Several brain researchers use the theory of evolution as the basis for research. While LeDoux (2002) and Izard and colleagues (2006) are mainly engaged in research into the cerebral cortex and cognitive functions (cognitive neuroscience), other researchers (Panksepp, 2003; Panksepp & Biven, 2012; Damasio, 2010) focus on deeper brain structures (the subcortical areas), looking for the primary origin of emotions and their influence on overall psychosocial development. Still other researchers are engaged in social development by investigating the function of the cerebral cortex (social neuroscience) (Happé & Frith, 2013).

2.1 Brain science and emotions

Within brain science, emotions are studied through cognitive, social and affective neuroscience. This is made possible through the application of advanced imaging (brain imaging) technology[2] to human and animal subjects.

2 Imaging ('brain imaging') technology is a technology for investigating the structure (e.g. through MRI, magnetic resonance imaging) and function (e.g. through FMRI, functional MRI) of the brain.

2.1.1 Cognitive neuroscience

According to cognitive neuroscientists (LeDoux, 2002, 2015; Kandel *et al.*, 2000; Izard *et al.*, 2006), the primary function of emotions is the adaptation of the individual to the environment. Emotions are also seen in this field of science as a primary motivational system that plays an important role in the behaviour of the individual (Izard & Harris, 1995; Izard *et al.*, 2006).

Cognitive neuroscientists speak of four universal basic emotions: pleasure, fear, anger and social interest. These emotions arise from neural systems responsible for survival functions (nutrition, defence, reproduction and social contact). According to Kandel (2006), the activation of emotions has three stages: 1) unconscious, implicit evaluation of the stimulus (for example danger or stress), followed by 2) a physiological (via the autonomic nervous system) reaction (for example a stress reaction), possibly turning into 3) a conscious experience (feeling) of the state of one's own body (e.g. fear, panic).

The amygdala and the hippocampus, two nuclei of nerve cells located deep in the temporal lobe, play an essential role in the experience of emotions. The amygdala is primarily responsible for negative emotions, such as fear or anger at danger. LeDoux (2002) has created a scheme of responses of the amygdala to stimuli similar to the scheme described above of Kandel's activation of emotions. Danger signals, which the amygdala receives as sensory stimuli through the thalamus, can be sent directly to the hypothalamus, which causes a stress response by activating the person's autonomic nervous system via the HPA (hypothalamic–pituitary–adrenal) axis. In this reaction, the cortex is not turned on, and the reaction proceeds quickly and unconsciously. LeDoux (2002) calls this reaction the low road of emotions. In these cases it is also referred to as the fight-or-flight response. If the signals are not seriously threatening, the hippocampus is also involved in the processing of the stimuli. It filters, as it were, the signals, distinguishes between really dangerous and apparently dangerou, and important and less important signals, and sends the relevant signals to the prefrontal cortex (the front cerebral cortex). Only now does the person become aware of the signals, and the person gets a feeling about what is happening, for example fear or anger. In cases where people become aware of the experience, LeDoux speaks of the high road of emotional reactions. While a person responds automatically and quickly in a low-road reaction, in a high-road reaction the person has the opportunity to consciously plan their own behaviour (Došen, 2014) (see figure 2.2).

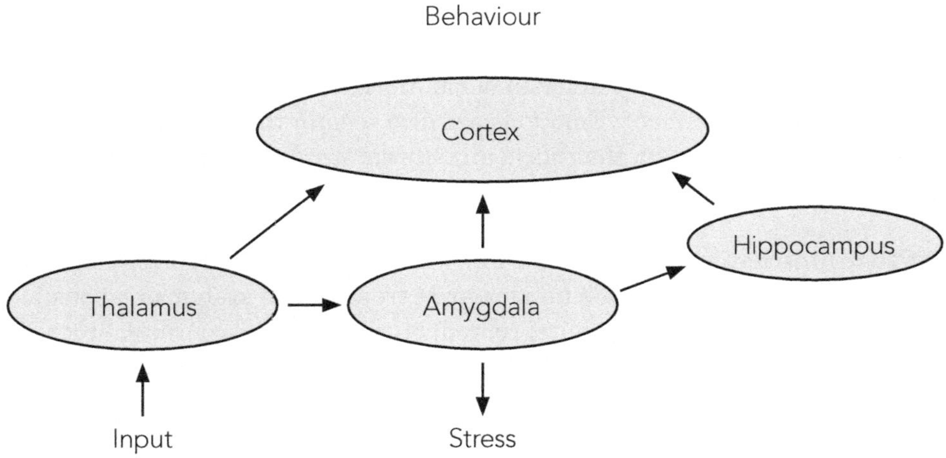

- thalamus–amygdala: low road, HPA axis, stress
- thalamus–amygdala–hippocampus–cortex: high road, behaviour

Figure 2.2: Unconscious and conscious behaviour (LeDoux, 2002) (source: Došen, 2014)

People with an immature or functionally weak cortex, such as people with intellectual disabilities, can expect the low road to be activated more often than those with a functioning cortex.

2.1.2 Affective neuroscience

Damasio (2010) sees emotions as evolutionary programmes of action that lead on the one hand to changes in the body (such as changes in facial expression, body posture, intestinal function, respiration and heart rate), and on the other to the activation of the cognitive system, which results in feelings, ideas, ways of thinking and motivations.

Jaak Panksepp (Panksepp & Biven, 2012), one of the founders of affective neuroscience, searches for the neurological basis of emotions in the subcortical areas. He situates primordial emotions in the brainstem, to be precise in the periaqueductal grey. These emotions arise in a survival process and are not the product of learning but an innate consequence of evolution. Panksepp recognises seven basic emotions: seeking, fear, rage (anger), lust (pleasure), care, panic/grief (sadness) and play. Neural systems for these emotions are located in different parts of the brain: the brainstem, the midbrain (hypothalamus), the subcortical nuclei (amygdala, hippocampus, striatum), the limbic cortex and the prefrontal cortex (see figure 2.3).

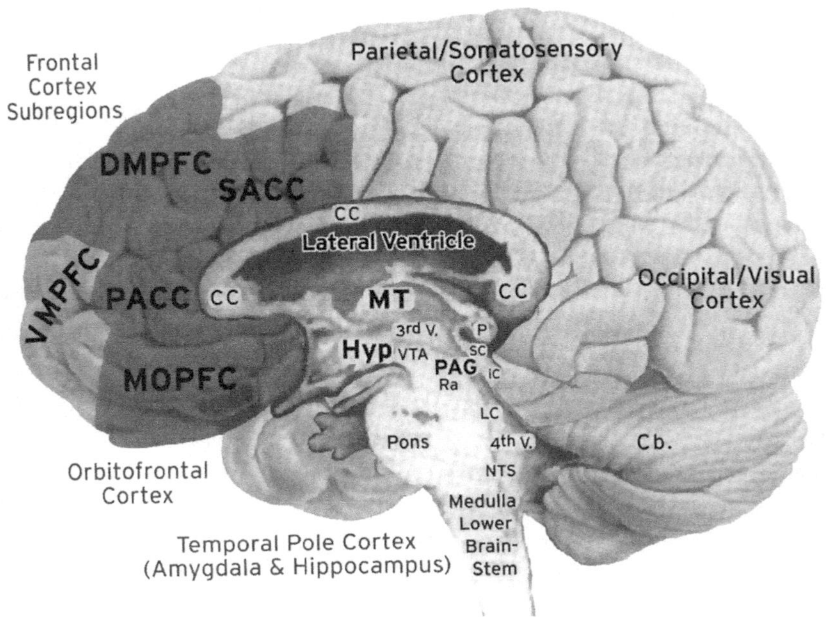

Figure 2.3: Emotions are the product of the brainstem and the upper brain areas (source: Panksepp & Biven, 2012, p.3).

Each of these emotions arises from specific internal or external stimuli, which activate a specific neural system in the brainstem and the midbrain. This may then lead to the activity of higher brain systems: the subcortical nuclei and the cortex. Some of these emotions are active at birth (e.g. seeking, fear, rage and lust), while others, such as panic/grief and play, become active later (depending on the maturation of the neural system in question).

Panksepp distinguishes between three brain levels, on which three types of emotional processes take place.

- The first level consists of the brainstem and the hypothalamus. This is the primary emotional system. At this level, primary emotional processes develop that allow for the perception of sensory stimuli and instinctive (survival) responses to stimuli. Panksepp calls this neural system the unconditioned 'integrative brain-mind system'.
- The second level consists of the amygdala, the hippocampus and the striatum. These brain regions allow for secondary emotional processes, which are aimed at the initiation of simple emotional learning, including operant conditioning.

- The third level consists of the limbic system and the medial frontal cortex, where tertiary emotional processes take place. Here, affective cognition, social emotions, feelings, thoughts and the associated behaviour are established.

According to this scheme, the stimuli (e.g. sensory stimuli) received by sensory organs are initially processed by the primary emotional system. A perception of the stimulus arises, possibly followed by an unconscious (instinctive) physical reaction (the primary emotional process). At the same time, the information about the stimulus is forwarded to the second level (the amygdala and hippocampus), where secondary emotional processes take place, knowing and recognising the stimuli and assessing the meaning of the stimulus (dangerous or not dangerous) and determining the physical response to the stimulus. At this level, learning, conditioning and the beginning of cognitive development arise. The emotional experiences of this level are transmitted to the cortical areas, where the experience becomes conscious (the tertiary emotional process). The emotional and cognitive experiences that arise from the activity of the subcortical nuclei and the brainstem are unconscious, but they can result in striking physical reactions and behaviours. A conscious experience of the stimuli only arises after the information about the stimulus has been sent to the cortex by the two lower emotional systems (LeDoux, 2015).

2.1.3 Social neuroscience

According to social neuroscience, the social brain develops on the basis of emotional and cognitive experiences. Happé and Frith (2013) indicate that social cognition arises from the activity of certain neural systems in the prefrontal cortex, areas of the temporal lobes, the insula and the amygdala. The activity of these neural systems results in empathy, mentalisation, mirror activity[3] and the detection of danger and threat. Social development occurs when the relevant brain areas are sufficiently mature. This means that social cognition arises later than emotional and cognitive skills. Researchers on the Romania's Abandoned Children project (Nelson, *et al.*, 2014) found that children who stayed in Ceaușescu's boarding schools, where the children were severely neglected (psychosocially) in the first six months of their lives (but no longer), had relatively little damage to their later development (attachment). According to the authors, this means that the sensitive phase for attachment begins after the sixth month of life, but only when certain brain areas are sufficiently mature. This may explain the relatively late (usually after the first year of life) onset of autism symptoms (for example, avoidance of physical contact and unexplained anxiety).

3 Mirror activity arises as a function of mirror neurons, which make possible mirror behaviour.

Happé and Frith (2013) emphasise that, in addition to our innate predisposition to social development, learning in contact with other people plays an essential role in the development of our social brain. Social learning starts very early after birth through reciprocal stimulation between mother and child (movements, facial expressions, sounds and eye contact) and leads to attachment behaviour and attachment. Affective synchrony between mother and child (that is, attention and response to signals that the child sends), play, verbal dialogue, the regulation of affect and arousal, tempo, rhythm of activity and passivity are indispensable for optimal attachment.

2.1.4 Positive emotions

In addition to the nuclei that mainly cause negative emotions, such as the amygdala, there are also brain nuclei that provide positive emotions. This neural system is called the reward system. Positive emotions, such as pleasure, confidence and empathy, are mainly co-ordinated by the striatum (figure 2.4) and the prefrontal cortex. Fundamental sensory pleasure arises from stimulation of the striatum (the ventral pallidum and nucleus accumbens), while higher-order pleasure (e.g. satisfaction and happiness) arises from the activity of the orbitofrontal cortex and the limbic system.

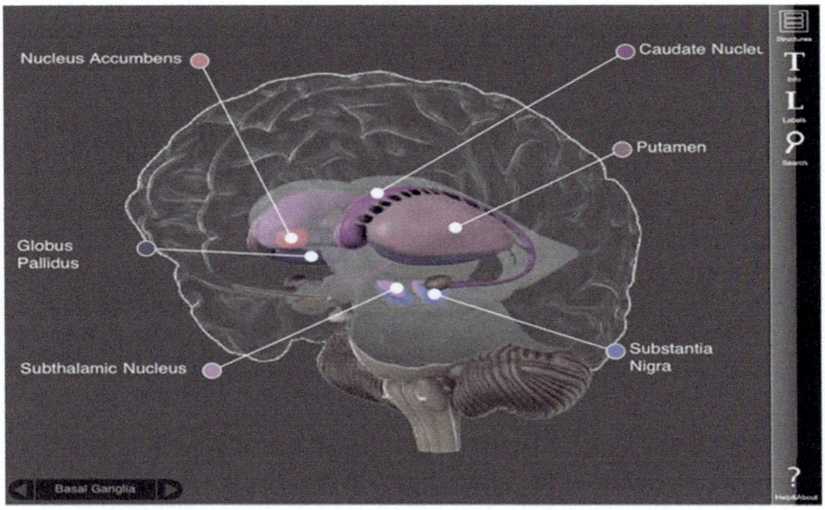

Figure 2.4: The striatum (consisting of the nucleus accumbens, the globus pallidus, the nucleus caudatus and the putamen) is a nucleus of nerve cells located deep in the hemispheres of the brain.

The active reward system (experience of pleasure) provides the motivation to adapt to the circumstances. A balance of activity between neural systems for positive and negative emotions is important for healthy mental development (Berridge & Kringelbach, 2013). It should be emphasised here that the experience of pleasure and joy does not depend on the level of development; it arises very early in development and depends on the stimulation of the reward system. This means that people with a very serious developmental delay can still have fun if they are adequately stimulated.

3 Emotional development

While emotions have been the subject of scientific studies for a relatively long time, it is curious that their development (especially in people with intellectual disabilities) has so far received very little scientific attention. However, a change is visible. An important recent discovery by brain scientists is that the emotional system and the cognitive system are two separate neural systems that can to some extent develop independently of each other (LeDoux, 2002; Panksepp, 2002; Izard *et al.*, 2006; Kandel, 2006; Damasio, 2010). It is believed that the social neural system is also a separate system that, although strongly linked to the emotional and cognitive systems, can to some extent present and develop independently of them. An example of this can be found in people with Down's syndrome. The social skills of these individuals may exceed their cognitive level, while their emotional level may be significantly below their cognitive level (Došen, 2014).

These findings can be considered revolutionary because they will change traditional thinking in psychology and psychiatry about cognitive supremacy[4] in psychosocial development and psychic life.

As mentioned earlier, the emotional, cognitive and social neural systems are interconnected and influence each other's development. Izard *et al.* (2006) emphasise: 'When these connections [between emotions and cognition] fail to develop, problem behaviours are likely to emerge.'

The development of each of these systems, as well as the connections between them, can be disrupted for several reasons. This can lead to a discrepancy in the development of these systems (one system is delayed while the development of another system continues), with significant consequences for overall psychosocial development. In our practice, we found a striking discrepancy between emotional and cognitive development in people with intellectual disabilities and behavioural and psychiatric disorders. The level of emotional development in these people was often significantly lower than that of their cognitive development (Došen, 2014). Other authors also report a discrepancy in development in certain genetic syndromes, in abused children and in people with autism spectrum disorder (ASD)

4 The cognitive aspect has predominated in psychology for a long time.

(Izard *et al.*, 2006). The discrepancy between emotional and cognitive development results in an unbalanced personality, vulnerable to the development of problem behaviour and mental disorders (Došen, 2014).

In practice it is striking that the level of emotional development can determine the behaviour of the person. Every stage in age development has a certain personality development (referred to in the literature as a personality level, personality structure or personality layer), in which the level of emotional development determines the style of action and reaction, affect control, aggression regulation and the way of interaction. These are referred to as the personality traits that are characteristic of a certain level of emotional development (Došen, 2014).

It is assumed that personality development in people with intellectual disabilities follows the same trajectory as it does in all other people (Hodapp & Zigler, 1995; Greenspan, 1997). Piaget's (1953) theory of cognitive development serves as a background here. Recognition of the developmental level of the personality (the level of emotional and cognitive development) can then say a lot about the behavioural traits, the reaction patterns, the ways of communicating and the behavioural problems of people with intellectual disabilities.

However, measuring this personality development is a major problem. This is mainly due to the lack of tools for measuring emotional development. Practitioners in the field are forced to use certain schemes instead of measuring instruments in order to gain insight into the results of someone's personality development.

In our practice we use the Scale of Emotional Development (SED) (Došen, 1990; 2014), which provides insight into a person's level of emotional development. The SED has recently been revised and validated (the Scale of Emotional Development – Revised2) (Morisse & Došen, 2016), making the scale more applicable for assessment in this population (see chapter 13).

4 Conclusion

Recently, providers of care for people with intellectual disabilities have increasingly focused on emotional development. Many behavioural scientist in the Netherlands, Belgium and a number of other European countries have found that knowledge of the level of emotional and personality development is valuable in care provision. Knowledge of the level of emotional development allows practitioners to better understand the inner world of the client and to discover their basic emotional needs. Adapting the environment to these needs is essential to supporting the health and high quality of life for people with intellectual disabilities. For behavioural and psychological problems in these people, knowledge of the level of emotional development can be an important tool in recognising the mechanism of the problem, as well as in the diagnosis and planning and execution of the treatment.

Knowledge of the biological basis of emotional development is indispensable for understanding the overall psychosocial development of these people. It is important to know how their development processes have progressed, at what time in development and in which neural system a disorder has developed and what the consequences of their disorders are for other aspects of development.

The order of psychosocial development is:

- emotional development (the basis of psychosocial development)
- cognitive development
- social development, as 'superstructure'.

Each of these developmental aspects arises as the respective neural system matures. There are basic needs at each of these three levels that must be satisfied for further development.

In care provision one should therefore discover the basis of the problem and start the support and treatment from there. For example, the disruption of Panksepp's first emotional system (the brainstem) can have far-reaching negative consequences for both the cognitive and social development of the individual. We assume that this is often what has happened in children with ASD. In this case, the assistance should initially focus on strengthening the emotional skills (the level of the first emotional system), and only after progress in that area should it proceed to cognitive and social training. Disruption of higher neural systems (the subcortical nuclei and cortex) would mainly hinder cognitive development. The delay in cognitive development in the disturbance of the tertiary emotional system (for example, a mild intellectual disability) only becomes apparent after the relevant cortex areas have matured (at school age). In these situations, too, the counsellor should take into account the level of emotional development, for this level provides the motivation to learn from the person and creates opportunities for adequate support for social behaviour.

References

Berridge K, & Kringelbach, M (2013) Neuroscience of affect: Brain mechanisms of pleasure and displeasure. *Current Opinion in Neurology* **23** (3) 294–303.

Cicchetti D & Cohen, DJ (Eds) (2006) *Developmental psychopathology: Vol 1, Theory and Method* (2nd edition). New York: Wiley.

Damasio, A (2010) *Het zelf wordt zich bewust*. Amsterdam: Wereldbibliotheek.

Došen, A (1990) *Psychische en gedragsstoornissen bij zwakzinnigen: Een ontwikkelingsdynamische benadering*. Amsterdam: Boom.

Došen, A (2014) *Psychische stoornissen, gedragsproblemen en verstandelijke handicap*. Assen: Van Gorcum.

Greenspan, SJ (1997) *Developmentally based psychotherapy*. Madison, CT: International University Press.

Happé, F & Frith, U (2013) Annual Research Review: Towards a developmental neuroscience of atypical social cognition. *Journal of Child Psychology and Psychiatry* **55** (6) 553–577.

Harris, JC (1998) *Developmental neuropsychiatry, Vol. 1*. Oxford: Oxford University Press.

Hodapp, RM & Zigler, E (1995) Past, present and future issues in the developmental approach to mental retardation and developmental disabilities. In: D Cicchetti and DJ Cohen (Eds) *Developmental psychopathology: Vol. 2, Risk, disorder, and adaptation* (pp299–331). New York: Wiley.

Izard, CE & Harris, P (1995) Emotional development and developmental psychopathology. In: D Cicchetti and DJ Cohen (Eds) *Developmental Psychopathology: Vol 1, Theory and Method* (pp467–504). New York: Wiley.

Izard, CE, Youngstrom, EA, Fine, SE, Mostow, AJ & Trentacosta, CJ (2006) Emotions and developmental psychopathology. In: D Cicchetti & DJ Cohen (Eds) *Developmental Psychopathology: Vol 2, Risk, disorder, and adaptation* (2nd edition) (pp149–158). New York: Wiley.

Kandel, ER (2006) *In Search of Memory: The emergence of a new science of mind*. New York: Norton.

Kandel, ER, Schwartz, JH, Jessell, TM, Siegelbaum, SA & Hudspeth, AJ (Eds) (2000) *Principles of neural science*. New York: McGraw-Hill.

LeDoux, JE (2002) *Synaptic Self: How our brains become who we are*. New York: Macmillan.

LeDoux, JE (2015) *Anxious: Using the brain to understand and treat fear and anxiety*. New York: Viking.

MacLean, PD (1993) *The Triune Brain in Evolution: Role in paleocerebral functions*. New York: Plenum Press.

Morisse, F & Došen A (Eds) (2016) *SEO-R² Schaal voor Emotionele Ontwikkeling bij mensen met een verstandelijke beperking – Revised²*. Antwerpen/Apeldoorn: Garant.

Nelson, C, Fox, N & Zeanah, C (2014) *Romania's Abandoned Children*. Cambridge, MA: Harvard University Press.

Panksepp, J (2003) At the Interface of the Affective, Behavioral and Cognitive Neurosciences: Decoding of emotional feelings of the brain. *Brain and cognition* **52** (1) 4–14.

Panksepp, J & Biven, L (2012) *The archaeology of mind: Neuroevolutionary Origins of Human Emotions*. New York: Norton.

Piaget, J (1953) *The Child's Construction of Reality*. London: Routledge.

Rutter, M (1980) *Developmental Psychiatry* London: Heinemann.

Sroufe, L, Egeland, B, Carlson, A, & Collins, A (2005) *The Development of the Person: The Minnesota study of risk and adaptation from birth to adulthood*. New York: Guilford Press.

Chapter 3
Seven stages of emotional development, from birth to adulthood

Jolanda Vonk

Summary

The development of children into adults can be described in stages. Stages follow each other and accumulate behaviour: behaviour is not so much replaced as extended. Children go through sensitive periods in their development: a stage where they are most receptive to a specific developmental task. Each child develops at its own pace. Because stages stack up, disruptions in the early stages of life often have major consequences for the later stages. That is why the first years are crucial for building a stable personality.

For children with intellectual disabilities, this development will often be more delayed and will rather flatten. In order to recognise unmet basic emotional needs and identify delays in children and adults with intellectual disabilities, it is important to have adequate knowledge of healthy emotional development. This chapter describes the seven stages of emotional development from birth to adulthood. As a framework for this description, Došen's developmental dynamic approach is used.

1 Introduction

Emotional development can be seen as a developmental domain just like cognitive and sexual development. A definition of emotional development was given in 2009:

> *A dynamic process in which the basic primary emotions will develop into a differentiated emotional life and thus make a major contribution to the formation of the personality. Emotional development plays an essential role in the perception and behaviour of the individual throughout life.* (Vonk & Hosmar, 2009, p.24)

According to Anton Došen's developmental dynamic approach, emotional development is a central aspect of growing up.

> *In order to find a starting point for practical action, an approach to emotional development is chosen from a multidimensional perspective. Emotional development is discussed here in the context of social interactions and cognitive development, with the aim of gaining insight into the process of personality development.*
>
> *Our model of emotional development links biological and psychosocial aspects of development. The following theories are involved: neurophysiological theory, self-development theory, neuropsychological theory, cognitive theory, psychodynamic theory, self-development theory, attachment theory and ego and social development theories.* (Došen, 2014, p. 57)

Emotional development is a concrete elaboration of an ongoing process from birth to adulthood and is characterised by developmental tasks and basic needs, divided into distinctive stages. In this chapter a description is given of the seven stages of emotional development. These stages are essential in the evaluation and assessment of emotional development. Knowledge of emotional development creates an awareness of underlying basic needs (Sappok *et al.*, 2016). When professionals are aware of the current basic needs of people with intellectual disabilities entrusted to their care, they will be more readily able to adjust in a respectful way in daily social interaction.

Alicia is 19 years old. She has been raised by her father and sister. Her mother left the family when Alicia was eight. Her father took care of his daughters as best as he could, but at the same time he had to work all day and the girls were often left at home alone. Alicia was delayed in her development: she was late in reaching developmental milestones like walking and talking. At kindergarten she had trouble getting used to the demands and rules of the teacher. When she was six, she dropped out and went into special education. In a classroom with fewer children and with an understanding teacher, things went well for some time and Alicia liked going to school, although she continued to have problems with rules and demands, especially when she did not like the task or was not good at it. In such cases she had temper tantrums. After her mother left, her problem behaviour increased, and by the age of 12 the conflicts with her sister and father had grown to the point of physical aggression, on the part of Alicia as well as her father. She then left home and moved to a family home with other children with behavioural problems and intellectual disabilities. At present, she lives in a home for young people with mild intellectual disabilities. She wants to look for a job and is preparing for supported living in an apartment. Alicia is very present in the group: when she is happy, she is social and always up for a joke. When she is familiar with her caregivers, Alicia is willing to listen and to do what is expected of her. When caregivers are uncertain and hesitant, Alicia will become dominant and rebellious. In such situations, Alicia will talk very loudly, and she shouts when things go differently from how she had expected they would. She slams the door very angrily and withdraws to her room. If the caregiver starts to argue with her, Alicia will start kicking, hitting and calling the caregiver names.

2 Emotional development according to Anton Došen

When Došen started his career as a child psychiatrist caring for people with intellectual disabilities, in the Netherlands, he was genuinely interested in the inner world of these children (Došen, 1990). He wanted to understand how they experienced the world around them and why they behaved in the way they did. He wanted to discover the essential characteristics and basic needs of these children. From 1980 onwards, Došen compared several theories that describe development in sequential stages. Those theories are well known: Piaget's developmental stages of cognition, Mahler's separation-individuation theory, Erikson's stages of psychosocial development and Kohlberg's theory of moral development. In Došen's opinion, emotional development is the most essential domain of development. Because no suitable instruments were available, he decided to create one himself with the support of colleagues from the Hondsberg Observation Centre. This marked the start of the Scale of Emotional Development (SED), or SEO in Dutch (SEO 1986). The first SED described five stages of emotional development up to 12 years of age.

In Došen's theory, there are some basic assumptions:

- A child/human being will feel good if the cognitive, social and emotional development are in balance, no matter the level of functioning (normal intelligence or intellectual disability).
- It is rare for the level of emotional development to be higher than the level of cognitive development.

- Because people with an intellectual disability rarely have a developmental age higher than 12 years in cognition, he did not feel the need to describe stages for emotional development beyond 12 years at that moment.
- Trauma, illness or any kind of crisis/setback will create a disturbance in emotional development. Emotional development may come to a standstill (stagnation), fall back (regression) or be delayed (retardation).

Figure 3.1: From birth to adulthood

3 Description of the seven stages

Using stages to describe emotional development is a useful way of sketching the development from birth to adulthood. Stages can be distinguished on the basis of specific competencies in critical periods and associated development tasks. In the stages described below the emotions and milestones are intertwined with physical, cognitive and relational aspects (Verhulst, 2005).

Since the SED has come to be used, in the Netherlands and beyond, in the care of people with intellectual disabilities, and increasingly in other healthcare sectors, there is a growing need to describe two additional stages, stages six and seven. After all, people with mild intellectual disabilities or psychological problems and normal intelligence may also benefit from a description of their resilience, expressed in basic needs. Another reason for adding these stages is the fact that normal development continues up to 25 years, the age at which the brain has achieved maturity and children have grown into adults (Vonk, in press).

3.1 Stage one: homeostasis or adaptation (birth to six months)

When a child is born, sensory perception is still total and diffuse. The baby primarily responds to lust and distress. The baby does not consciously experience themselves as separate from the other. Within this context, homeostasis means 'co-ordinated processes that keep conditions necessary for life within certain limits'. It means that a baby can adjust physically to conditions outside the womb, such as breathing, digestion and temperature regulation. The child also learns to receive and process sensory stimuli from the environment. The way this happens is determined by the temperament of the child and the responsiveness of the environment. If babies are not experiencing stress (pain, hunger or tension), they will have time and energy left to discover their own bodies and will try to repeat pleasant experiences. Babies can be fascinated by their own hands and fingers: they put their toes and fingers in their mouths and turn their heads towards light, sound or movement. Everything is still primarily sensory. Touch, taste and smell develop first, then sight and hearing, followed by the combination of the various senses at the same time. A baby sleeps a lot in the beginning, soon seeks for food, wants to be held against the body of a loving, trusted caregiver. In the interaction between baby and caregiver, a pattern emerges by itself: a rhythm of rest and activity and therefore a predictable regularity. It is important for parents to experience that they can satisfy their own child: being together without the need for verbal communication, where a baby feels that their presence is appreciated.

Relaxation and fun become visible in the baby's laughter and relaxed body. Pain and stress are expressed through crying and cramping. In fact, emotions are still diffuse. Touch and experiencing with the whole body are basic to the further differentiation of the emotions. Hunger and thirst are necessary survival mechanisms. The sucking reflex, the turning of the mouth towards the breasts, which is stimulated near the mouth, is of vital importance in the first months. Groping with the mouth is the most primitive way of exploring objects. One often sees older children as well as adults unconsciously making the natural gesture of bringing their thumbs or hands to their mouth. It calms them when they are anxious, scared or tired. Kissing or hugging beloved people can be traced to this fact: a basic need and an expression of intimacy.

Babies experience themselves as a whole: they are their bodies. Sucking, biting or unconsciously touching pleasant spots on their bodies happens naturally and without intention. 'Skin hunger' is a basic need that underlies the development of intimacy and the feeling of being and staying connected with others. Cuddling and touching make a baby feel safe.

Figure 3.2: The obvious closeness between mother and child

In summary, in this first stage, basic emotional needs are linked to the regulation of physiological needs; integration of sensory stimuli; structure of place, time, persons and activities; constency in the environment; and stimulation of attachment behaviour and physical contact.

Characteristic for this first stage is homeostasis versus dysregulation.

- The child finds a balance in rest, rhythm and regularity: balances between effort and relaxation, day and night, eating and sleeping, being awake and playing are gradually formed.
- The 'other' is important: the parent/caregiver is nearby and direct physical contact is desirable and much needed.
- The child still feels connected to and not separate from the parent/caregiver.
- Appropriate dosage of sensory stimuli and impressions is important.
- The proximity senses (like taste, smell and touch) and the whole body are used to explore and experience the nearby environment little by little.
- Emotions are still basic and diffuse: tension and stress are expressed with the whole body, and the child experiences cramping, crying and screaming. Relaxation and pleasure are expressed in eye contact, laughter, cooing, wordless togetherness and the relaxation of the body.

3.2 Stage two: attachment or first socialisation (six to 18 months)

The baby has a more steady rhythm and can tolerate more time between feedings, and there is a transition from liquid to solid food. The child is awake for longer and has more time to perceive the surroundings and to move. For example, the child will experiment with rolling, raising the head, practising the use of the arms and legs, sitting, crawling and expanding their world. The motor skills mature neurologically and increasingly enable the above activities. The period from one to two years of age is the stage when children gain the most basic movement experiences. It is the period in which simple patterns are developed: grasping an object and moving through space while maintaining balance. These simple movement patterns are united into a functional whole. Emotionally, a child begins to learn that there are limits to movement: that action has an effect and can cause a reaction in the environment.

These experiences are the precursors of a later self-awareness, knowing that there is a connection between yourself and the environment and that 'I' can be responsible for events in the environment (Rygaard, 2007). Through 'trial and error' the child will automatically discover what has an effect. The child will repeat whatever is funny and pleasant, whereas they will try to avoid whatever is fearful or painful. This is pre-eminently the period of playing 'in the playpen', which is a safe and structured playing environment. Toys with sounds and effects are funny, and stacking cups and books with simple pictures are enjoyable. Babies increasingly recognise the things that occur in their daily lives. Furthermore, 'peek-a-boo' and endless games of 'in and out' are enjoyed; playing with sand, water, rice and finger paints also suits this stage. The child is increasingly aware of patterns and at some point knows what comes next. In communication, eye contact and babble with the important caregiver increases; this is pre-eminently the period of pleasure in action–reaction and reciprocal contact. The baby will laugh purposefully and will recognise familiar people. The baby also gets a sense of departure: they know that 'gone' is indeed gone. This 'object permanence' or 'person permanence', when it comes to objects or people, respectively, heralds the stage of attachment with the important other (parent or caregiver).

In this period basic security and confidence are formed. As a sign of this attachment, some children become more wary at this stage: they turn away when an untrusted person approaches or touches them. Children can then only be comforted or reassured by the trusted mother, father or caregiver. Other signs of this attachment are signs of uneasiness, anger, fear or sadness when the trusted person leaves. Cuddly toys become important, especially as replacement objects for caregivers if they are not physically present. In psychoanalytic and psychodynamic theory, this is called a 'transitional object' (Winnicott, 1953). Cuddly toys provide comfort, a sense of familiarity and the feeling that the baby can control the toy. Emotions that belong to this stage are lust/discomfort, love (reciprocity in close contact), separation anxiety, panic in unknown situations and temperamental behaviour in the form of screaming and crying loudly. Again, predictable patterns mean safety and the absence of stress. The baby will make the first targeted sounds, babble, scream and use words. This is the stage where one can name everything one sees and does.

At this stage, children's vocabulary matures without them being able to use all the words: the understanding of language precedes its use. During this period, children want to be with the caregiver all the time, so caregivers can hardly be absent, for example, to go to the toilet. Children are focused on being together, a kind of natural attachment and necessary symbiosis. This is also pre-eminently the period in which the child's attention can be focused by naming what one is doing, for example by taking the child on one's lap and looking at pictures together or reading simple stories. The creation of shared attention ('joint attention') is an important condition for concentration and learning in later school development (Tomasello, 1986).

Figure 3.3: Shared attention and togetherness

Children use their bodies to explore the world, understand what body parts are called, make repetitive movements and reach the first developmental milestones such as sitting, crawling, walking, drinking from a cup or eating with cutlery. Children feel their genitals if they feel comfortable doing so. There is no embarrassment about this for them; it is just experienced as a relaxed, pleasant feeling.

In summary, in this stage, the basic emotional needs are physical contact, interaction and reciprocity, the presence of the important 'other', attachment, security and trust, social stimulation and the handling of objects.

Characteristic of the second stage is trust versus mistrust.

- There is a need to be together and connected, regardless of what the activity is, a kind of natural and necessary symbiosis.
- The important other person is within reach and preferably always in sight and available.
- The child takes pleasure in action and reaction: reciprocity in contact, activities and communication and play.

- The basis of attachment is formed: security and confidence.
- There is the beginning of joint attention.
- The world is explored through games and regularly recurring activities.
- The basic theme is building feelings and an awareness of safety and trust.

3.3 Stage three: autonomy or first individuation (18 months to three years)

Children discover their own will, fight for autonomy and are afraid of losing it, want to do things by themselves and frequently say 'no!' Children are confronted with the opposition of autonomy (doing what they want) and dependence (doing what others want). This is the famous toddler stubbornness or 'the terrible twos'. The child enlarges their world, but must know that the caregiver is nearby. There is interaction with peers, albeit next to each other rather than really with each other.

Emotions like fear, pride, sadness, jealousy and love start to play an important role. Communication is more mediated by language. Characteristic of this period is the intense focus on oneself (egocentric behaviour) and the difficulty in controlling all kinds of feelings. A toddler can quickly feel hurt or misunderstood if one is joking: they feel laughed at. Imitation is an important way of learning things. As a caregiver/parent, one is important as a role model.

There is no internal conscience yet. The outside world must therefore uphold the rules: when you walk out the door, the conscience, as it were, walks out with you. This age is also known as the stage of stubbornness or prepuberty. Children are stubborn because they constantly conflict with their environment and themselves. This causes inner tension. Above all, children want to decide for themselves; everything has to be done their way. On the other hand, the toddler is still very dependent.

Furthermore, this is typically the beginning of the 'why' stage: wanting to know everything but not yet being ready for very detailed information. The vocabulary is expanding. Language has become an important means of communication. Imitation also begins. The toddler is looking for boundaries and tries them out regularly. There is a need for clarity and a framework. If these are given, this is often a reason to resist and get angry. In this way one can easily, and more often than is desirable, enter into a battle with children in this stage. By being consistent in the rules provided (repeating them regularly and quietly, without anger), children learn where they stand, even if they protest at first. This provides a safe framework with room for negotiation and choice. However, thinking is young, concrete and linked to the here and now. The child mainly thinks from their own perspective: children are not yet able to adopt the perspective of the other.

The toddler becomes toilet trained during this stage: the child experiences that the sphincter muscles of the bladder and anus can be held and released. This is the first physical experience children have of control and power over themselves, something that is not easy to give up and is not experienced everywhere. It has been observed that children do not like to poo in strange places (many adults do not either). This is the very first experience of having to let go of something from oneself. In addition, children can be very proud of their own product, and it is of course very interesting for them to talk a lot about poo and pee.

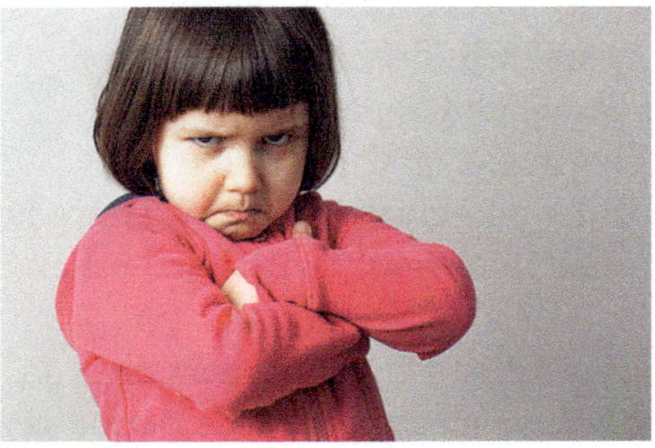

Figure 3.4: Toddler disagreeing

The experience of the will arises: the ability to make choices. The self, concretely denoted as 'I' or 'me', is central. This is the stage at which autonomy and the beginning of a person's own identity are formed. If this stage is completed properly, a sense of autonomy is well developed. If not, feelings like shame and doubt are more prominent. If children are not given the opportunity to develop their own will, they will be ashamed of their will. The child will want to please others rather than be driven by their own motivations. The child will constantly practise holding and letting go. In fact, the child will ask: is my 'self' worth it? At this stage, the child experiences that other people have their own identities.

Almost all healthy children can walk during this stage. They play in the sandbox, ride tricycles and start painting, scratching on paper and the first puzzles are completed (first inlay boards and then puzzles of four to nine pieces). They build with blocks (e.g. Duplo and Lego) or play with toy cars, trains and dolls. This is the period in which children learn to sing songs and are able to understand many more stories read to them by caregivers. Children see pictures and thus expand their vocabulary enormously. The use of language is now exploding. One-word sentences are used to indicate what they see or want. Just think of 'beep beep' for a car. Whereas one child continues to babble for a long time and gradually learns to speak better and better, another child will be silent for longer and then suddenly speak in clear words. As a role model, it is always important to mention what you are doing. In this way, children quickly learn their native language and joint attention is increasingly stimulated. Children start to get a sense of self-awareness and all-powerfulness about their bodies. There is an awareness of the different appearances of boys and girls. Their own bodies and those of others are discovered. The use of words such as 'poo' and 'willy' is very interesting, and, partly inspired by the rules imposed by caregivers, there is the beginning of an awareness of what is and is not acceptable. There is no sense of shame yet, and touching genitals can provide a soothing and relaxing feeling.

In summary, in this stage, the following basic emotional needs are central: more distance from caregivers while still having them in the picture, confirmation of a certain degree of autonomy and reward for social behaviour.

Characteristic of the third stage is autonomy versus dependence.

- There is a search for autonomy and the beginnings of identity.
- The 'self' is central.
- There is an increase in the use of language.
- The child looks for boundaries and an underlying clarity and safety.
- The child says 'no' but cannot offer sensible alternatives.
- The key emotions and characteristics are a quick temper, anger or jealousy, trouble sharing, feelings of omnipotence and impulsiveness.
- The important other can negotiate and offer options from which to choose.
- The important other is nearby, can intervene/steer if necessary and provides natural boundaries.

3.4 Stage four: identification (three to seven years)

In this stage, children can be separated for longer periods from the important other, on the condition that the environment is familiar. This means that they are emotionally able to attend school.

Assuming normal development, most children are toilet trained at this stage. They speak in sentences and sometimes come up with their own fantasy words to describe existing things for which they do not yet know the right words. The ego continues to develop. Thought is still self-centred and all-powerful: children cannot really imagine that someone else can think differently from them. Their ideas are true. This is also the time of fantasy and fairy tales: this is reflected in the immersion stories and games. 'Magical thinking' fits into this: truth and fantasy are not yet separated. Whatever they come up with is perceived as really true: a fantasy boyfriend is as real to them as a real boyfriend. Playing doctors, pretending to be mummy or daddy and dressing up are fun activities. The child is able to accept and understand simple rules about social behaviour. It is only during this stage that children start to play together reciprocally. They imitate the behaviour of their caregivers, teachers and identify with members of the same sex. In this stage, simple board games can also start to be played (such as Lotto and dominoes).

Figure 3.5: Identification with Superman

Children become creative: they are going to build and construct and not just imitate. In the kindergarten classroom you see a doll's corner and a construction corner. Drawing skills develop, with children creating simple figures and objects such as balls, houses, etc. The gross and fine motor skills develop rapidly. This is the period in which 'spatial skills' are central. A child learns to walk and run, play hopscotch, cycle, swing, ride on play cars and go-karts, play hide-and-seek and pass the ball. Preschoolers can have fun with the movement itself: training and acquiring the skills provide them with intrinsic pleasure and can therefore continue indefinitely. One can observe clearly how important movement experiences offer a basis for the development of feeling and thinking. Using iPads, computers or smartphones is often just as attractive for these children and keeps them quietly busy. Finding a balance between physical movement and playing on the one hand and sitting still on the other hand is an important consideration in education.

There is the beginning of the development of conscience: knowing what is and what is not allowed and understanding the effort it takes to comply if the important other/parent is not around. Fear of failure can also arise during this period: the fear of not being accepted by the caregiver. Feelings that characterise this stage are happiness, (a nascent) empathy, a fear of failure and shame. This stage is characterised by playing, through which children acquire many skills. Girls strongly identify with mum and the female teacher at school and boys with their father or male teacher. Children fall in love and they experience that feeling as a special friendship. They can fall in love with someone of the same or opposite sex. Nightmares are very common during this period. Children experience a lot of things and think a lot too, but they often do not yet fully understand how things work. It is not yet possible to distinguish between reality and fantasy, and they can take everything concretely and literally. Thanks to this 'magical thinking' the world is very exciting. Scary dreams are a means of dealing with these tensions.

Preschool children are aware that there is a difference between the sexes and that their sex will not change. Partly because of the arrival of younger brothers or sisters, they start to have some knowledge about pregnancy and birth. There is an increasing idea of what is private and of boundaries. Preschoolers can name their genitals and know where to touch and not to touch. Feelings of shame can increase. Physical contact remains important, although it takes place less often in public. Young children like to play doctor. They are curious and thus discover each other's bodies together. This is part of their development, but it is important that caregivers lay down some rules about what is permissible and what will not be tolerated.

To summarise, in this stage, the basic emotional needs are the presence of an identification figure, the experience of social acceptance and social competence. Characteristic of the fourth stage is initiative versus inhibition.

- Children start to be aware of social rules.
- There is the beginning of empathy and friendship.
- Children identify with important role figures.
- Children inhabit a magical world: fantasy and reality merge.
- Children become creative, take pleasure in building within games and activities and enjoy role playing.
- The key emotions are love, fear of failure, shyness.
- Conscience begins to develop.
- An important other is there every day at recurring moments, but does not always have to be physically present.

3.5 Stage five: reality awareness (seven to 12 years)

At this stage, the child is mainly active in the intellectual field. From the age of seven, children learn school skills such as calculating, reading and writing. The everyday world becomes a natural pattern in which a child can usually function independently. Children only need a parent/caregiver nearby in case of arguments or panic, to share what happened that day or to arrange things that are out of the ordinary. Children can fully express themselves through language; only with unusual or more abstract words will they ask for an explanation. Real friendships are developed during this period. Girls are often more attracted to girls, and boys only want to play with boys. Measuring physical performance becomes important. This is the period when children start to play sports (and develop skills and discipline through them) or musical instruments. There is an urge to compete with peers, and the child develops their own interests, needs and wishes.

Figure 3.6: Soccer playing in a team, exercising with competence and competition

Children know very well the difference between reality and fantasy now. This is the stage in which the belief in Santa Claus disappears – usually around age eight or nine. The development of conscience continues: children can adhere to rules, even if the important other is not present, because their own conscience has been internalised. During this period the child develops a religious ego (a sort of awareness of God) if religion is a part of daily life: 'it is crazy that we exist and there is more than what I can see around me.' In addition, there is a realisation that there was a time when they were not yet there. Interest in and understanding of history, geography and biology increases.

Just like at the age of two to three, there is an inner struggle: children try to free themselves (real prepuberty) from the dependence on their important others and want to take responsibility for their own behaviour. This can lead to worry or some nervous habits. In general, this is a quiet period emotionally for both children and parents, in which children can play endlessly, play sports, read and increasingly play games on the computer or become active on social media with a smartphone.

In terms of physicality and sexuality, it seems like a quiet period, but there is an increase in knowledge. In the primary school curriculum in the Netherlands, attention is paid to sexuality from the age of ten. Children are increasingly aware of pregnancy, reproduction, sexual intercourse and masturbation, and they know the right words for these things. Children are the most receptive to sex education just before the onset of puberty. It helps if boys and girls know what to expect around the physical changes that will come with puberty. The availability of the internet means children may see images that are explicitly sexual at an early age and may come into contact with porn websites. Parents and caregivers should discuss this with them to indicate what is real and what is appropriate in which situation. Talking about sex reduces discomfort. For boys and girls in this stage, the differences between friendship, relationships and love are clear. There is an increasing interest in adult sexuality, and children may increasingly stimulate their own genitals. Physically, the first signs of puberty can become apparent (such as pubic hair, nipple growth, first ejaculation or menstruation). At the end of primary school, children may experience exciting events such as falling in love, their first 'courtship', going to camp, performing a musical and saying goodbye to primary school and moving to a larger school, often a little further from home.

To summarise, in this stage, the basic emotional needs are the recognition of one's own achievements, productivity and creativity in dealing with the material world and fixed rules of social behaviour, also referred to as 'golden rules of interaction'.

Characteristic of the fifth stage is self-confidence versus inferiority.

- Children are able to distinguish between fantasy and reality.
- Children are focused on competence and competition.
- There is an increase in cognitive growth around general knowledge.
- Children are aware of the fixed rules of social interaction; the 'golden rules' have been internalised.
- There is an important other, but this caregiver is not involved in all day-to-day matters.
- Friendships become closer: girls are drawn towards other girls and boys towards other boys.
- Emotionally, it is a relatively quiet period.
- Initial knowledge and interest in courtship, infatuation and sexuality emerges.

3.6 Stage six: social autonomy (12 to 17 years)

Puberty, as the beginning of adolescence, is a stormy period that involves physical, emotional and mental changes. Children are going through a growth spurt: first the hands and feet and then the back, legs and arms. Girls overtake boys physically and are often taller and physically more mature around 12 years of age. The young person develops both primary sexual characteristics (growth of the genitals) and secondary sexual characteristics, such as hair around the genitals, armpit hair, beard growth and a lower voice (in boys) and breasts (in girls). Sexuality and body experience become very important, partly because of all the changes taking place in the body. Thinking and talking about all of this, and making fun of it, is common. The development and perception of sexuality differs from child to child, and is also related to differences in culture and environment. Girls have their first period; boys have their first ejaculation. Both boys and girls experience more sexual arousal and masturbate more frequently. Appearance becomes very important: it is all about seeing and being seen. Embarrassment, blushing and shyness around the opposite sex fit into this picture, as do turning endlessly in front of the mirror and making sure you are well dressed so as to fit in with the group and not stand out too much. Clothing from well-known brands is important for many adolescents.

Parents face a hard time at this stage because children explore boundaries when it comes to household rules, norms and values. Competing against parents and identifying with peers are at the forefront. Feeling misunderstood fits into this period. There are also adolescents who withdraw: they spend a lot of time in their rooms, hardly interact with their environment and live very much in their own worlds, and home functions as a kind of hotel, a place to sleep, to get clean clothes, to eat food and, above all, to be able to go their own way and be left alone. Adolescents who already had good relationships with their parents will still be able to share their feelings of stress and doubt and their experiences with them. Young people with a less good relationship with their parents use their freedom and space to avoid, reject or constantly argue with them, which can be at the expense of their own well-being and mental health. The family and relatives continue to play an important role in adolescents' search for their own roles and identities, with young people either identifying with or opposing their elders. It can be hard for parents to let go of their children, especially if they believe that their children are not doing useful things. Still, it is important to instil confidence and to provide them with their own space. The best way to face the expanding world is by noticing your own experience of what works and what does not. At this stage, parents are literally and figuratively standing on the sidelines. It remains important to be there and to have 'coaching' conversations when things are difficult.

Figure 3.7: Adolescents lost in their own world

Adolescents spend a lot of time on social media or gaming on smartphones, iPads, laptops, notebooks or computers. Their attention is focused, more than ever, on a digital world. This can be relaxing, but it can also lead to avoidance, depending on the extent to which this happens and disturbs other things in daily life. The internet is also a source of information, which is necessary for study. Schools are also increasingly providing 'online learning' through their own websites or teaching programmes. For many young people the internet has replaced television as a way of becoming informed about the world, playing games or relaxing (by watching their favourite series or YouTube channels). Under the influence of an increase in hormones and a changing body, as well as the rapid growth and maturation of the brain, adolescents experience a rapid alternation of (strong) emotions and seem to have an overactive emotion system. This can lead to impulsive action and thoughtless behaviour. There is a stronger urge to get emotional kicks or quick rewards. Because of the discomfort and changes they are experiencing, there is also great uncertainty and an intense focus on themselves, just like in the third stage. The difference is that there is much more need for a private territory in which parents have no business, both physically and in the psychological space. How peers or friends react, in real life and virtually, becomes very important. 'Do I belong to the group, can I participate and how am I seen by others?' The peer group and group culture become the most important social context in this period of life.

Sport remains important for many young people. They also need more money, to buy sweets and snacks at school, for cigarettes, for drinks, to go out or go for dinner, for smartphones or for clothing that is currently trendy. They have their first jobs, such as babysitting or working in a store.

The development from concrete operational thinking to abstract thinking take place: the young person is able to think in images and concepts and to make logical and theoretical connections. In this way, adolescents gain more insight into the functioning of their own neighbourhoods, countries and societies. Adolescents are able to take in a lot of knowledge, but at the same time they are often mentally lazy; their brains are 'off'. It is quite an art to stimulate and motivate them to learn or do their homework. For many, school is an obligation and by definition 'boring'. The young person is increasingly able to see complex connections. In this period a critical ego and an ideal ego are developed: the young person does not accept everything blindly, but thinks about what their opinion will be. Young people also have an idea about themselves, or an ideal image. This is also the period in which idols (e.g. sportspeople, musicians and YouTube, Instagram or vlog personalities) play a major role.

Boys and girls experiment with flirting and kissing. For a healthy development it is preferable that there is step-by-step experience with sexuality, that there is space and privacy for exploring and experiencing one's sexuality with oneself or with someone else. There is usually a build-up from (French) kissing and the groping of each other's bodies and genitals to sexual intercourse. How this path develops depends on the previous experiences of the adolescents. Do they have a positive body image? What are their beliefs about sex (possibly based on frequently heard messages at home)? How will they react under peer pressure? Media such as television, the internet and youth programmes draw a fairly sexualised picture of boys and girls, which is a risk for young people who are unable to handle the borders in this area properly.

During this period, boys or girls often find out for themselves whether they are heterosexual, gay or bisexual. With increasing experiences of falling in love, many young people come to understand to whom they are attracted. Depending on the tolerance in the family and local community, it is more or less easy to make this known. Ultimately, parents remain the most important and stable support figures for children, and this support is related to a successful transition to adulthood.

At this stage, the basic emotional needs are belonging to a peer group, a focus on one's own body (physical growth), retreating into one's own territory, distancing oneself from parents and looking for one's own identity/sexual orientation.

Characteristic of the sixth stage is identity versus role confusion.

- Young people are very concerned with appearance and body (seeing and being seen) and with love.
- Young people want to belong to the group and to blend into group culture.
- Young people are immersed in their own worlds and have a need for their own territory.

- Young people compare themselves with parents and still need them at the same time.
- Young people search for their (sexual) identity and orientation.
- Young people explore their sexuality with others and with themselves.
- There is an increase in cognitive skills (abstract thinking).
- The key emotions are insecurity, rapid mood swings and storms of emotions.
- There is experimentation with things that are exciting or not allowed.
- There is an increase in inhibitory capacity.
- Young people increasingly use the digital environment (e.g. smartphones and social media).
- The important other stands on the side, has a coaching presence within a good relationship and continues to indicate the limits in what is and is not healthy.

3.7 Stage seven: social responsibility (17 to 25 years)

This stage is characterised by increasing personal responsibility, with the parent or caregiver no longer having to be present every day to supervise or control. Young people are now physically at their peak to achieve in sports: this is reflected in professional football, where young people around the age of 21 already perform at the top level.

In the development of the brain, there is mainly the maturation of the frontal cortex, which is expressed in increasing executive functioning. There is an increase in inhibition, working memory, planning and flexibility. In short, these developments are about skills that are required to function independently. The brain is also becoming more creative as a result of the emergence of increasingly integrated and flexible connections. There is also an increase in adventurous behaviour: more risks are taken. Young people quickly think that something is possible and will be fun; they are looking for kicks (Crone, 2018).

More social and political awareness is also being developed (principled and critical ego), generating interest in discussion, debates and social themes. Today, there are young people who protest against gun violence in the United States or who protest against governments' climate policies and are concerned about global warming and environmental depletion.

Figure 3.8: Young people protesting

Really complex emotions, such as surprise or love, can now be recognised. In addition, there is an increase in emotion regulation during this stage; young people can now intrinsically control emotions themselves. But at the same time young people can still take great risks during this stage, especially if they are surrounded by friends who spend a lot of time engaged in risky activities. This is particularly difficult when there is a promise of reward and they think 'nothing bad will happen to me', which is still common at this stage. Parental influence can help to prevent this risky behaviour. At the end of this stage, the warning system has matured.

Most young people still ask their parents for advice with important matters or choices that have to be made. When something bad happens, most of them usually fall back on the safe nest that the parents have always been for them. Parents can be there, listen and support, but the young person makes their own choices.

Only at this stage are young people able to reflect on themselves and what has happened. This makes them ask 'who am I, what can I do and what do I want?' This is important for their search for their own adult identities. There can be considerable uncertainty about this, as adult life is imminent. Not everyone has a clear intrinsic goal or plan to create their own future. In this stage, young people enjoy their freedom and use it to gain experience with relationships and sexuality. Following their experiences in puberty, young people continue to take steps in sexual development. Young people may be quick to share their bed with one another, although there are large differences in the degree to which and speed with which this will happen. While it was customary 50 years ago to wait until after marriage to have sexual intercourse (which is still the case in more dogmatic religious settings), there is nowadays a lot more tolerance with regard to losing one's virginity. Partly because of the availability of contraception, many parents in the Netherlands prefer that sex take place under their roof rather than outdoors and in secret. In terms of sexual freedom, the Netherlands has thus become one of the most progressive countries. Yet there is a new kind of taboo among young people about saying too quickly that they are in a relationship. Less well educated young people often explore sexuality earlier and may settle faster into a steady relationship and move in with partners. This is partly due to the fact that this means they will enter the labour market faster, become financially independent and therefore have the opportunity to organise their own lives.

More well educated youngsters may start experimenting later with relationships and sexuality, but may also continue to do so for longer. As a result of having a longer period of education, they will often settle down and commit to permanent relationships later. There are adolescents who live together at these stages and may or may not marry afterwards. However, in terms of biological maturation, this period is very suitable for getting pregnant and having children. Many Dutch youngsters are only ready for this later. On average, the age at which people in the Netherlands have their first child is 29.8 years for women and 32.7 years for men (NJI, 2017).

The freer norms with regard to sexuality are partly reinforced by the use of social media, which allows people to find dates via the internet. Within Dutch society experimenting with relationships and sexuality is often accompanied by alcohol consumption. Although the use of cigarettes seems to be decreasing, there is a trend towards more alcohol use and the use of substances such as MDMA and GHB, especially at festivals. Nightlife has broadened from the café, terrace or disco to large festivals or dance events. It should be clear that there is more disinhibition as a result of substance use. It is known that this creates risks of addiction. Young people with a better self-image, a goal in mind, a stable social network and parents with whom they have built up a good relationship are less likely to develop addictions. Ultimately, most youngsters grow into pleasant and reasonable adults.

In summary, the basic emotional need within adolescence is to stand on your own two feet, to find your own identity and to take responsibility with regard to education, work and relationships and friendships. This stage involves the longing for intimacy and autonomy.

Characteristic of the seventh stage is intimacy and responsibility versus isolation.

- Young people take responsibility for their own health, relationships and long-lasting friendships.
- Executive functioning matures: reflection on emotions and emotion regulation is acquired.

- Young people are at their peak in terms of sports and motor skills.
- Young people form a critical and social ego.
- There is more experience of and control over sexuality.
- Young people pursue vocational education and transition to work.
- There is a transition from casual sexual intercourse to permanent relationships.
- Parents act as a fallback in situations of crisis and distress.
- The mentality is based on the thought that 'nothing bad will happen to me.'

4 And now back to Alicia

In the home in which she is living, the psychologist used the Scale of Emotional Development – Short (SED-S) to collect information about Alicia's basic needs by asking questions about her behaviour and way of reacting in various situations. She talked with Alicia's father and sister and with the caregivers involved with Alicia. The discussions with and collective experience of the respondents led to more understanding of the way Alicia is dealing with daily life. The SED-S profile is shown in figure 3.9.

The overall stage of emotional development is three, which means that Alicia will benefit from the support that is appropriate to the needs of the third stage. Although Alicia is 19 years old, physically in the seventh stage, able to manage herself in a familiar situations and communicate about her activities (which is more characteristic of the fourth stage), she needs an important other nearby to feel safe and relaxed. When stress occurs, she needs the support and availability of her father or caregivers she trusts. Alicia benefits from clarity and boundaries, although she opposes them loudly at the moment they are provided. In good moods she honestly admits her need to be close to important others. She enjoys the good atmosphere.

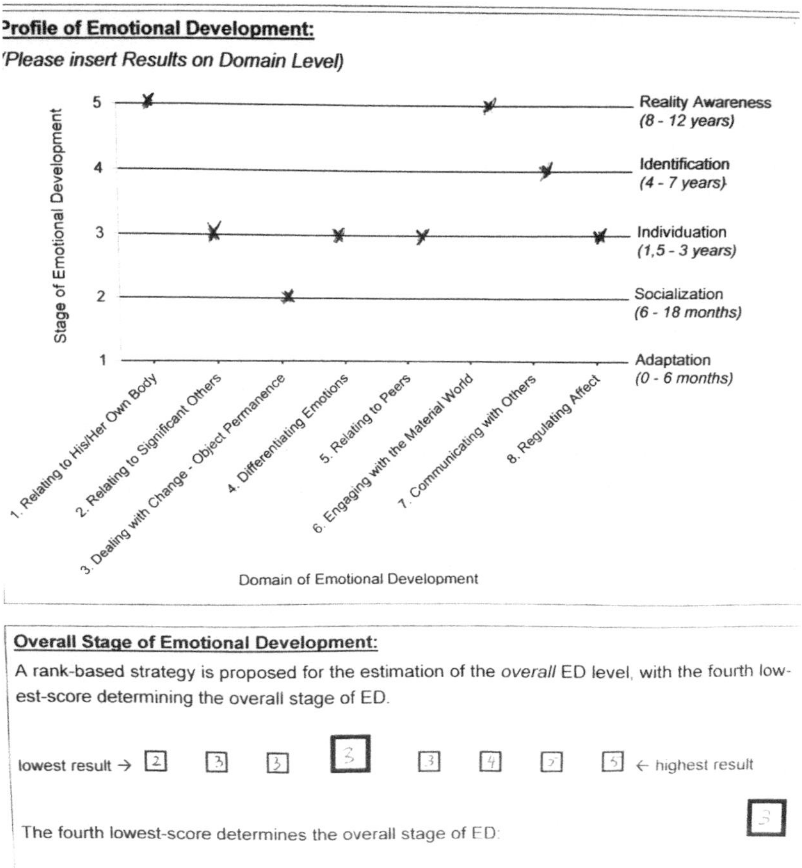

Figure 3.9: Profile of Alicia on the SED-S

5 Conclusion and discussion

This chapter has described how stages of emotional development contribute to the recognition and awareness of underlying basic needs within Anton Došen's developmental dynamic approach. To achieve this, the stages have been described in detail. Although the diagnostic scales in relation to emotional development still include five stages (the SED-S and the Scale of Emotional Development – Revised[2], described in chapters 12 and 13 of this book), the choice has been made to expand these to seven stages so that the entire development of children and young people can be described with regard to the milestones of emotional development from birth to adulthood. This description offers a tool for further developing the SED-S in future by adding stages six and seven.

Some colleagues have difficulty with the linear character of the description of the stages: it seems too static and not in line with the complexity of the lives of people with intellectual disabilities (Vugts- de Groot & Wijnroks, 2017). This could be a danger if too much emphasis is placed on the linearity of the development. In my experience of working in daily practice with professionals caring for people with intellectual disabilities, a description of normal emotional development is very helpful in recognising what is going on, especially when there are a lot of behavioural problems. Young parents all recognise the underlying basic needs of their own children.

It is important to be aware of the life experiences of young people and adults with intellectual disabilities who are older in physical age but have basic needs comparable to people at lower stages of emotional development, often the first three stages of emotional development. Stages one, two and three are the basis of the construction of the personality in Došen's developmental-dynamic model. When the development of intellectual capacity is delayed or limited, basic needs like the needs for security and proximity are faster and more often felt, and they must be fulfilled. This does not mean that grown-up people with intellectual disabilities should be treated as children of that young age: it means that involved caregivers should be able to recognise the underlying needs and be aware of what kind of support is appropriate at that specific moment. Emotional development means that resilience can vary from better to worse periods. Unlike emotional functioning (which reflects a state of mind in a specific moment), the concept of emotional development involves a broader range (bandwidth) and demonstrates a profile of functioning in several domains, sometimes in several stages. Recognition of the core aspects of the stages and the associated basic needs helps to contribute to the well-being of people with intellectual disabilities. Within diagnostics it is important to describe the profile of emotional development and integrate it in the total description of a person in which all important aspects are associated with each other.

References

Crone, EA (2018) *Het puberende brein: over de ontwikkeling van de hersenen in de unieke periode van de adolescentie*. Amsterdam: Prometheus.

Došen, A (1990) *Psychische en gedragsstoornissen bij zwakzinnigen*. Meppel/Amsterdam: Boom.

Došen, A (2014) *Psychische stoornissen, probleemgedrag en verstandelijke beperking Een integratieve benadering bij kinderen en volwassenen* (5th edition). Assen: van Gorcum.

Nederlands Jeugdinstituut (2017) *Figures on Youth and Education* [online]. Available at: https://www.nji.nl/nl/Databank (accessed March 2021).

Rygaard, NP (2007) *Hechtingsstoornissen: praktijkgericht therapiehandboek voor ernstige hechtingsstoornissen bij kinderen*. Amsterdam: SWP.

Sappok, T, Barrett, BF, Vandevelde, S, Heinrich, M, Poppe, L, Sterkenburg, P, Vonk, J, Kolb, J, Claes C, Bergmann T, Došen, A & Morisse, F (2016) Scale of emotional development – Short *Research in Developmental Disabilities* **59** 166–175.

Tomasello, M & Farrar, MJ (1986) Gezamenlijke aandacht en vroege taal. *Kinderontwikkeling* **57** (6) 1454–1463.

Verhulst, FC (2005) *De ontwikkeling van het kind*. Assen: van Gorcum.

Vonk, J & Hosmar, A (2009) *Emotionele ontwikkeling bij mensen met een beperking Een denk- en handelingskader voor de praktijk*. Leuven/Den Haag: Acco.

Vonk, J (in press) *Emotionele ontwikkeling: over basisbehoefte en draagkracht, kwetsbaarheid en plezier Een denk- en handelingskader voor de praktijk*. Leuven/Den Haag: Acco.

Vugts-de Groot, B (2017) Een reflectie op het gebruik van ontwikkelingsleeftijden binnen het domein van emotioneel functioneren. In: J de Bruijn, J Vonk, A v d Broek & B Twint (Eds) *Handboek emotionele ontwikkeling & verstandelijke beperking* (pp53–69). Amsterdam: Boom.

Wijnroks, L (2017) De relatie tussen cognitie en emotie bij mensen met een verstandelijke beperking: een neurocognitieve benadering. In: J de Bruijn, J Vonk, A v d Broek & B Twint (Eds) *Handboek emotionele ontwikkeling & verstandelijke beperking* (pp85–105). Amsterdam: Boom.

Winnicott, D W (1953) Transitional objects and transitional phenomena. *International Journal of Psycho-Analysis* **34** 89–97.

Chapter 4 Emotional development, stress and adaptation

Albert Ponsioen

Summary

Using a single IQ (intelligence quotient) score to determine the type and severity of intellectual disability was until recently common practice (and it sometimes still is). The strengths and weaknesses in the various domains of development can and must not be inferred from an IQ score. Another fallacy is the suggestion that these domains of development have not only theoretical but also practical relevance, as if the levels of cognitive, emotional, social and physical development could be assessed independently in a person. There is an alternative view that does more justice to the individual characteristics of especially persons who are indicated with the terms 'borderline intellectual functioning' and 'mild intellectual disability'.

1 Introduction

In somatic health care, the patient's complaint is central, and the diagnostics focus on the nature and seriousness of the complaint and the possible causes thereof. The patient tells their story in the doctor's office, not only about the complaint itself but also about their living conditions, history and thoughts and feelings. The doctor often focuses, however, on the somatic aspects of the complaint. The story of the patient is often of secondary importance, or is not addressed at all. There are even doctors who just find it bothersome that, besides an inflamed bowel, a hernia or a tumour, a thinking and feeling human being has walked into their office.

In mental health care the situation is fundamentally different. The thinking and feeling of the person are now the central issues. And if someone is less capable of expressing thoughts and feelings, the actions of the person must tell the story and allow the practitioner to infer the core problems. However, even if a person does not have any problems in verbalising the main reasons for seeking help, a major part of the manifest behaviour of that person will be the starting point of the therapist.

And with a little help from the *Diagnostic and Statistical Manual of Mental Disorders* (fifth edition) (DSM-5) (APA, 2014), a classification of the dysfunctional behaviour is made and a specific intervention justified.

But the behaviour of a person gives little information about the underlying causes of that behaviour. A very impulsive and distracted person can meet the criteria for attention deficit hyperactivity disorder (ADHD), but this classification (as well as classifications in general) has no explanatory power. ADHD is not caused by ADHD; it is only a summarising term for a cluster of behavioural symptoms. Similarly, the reading problems of a child can meet the criteria for dyslexia, but are not caused by dyslexia. Learning disabilities are not explained by a low IQ score; this IQ score is merely a confirmation of the learning disabilities. A common and persistent pitfall is the so-called reification of classification terms, as if these terms were latent factors causing the manifest symptoms. To cite Borsboom (2011): 'If you want to find the cause of the synchronized flight of a flock of starlings, you must not look for the latent bird.'

2 The network approach to mental disorders

A way of avoiding falling into the classification trap is to conceptualise mental disorders as dynamic networks of intrapersonal symptoms, interpersonal relations and external factors, with all kinds of feedback loops (Borsboom, 2017). Došen (2005) makes a distinction in this regard between personality (the motivational, cognitive and emotional foundation of adaptive behaviour) and temperament (the intensity of the behaviour). It is not only important to differentiate between the 'latent factor' and the 'network' approaches for theoretical reasons; it also has methodological and pragmatic implications: 'For the greater part of the scientific history of clinical psychology, the common cause idea – by which a common latent disorder determines a set of symptoms – was simply the only psychometric game in town' (Borsboom & Cramer, 2013, p. 93)[5]. Figure 4.1 shows the latent factor approach and the network approach. Figure 4.2 is an illustration of an elaborated network of ADHD behaviour in which the factors underlying the core symptoms are translated into behavioural characteristics, and only the strongest interconnections are included.

5 In 2010 a complementary classification system was developed, the Research Domain Criteria (RDoC). Unlike the DSM-5 the RDoC contains information about the aetiology of disorders (https://www.nimh.nih.gov/research/research-funded-by-nimh/rdoc/definitions-of-the-rdoc-domains-and-constructs.shtml).

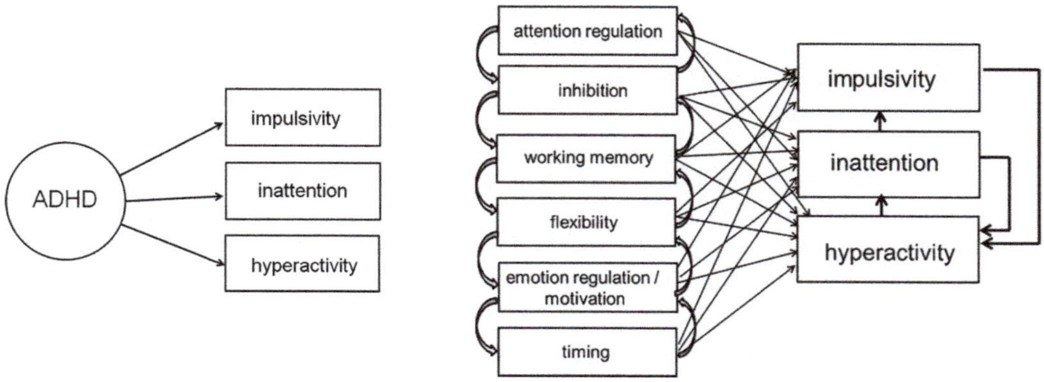

Figure 4.1: The latent factor approach (left figure) and the network approach (right figure) to ADHD.

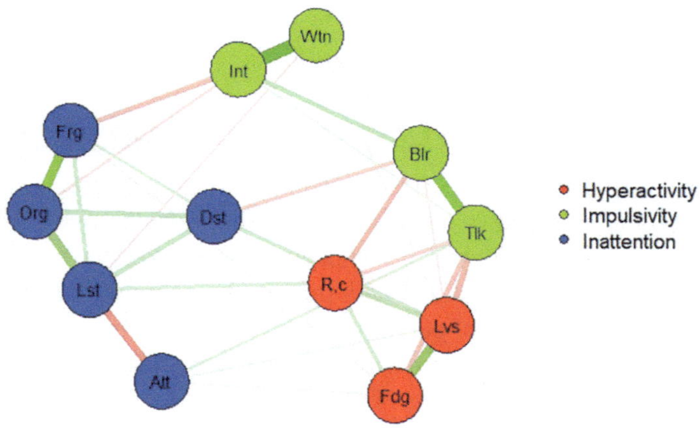

Figure 4.2: The network approach to ADHD with examples of behaviour operationalising the relevant factors underlying the core symptoms.

Att = attention difficulties, Lst = often does not seem to listen, Org = difficulty organising tasks and activities, Dst = is often easily distracted by extraneous stimuli, Frg = is often forgetful in daily activities, Fdg = often fidgets hands or feet, Lvs = often leaves seat in situations when remaining seated is expected, R,c = often runs about or climbs in situations where it is inappropriate, Tlk = often talks excessively, Blr = often blurts out an answer before a question has been completed, Wtn = often has difficulty waiting their turn, Int = often interrupts or intrudes on others (based on: Martel, Levinson, Langer & Nigg, 2016).

The network approach to psychopathology explains the high prevalence rates of comorbid disorders (Jensen & Steinhausen, 2015). The clinical consequence of this approach is to focus not only on the behavioural core symptoms but also on all known underlying internal and external factors.

The network approach is not only applicable on psychopathology. Every person can be characterised by more or less stable patterns of behaviour, a certain mindset and emotional and motivational tendencies. The degree of resilience of these patterns of behaviour, cognitive functions, emotions and motivational factors can be an indication of the risk of developing maladaptive behaviour. A network of these factors can lead to adaptive problems if an external trigger is strong enough to activate a few negative factors (symptoms). If the negative factors are weakly interconnected, the adaptive problems will not long endure after the external trigger is extinguished. If there are strong interconnections with other negative factors, this network of symptoms can be sustained even when the external trigger is long gone (Borsboom, 2017). In this way the distinction between adaptive and maladaptive behaviour is more gradual than sharp. Later in this chapter the clinical implications of the network approach applied to (mild) intellectual disability will be discussed.

3 Mental disorders and intellectual disability

Došen (2005) approached psychopathology in persons with mental retardation from a multidimensional perspective. Došen's model of personality development is an integration of models of neurophysiological, neuropsychological, cognitive, psychodynamic and social functioning, and of the development of attachment and the self. This resulted in a scheme of phases of personality development from birth to twenty-five years of age (Došen, 2005, p. 53). Mental disorders can be a consequence of a discrepancy between the developmental levels of the aforementioned personality domains. Especially when the emotional development is out of step with the cognitive development, maladaptive behaviour can emerge (Došen, 2005).

However, this so-called discrepancy hypothesis is increasingly being questioned. The aforementioned personality domains (patterns of behaviour, cognitions, emotions, motivation) can in theory be considered separately from each other, but the assessment of each developmental trajectory is a complex endeavour. Especially difficult, if not impossible, is measuring emotional development independently of cognitive development, despite the validity of instruments like the Scale of Emotional Development (Sappok et al., 2016). In diagnostic reports the use of mental ages for the different domains can suggest that (i) domains can develop at different tempos and (ii) the separate domains can be assessed in a sufficiently reliable and valid way. This suggestion seems to be an echo from the time when localised brain functions were still considered to exist. A theoretical point of view can be a useful description of a realistic situation but should not be confused with reality itself. An alternative to the discrepancy hypothesis is needed (see chapter 5, Wijnroks).

4 In search of an alternative hypothesis

Let us therefore revert to theoretical frameworks that better reflect the strong interdependence between the emotional development domain and the other domains. It is possible that the network models for conceptualising psychiatric disorders can also be of value in this context. Perry (2007) describes the development of neural networks from the first movement of the foetus in the womb to adulthood and demonstrates with impressive case studies the consequences of a less optimal development trajectory. In order to gain a better understanding of the relationship between emotional development and the development of social adaptive behaviour, a core concept in the context of (mild) intellectual disability, a look 'under the hood' of behaviour is useful. We therefore go back to basics: the development of brain functions (Ponsioen, 2014).

4.1 The development of brain functions

An illustration of the main brain structures and functions is given in figure 4.3. The development starts from the brainstem in the centre of the brain. From this area ('the reptilian brain'), the vital autonomous life functions (breathing, sleep/wake rhythm, blood circulation) and automatic behaviour (reflexes) are controlled. The development of this area takes place early in pregnancy.

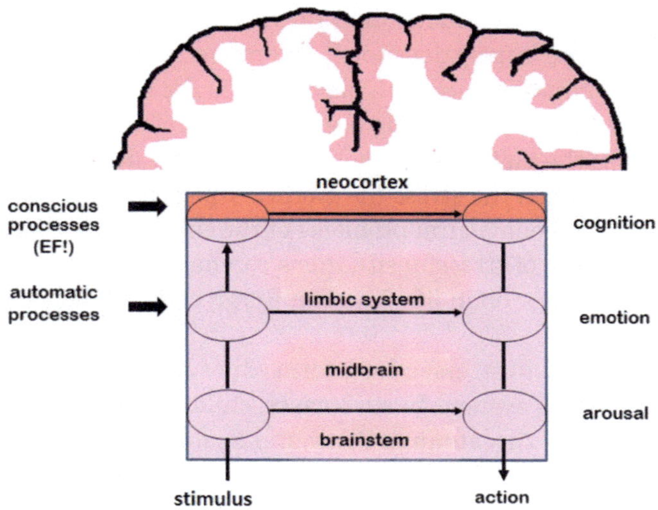

Figure 4.3: Layering of brain structures and functions (Van Cranenburgh, 1999)

Later in pregnancy, the brain structures that belong to the midbrain and the limbic system ('the mammalian brain') develop. These structures are important for giving emotional meaning to behaviour and memory processes. In the outermost layer of the brain, the neocortex ('the human brain'), development continues into adulthood. The neocortex consists of a back part (the posterior part) and a front part (the anterior part), separated by a central groove (the sulcus centralis) that runs across the brain. In the rear part, sensory perceptions are processed; in the front part, motor actions are prepared. This is not to say that our actions are driven solely by the neocortical areas. Most actions take place at a lower brain level and therefore largely outside of our consciousness. When someone calls your name in the street, your attention is reflexively drawn and you turn your gaze directly to the calling person. Subsequently, a feeling of recognition may (or may not) be evoked, after which a positive (or negative) emotion may arise on the basis of which actions are prepared (do you approach that person or pretend you do not know them?) Finally, an extensive search in our memory takes place if we cannot come up with the name of the person directly. And so all of the levels in figure 4.3 are often involved in our actions. In 'normal' development, the higher, later developing regions have a regulating function on the lower regions. The areas that develop into adulthood, the prefrontal cortex, direct the cognitive functions that give people conscious control over action: the so-called self-regulating executive functions (EFs). If these functions are less optimally developed, a person is less able to regulate the underlying functions (emotions and automatic behavioural patterns) when it is required in a situation.

4.2 The role of stress

The areas in the neocortex, especially those prefrontal areas that are still developing in a child, appear to be very sensitive to environmental influences. The optimal development of these areas is therefore largely dependent on optimal learning situations. Even during pregnancy, circumstances can play a role in the development of the brain of the foetus, not only alcohol and/or drug use on the part of the mother (e.g. Butcher & Fock, 2011) but also the mother's psychological condition during pregnancy. There is a correlation between the stress the mother experiences during her pregnancy and the emotional and behavioural problems of the child later in life (Swaab, 2014). The mother's experience of stressful situations can negatively affect the child's ability to cope with stress later on in life (Van den Bergh et al., 2005).

But even without an innate sensitivity to stress, a long-term exposure to unsafe situations can disrupt the child's stress system. In such cases, children can react to ordinary experiences as if they were threatening. Perry and Szalavitz (2007) describe the neurosequential approach in which traumatic experiences in early childhood can lead to dysfunction in different areas of the brain and brain functions. And if this dysfunction mainly concerns self-regulating EFs, the child is less able to contain their impulses (deficient inhibitory ability), is guided more by here-and-now thinking (deficient working memory) and more often 'gets stuck' in one pattern of action (lack of flexibility or switch ability).

These deficient functions concern the core EFs, also referred to as the 'cold EFs' (Ponsioen & Ten Brink, 2014). In people with these deficiencies, the emotions overly determine the action (figure 4.4). The EFs involving emotional and motivational processes, such as in social situations, are also referred to as the 'hot EFs' (Ponsioen & Ten Brink, 2014). As shown in figure 4.3, automated processes determine an important part of our actions. The brain learns to a large extent as a result of pattern-based, repetitive activity (Perry & Szalavitz, 2007). Connections are created between networks of neurons in the brain when these networks are activated simultaneously and repeatedly. Figure 4.5 shows how the development of the brain functions depicted in figures 4.3 and 4.4, in interaction with environmental factors, leads to ingrained patterns of feeling, thinking and acting (this is what the IWM, or internal working model, in figure 5.5 refers to). These patterns eventually lead to a more or less stable self-image, an awareness of the person's own identity and, later on, the personality characteristics of the individual. The emotional areas in the brain give an extra 'charge' to these connections. Children who already have less well developed EFs because of negative parenting situations during their development, also run the risk of developing a negative self-image. Therefore situations that call on problem-solving skills can automatically evoke feelings of failure and negative thoughts like: "This is way too difficult for me! I can't do this!", another negative experience on top of less optimally developed EFs.

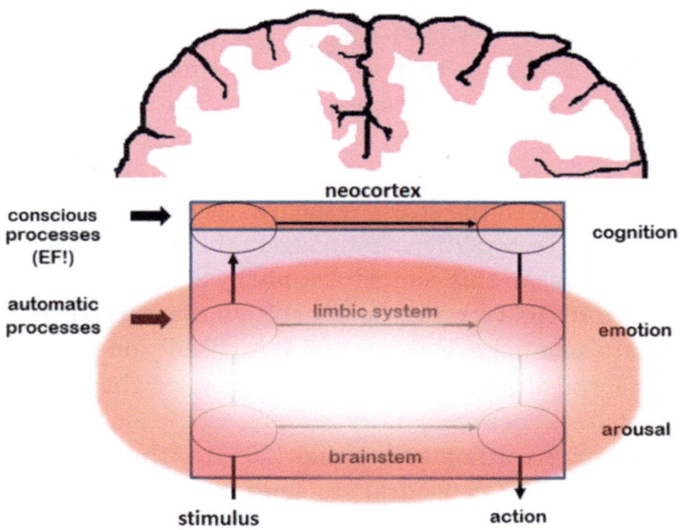

Figure 4.4: Brain-functions with failing executive functions (EFs)[6] (Van Cranenburgh, 1999)

6 Inspired by the work of Bruce Perry (https://www.youtube.com/watch?v=1uCn7VX6BPQ).

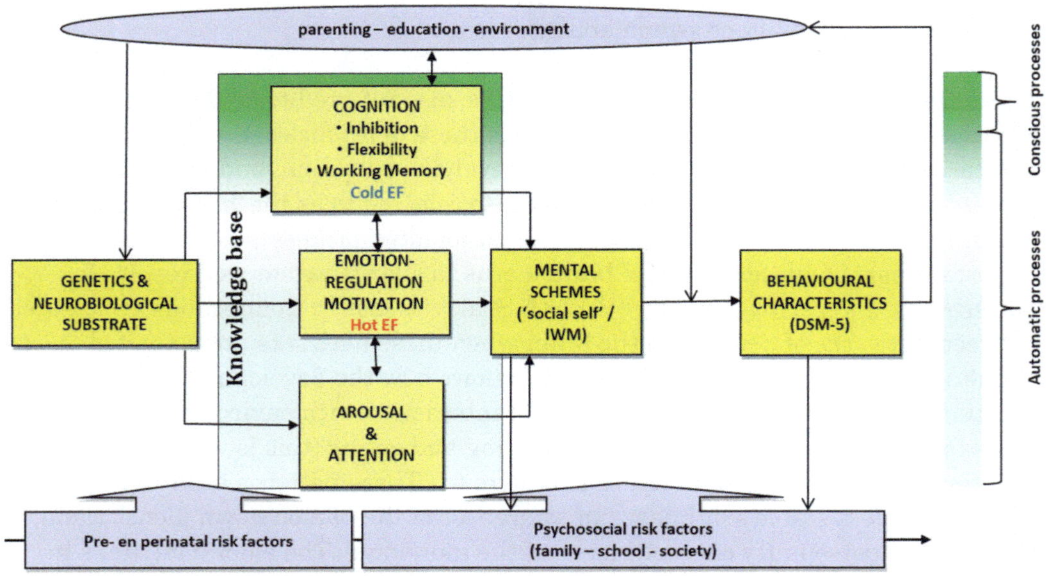

Figure 4.5: Transactional model of development (see Ponsioen & Ten Brink, 2014; EF = executive functions, IWM = internal working model)

4.3 A question of overloading or stress?

Wijnroks (2013) argues, however, that the concept of overloading can lead to confusion because it concerns a tuning problem between the situational demands and the skills of a person. It is not always clear whether by 'overloading' we refer to those demands or to the response of someone to those demands. And often one can conclude only afterwards, when it is clear that a person failed to meet the demands, that this was a case of the person being overloaded. Wijnroks therefore finds it more meaningful to talk about stress, because this concept makes the entire process more clear. A distinction is made between the stress response (the response to a demanding situation), the stressor (the condition that triggers the response) and the stress (the process). Wijnroks cites in this context a study by Swabe and Wolf (2013) in which chronic stress led to rigid stress responses. High concentrations of the stress hormone cortisol are said to have a toxic effect, especially on the prefrontal cortex, and, in people who already have limited EFs, even light stressors can lead to extreme stress responses. These may include fears, compulsions, mood problems and aggressive behaviour. According to Wijnroks (2013), if the stress hypothesis is placed at the centre of the behavioural problems of people with cognitive problems, there is no reason to use discrepancies between the different development domains as an explanatory model.

The neurosequential approach of Perry and Szalavitz (2007), already discussed in the previous section, offers insight into the consequences of extreme situations that have occurred at different stages of development in severely traumatised persons. As with everyone, fear is 'a bad counsellor'; in other words, fear makes it very difficult to think carefully. From an evolutionary point of view, switching from the prefrontal areas of the brain to the lower areas of the brain in a threatening situation is a good thing, because it means that the cause of the threat can be reacted to quickly ('fight or flight'). However, if this feeling of fear persists and leads to a chronic stress response even when the person is no longer in the situation that gave rise to the stress, a maladaptive behavioural pattern has emerged. As a result, children can be extra sensitive to stressors and can remain so as adults. This can then lead to a state of hyperarousal (increased heart rate, muscle tension), in which the midbrain is mainly active (figure 4.4). Sometimes, however, the oldest areas of the brain, in the brainstem, can take over, with 'freezing' rather than fleeing or fighting now the only option. There is then a reduced heart rate and an anaesthetic effect that reduces the painful feelings, a dissociative reaction pattern.

5 Practical implications

Wijnroks (2013; see also chapter 5 in this book) argues that clinical practice should focus more on determining sensitivity to stress and mapping the stressors that can affect someone in certain situations. This view is closely related to that of Perry (2009), who tailors treatment to information about the development of the brain. At certain stages of the child's development, the environment may have had a negative impact on, as Perry calls it, the neurosequential development. As a result, the highest cognitive functions can play too small a role in the actions and the emotions, and other automatic behavioural patterns can play too dominant a role.

However, it is striking how little use is made of these concepts in clinical practice. Searching for publications about stress and (mild) intellectual disability or intellectual disabilities mainly yields articles about the experience of stress by the parents or the caretakers of persons with intellectual disabilities; almost nothing can be found about the influence of stress on the persons with intellectual disabilities themselves. Much is known about the often stressful parenting situations in which many of the children and young people who are admitted to orthopedagogical treatment centres grow up (see, among others, Schuiringa, Van Nieuwenhuijzen, Orobio de Castro & Matthys, 2015). And much is known about the risks that these parenting situations pose for the development of a secure attachment (Giltaij *et al.*, 2015, or chapter 6, Sterkenburg & Zaal).
And by placing children and young people with similar problematic backgrounds in groups, the unsafe attachment history seems to be repeated (Bakermans-Kranenburg *et al.*, 2011). It could benefit treatment if the stress parameters (stressors, stress

responses) were measured systematically. In any case, it is important that guidance and treatment aim at reducing the stress experienced by children and young people. It is precisely the (hot) EFs among these youngsters that will often fall short when it comes to using them in daily social situations. It is therefore important to make sure that the social situations in which children and young people find themselves within residential treatment settings do not trigger the stress responses that activate the 'emotional brain'. Researchers and practitioners who focus on children with attachment problems could be consulted to help with this. The three basic human needs from the self-determination theory also provide starting points for setting up a living and learning environment that contributes to the development of children: autonomy, competence and social cohesion (Deci & Ryan, 2000). Autonomy means that you experience a sense of psychological freedom and choice in the performance of an activity, and it can be fostered by offering children choices appropriate to their age. Competence means that a child feels capable of achieving a desired result. Setting feasible challenges (also called 'adaptive learning') can help promote competence. Social cohesion refers to experiencing warm relationships with others and feeling included in a broader social network. One may wonder whether these conditions are currently being met in many care centres, where, in addition to the pressure-cooker effect created by behavioural problems, the chances of establishing a relationship of trust with an adult are, putting it mildly, not optimal. The teams in residential care centres often change, because of the age of the mentors combined with the strenuous job demands. A stable environment is particularly important for children and young people who have developed a sensitivity to stressors (see e.g. Perry & Szalavitz, 2009). In a clear, well-organised and predictable living environment, the chances of reversing an unsafe attachment development are greater. And this offers opportunities for developing a more positive self-image and for establishing reciprocal social relationships.

In order to know more about the adaptive vulnerability of children and young people, IQ scores and the use of questionnaires based on models of distinguishable domains are not very useful. In line with the network approach in psychiatry, the perspective on children and youngsters who are still classified with the labels 'borderline intellectual functioning' (BIF) and 'mild intellectual disability' (MID) should also be adjusted. If the child's IQ score is below average and if the child does not keep up well in regular schools, these labels are too readily and too often regarded as an explanation of the child's behavioural and learning problems. Figure 4.6 illustrates a classical and a network approach to BIF and MID. Individuals may share a cluster of elements or 'nodes' of symptoms and other factors, but the strengths, directions and valences of the interconnections of the elements can vary between individuals (see figure 4.7).

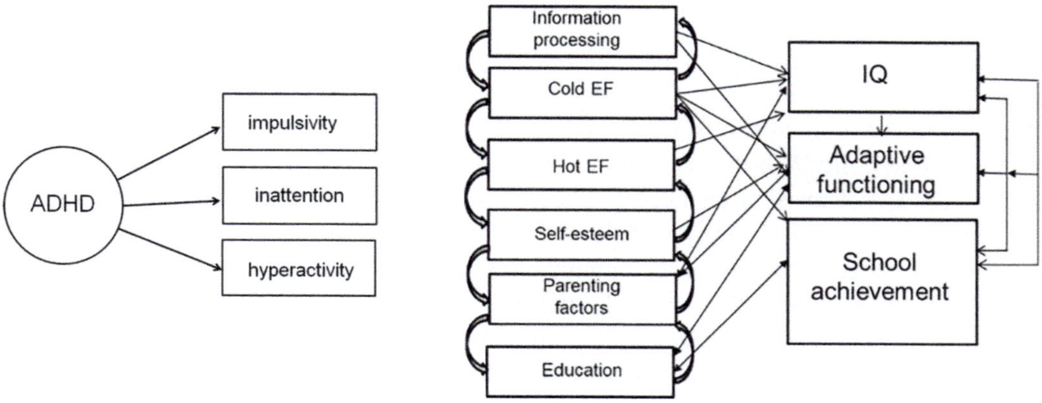

Figure 4.6: The latent factor approach to mild mental retardation (left figure) and the network approach (right figure), with some examples of relevant factors underlying the core symptoms (BIF = borderline intellectual functioning, MID = mild intellectual disability, EF = executive functions)

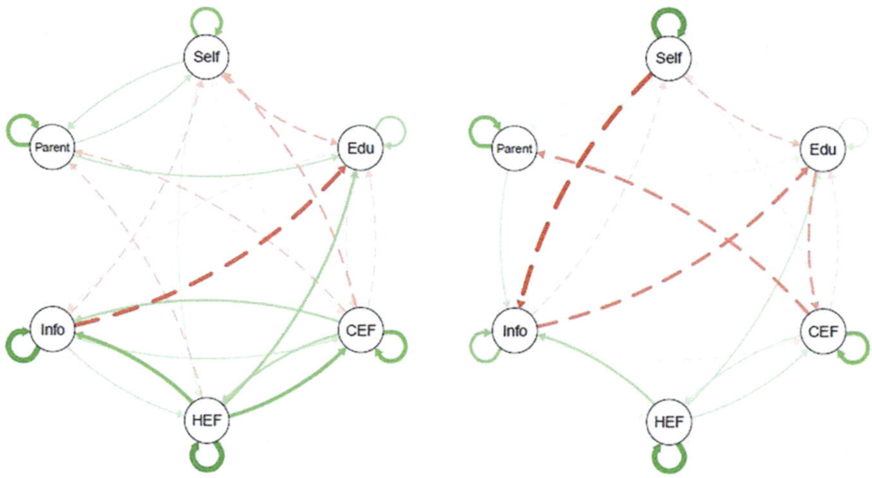

Figure 4.7: Individual networks (Self = self-esteem, Edu = education, CEF = cold EF, HEF = hot EF, Info = information processing, Parent = parenting factors).

The arrows signify the strength, direction and valence of the connection between two elements of nodes; the circular arrows signify the strength of the autocorrelation of an element (the stronger this autocorrelation, the more dominant this element in the network).

6 Conclusion

Diagnostics should focus more on the adaptive vulnerability of a child (Ponsioen & Nelwan, 2014; Ponsioen, 2014). Where does this vulnerability come from? What are the real limitations of the child? What are the potentially unexploited strong skills of that same child? What is the explanation of the problem behaviour, and would the 'stress hypothesis' offer more starting points for guidance and treatment than thinking in terms of different developmental ages (the 'discrepancy hypothesis')? Should not more specific biophysiological markers of stress responses (heart rate, skin resistance, cortisol) also be included in diagnostic assessment (see, for example, Wijnroks, 2013, and chapter 5 in this book)? For example, would an anti-cortisol agent such as oxytocin be a more targeted addition to the current often 'ex juvantibus' (deriving a diagnosis from the efficacy of a therapy) medication arsenal (Rueda et al., 2009; Scheifes, 2015)? And should the conclusion be that the terms MID and BIF are no longer adequate? After all, they concern adaptively vulnerable children, and it is important properly to investigate the nature and the reasons for these vulnerabilities (Ponsioen et al., 2016) and then to draw up targeted guidance and treatment advice based on this targeted diagnosis.

References

American Psychiatric Association (2013) *Diagnostic and Statistical Manual of Mental Disorders* (5th edition): DSM-5TM. Washington: Auteur.

Bakermans-Kranenburg, M J, Steele, H, Zeanah, C H, Muhamedrahimov, R J, Vorria, P, Dobrova-Krol, N A … Gunnar, M R (2011) Attachment and Emotional Development in Institutional Care: Characteristics and catch-up. *Monographs of the Society for Research in Child Development* **76** 62–91 doi: 101111/j1540-5834201100628x.

Borsboom, D (2011) *Presentation at the APS 23rd Annual Convention, 'The Many Faces of Network Analysis'* [online]. Available at: https://www.psychologicalscience.org/publications/observer/obsonline/network-analysis-a-better-way-to-represent-data.html (accessed March 2021).

Borsboom, D (2017) A network theory of mental disorders. *World psychiatry* **16** (1) 5–13.

Borsboom, D, Cramer, AOJ, Schmittmann, VD, Epskamp, S & Waldorp, LJ (2011) The small world of psychopathology. *PLoS ONE* **6** (11) e27407 doi: 101371/journalpone0027407.

Borsboom, D & Cramer, AOJ (2013) Network analysis: an integrative approach to the structure of psychopathology. *Annual review of clinical psychology* **9** 91–121.

Butcher, P & Fock, A (2011) Ontwikkeling van de hersenen. In: H Swaab, A Bouma, J Hendriksen & C König (Eds) *Klinische kinderneuropsychologie* (pp41–77). Amsterdam: Boom.

Deci, EL & Ryan, RM (2000) The 'what' and 'why' of goal pursuits: Human needs and the self-determination of behavior. *Psychological Inquiry* **11** (4) 227–268.

Došen, A (2005) *Psychische stoornissen, gedragsproblemen en verstandelijke handicap Een integratieve benadering bij kinderen en volwassenen*. Assen: Van Gorcum.

Giltaij, HP, Sterkenburg, PS & Schuengel, C (2015) Psychiatric diagnostic screening of social maladaptive behaviour in children with mild intellectual disability: Differentiating disordered attachment and pervasive developmental disorder behaviour. *Journal of Intellectual Disability Research* **59** (2) 138–149 doi: 101111/jir12079.

Jensen, CM & Steinhausen, HC (2015) Comorbid mental disorders in children and adolescents with attention-deficit/hyperactivity disorder in a large nationwide study. *ADHD Attention Deficit and Hyperactivity Disorders* **7** (1) 27–38.

Martel, MM, Levinson, CA, Langer, JK & Nigg, JT (2016) A network analysis of developmental change in ADHD symptom structure from preschool to adulthood. *Clinical Psychological Science* **4** (6) 988–1001.

Perry, BD (2009) Examining child maltreatment through a neurodevelopmental lens: Clinical applications of the neurosequential model of therapeutics. *Journal of Loss and Trauma* **14** (4) 240-255 doi: 101080/15325020903004350.

Perry, BD & Szalavitz, M (2007) *The Boy Who Was Raised as a Dog and Other Stories from a Psychiatrist's Notebook: What traumatized children can teach us about life, loss and healing.* New York: Basic Books.

Ponsioen, AJGB (2014) Adaptatie. In: J de Bruijn, W Buntinx & B Twint (Eds) *Verstandelijke beperking: definitie en context* (pp91–100). Amsterdam: SWP.

Ponsioen, AJGB, Groot, A de, & Maes, B (2016) Leerlingen met een licht verstandelijke beperking. In: K Verschueren & H Koomen (Eds) *Diagnostiek in de leerlingenbegeleiding: Kind en context* (pp339–358). Antwerpen: Garant.

Ponsioen, AJGB & Nelwan, M (2014) Van intelligentieonderzoek naar intelligent onderzoek. In: J de Bruijn, W Buntinx & B Twint *Verstandelijke beperking: definitie en context* (pp81–90). Amsterdam: SWP.

Ponsioen, AJGB & Ten Brink, EL (2014) *Zelfregulatie Diagnostiek en behandeling van executieve functies bij kinderen Trainershandleiding*. Tielt: Lannoo.

Rueda, JR, Ballesteros, J & Tejada, MI (2009) Systematic review of pharmacological treatments in fragile X syndrome. *BMC neurology* **9** (1) 53 doi: 101186/1471-2377-9-53.

Sappok, T, Barrett, BF, Vandevelde, S, Heinrich, M, Poppe, L, Sterkenburg, P & A Došen (2016) Scale of Emotional Development – Short. *Research in Developmental Disabilities* **59** 166–175.

Scheifes, A (2015) *Psychotropic drug use in people with intellectual disability: Patterns of use and critical valuation* (PhD thesis). Utrecht: Universiteit Utrecht.

Schuiringa, H, Nieuwenhuijzen, M van, Orobio de Castro, B, & Matthys, W (2015) Parenting and the parent-child relationship in families of children with mild to borderline intellectual disabilities and externalizing behaviour. *Research in Developmental Disabilities* **36** 1–12

Schwabe, L, & Wolf, O T (2013) Stress and multiple memory systems: From 'thinking' to 'doing'. *Trends in Cognitive Sciences* **17** (2) 60–68 doi: 101016/j tics201212001.

Swaab, H (2014) Klinische ontwikkelingsneuropsychologie. In: P Prins & C Braet (Eds) *Handboek klinische ontwikkelingspsychologie* (2nd edition) (pp57–76). Houten: Bohn Stafleu van Loghum.

Van Cranenburgh, B (1999) *Neuropsychologie Over de gevolgen van hersenbeschadiging*. Maarssen: Elsevier Gezondheidszorg.

Van den Bergh, BR, Mulder, EJ, Mennes, M & Glover, V (2005) Antenatal maternal anxiety and stress and the neurobehavioural development of the fetus and child: Links and possible mechanisms, a review. *Neuroscience and Biobehavioral Reviews* **29** (2) 237–258.

Wijnroks, L (2013) Kritische kanttekeningen bij de discrepantiehypothese en het concept overvraging Het stressmodel als alternatief. *NTZ – Nederlands Tijdschrift voor de Zorg aan mensen met verstandelijke beperkingen* **39** (2) 99–113.

Chapter 5
The relationship between cognition and emotion in people with an intellectual disability: a neurocognitive approach

Lex Wijnroks

Summary

In this chapter, recent empirical results and theories about the relationship between cognition and emotion are discussed. As much as it appeals to the imagination, the idea that the brain can be divided into an emotional brain, a cognitive brain and possibly a social brain is not supported by recent neuroscientific research. They are only psychological metaphors at best. The conclusion that can be drawn from this is that cognition and emotion are not independent processes. This means that the distinction, commonly used in the care of people with intellectual disabilities, between 'being able' and 'being able to cope' may actually be a false dichotomy. These new insights should not only lead to a different view of scientific and diagnostic research into the emotional development of people with intellectual disabilities, but also contribute to a better practice of care.

1 Introduction

Practitioners caring for people with intellectual disabilities in the Netherlands and Flanders usually make a distinction between 'being able' and 'being able to cope'. Generally, the concept of 'being able' refers to a person's cognitive abilities and knowledge, and the concept of 'being able to cope' to a person's social-emotional development or adaptive skills. An important assumption is that cognition and emotion are two independent processes, but in some people these processes are not developed to the same level. When such a discrepancy occurs, there is a risk that the person's social environment will overestimate or underestimate the person's adaptive skills (Došen, 2005; 2014). Furthermore, Došen (2005; 2014) believes that this discrepancy is the underlying mechanism that can explain the higher incidence of behavioural problems and psychiatric disorders in this population (Došen, 2005). In a paper published in 2013, I argued that this so-called discrepancy hypothesis is not supported by empirical research and the latest insights from neuroscience (Wijnroks, 2013a). It seems more likely that experiencing discrepancies between one's competencies on the one hand and the requirements and expectations of the environment on the other (in terms of living, learning and working situations; relationships and communication with other persons; and participation in society) is actually a general characteristic of people with intellectual disabilities, rather than a risk condition and an indirect cause of behavioural problems and psychiatric disorders. This discrepancy is what gives rise to 'support needs' and makes necessary support to reduce this discrepancy (Buntinx, 2016; Wijnroks, 2013a). If the idea of discrepancies between cognitive and emotional development in people with intellectual disabilities is no longer tenable, is diagnostic research into emotional development still useful, and can it contribute to an explanation for, for example, problem behaviour or psychiatric disorders? To answer this question, this chapter examines the relationship between cognition and emotion and argues that both processes are difficult to assess independently and that even at the brain level they are difficult to distinguish. This has consequences for studying emotional development in people with intellectual disabilities. The idea of a separate emotional brain, cognitive brain and social brain is intuitively attractive, but we will see that this idea is not consistent with the results of modern brain imaging. Our brains consist of complex large and small-scale networks, which not only continuously interact with each other but also are in competition with each other. These networks help us to understand the world and respond adequately to stimuli (Wijnroks, 2015).

The chapter begins with the question of what emotions are. Ideas about what emotions are have changed dramatically in recent years. An important discussion is whether emotions are separate processes that can be linked to specific brain areas that are part of an emotional brain, or whether they are constructions that are determined by the perception of physical reactions, the context and previous experiences. The chapter continues with a summary of research into the emotional competence of children and adults with intellectual disabilities. Researchers have questioned whether the problems in the emotional development of people with intellectual disabilities can be interpreted as a developmental delay, as Došen (2005; 2014) interprets them, or as a specific disorder, whether linked to a particular syndrome or not. Research in recent years seems to support the latter view in particular. Next, some new insights into how the brain is organised and how it deals with sensory sensations that can lead to emotions are discussed. These insights are applied in the new constructivist theories of emotions, which consider emotions to be socially constructed processes that depend on the perception of interoceptive or body signals, the context, and knowledge about the emotions. The chapter closes with some conclusions and recommendations.

2 What are emotions?

Although there are countless theories about emotions, and these are very different from each other, there is consensus on a number of core ideas. Most emotion researchers agree that emotions have an evolutionary adaptive function in that the development of emotions has contributed to the development of the human species. Furthermore, it is clear that emotions consist of several aspects: they contain both conscious and unconscious processes; they play a role in the relationship between the brain and certain body sensations (caused by the autonomic nervous system); and some, if not all, emotions are constructed on the basis of affective and cognitive processes. Most researchers also agree on the existence of separate emotions, such as fear and anger, as well as on the distinction between these basic emotions and higher-order or social-moral emotions, such as shame and pride. An important difference of opinion concerns the question of whether the basic emotions are innate (natural kinds) and are therefore independent of cultural processes, or whether they are constructed from a combination of certain basic processes that are not emotions themselves (building blocks or core processes, such as reward and punishment, arousal, pleasure) (see Barrett *et al.*, 2007; Gross & Barrett, 2011; Lindquist, 2013). The American psychologist Paul Ekman distinguishes six basic emotions, in which each emotion can be traced back to very specific facial expressions that are expressions of the inner emotional state. According to Ekman, these emotions and facial expressions are recognised in every culture, and must therefore be innate (Ekman & Cordaro, 2011).

With the exception of joy, each basic emotion can be linked to specific brain areas. Anxiety is linked, for example, to the amygdala, anger to the orbitofrontal cortex and gyrus cinguli anterior, sadness to the amygdala and right temporal pole, and disgust to the insula anterior and gyrus cinguli anterior. Today, however, there is much doubt about the idea that each basic emotion can be linked to its own unique set of brain regions or networks. There does not seem to be a one-to-one relationship between the perceived emotional expression, the subjective experience, the brain areas involved and the physiological processes in the body (Barrett & Satpute, 2013; Lindquist *et al*, 2012; Touroutoglou *et al*, 2015). Before discussing these new ideas, I will first summarise the research into the emotional functioning of children and adults with intellectual disabilities.

3 The development of emotional functioning in people with intellectual disabilities

Usually, the statement 'not being able to cope with something emotionally' refers to a multitude of problems at an emotional level, such as emotion perception and emotion regulation, also known as emotional competence (Twint & Veenstra, 2015). Emotional competence generally refers to one's ability to perceive, understand and regulate one's own emotions and to perceive and understand the emotions of other people (Baurain & Nader-Grosbois, 2013; Baurain *et al.*, 2013; Pons & Harris, 2005). It is important for the social functioning of children that they have good emotional competence (Harris, 2008). Problems in emotional competence are considered by many researchers to be an important predictor of all kinds of psychopathology (see e.g. Kret & Ploeger, 2015) and externalising and internalising problems (Trentacosta & Fine, 2010).

The idea of measuring the emotional development of people with intellectual disabilities is attractive to many behavioural practitioners who work with these people. The instruments that are currently widely used in this field, the Scale of Emotional Development – Revised^2 (SED-R^2) and the Experimentele Schaal voor de beoordeling van het Sociaal Emotionele Ontwikkelingsniveau (ESSEON-R), take as a starting point the observations of the person's behaviour by informants, so they mainly have a descriptive and not an explanatory function. If they are used in an explanatory sense, then the pitfall of circular reasoning threatens (Wijnroks, 2013a). In a number of studies, a group of researchers, in collaboration with Anton Došen, showed that the level of emotional development as measured with the SED-R^2 is related to problem behaviour (Sappok *et al*, 2014). Looking at differences in emotional development allowed researchers to distinguish between adults with an intellectual disability who have autism and adults with an intellectual disability who do not (Sappok *et al*, 2013). Unfortunately, this research does not provide any insight into emotional functioning itself.

Research into the emotional competence of children with an intellectual disability or developmental delays has taken place more recently and has increased in recent years. In many cases, the research focuses on specific syndromes, such as Down's syndrome, fragile X syndrome and Williams syndrome, or on disorders such as autism. Research into the development of the emotional functioning of children with developmental delays (see for a review: Kasari *et al.*, 2012; Niccols *et al.*, 2012) and adults with an intellectual disability (see for a review Scotland *et al.*, 2015) is still quite limited. The scarce research mainly focuses on emotion recognition and emotion understanding. Little research has been conducted into emotion regulation (see for an exception Baurain & Nader-Grosbois, 2013), and thus far there is no research into a person's perception of their own emotions among members of these target groups.

After a review of a study of children with an intellectual disability as a result of a specific syndrome, Kasari and colleagues (2012) concluded that these children have difficulty perceiving emotions in others and expressing emotions compared to typically developing children of the same mental age, but that these problems depend on the type of syndrome. For example, compared with other children with intellectual disabilities and typically developing children, children with Down's syndrome have more difficulty perceiving anxiety, show fewer emotional expressions and are also considerably slower in showing emotional expressions. Presumably, other restrictions also play a role here, such as problems with muscle tension and motor speed. Children with fragile X syndrome have no specific limitations in the recognition of emotions, but they do have limitations in the regulation of emotions (Kasari *et al.*, 2012). Another emotional skill is the degree to which one responds adequately or empathically to another's emotional expressions. In typically developing children, this skill arises simultaneously with the ability to recognise and understand the meanings of emotions in themselves and others. Children with Down's syndrome are more likely to show anxiety, prosocial and comfort behaviours than other children with developmental delays and typically developing children, although in a hypothetical situation they do not seem to understand the abstract concept of empathy. A recent review article on emotion recognition in adults with intellectual disabilities concludes that they have more difficulty perceiving and recognising emotions compared with other adults and typically developing children (Scotland *et al.*, 2015). There are two possible explanations for these findings. The first is the *emotion specificity* hypothesis, which says that the poor performance on emotion recognition tasks points to a specific limitation in emotion perception that cannot be explained in terms of general cognitive limitations. The second explanation is that the perception of emotions is intact, but the poor performance is due to problems in general information processing and intelligence. A recent study by Scotland *et al.* (2016) tested both hypotheses. The results appear mainly to support the *emotion specificity* hypothesis.

An important question is whether problems in emotional functioning are related to behavioural and social problems in children and adults with an intellectual disability. In a longitudinal study, Berkovits and Baker (2014) investigated to what extent problems in emotion regulation were linked to social problems in children with developmental delays and typically developing children. The children were tested at the ages of seven, eight and nine years. The results showed that children with developmental delays had more problems in emotion regulation and more social problems, but that problems in emotion regulation were not a significant predictor of later social problems, which was the case in the typically developing group. The researchers assumed that, in children with developmental delays, other factors play a more important role than emotion regulation in the development of social behaviour. After a systematic review of the literature, Davies *et al.* (2015) concluded that there is no relationship between the ability to recognise emotions and *challenging behaviour* in adults with intellectual disabilities. In summary, there is no scientific evidence that difficulties in the emotional functioning of people with intellectual disabilities is an important factor in the development of behavioural problems and/or psychiatric disorders.

The clinical literature describes patients who are unable to distinguish between, and cannot describe or label, their own emotions (Kret & Ploeger, 2015; Smith & Lane, 2015): they literally have no words for feelings. This disorder is called alexithymia. People with this disorder have a hard time distinguishing feelings and body sensations and have difficulty naming and communicating emotional experiences. Alexithymia can develop as a result of early child abuse and other forms of early trauma, as well as an insecure attachment relationship. The disorder has been linked to drug use and especially to violent behaviour, directed against others but also against oneself (Smith & Lane, 2015). The disorder was described by Sifneos in the early 1970s, but little research has been done since then. Today there is a renewed interest in this disorder. An interesting hypothesis to investigate is whether alexithymia can explain the problems with emotion recognition in people with intellectual disabilities. To my knowledge, only one study has been conducted on alexithymia in this target group (Davies *et al.*, 2015b). As expected, the researchers found a significant relationship between alexithymia and challenging behaviour, but only if both were assessed by professionals and not if the clients assessed themselves. Although it was a correlational study, it appears that challenging behaviour can be partly explained by an inability to perceive and describe one's own emotions and those of others (Davies *et al.*, 2015b).

An explanation for general problems with emotional competence is still lacking, however. In an earlier publication, Wijnroks introduced Daniel Kahneman's two systems model (2011) to help explain why many people with intellectual disabilities develop behavioural and psychiatric disorders (Wijnroks, 2013b). It might still be viewed as an important model, but it mainly explains why problems in behavioural regulation (including emotion regulation) can arise and does not say anything about the perception of emotions themselves. The next section discusses a number of findings from the neuroscientific literature that can provide more insight into the 'why' of these problems.

4 Cognition and emotion: the limbic system concept[7]

The idea of an emotional brain was introduced in the 1950s by the American neuroscientist Paul MacLean, who assumed that emotion is in the medial and the so-called 'older parts' of the cortex (for example the hippocampus and the gyrus cinguli) and cognition in the lateral and what he called the 'newer parts' of the cortex (LeDoux, 2012b). MacLean thought that the specific emotions, such as anger, fear and love, are products of the limbic system. He attributed the cognitive functions, such as thinking and language, to the neocortex. He included both the limbic system and the neocortex among the evolutionarily later parts of the anterior brain structures. These structures lie on top of the so-called reptilian brain (the basal ganglia and brainstem), and according to MacLean they have only developed in mammals and not in other vertebrates. However, MacLean's idea of an old and a new cortex was based on the knowledge of the neuroanatomy of the time (the 1950s and 1960s) and has now become obsolete (LeDoux, 2012b). In the first place, the precursors to the brain regions that MacLean tagged as 'new' are also found in reptiles and birds, and the limbic system not only has emotional functions but consists of different structures with both emotional and cognitive functions. One of those structures, the hippocampus, is considered as a core structure of the limbic system, but this area mainly has a cognitive function, including storing events in episodic memory and spatial information about the environment (Rolls, 2015). There is also no evidence that the parts of the limbic system function as one coherent emotional system (LeDoux, 2012b).

Most scientists were convinced, and some still are (including Ekman and Panksepp), that anger, fear, sadness, joy and disgust are not only separate emotions but also the product of separate, innate and culturally universal modules in the brain (for a review, see Lindquist *et al.*, 2012). Researchers such as Ekman and Panksepp claim that each basic emotion can be linked to a specific brain area, for example fear to the amygdala and disgust to the insula (Ekman & Cordaro, 2011; Panksepp & Watt, 2011). But the amygdala and insula, as well as other brain areas, show increased activity in a variety of different emotions. The amygdala not only appears to be involved in anxiety conditioning but is essentially a much

7 For a visualisation of the brain systems see chapter 2 and chapter 4.

more complex system than previously thought (Pessoa, 2015). A core function of the amygdala is that it contributes to selective information processing, because it is involved in systems that contribute to recognising a stimulus. But the amygdala also determines the importance of a stimulus for the person in question, for example in the case of an unexpected or surprising event. Finally, the amygdala is involved in systems that decide on what to do, because it contributes to the representation of the value of the stimulus (how relevant is the stimulus to me?) and in decision-making (Pessoa, 2015). Specific brain circuits have been found that play a role in behaviours such as fighting, fleeing or freezing, but the question is whether these are emotional behaviours as they can all be triggered by the same 'fear' stimulus (LeDoux, 2012b). Because these behaviours contribute to emotions themselves, they are also referred to as emotional primitives (Anderson & Adolphs, 2014) or core affects (Barrett, 2012, 2014).

The idea that the brain can be divided into an emotional brain, a cognitive brain and possibly a social brain is not supported by recent neuroscientific research. They are no more than psychological constructs; they are not specific brain systems or networks. According to Pessoa, cognition and emotion are the result of dynamic interactions between so-called *large-scale brain networks* (Pessoa, 2015). In the next section, these large-scale networks are discussed and explained in further detail and their relationship to the development of emotional functions is examined.

5 Large-scale complex networks in the brain

New brain research using imaging (especially functional magnetic resonance imaging) and complex statistical techniques reveals a completely different picture from the traditional division into an emotional brain, cognitive brain and social brain. Bressler and Menon (2010) even speak of a new paradigm. Simply put, the research of the last 10 years shows that the brain is organised into various large-scale and small-scale networks. Although the word 'network' is a formal term, in brain research it refers to a collection of sometimes anatomically widely spaced brain regions that are not only linked by long white matter tracts but also activated simultaneously when someone is at rest, during the performance of certain tasks or when someone observes something interesting. According to this paradigm, optimal brain function depends on a balance between processes at the local level (i.e. within a brain region that has a specialised function, also called a module) and the integration of these processes at a global level (in a large-scale network). According to these new insights, both cognitive and emotional functions arise through a dynamic interaction between processes in cortical and subcortical networks. They are therefore not the 'product' of one specific brain area. Several large-scale networks have been described. The simplest division is that provided by Bressler and Menon of three networks: the default mode network (DMN), the salience network (SN) and the central executive network (CEN). As mentioned before, none of these networks has a specific emotional, cognitive or social function. The DMN can be translated as the resting state network, because the brain areas that belong to this network are active (relative to other brain areas) when one thinks or reflects on oneself and others (Barrett & Satpute, 2013). The DMN is therefore an integrated system for autobiographical, self-reflective and social-cognitive functions. The main function of the SN is to focus attention on interesting or relevant external perceptions (for example, seeing an angry face) or internal, physical sensations (for example, a quickened heartbeat after seeing an accident). The main function of CEN is to plan, direct and monitor targeted behaviour.

Several researchers have pointed to the relationship between abnormalities in these functional networks and psychopathology, such as depression, schizophrenia, autism and attention deficit hyperactivity disorder (for a recent review, see Zhao & Castellanos, 2016). Moreover, the new paradigm has implications for the way we view different disorders. Rather than considering disorders as separate categories, they can be better described as dimensional constructs that can be linked to the functions of the different networks, so that we do more justice to the complexity and heterogeneity of psychiatric disorders (Casey *et al.*, 2014). Now that we have seen that the brain cannot be divided into brain areas with specific cognitive, emotional or social functions, we will look at how the brain deals with incoming stimuli and how this can lead to an emotional response.

6 The predictive brain

Most of us will agree with the statement that we live in an uncertain world, full of ambiguous stimuli and events about which we are unsure. The better prepared we are, the more efficiently we can respond to these stimuli (Bar, 2009). A well-known assumption is that, if we observe an object, we must first analyse the object's perceptual characteristics (for example, the contour, colour and surface texture) before we have built up a complete mental representation of the object and are able to recognise it. Furthermore, the input process depends only on an information flow that starts from the senses, in this case the eyes, and is further processed in the different brain areas, such as the primary visual cortex and ultimately the association areas, where the 'recognition' takes place. In other words, we interpret the world, according to this assumption, by analysing incoming information. But that is not what actually happens; as soon as we perceive something (for example, an object, a person or a situation), our brains continuously wonder whether the input resembles what we already know (Bar, 2009; Howry, 2012). Our brains work most efficiently if we can use our knowledge from previous experiences to make predictions about what will happen, and thus minimise surprises. We therefore speak of the *predictive brain*. Some of these previous experiences are preprogrammed or innate in many animal species, including humans, and do not require learning, such as bonding to individuals and a preference for looking at faces. At the same time, these preprogrammed predictions are not very flexible. This means that within certain margins the variations in facial configurations still lead to the recognition of a face, but larger deviations are seen as 'strange' or 'different'. The brain proactively and continuously generates predictions that are compared to the input, however rudimentary or incomplete that input might be. For example, we only need to see part of an object, even from an unusual angle, to recognise it instantly. Once an analogy (something similar to what has been previously observed) is found, the associated representations (objects stored in memory) are immediately activated, and this in turn leads to new predictions about what will happen next or what can be done (Bar, 2009). Bar sees the process from analogy to associations to predictions as a universal principle: analogies activate associations, which in turn form the building blocks for further predictions. Because our (social) environment is very complex, multiple analogies can be found simultaneously, and these can be combined again into more complex predictions. Predictions act as hypotheses about the world that can be tested against the sensory signals that enter the brain. When a difference is observed, we speak of a *prediction error*. According to many neuroscientists, the brain focuses on minimising the discrepancy between predictions and actual experience.

This description shows that the boundary between perception and cognition cannot be drawn sharply. Our perception of the environment depends as much on memory as on incoming information. In other words, sensory information interacts with existing representations for the purpose of perception. Constructivist theories hold that prediction errors can lead to changes in bodily processes, which in turn can form the basis for emotions (Barrett & Simmons, 2015). The next section deals with this.

7 Modern constructivist theories of emotions

Constructivist theories, such as Barrett's conceptual act theory (2014), assume that all mental states, regardless of whether they are experienced as an emotion, are the result of more basic, domain-general psychological processes. The brain makes a first rough prediction about the meaning of the sensory input in the context, and the error between the first top-down prediction and sensory activity is directly reduced (Barrett & Simmons, 2015). Lindquist and Barrett (2012) assume that the salience network plays an important role in this. Emotions arise when someone uses previous experiences to give meaning to the sensory input from the body and from the world around them. In other words, emotions become conscious when someone perceives a change in internal (physical) and external (visual, auditory, tactile, etc.) stimuli and categorises these stimuli into separate emotion categories, such as anger or fear (Lindquist, 2013). Lisa Feldman Barrett calls this change a *core affect*, and with this term she refers to the mental representation of changes in the body, which are sometimes experienced as pleasant or unpleasant (valence) and are accompanied by a certain level of arousal or intensity (arousal). Many researchers hypothesise that the two dimensions of valence and arousal underlie all emotional experiences and perceptions (Russell, 2003).

Changes in a core affect do not necessarily have to be caused by psychological processes but can also be caused by the production of sex hormones when an organism perceives the scent of a partner, by the release of neuropeptides after a bacterial infection or by an increase in blood sugar levels after eating food. External stimuli can also cause changes in core affect through the principles of associative learning (Lindquist, 2013). An unconditioned response (an unpleasant feeling) can be linked to a conditioned stimulus (e.g. someone's negative comment about your appearance), so that the conditioned stimulus acquires a core-affective value (negative). But it may also be that a stimulus is associated with a core-affective value through purely symbolic meanings (for example, a parent telling a child that he is not doing his best).

But emotions are more than just core affect (Lindquist, 2013). The second step in the basic psychological process is that internal sensory signals or the associated affective feelings (pleasant or unpleasant) are provided with meaning automatically and without any effort (Barrett, 2014; Lindquist, 2013). This is a form of categorisation. Emotion concepts or what someone knows about emotion are, according to Barrett and Lindquist, constructed psychological concepts that can be distinguished from each other. Emotion concepts use the core affect system in different ways, and are also linked to different types of information that are processed outside the core affect system, such as executive control (for regulating and interpreting emotions), language (for categorising and labelling), *theory of mind* (for understanding and interpreting emotions in others) and so on. Culturally specific experiences directly influence the process (Lindquist *et al.*, 2015). For example, the emotion 'pride' has a meaning in American culture (positive) that is different from that in East Asian cultures (negative). The cultural context partly determines how sensory sensations from the body are linked to the context and lead to subjective experience.

According to Barrett (2012), the reliable perception of an emotion by means of facial expressions in another person is only possible if we also know the context. This contradicts the basic emotion theory of, for example Ekman, who assumes that the basic emotions are directly deducible from facial expressions. However, if someone does not have certain linguistic emotion concepts, this person cannot perceive those emotions in the faces of others, even if language is not explicitly needed to perform this task (Lindquist, 2013).

Emotion words, such as the words 'fear' and 'anger', are abstract categories that are socially constructed. Emotion words or emotion labels develop in childhood by linking recurring core affect situations and perceptions to words used by parents. If we translate this into Bressler and Menon's large-scale network model, this process refers to the DMN (Lindquist *et al.*, 2012). Emotion words help us construct perceived affective feelings because the feelings themselves are not based on statistical regularities in the real world. They do not have clearly natural categorial boundaries that create a one-to-one relationship between perceived physical sensations, events in the outside world and the experienced emotion (see also Hellendoorn, Wijnroks & Leseman, 2015). A simple example can clarify this. Someone suddenly startles you. Your response is usually a mixture of fear (the first response to the stimulus) and anger (the perception of the source of the stimulus), and it is difficult properly to distinguish and interpret the feelings experienced. The emotion words that someone uses have been learned from previous experiences in the cultural context. Culture does not *cause* the emotions, but emotions are cultural skills that are transferred through parenting and education. For the emergence of emotions, someone must be part of a group of people who agree that certain events (for example, a bodily sensation or action) have specific functions (for example, to understand the world, to communicate intentions and to control the behaviour of others).

We have seen that, according to modern constructivist theories, the brain continuously links information from the body (core affect), from the outside world and from the context (exteroceptive sensory information) to representations of previous experiences (conceptualisations). This construction process must be regulated, for which the activity in the other networks must be controlled, but some sensations must also be selected for conscious perception and others suppressed. This involves the CEN. The CEN also checks which exteroceptive sensory information takes precedence over other processing operations and whether the core affect comes to consciousness. It is not yet known what exactly these core affects are, but an example is approaching and avoiding, which in turn can be linked to specific actions, such as fighting, fleeing or freezing (LeDoux, 2012a).

If core affect and conceptualisation are necessary to experience an emotion, then a logical conclusion would be that a disturbance in either system can cause a person to experience no emotions. We have already discussed the alexithymia disorder, but semantic dementia is another example in this context. This disorder means that one cannot perceive emotions such as fear, anger and sadness in the face of another person, but one is able to sort faces into negative, positive and neutral valences (Lindquist, 2013).

The consequence of modern constructivist theories is that any changes in proprioception (for example, a touch or tap), in the movements of the facial muscles (for example, a raising of the eyebrows or facial spasm), in peripheral physiology (for example, a quickened heartbeat or a tightness of the chest) and in one's awareness of changes in one's own body (for example, their being perceived less consciously because of aging) can lead to a change in the experienced emotion. The extent to which someone understands emotions and possesses complex emotional knowledge determines how this person perceives and experiences their own core affect (Barrett, 2012; Lindquist, 2013).

8 Final remarks and recommendations

In this chapter it has been argued that the distinction between 'being able' and 'being able to cope' is not only vague but actually a false dichotomy. Processes such as cognition and emotion are difficult to distinguish from one another. There are heated discussions in the scientific literature about what an 'emotion' is; how we can distinguish it from other mental processes, such as cognition and perception; and how we can measure emotions (see for example the many discussions in the scientific journal *Emotion Review*). Based on this, some researchers have proposed avoiding the term 'emotion' altogether (e.g. Russell, 2003). If we disagree on what an emotion is and we cannot distinguish emotions from other psychological processes, how can we research how emotions develop? Of course, emotions really exist and have evolved for some purpose during evolution, mostly as basic processes or core affects that humans use to respond flexibly to the world around them (Barrett, 2012). And, of course, emotions also have consequences for social behaviour, relationships, decision-making and even health (Lindquist, 2013).

The explanation that constructivist theories would give for the problems in emotional competence in children and adults with intellectual disabilities is that they are the result of a multitude of factors. For example, problems may arise in the perception of core affect (body sensation) or in associating core affect with the context (the situation) or emotion knowledge (conceptualisation). Emotion knowledge itself again depends on the development of language and on the culture in which one has grown up and been raised. Children already show the basic emotions, such as joy, sadness, anger, disgust and fear, in their first year of life, but that does not mean that they also experience the emotions in the same way as older children and adults. Also, when a baby exhibits a rapid automated response in the form of characteristic facial expressions, combined with turning away or moving away from the source after an externally perceived stimulus, such as smelling a foul odour, it does not mean that the baby experiences the emotion 'disgust'. Rather, this is a reflex in response to a perceived physical sensation. Young children gradually learn to link the consciously perceived physical sensations to external and internal events and only later do they also learn the emotional concepts belonging to these experiences. Children of parents who talk a lot about emotions with their children develop better emotion perception and emotion awareness (Harris, 2008). The social-moral emotions, such as shame and guilt, which develop later, are also learned emotions that develop in a social context.

If we extend this knowledge to people with intellectual disabilities, it will come as no surprise that they experience problems in the perception of emotion and in the development of social-moral emotions and emotion regulation. These problems are not delays in emotional development but rather impairments that result from cognitive and perceptual problems, from language problems, from parents not communicating about emotions, from temperament and from the development of an insecure attachment caused by less sensitive parenting or abuse.

Wijnroks (2013b) pleads for us to no longer put energy into determining the cognitive and emotional developmental ages of adults with intellectual disabilities. A drawback of determining developmental ages is that they are usually estimated by averaging over a large number of different items, so that information about underlying profiles is not included and therefore remains invisible[8]. Nor does it make sense to determine the emotional level of a person with an intellectual disability, particularly in terms of 'ages'[9], because this suggests that we know what is normal and what is abnormal and how a 'normal' development of the processes involved in emotions proceeds. However, our knowledge of normal emotional development is still limited (Chronaki *et al.*, 2014; Harris, 2008), at least too limited to produce valid and reliable measurements of these developments.

In Došen's view, emotional development is primarily a process of maturation in which the influence of language and education is taken for granted but not as an essential part of emotions themselves. Research into people with an intellectual disability as a result of a specific syndrome shows that many syndromes have a characteristic profile of strengths and weaknesses in the development of the psychological functions, and we should take this into account in supporting them (Wijnroks, 2013b). Sometimes 'weak' means that there is a developmental delay, but it can also indicate a structural defect. Challenging behaviour has little to do with a lag in emotional development but is most likely the result of genetic factors and/

8 Došen is interested in profiles, but only from a developmental perspective that looks for differences in levels of development for the different social-emotional skills.

9 The American Association on Intellectual and Developmental Disabilities has not used the term 'mental age' to refer to general intelligence in its manuals since 2002, in part because such an estimation suggests that the person in question is actually functioning cognitively at a level corresponding to a stage of normal development, but mainly because having a 'lower mental age' invites others to approach people with an intellectual disability as children and to treat them in ways that do not correspond with what is common in society for someone of their chronological age.

or congenital abnormalities in brain development, in combination with experiences gained in the social context (see for a review: Hastings & Lloyd, 2007).

Does it make sense to look at the social-emotional functioning of people with an intellectual disability at all? It is conceivable that we will better understand why someone demonstrates challenging behaviour when we know whether this person is able to interpret emotions and whether they can perceive emotions and behavioural intentions in others (empathy), but it is misleading to think that we have measured functions that are independent of cognitive functions, such as language, or of the person's experiences and cultural context. It may certainly make sense to study people with an intellectual disability who can communicate about their perceptions of emotions in others as well as in themselves, about emotion awareness and emotion understanding. No evidence, however, has been found that the behavioural problems of people with an intellectual disability can be explained by problems in their emotional competence. For people with a severe intellectual disability, the situation is even more complex. Since we cannot reliably infer emotions from the behaviour itself, and since the subjective perception of the perceived core affect depends on language, culture, parenting, education and previous experiences, we will probably never know what emotions are experienced by people who function at a low intellectual level. If you want to know more about how they perceive the inner world and the outer world, it would be wise to look at the emotional primitives, such as fighting, fleeing or freezing, assess the valence and intensity that are visible in their behaviour and check whether we can link our observations to the context. By using physiological measurements, such as heart rate, skin resistance and respiration, it is possible to determine intensity (see also Anderson & Adolphs, 2014). Depending on the context, a measured high level of arousal may be a signal of an upcoming difficulty in understanding or instance of challenging behaviour. These types of systems are available and affordable (see for an example the EQ-Radio developed by the Massachusetts Institute of Technology). It would be incorrect to simply define the aforementioned emotional primitives, such as fighting and flight, as problem behaviour. It would be better to see them as the results of associations between the perceived core affect, the context and previous experiences, without there being a 'real' emotional experience as we understand it.

References

Anderson, DJ & Adolphs, R. (2014) A framework for studying emotions across species. *Cell* **157** (1) 187–200 doi: 10.1016 / j.cell.2014.03.003.

Bar, M (2009) The proactive brain: Memory for predictions. *Philosophical Transactions of the Royal Society of London, Series B: Biological Sciences* **364** 1235–1243 doi: 10.1098 / rsb.2008.0310.

Barrett, LF (2012) Emotions are real. *Emotion* **12** (3) 413–429 doi: 10.1037 / a0027555.

Barrett, LF (2014) The conceptual act theory: A précis. *Emotion Review* **6** (4) 292–297 doi: 10.1177 / 1754073914534479.

Barrett, LF, Mesquita , B, Ochsner, KN & Gross, JJ (2007) The experience of emotion. *Annual Review of Psychology* **58** (1) 373–403 doi: 10.1146 / annurev.psych.58.110405.085709.

Barrett, LF & Satpute, AB (2013) Large-scale brain networks in affective and social neuroscience: Towards an integrative architecture of the human brain. *Current Opinion in Neurobiology* **23** (3) 361–372 doi: 10.1016 / j.cob.2012.12.012.

Barrett, LF & Simmons (2015) Interoceptive predictions in the brain. *Nature Reviews Neuroscience* **16** (7) 419–429 doi: 10.1038 / nrn3950.

Baurain, C & Nader-Grosbois, N (2013) Theory of mind, socio-emotional problem-solving, socio-emotional regulation in children with intellectual disability and in typically developing children. *Journal of Autism and Developmental Disorders* **43** (5) 1080–1097 doi: 10.1007 / s10803.012.1651.4.

Baurain, C, Nader-Grosbois, N & Dionne, C (2013) Socio-emotional regulation in children with intellectual disability and typically developing children, and teachers' perceptions of their social adjustment. *Research in Developmental Disabilities* **34** (9) 2774–2787 doi: 101016 / jridd201303022.

Berkovits, LD & Baker, BL (2014) Emotion dysregulation and social competence: Stability, change and predictive power. *Journal of Intellectual Disability Research* **58** (8) 765–776 doi: 101111 / jir12088.

Bressler, SL & Menon, V (2010) Large-scale brain networks in cognition: Emerging methods and principles. *Trends in Cognitive Sciences* **14** (6) 277–290 doi: 101016 / jtics201004004.

Buntinx, W (2016) Adaptive behavior and support needs. In: A Carr, Ch Lineman, G O'Reilly, P Noonan Walsh & J McEnvoy (Eds) *The Handbook of Intellectual Disability and Clinical Psychology Practice* (pp107–135). London: Routledge.

Casey, BJ, Oliveri, ME & Insel, T (2014) A neurodevelopmental perspective on the Research Domain Criteria (RDoC) framework. *Biological Psychiatry* **76** (5) 350–353 doi: 101016 / jbiopsych201401006.

Chronaki, G, Hadwin, JA, Garner, M, Maurage, P & Sonuga-Barke, EJS (2014) The development of emotion recognition from facial expressions and non-linguistic vocalizations during childhood. *British Journal of Developmental Psychology* **33** (2) 218–236 doi: 101111 / bjdp12075.

Davies, BE, Frude, N, Jenkins, R & Hill, C (2015a) The relationship between emotional recognition ability and challenging behavior in adults with an intellectual disability: A systematic review. *Journal of Intellectual Disabilities* **19** 393–406 doi: 101177 / 1744629515581730.

Davies, BE, Frude, N, Jenkins, R, Hill, C & Harding, C (2015b) A study examining the relationship between alexithymia and challenging behavior in adults with intellectual disability. *Journal of Intellectual Disability Research* **59** (11) 1022–1032 doi: 101111 / jir12186.

Došen, A (2005) *Mental Disorders, Behavioral Problems and Intellectual Disability: An integrative approach in children and adults*. Assen: Van Gorcum.

Ekman, P & Cordaro, D (2011) What is meant by calling emotions basic? *Emotion Review* **3** (4) 364–370 doi: 101177 / 175407391140740.

Gross, JJ & Barrett, LF (2011) Emotion generation and emotion regulation: One or two depends on your point of view. *Emotion Review* **3** (1) 8–16 doi: 101177 / 1754073910380974.

Harris, PL (2008) Understanding emotion. In: M Lewis, JM Haviland -Jones & LF Barrett (Eds) *Handbook of Emotions* (3rd edition). New York: Guilford Press.

Hastings, RP & Lloyd, T (2007) Expressed emotion in families of children and adults with intellectual disabilities. *Mental Retardation and Developmental Disabilities Research Reviews* **13** (4) 339–345 doi: 101002 / billion20173.

Hellendoorn, A, Wijnroks, L & Leseman, PPM (2015) Unraveling the nature of autism: Finding order amid change. *Frontiers in Psychology* **6** 1–16 doi: 103389 / fpsyg201500359.

Howry, J (2012) Attention and conscious perception in the hypothesis testing brain. *Frontiers in Psychology* **3** 1–14 doi: 103389 / fpsyg201200096.

Kahneman, D (2011) *Our Fallible Thinking*. Amsterdam: Business Contact.

Kasari, CL, Jahromi, LB & Gulsrud, AA (2012) Emotional development in children with developmental disabilities. In: JA Burack, RM Hodapp, G Iarocci & E Zigler (Eds) *The Oxford Handbook of Intellectual Disability and Development* (pp239–253). New York: Oxford University Press.

Kret, ME & Ploeger, A (2015) Emotion processing deficits: A liability spectrum providing insight into comorbidity of mental disorders. *Neuroscience and Biobehavioral Reviews* **52** 153–171 doi: 101016 / jneubiorev201502011.

LeDoux, J (2012a) A neuroscience perspective on debates about the nature of emotion *Emotion Review* **4** (4) 375–379 doi: 101177 / 1754073912445822.

LeDoux, J (2012b) Rethinking the emotional brain. *Neuron* **73** (4) 653–676 doi: 101016 / jneuron201202004.

Lindquist, KA (2013) Emotions emerge from more basic psychological ingredients: A modern psychological constructionist model. *Emotion Review* **5** (4) 356–368 doi: 101177 / 1754073913489750.

Lindquist, KA & Barrett, LF (2012) A functional architecture of the human brain: Insights form the science of emotion. *Trends in Cognitive Sciences* **16** (11) 533–540 doi: 101016 / jtics20129005.

Lindquist, KA, Satpute, AB & Gendron, M (2015) Does language do moretham communicate emotion? *Current Directions in Psychological Science* 2499–108 doi: 101177 / 0963721414553440.

Lindquist, KA, Wager, TD, Kober, H, Bliss-Moreau, E & Barrett, LF (2012) The brain basis of emotion: A meta-analytic review. *Behavioral and Brain Sciences* **35** (3) 121–143 doi: 101017 / S0140525X11000446.

Mesquita, B, Boiger, M & De Leersnyder, J (2016) The cultural construction of emotions. *Current Opinion in Psychology* **8** 31–36 doi: 101016 / jcopsyc201509015.

Niccols, A, Thomas, K & Schmidt, LA (2012) Socioemotional and brain development in children with genetic syndromes associated with developmental delay. In: JA Burack, RM Hodapp, G Iarocci & E Zigler (Eds) *The Oxford Handbook of Intellectual Disability and Development* (pp254–274). New York: Oxford University Press.

Panksepp, J & Watt, D (2011) What is basic about basic emotions? Lasting lessons from affective neuroscience. *Emotion Review* **3** (4) 387–396 doi: 101177 / 1754073911410741.

Pessoa, L (2015) Précis on the cognitive-emotional brain. *Behavioral and Brain Sciences* 1–66 doi: 101017 / S0140525X14000120.

Pons, F & Harris, P (2005) Longitudinal change and longitudinal stability of individual differences in children's emotion understanding. *Cognition and Emotion* **19** (8) 1158–1174 doi: 101080 / 02699930500282108.

Rolls, ET (2015) Limbic systems for emotion and for memory, but not a single limbic system. *Cortex* **62** 119–157 doi: 101016 / jcortex201312005.

Russell, JA (2003) Core affect and the psychological construction of emotion. *Psychological Review* **110** (1) 145–172 doi: 101037 // 0033-295X1101145.

Sappok, T, Budczies, J, Bölte, S, Dziobek, I, Došen, A & Diefenbacher, A (2013) Emotional development in adults with autism and intellectual disabilities: A retrospective, clinical analysis. *PLoS ONE* **8** (9): e74036.

Sappok, T, Budczies, J, Dziobek, I, Bölte, S, Došen, A & Diefenbacher, A (2014) The missing link: Delayed emotional development predicts challenging behavior in adults with intellectual disability. *Journal of Autism and Developmental Disorders* **44** (4) 786–800 doi: 101007 / s1080301319335.

Scotland, JL, Cossar, J & McKenzie, K (2015) The ability of adults with an intellectual disability to recognize facial expressions of emotions in comparison with typically developing individuals: A systematic review. *Research in Developmental Disabilities* **41-42** 22–39 doi: 101016 / jridd201505007.

Scotland, JL, McKenzie, K, Cossar, J, Murray, A & Michie, A (2016) Recognition of facial expressions of emotion by adults with intellectual disability: Is there evidence for the emotion specificity hypothesis? *Research in Developmental Disabilities* **48** 69–78 doi: 101016 / jridd201510018.

Smith, R & Lane, RD (2015) The neural basis of one's own conscious and unconscious emotional states. *Neuroscience and Biobehavioral Reviews* **57** 1–29 doi: 101016 / jneubiorev201508003.

Touroutoglou, A, Lindquist, KA, Dickerson, BC & Barrett, LF (2015) Intrinsic connectivity in the human brain does not reveal networks for 'basic' emotions. *Social Cognitive and Affective Neuroscience* **10** (9) 1257–1265 doi: 101093 / scan / nsv013.

Trentacosta, CJ & Fine, SE (2010) Emotion knowledge, social competence, and behavior problems in childhood and adolescence: A meta-analytic review. *Social Development* **19** (1) 1–29 doi: 101111 / j1467-9507200900543.

Twint, B & Veenstra, A (2015) *Guiding with Insight: About being able and able to cope with people with an intellectual disability*. Amsterdam: Boom.

Wijnroks, L (2013a) Critical comments on the concept of transfer and the discrepancy hypothesis: The stress model as an alternative. *NTZ - Dutch Magazine for the Care of people with intellectual disabilities* **39** (2) 99–113.

Wijnroks, L (2013b) The fallible thinking of people with intellectual disabilities. *NTZ - Dutch Magazine for the Care of people with intellectual disabilities* **39** (4) 233–253.

Wijnroks, L (2015) Do neurosciences have anything to offer us? *Research & Practice* **13** (2) 39–42.

Zhao, Y & Castellanos, FX (2016) Annual research review: Discovery science strategies in studies of pathophysiology of child and adolescent psychiatric disorders – promises and limitations. *Journal of Child Psychology and Psychiatry* **57** (3) 421–439 doi: 101111 / jcpp12503.

Part II
Themes of emotional development

Chapter 6 Development of emotion regulation and the role of the attachment relationship

Paula Sterkenburg, Sandra Zaal and Paula Dekkers-Verbon

Summary

In this chapter, the development of emotion regulation and the role of the attachment relationship are described. The attachment development is of great importance for the regulation of emotions. This starts early on, with stress regulation in babies, where the reactions of the parent contribute to the emotional self-regulation and emotional balance of the child. When parents function as a secure base and safe haven for their child, the child will learn to regulate their emotions and be able to take new steps in exploration. Both parental and child factors can contribute to a disturbed or absent development of the internal attachment representation. For a very long time people thought that, when no attachment relationship with a parent develops during the child's early developmental stages, the child will never be able to engage in an attachment relationship later on in life. But nowadays, research studies show that this is possible (Schuengel *et al.*, 2009). Thorough assessment is necessary in order to understand the specific problems in the reactive regulation of emotions and then to match the specific intervention to the specific problem. The way to assess problems in emotion regulation and how to match the intervention to the problem will be illustrated in two case studies. Finally, we describe the possibilities for the treatment of problems concerning emotion regulation within relationships.

Case: Maria[10]

Maria is forty-seven years of age and has a moderate intellectual disability. She became blind later in life and has an auditory impairment, for which she refuses to use a hearing aid. She comes from a family of nine children. Her mother passed away when Maria was seven and in the same year Maria moved to a group home, living together with other children with moderate intellectual disabilities. Maria has type one diabetes. There are frequent escalations in her behaviour. For the other persons in her group home, her screaming and slamming of doors is very disturbing. Maria withdraws from contact with others by going to her room, where she self-harms.

Case: Edward

Edward is forty-eight years of age. He is blind and has a severe intellectual disability. From a young age onwards, he has had behavioural problems like screaming, self-mutilation, pulling others' hair and pushing, pinching or biting others. Because his parents could not be sufficiently emotional available and could not adequately take care of him, he was removed from their care at the age of four. The contact between him and his parents has always been limited.

Both Maria and Edward have difficulties regulating their emotions. Furthermore, there are several factors that contributed to the disturbance of attachment development. As we will demonstrate below, this development is of great importance for emotion regulation in general.

1 Development of emotion and stress regulation

Immediately after birth, a baby experiences all kinds of sensations, including discomfort, hunger and pain. The parents[11] help the baby to overcome these discomforts; they are the most important persons to help the baby with regulating stress or recovering emotional balance (homeostasis). Schore (2001) describes how parents who prevent their child's stress levels from becoming too high contribute to the development of the child's self-regulation of emotions. A parent who interacts with their child helps the child to regulate the stress and also supports the child to restore balance.

For most parents, helping to regulate the baby's emotions is an automatic response. When stress levels seem to become too high, the child will avert their gaze, will

10 The cases have been anonymised.

11 For the sake of readability the word 'parent(s)' is used in this chapter. However, this can in any instance be replaced with 'primary caregiver(s)'.

pick something up; their facial expressions will decrease and they push their chest forward. An observant parent who is focused on the child will notice (consciously or unconsciously) that at this moment everything is too much for the child, and the parent will subsequently alter their own behaviour. Beebe and Lachmann (2002) describe this process of stress regulation as 'interactive stress regulation'. A sensitive, well-attuned parent will react within seconds, resulting in the development of the effective emotional self-regulation of the baby. This is because, when the parents sensitively react to the child's needs, the baby learns to expect that when this particular caregiver is present the experienced discomfort will remain within bearable limits. The stimuli will not overwhelm the baby and the baby can remain calm and wait for the parent's expected reaction or give another hint (some kind of behaviour) to the parent concerning their needs.

The American developmental and clinical psychologist Edward Tronick has developed the still-face paradigm, with which he shows how important this interactive regulation is. An example of this is the 'Still Face Experiment', which can also be found on YouTube (Tronick, 2009), in which he asks a mother not to react to the signals of her baby – not to react sensitively to the baby's signals of discomfort. What is striking is that the baby will do anything to elicit a sensitive reaction from the parent. In turn, the baby will smile at the parent, wave their arms, point to something in the surroundings, arch their back, scream, turn away, forcefully move their body and, eventually, cry. This process is completed within two minutes. The baby is overwhelmed by stress and, since the parent does not help regulate them, the baby cannot regulate their own stress. Without interactive regulation, the baby will be emotionally out of balance; the child cannot self-regulate their emotions as they are overwhelmed by them.

During times of pain or discomfort, a sensitively and adequately reacting (responsive) parent helps regulate stress, whereupon the child gradually learns to regulate their own stress level. A sensitive parent mirrors the emotion of the child. When a child hurts themselves, the parent will non-verbally and verbally let the child know that they understand that the child is experiencing pain. The mirroring of emotions is an interactive process. The mirroring neurons of the parent are activated, which stimulates empathy for the emotions of the child; in this way, the parent can mirror the correct emotion of the child. Mirroring neurons reducee in particular brain areas that become activated when an emotion or behaviour of someone else is noticed (Šešo-Šimić *et al.*, 2010). Because the parent is aware of the emotion of the child, the parent can then help to regulate the emotion by comforting the child. After that, the parent will help the child to move on with a new activity, thus stimulating exploration (Ainsworth, 1973).

Powell and colleagues (2016) describe this process of reacting as following the 'circle of security'. The parent functions as a safe haven: they express the emotions of the child in words, give meaning to them and put them into place (containment). In addition, the parent functions as a safe base, which stimulates the child to start exploring once more. Because of the predictable reaction of the parent, a child learns to organise their experiences and feelings and learns to regulate their emotions themselves or within a relationship (Powell *et al.*, 2016). Such a predictable and stress-regulating relationship is called a secure attachment relationship, and the predictable, stress-regulating person, most of the time the mother and/or father, is called the attachment figure. With a secure attachment relationship, a child focuses on the attachment figure when they are in pain, are sad or are experiencing other discomfort and are seeking consolation. When comforted, the child can proceed to explore once again. An example of this can be seen in the case of Ilona.

Case: Ilona

Ilona is twenty years of age and has a moderate intellectual disability. She likes to go to the public swimming pool with her caregivers. Besides taking a lovely swim, she can also go down the water slide and immerse herself in a steam bath. She always enjoys the swimming. Last month, she went swimming together with her caregiver, Caro. Ilona slipped in a puddle of water. Because of the shock and the pain in her leg, she started to cry. Her caregiver saw what happened and noticed the shock and pain on Ilona's face. Caro showed Ilona that she understood, comforted her and encouraged her to sit upright. After a while, the crying turned into laughter. Together, they were laughing about what had just happened and how funny it had looked. Caro noticed Ilona's emotional reaction and thereafter encouraged Ilona to continue her swim. Caro was the safe haven and secure base, just what Ilona needed at that point in time. That night, and many days after, they would still talk about what had happened at the swimming pool.

Around the age of nine months, a baby starts to use the parent to regulate their own stress. When the baby is anxious, tired or tense, they will 'ask' the sensitive and responsive parent for support, help or understanding (Bowlby, 1984). An infant does this by crying, which over time changes to seeking close proximity and making contact with the parent. The parent mirrors the emotions of the child (helps to regulate stress), creating room for exploration (Ainsworth, 1973). In this way, adequate emotion regulation (the restoration of emotional balance) arises, and opportunities for further development and growth open up. The attachment figure thus functions as a buffer for the stress experienced by the child (Sterkenburg & Schuengel, 2011). When the child 'uses' the parent in an adequate way to reduce their own stress, thus for regulation, this parent is a secure attachment figure for the child.

Within an attachment relationship the child seeks out a specific adult, the attachment figure, to share joy and to deal with stress, helping to regulate the child's emotions and return to exploration. If children do not use the attachment figure to regulate stress, specific interventions can be used to support the development of attachment relationships. For example, after a protocolled treatment, the Integrative Therapy for Attachment and Behaviour (ITAB), it was found that, during times of stress, the children who received the intervention used an attachment figure to regulate their stress by seeking proximity (Schuengel *et al.*, 2009). ITAB is conducted by sensitive and responsive therapists who focus on developing an attachment relationship (again or for the first time) in children up to eighteen years of age with a severe intellectual disability. This reduces the children's stress levels, and they exhibit fewer behavioural problems and more exploration and development with the attachment figures than with persons with whom they have only functional contact (Sterkenburg *et al.*, 2008). Because of the stress buffering action of the relationship, the child can increasingly regulate their stress and explore the environment. Up until now, there has been no scientific research into the stress buffering action of ITAB within a relationship for persons with a disability over eighteen years of age. However, considering the theoretical background of ITAB, the results could be similar.

When a child has a secure attachment relationship with a parent, the child knows they can always turn to the parent to help regulate their emotions. Because of the consequent behaviour of the attachment figure, the child can create an internal representation of (emotional connection with) people and the surroundings. Bowlby (1984) named this representation the 'internal working model'. When a child has such a secure internal working model, they can better endure being separated from their parent because they have an internal realisation that they can seek the attachment figure when needed. At first the endurance of separation occurs when the parent is in another room, and then much later when the child plays at a friend's house, etc. When a child is a bit older, they can comfort themselves with the words a parent usually uses, for example: 'It hurts, but it will pass soon.' The child can also postpone the proximity-seeking behaviour: 'When I see Mummy again, I will tell her what happened.' Because of the internal representation of the attachment relationship, the child knows the attachment figure is there and they can always rely on them.

2 Risk factors in the development of attachment in children

Disturbed or absent development of a secure internal attachment representation can occur because of specific parental and child factors related to the intellectual disability of the child. An important child factor is the presence of a disability. Gunther (2004) describes the fact that the development of attachment in children with visual and intellectual disabilities takes longer; and Gringhuis and colleagues

(1996) and Egan (1979) find that the phase of separation anxiety and fear of strangers is longer in children with a visual impairment. Separation anxiety is a phase in the development of the internal representation of the attachment figure. After all, the child has to learn that the attachment figure still exists, even if they are not present at that moment (person permanence) and that the child themselves can seek the attachment figure to help regulate stress. For children with an intellectual disability, the concept of person permanence is difficult to learn. If they do not learn this abstract concept at a later age, they continue to experience separation anxiety (Janssen *et al.*, 2002). They are able to use the attachment figure for regulating stress but are anxious when this person is absent (Hoffman *et al.*, 2017). When children have a severe visual impairment as well, this concept is even more difficult to learn.

When a child with an intellectual disability is admitted to hospital, it is more difficult for parents to always be emotionally available (Biringen, 2000), even more so if there are many children in the household. For the parent it can also be difficult to be sensitive and responsive when the parent – because of the disorder or disability of the child – does not understand the signals the child is sending about their needs. For instance, when a blind child turns their face away from the parent, bringing the ear closer to the parent so they can perceive the parent better, the parent can interpret this turning away of the face as indicating that the child does not want the parent's consolation. Also, for a child with a visual impairment, the inability to see non-verbal cues makes it difficult to perceive the mirroring of emotions by the parent (Dekker-van der Sande & Sterkenburg, 2016). Children with intellectual disabilities often have delayed reactions, and because of this parents may fail to notice attachment behaviour on the part of the child. Children with (visual and) intellectual disabilities are therefore at risk of insecure attachment (Atkinson *et al.*, 1999).

Schuengel and Janssen (2006) also mention parental factors that could disturb the development of attachment in children with an intellectual disability. When parents learn that their child has a disability, they can experience loss and grief. For some parents this grief is recurrent, and it can last for years or even a lifetime (Brown, 2016; Kandel & Merrick, 2003). It can then be difficult for parents to focus on the child while dealing with their own coping process. The consequence can be that parents are less emotionally available (De Belie & Van Hove, 2005). Also, the care for a young child with special needs requires a lot of time and energy from the parents – 24 hours a day. It is not uncommon for these parents to be chronically sleep deprived (Lee *et al.*, 2018; Safe *et al.*, 2012). Furthermore, in the first year of life, the nature of the disability and impact of the disability on the child's development are often unknown, which causes uncertainty about the child's future and sometimes also feelings of guilt in parents (Kandel & Merrick, 2003). Moreover, many parents of children with disabilities have limited social support and experience little understanding about their stress from others, which is associated with poorer parental health (Gallagher & Whiteley, 2012) and parental social isolation (Boushey, 2001; Currie & Szabo, 2020). The combination of (recurrent) grief and excessive (emotional and physical) parental stress can affect the sensitive and responsive parenting of children with an intellectual disability (Schuengel & Janssen, 2006). Among parents of children with developmental disabilities, burnout is common – practising mindfulness and using active coping strategies can help parents deal with stress (Donnchadha, 2017; Families Special Interest Research Group of IASSIDD, 2014; Hwang & Kearney, 2014). Furthermore, pathogenic environmental influences are associated with problematic attachment: neglect, abuse and frequent and early changes in primary caregivers.

Giltaij and colleagues (2016) show that children who have what the *Diagnostic and Statistical Manual of Mental Disorders* (fifth edition) describes as reactive attachment disorder (RAD) or disinhibited social engagement disorder (DSED) have a significant delay in their adaptive functioning, which can be explained with reference to their reduced ability to explore. The lack of a supporting, secure attachment relationship results in a delay in their development.

3 Problems with emotion regulation and attachment

Maria and Edward, described at the start of this chapter, both have problems with their emotion regulation. The behavioural problems are very undesirable, both for others and for themselves. They scream, slam doors, hit and bite others and self-mutilate. They clearly do not use an attachment figure to help regulate their emotions. Furthermore, from the brief descriptions we can see that in both cases there are several factors involved that increase the risk of developing a problematic attachment relationship. They both have a visual and intellectual disability and were removed from home at a young age, and in Edward's case the attachment figures were practically absent (his parents could not take care of him, and later they could not reach out to him much).

To gain insight into whether important others are used for emotion regulation, Dekker-van der Sande and Janssen (2010) have developed a step-by-step approach, in Dutch, based on the guidelines of the American Academy of Child and Adolescent Psychiatry (Boris *et al.*, 2005). This step-by-step plan was then incorporated into the Dutch guidelines about problematic attachment, published by the *Nederlands Jeugdinstituut* (Wolff *et al.*, 2014). In this step-by-step process, eight signals (affection, consolation, asking for help, co-operation, exploration, control, reaction at reuniting and reaction towards strangers: see table 6.1) of (disturbed) attachment behaviour (Boris *et al.*, 2005) are repeatedly used to examine (disturbed) attachment behaviour.

In this way, the use of (or failure to use) the attachment figure as a secure base and safe haven for stress regulation can be mapped. The scoring is repeated in various diagnostic situations, namely: while looking at the child's files, during an intake interview with parents or primary caregivers, during an intake interview with a familiar (to the person) caregiver, during an observation in a daily situation, during a clinical observation of attachment (COA) and during the 'disturbances of attachment interview'. Giltaij and colleagues (2017) show that it is important to use this very structured diagnostic process to come to a reliable diagnosis. Dekker-van der Sande and Janssen (2010) propose that, for clients, one might also consider a consultation of a (paediatric) psychiatrist and/or an observation conducted by a psychotherapist. When a remedial educationalist or (developmental) psychologist accurately goes through the diagnostic process, light is shed on the interactive regulation of emotions and tools for treatment are provided.

We have gone through this diagnostic process for the cases of Maria and Edward. Maria's scores can be found in table 6.1 and Edward's in table 6.2, where a score of 1 means adaptive attachment behaviour and a score of 5 is a signal of maladaptive attachment behaviour.

Table 6.1 Scores for signals of disturbed attachment behaviour, Maria

Signals	Intake	Group home observation	DAC* observation	Interview caregiver	Interview caregiver	COA**
Affection	1	1	-	1	1	1
Consolation	5	4	5	5	5	5
Asking for help	5	4	4	3	3	4
Co-operation	1	1	2	2	2	2
Exploration	3	-	3	5	5	4
Control	1	1	2	1	1	1
Reaction at reuniting	1	-	-	1	1	1
Reaction towards strangers	1	1	1	1	1	1
Total	18	12?	17?	19	19	19

*DAC = daycare centre, **COA = clinical observation of attachment

The results of the attachment diagnostics show low scores on affection for an important other adult person, co-operation with the important other and reaction with reuniting with the important other, and they indicate a hesitant and reserved attitude towards strangers. These results show that Maria distinguishes important others from strangers. She can use the attachment figure as a buffer for stress, but the high scores on seeking consolation, asking for help and exploration show that, when emotions increase and she has stress, she does not (sufficiently) use the attachment figure as a buffer. She does not look for the attachment figure when she is in need of consolation or if something is not working out. In a strange environment she stays close to her caregiver and she is afraid to explore.

Table 6.2 Scores for signals of disturbed attachment behaviour, Edward

Signals	Intake	Group home observation	DAC* observation	Interview caregiver	Interview caregiver	COA**
Affection	5	1	4	2	3	4
Consolation	3		5	3	3	4
Asking for help	4	-	4	4	4	4
Co-operation	1	1	4	3	4	4
Exploration	-	4	4	3	2	4
Control	1	2	3	3	2	1
Reaction at reuniting	-		-	2	3	3
Reaction towards strangers	5	3	3	3	2	3
Total	19?	11?	27?	23	23	27

*DAC = daycare centre, **COA = clinical observation of attachment

Edward receives high scores on most signals of disturbed attachment behaviour. For him, there is no clear distinction between familiar people and strangers. When he experiences stress, he has no buffer for it. Emotions will overwhelm him and he will not know who to go to for consolation and help. He has never had someone who taught him how to adequately regulate his emotions; he was not able to build up a secure internal working model of an attachment figure.

4 Treatment for problems in emotion regulation and disturbed attachment

When problems occur with emotion regulation, structured and thorough diagnostics can give a good indication for treatment. The type of intervention depends on the intellectual abilities of the person in question, on the context and on the results of the structured diagnostic process. With the necessary adjustments, most standard psychotherapeutic methods (e.g. psychoeducation, cognitive behavioural therapy, psychomotor therapy) can be used to treat psychological problems in persons with (visual and) intellectual disabilities. Adjustments predominantly entail creating a safe, comfortable and quiet therapy environment; taking enough time and using visual supportive materials when explaining the diagnosis and when providing psychoeducation; shortening assignments; using language that is easy to understand; and involving parents and caregivers when giving therapy to persons with moderate to severe intellectual disabilities (Sterkenburg & Braakman, 2019). Also, prior to the intervention, psychoeducation and the coaching of parents and/ or caregivers are important elements of the treatment (Morisse *et al.*, 2017; Zaal *et al.*, 2009). Furthermore, in the daily care of all persons with disabilities, attention should be focused on the resilience and vulnerability of caregivers and how to optimise their emotional availability (De Belie & Van Hove, 2013).

4.1 Children with a visual and/or intellectual disability under the age of five

Some parents, for example parents suffering from depression or adolescent parents, find it more difficult to act sensitively and responsively towards their child, even though responding sensitively especially helps with interactive regulation. Therefore, Juffer and colleagues (2007) have developed a method called 'video feedback to promote positive parenting' (VIPP), which is aimed at increasing the sensitivity and responsiveness of the parent. Because it is so difficult to understand the behaviour of children with a visual and/or intellectual disability, 'video feedback to promote positive parenting – visual or visual-and-intellectual disability' (VIPP-V) has been developed (Van den Broek *et al.*, 2017). The effect of VIPP-V was studied in a randomised controlled trial (Overbeek *et al.*, 2015). There was no direct benefit from VIPP-V on parental sensitivity or parent–child interaction quality. Nonetheless, parenting self-efficacy (in supporting and comforting their child) increased. This increase in parental experience could in future lead to higher parental sensitive responsiveness and more positive parent–child interactions (Platje *et al.*, 2018). To provide parents and caregivers of young children with visual and intellectual disabilities another tool to facilitate parent–child bonding, the interactive playmat was developed in a multidisciplinary collaboration. This multisensory playmat is designed to promote sensitive and responsive parenting behaviour and specifically to support mirroring parental play (Dekkers-Verbon *et al.*, 2019). When parents display these kinds of behaviours, parent and child will be more easily emotionally attuned to each other, which in turn makes the child feel understood and secure. In the long run, this emotional security promotes children's growth on all developmental levels.

4.2 Persons with a developmental age lower than nine months

With persons with intellectual and emotional capabilities comparable to a child under nine months of age, person permanence has not yet developed, and so neither has emotion regulation by a specific attachment figure. However, Vandesande *et al.* (2019) show that in times of stress, children with severe or profound intellectual disabilities make a distinction between consolations provided by parents and those provided by strangers. For their emotion regulation, people with severe intellectual disabilities are dependent on the sensitivity and responsiveness of the parent or caregiver. For example, when they experience discomfort, overstimulation, pain, boredom or stress, they are dependent on the parent or caregiver for the interactive regulation of stress to restore balance (homeostasis). During interaction, the development of this interactive regulation can be stimulated. In the workbook *Developing Attachment*, parents and caregivers can find tools to work on this (Sterkenburg, 2011). People in this group not only need parents or caregivers to be nearby but also should be stimulated to explore. It is important for them to have both a secure base and safe haven for exploration. Also, feedback on the physiological reaction of the person via an app (*de Slimme Sok* ('the Smart Sock') app and the Flower app) can contribute to sensitive and responsive caregiving by parents and caregivers (Frederiks *et al.*, 2015; Sterkenburg *et al.*, 2017). Furthermore, the Hi Sense m-learning tool (an e-learning tool specially designed for use on mobile devices; see www.embinbeeld.nl) can provide parents and caregivers with a deeper understanding of the signals of a person with severe intellectual disabilities, as has been found in the case of the caregivers of persons with a moderate or mild intellectual disability (Van Wingerden *et al.*, 2019).

4.3 Separation anxiety

When a person with a moderate or mild intellectual disability has stress because of the absence of their important other (separation anxiety), technology supporting therapy for separation anxiety (TTSA) (Jonker *et al.*, 2015; Hoffman *et al.*, 2017) turns out to be an effective intervention. For three months, both client and care worker(s) use a smartphone with the Shakem app. Using this special application, clients can send messages to let caregivers know how they feel and so get support from their caregivers. The caregiver's reaction to these messages causes the client to feel heard and to know that the caregiver still exists (person permanence). Later, at an appropriate moment, the caregiver and client will have a conversation about the messages. Repetition of this process in the daily environment means an abstract concept like person permanence can be learned (Hoffman *et al.*, 2017).

4.4 Persons with a severe intellectual disability with severe problems in emotion regulation and/or a disturbed attachment

Promoting positive interactions between the child and familiar persons is the basis of the treatment of a disturbed attachment (Boris *et al.*, 2005). By reacting in a sensitive and responsive way – through tuning affect, words and actions to what the child feels, does and experiences – the caregiver contributes to the awareness that contact with specific persons can help with emotion regulation (as a buffer against stress). ITAB, mentioned above, starts with attachment therapy, which consists of three consecutive subphases, namely 'bonding and making contact', 'symbiosis' and 'stimulation to individuation'. Experience shows that after these phases most problem behaviour disappears. After an analysis of any remaining problem behaviour there follows a phase of behavioural therapy, using the accessory attachment-based reaction protocol. This intervention lasts for three months and consists of learning desirable behaviour through positive rewards. During the phase of 'generalisation and completion' the network of relationships is expanded and the therapist gradually moves into the background (Sterkenburg, 2008; Sterkenburg & Schuengel, 2020).

Case: Edward

Edward's diagnostics show he has no secure internal working model of an attachment figure. Because emotions overwhelm him, he is not able to find support from an important other (attachment figure) when sad, anxious or agitated. He needs intensive treatment. To make sure he starts considering specific persons as important others, the recommended treatment for Edward is ITAB over the course of a year.

4.5 Persons with a moderate or mild intellectual disability with severe problems in emotion regulation and/or a disturbed attachment

Persons with a mild to moderate intellectual disability have the cognitive capabilities to consciously think about feelings, desires and thoughts. By reflecting on the reactions that are evoked by emotions, these persons can learn to regulate their own emotions. The recognition of emotions, putting them into words and interpreting them within a relationship with another, contributes to regulation. Children are able to 'mentalise' when they can postpone their reaction to the other person and when they are able to think about the consequences of their actions and alternatives to those actions. Persons who have difficulties with mentalising also have problems regarding emotion regulation. However, mentalisation can be learned. Dekker-van der Sande and Sterkenburg (2016) describe mentalisation based support (MBS), which is aimed at increasing the mentalising capacities of the client (Dekker-van der Sande & Sterkenburg, 2017). Alongside stimulating clients' mentalisation, the caregivers of persons with mild to moderate intellectual disabilities and (signals of) disturbed attachment can use the m-learning Hi Sense App-ID to improve on their theoretical knowledge about forming secure attachment relationships with their clients (Van Wingerden *et al.*, 2019). Furthermore, the game 'The World of Empa' has been developed, which is aimed at enhancing empathy and decreasing personal distress in caregivers of people with intellectual disabilities (Sterkenburg & Vacaru, 2018).

4.6 Persons with specific problems in emotion regulation and/or attachment

Some people have not experienced and learned how they can ask their important other person for help when they are having difficulties with their emotion regulation. These clients can be offered specific training to practise asking for consolation and help. In doing so, it is important that parents and caregivers are coached to function as secure bases and safe havens as well as possible – especially when the client (through behaviour or attention) appeals to the important other for support. Furthermore, coaching can be given on how to adapt caregiving to the level of emotional functioning as assessed using the Scale of Emotional Development – Short (Sappok *et al.*, 2016).

Case: Maria

Maria's diagnostics show that there are certainly important others in her life. However, she has not yet learned to go to them when she needs consolation. Therefore, an intervention is needed in Maria's daily life so she can practise seeking support and gain positive experiences. The reaction of the caregiver is of great importance. The caregiver uses the 'circle of security' during practise, contributing to the sense of safety Maria experiences. This caregiver contributes to Maria's secure internal working model, in which she perceives the caregiver as a buffer for stress.

5 Conclusion

Emotional functioning is not only determined by biological, psychological and social aspects but also by developmental aspects like interactive regulation. Persons with intellectual functioning comparable to a child below nine months of age are completely dependent on their parent or caregiver for the regulation of emotions.

Persons with higher cognitive functioning slowly develop a secure internal working model for emotion regulation, meaning the parent or caregiver does not have to be available all the time. With persons with a (visual and) intellectual disability there are factors that could block the development of such a secure internal regulating system. Medical and sensory aspects play their part, as do environmental influences. Thorough diagnostics are needed to be able to understand the specific problems in the reactive regulation of emotions and to adequately adjust interventions for these. There are various treatment options; however, further development and research in this area is needed. There is for instance a need for an effect study on ITAB for persons with a moderate intellectual disability (ITAB-MID) and on interventions that promote mentalisation. Also, further studies on the effects of psychoeducation and team coaching are needed. There is an increasing amount of knowledge of the effects of the attachment relationship and of the concept of mentalisation and the processing thereof in the brain. This creates opportunities to offer parents and caregivers even better explanations and tools they can use in the intensive support of their child's or client's emotion regulation.

References

Ainsworth, MDS (1973) The development of infant-mother attachment. In: B Caldwell & H Ricciuti (Eds) *Review of child development research* (3rd edition) pp1–94. Chicago, IL: University of Chicago Press.

Atkinson L, Chisholm VC, Scott B, Goldberg S, Vaughn BE, Blackwell BE … Tam F (1999) Maternal sensitivity, child functional level, and attachment in Down syndrome. In: J I Vondra & D Barnett (Eds) *Atypical Attachment in Infancy and Early Childhood among Children at Developmental Risk: Monographs of the Society for Research in Child Development* **64** (3) 45–66.

Beebe B & Lackmann FM (2002) *Infant Research and Adult Treatment: Co-constructing interactions*. London: The Analytic Press.

Biringen Z (2000) Emotional availability: Conceptualisation and research findings. *American Journal of Orthopsychiatry* **70** 104–114.

Boris NW, Zeanah CH & The Work Group on Quality Issues (2005) Practice parameter for the assessment and treatment of children and adolescents with reactive attachment disorder of infancy and early childhood. *Journal of the American Academy of Child & Adolescent Psychiatry* **44** (11) 1206–1219.

Boushey A (2001) The grief cycle – one parent's trip around. *Focus on Autism and Other Developmental Disabilities* **16** (1) 27–30. doi: 10.1177/108835760101600107.

Bowlby J (1984) *Attachment and Loss: Volume 1: Attachment*. London: Penguin.

Brown J M (2016) Recurrent grief in mothering a child with an intellectual disability to adulthood: Grieving is the healing. *Child & Family Social Work* 113–122. https://doi-org.vu-nl.idm.oclc.org/10.1111/cfs.12116.

Currie G & Szabo J (2020) Social isolation and exclusion: The parents' experience of caring for children with rare neurodevelopmental disorders. *International Journal of Qualitative Studies in Health and Well-Being* **15** (1) 1–10. doi: 10.1080/17482631.2020.1725362.

De Belie E & Van Hove G (2005) *Ouderschap onder druk: Ouders en hun kind met een verstandelijke beperking*. Antwerpen: Garant.

De Belie E & Van Hove G (2013) *Wederzijdse emotionele beschikbaarheid: Mensen met een verstandelijke beperking, hun context en begeleiders samen op weg*. Antwerpen/Apeldoorn: Garant.

Dekker-van der Sande F & Janssen C (2010) *Signaleren van verstoord gehechtheidsgedrag. Best practice voor het diagnosticeren van gehechtheidsproblemen bij kinderen / jongeren met een visuele en / of licht verstandelijke beperking*. Den Haag: Lemma.

Dekker-van der Sande F & Sterkenburg P (2016) Mentalization can be learned: Introduction to Mentalization Based Support (MBS). Bartiméus Series. Webedu.

Dekker-van der Sande F & Sterkenburg P S (2017) Learning from mentalization based therapy for mentalization based support in daily care. *Journal of Mental Health Research in Intellectual Disabilities* **10** (1) 104.

Dekkers-Verbon P, Toeters M, Baars M, Barakova E & Sterkenburg, P (2019) An interactive playmat to support bonding between parents and young children with visual (and intellectual) disabilities. *International Conference of the DRS Special Interest Group on Experiential Knowledge* (EKSIG) 23–24 September 2019, Tallinn, Estonia.

Donnchaddha, SO (2017) Stress in caregivers of individuals with intellectual or developmental disabilities: A systematic review of mindfulness-based interventions. *Journal of Applied Research in Intellectual Disabilities* **31** 181–192 doi: 10.1111/jar.12398.

Egan, DF (1979) The early development of visually handicapped children. In: V Smith & J Keen (Eds) *Visual handicap in children* (pp 137-144). London: William Heinemann Medical Books .

Families Special Interest Research Group of IASSIDD (2014) Families supporting a child with intellectual or developmental disabilities: The current state of knowledge. *Journal of Applied Research in Intellectual Disabilities* **27** 420–430 doi: 10.1111/jar.12078.

Frederiks K, Croes MJG, Chen W, Oetomo SB & Sterkenburg, P (2015) Sense – a biofeedback system to support the interaction between parents and their child with the Prader-Willi syndrome: a pilot study. *Journal of Ambient Intelligence and Smart Environments* **7** (4) 449-459. https://doi.org/10.3233/AIS-150327.

Gallagher S & Whiteley J (2012) Social support is associated with blood pressure responses in parents caring for children with developmental disabilities. *Research in Developmental Disabilities* **33** (6) 2099–2105. https://doi.org/10.1016/j.ridd.2012.06.007.

Giltaij HP, Sterkenburg PS & Schuengel C (2016) Adaptive behaviour, comorbid psychiatric symptoms, and attachment disorders. *Advances in Mental Health & Intellectual Disabilities* **10** (1) 82–91.

Giltaij HP, Sterkenburg PS & Schuengel C (2017) Convergence between observations and interviews in clinical diagnosis of reactive attachment disorder and disinhibited social engagement disorder. *Clinical Child Psychology and Psychiatry* **22** (4) 603–619. https://doi.org/10.1177/1359104517709049.

Gringhuis D, Moonen J & Woudenberg P van (1996) Kinderen die slecht zien: Ontwikkeling, opvoeding, onderwijs en hulpverlening. Houten: Van Loghum.

Gunther F (2004) *Diagnostiek en behandeling van mensen met een visuele en verstandelijke beperking*. Doorn: Bartiméus.

Hoffman N, Sterkenburg PS & Van Rensburg E (2017) The effect of technology assisted therapy for intellectually and visually impaired adults suffering from separation anxiety: Conquering the fear. *Assistive Technology* 98–105. doi: 10.1080/10400435.2017.1371813.

Hwang Y-S & Kearney P (2014) Mindful and mutual care for individuals with developmental disabilities: A systematic literature review. *Journal of Child and Family Studies* **23** 497–509 doi: 10.1007/s10826-012-9707-9.

Janssen CGC, Schuengel C & Stolk J (2002) Understanding challenging behavior in people with severe and profound intellectual disabilities: A stress attachment model. *Journal of Intellectual Disability Research* **46** 445–453.

Jonker D, Sterkenburg PS & Rensburg E van (2015) Caregiver-mediated therapy for an adult with visual and intellectual impairment suffering from separation anxiety. *Research in Developmental Disabilities* **47** (12) 1–13.

Juffer F, Bakermans-Kranenburg MJ & IJzendoorn MH van (Eds) (2007) *Promoting Positive Parenting: An attachment-based intervention*. New York: Erlbaum.

Kandel I & Merrick J (2003) The birth of a child with disability: Coping by parents and siblings. The Scientific World Journal 3 741–750 doi: 10.1100/tsw.2003.63.

Lee J, Spratling R & Helvig A (2018) Sleep characteristics in mothers of children with developmental disabilities. *Journal of Pediatric Health Care* **32** (1) 9–18 http://dx.doi.org/10.1016/j.pedhc.2017.08.002.

Morisse F, De Belie E, Blontrock M, Verhasselt, J & Claes C (Eds) (2017) *Emotionele ontwikkeling in verbinding. Coachingsmethodiek voor begeleiders met probleemgedrag*. Antwerpen: Garant.

Overbeek MM, Sterkenburg PS, Kef S & Schuengel C (2015) The effectiveness of VIPP-V parenting training for parents of young visual or visual-and-intellectual disabled children: Study protocol of a multicenter randomized controlled trial. *Trials* **16** 401.

Platje E, Sterkenburg P, Overbeek M, Kef S & Schuengel C (2018) The efficacy of VIPP-V parenting training for parents of young children with a visual or visual-and-intellectual disability: A randomized control trial. *Attachment & Human Development* **20** (4) 1–18 doi: 10.1080/14616734.2018.1428997.

Powell B, Cooper G, Hoffman K & Marvin B (2016) *The Circle of Security Intervention: Enhancing attachment in early parent-child relationships*. New York City: Guilford Publications.

Safe A, Joosten A & Molineux M (2012) The experiences of mothers of children with autism: Managing multiple roles. *Journal of Intellectual & Developmental Disability* **37** (4) 294–302.

Sappok T, Barrett B, Vandevelde S, Heinrich M, Poppe L, Sterkenburg P, Vonk J, Kolb J, Claes C, Bergmann T, Dosen A & Morisse F (2016) The Scale of Emotional Development – Short. *Research in Developmental Disabilities* **59** 166–175.

Schore AN (2001) Effects of a secure attachment relationship on right brain development, affect regulation, and infant mental health. *Infant Mental Health Journal* **22** (1-2) 7–66.

Schuengel C & Janssen CGC (2006) People with mental retardation and psychopathology: stress, affect regulation and attachment: A review. *International Review of Research in Mental Retardation* **32** 229–260.

Schuengel C, Sterkenburg PS, Jeczynski P, Janssen CGC & Jongbloed G (2009) Supporting affect regulation in children with multiple disabilities during psychotherapy: A multiple case design study of therapeutic attachment. *Journal of Consulting and Clinical Psychology* **77** (2) 291–301.

Šešo-Šimić Đ, Sedmak G, Hof P R & Šimić G (2010) Recent advances in the neurobiology of attachment behavior. *Translational Neuroscience* **1** 148–159.

Sterkenburg PS (2008) *Intervening in Stress, Attachment and Challenging Behaviour: Effects in children with multiple disabilities* (dissertation). Doorn: Bartiméus.

Sterkenburg PS (2011) *Developing Attachment: A workbook for building up a secure relationship with children or adults with severe intellectual or multiple disabilities*. Bartiméus Reeks: Microweb Edu, Doorn.

Sterkenburg PS & Braakman J (2019) Psychotherapie bij mensen met een verstandelijke beperking. *Tijdschrift voor Psychiatrie* **61** (11) 792–797.

Sterkenburg P, Frederiks K, Barakova E, Chen W, Peters P & Feijs L (2017) A bioresponse system for caregivers of adults with severe or profound intellectual disabilities. *Conference: 11th European Congress Mental Health in Intellectual Disability* https://doi.org/10.1080/19315864.2017.1368259.

Sterkenburg PS, Janssen CGC & Schuengel C (2008) The effect of an attachment-based behaviour therapy for children with visual and severe intellectual disabilities. *Journal of Applied Research in Intellectual Disabilities* **12** 126–135.

Sterkenburg PS & Schuengel C (2011) De gehechtheidsrelatie als buffer tegen stress. In: J Zevalkink & P Sterkenburg (Eds) *Voor de verandering: Een psychodynamische kijk op ontwikkeling* (pp87-100). Assen: Van Gorcum.

Sterkenburg PS & Schuengel C (2020) Integratieve Therapie voor Gehechtheid en Gedrag: behandelprotocol. In: C Braet & S Bögels (Eds) *Protocollaire behandelingen voor kinderen en adolescenten met psychische klachten* (pp767–792). Amsterdam: Boom.

Sterkenburg PS, Schuengel C & Janssen CGC (2008) Developing a therapeutic relationship with a blind client with a severe intellectual disability and persistent challenging behaviour. *Disability and Rehabilitation* **30** (17) 1318–1327.

Sterkenburg PS & Vacaru VS (2018) The effectiveness of a serious game to enhance empathy for care workers for people with disabilities: A parallel randomized controlled trial. *Disability and Health Journal* **11** 576–82.

Tronick E (2009) Still Face Experiment. Available at: https://www.youtube.com/watch?v=apzXGEbZht0.

Van den Broek EGC, van Eijden AJPM, Overbeek MM, Kef S, Sterkenburg PS & Schuengel C (2017) A systematic review of the literature on parenting of young children with visual impairments and the adaptions for Video-feedback Intervenion to Promote Positive Parenting (VIPP). *Journal of Developmental and Physical Disabilities* **29** 503–545 https://doi-org.vu-nl.idm.oclc.org/10.1007/s10882-016-9529-6.

Vandesande S, Bosmans G, Sterkenburg P, Schuengel C, Van Den Noortgate W & Maes B (2019) Comfort provided by parents versus strangers after eliciting stress in children with severe or profound intellectual disabilities: does it make a difference? *Attachment & Human Development* doi: 10.1080/14616734.2019.1659835.

Van Wingerden E, Wouda M & Sterkenburg P (2019) Effectiveness of m-learning HiSense APP-ID in enhancing knowledge, empathy, and self-efficacy in caregivers of persons with intellectual disabilities: A randomized controlled trial. *Health and Technology* **9** 893–901 doi: 10.1007/s12553-019-00361-0.

Wolff M de, Dekker-van der Sande F, Sterkenburg PS & Thoomes-Vreugdenhil A (2014) *Richtlijn Problematische Gehechtheid*. Utrecht: Nederlands Jeugdinstituut. http://www.richtlijnenjeugdhulp.nl/problematische-gehechtheid/.

Zaal S, Boerhave M & Koster M (2009) *Hechting, basisveiligheid, basisvertrouwen. Begeleiding en behandeling*. Amsterdam: Cordaan/Amsta.

Chapter 7
Emotional development in autism spectrum disorders

Tanja Sappok and Els Ronsse

Summary
Individuals with intellectual disability are at risk of additional autism spectrum disorders (ASDs). In adults with ASD combined with an intellectual disability, the level of emotional development differs from that of adults with only an intellectual disability. This is noticeable in the overall level and in the domains 'relating to peers', 'differentiating emotions' and 'regulating affect'. The ASD-specific Scale of Emotional Development (SED) profiles can be supportive in the diagnostic process in assigning ASD group membership in adults with an intellectual disability. The recognition of delays in emotional development contributes to our understanding of the emotion-related impairments and maladaptive behaviours in adults with an intellectual disability and ASD. Assessment of emotional development may add value to diagnoses of ASD in adults with an intellectual disability and can form a basis for the treatment and support plan (Došen & De Groef, 2015).

1 ASD and emotional development: theoretical background
Individuals with an intellectual disability have an increased risk of ASD compared to the general population (25% v. 1%) (Böhm *et al.*, 2018). According to International Classification of Diseases (10th revision) (ICD-10) criteria, ASD is a pervasive developmental disorder that is defined by early onset impairments in social reciprocity alongside restricted, repetitive behaviours. Cognitive concepts such as executive malfunctions (Barnard *et al.*, 2008), weak central coherence (Happé & Frith, 2006) and problems with 'theory of mind' (Baron-Cohen *et al.*,

1985) attempt to explain the basis of autistic symptomatology. Other psychological theories propose emotion-processing alterations as the core ASD deficits. For example, Hobson *et al.* (1986) describe difficulties in the perception, recognition, understanding, expression and regulation of emotions. Leo Kanner (1943) himself first delineated alterations in the emotion system, which he summarised as a lack of 'affective contact'.

The emotion and the social cognition systems are closely related networks (Pessoa, 2010). Impairments in social reciprocity, such as lack of joint attention, reactive smiling, imitation and eye-gaze processing, are precursors of the 'theory of mind' deficits observed in ASD. They also reduce opportunities to share emotional experiences with others (Baron-Cohen *et al.*, 1985). These missed opportunities result in reduced social competencies and the impoverished maturation of socio-emotional abilities. Cognitive theories might not therefore be sufficient to fully account for the psychological nature of ASD. The impact of the autistic disorder itself and environmental causes on the difficulties in the regulation of emotions has not yet been clarified. Delays in emotional development may be understood as 'part of the autistic disorder', a collateral effect of ASD. As ASD is a pervasive developmental disorder, the probability of delays in emotional development can be presumed. Therefore some aspects of emotional functioning may develop differently and play a protective role, as we see in children with ASD and normal intelligence (Rieffe *et al.*, 2011).

2 The level of emotional development is delayed in adults with an intellectual disability/ASD combined compared to adults with an intellectual disability only

Adults with an intellectual disability and ASD showed significantly lower levels of emotional development compared to adults with an intellectual disability only. In a study assessing N = 289 adults with an intellectual disability in Berlin, the overall level of emotional development was not higher than the third phase of emotional development in individuals with ASD and an intellectual disability, which corresponded to the emotional development of normally developing infants aged 18 to 36 months (individuation), while those with only an intellectual disability achieved an overall developmental level of not higher than the fourth phase of emotional development, which is analogous to children aged three to seven years (identification) (Sappok *et al.*, 2012). Similar lower levels of emotional development were found in a small study of a group of normal-functioning youngsters with ASD (Ronsse, 2015).

In the Berlin research, individuals with mild intellectual disability showed more advanced levels of emotional development (mean score on the SED = 4.4) than those with mild intellectual disability and additional ASD (mean SED = 3.6). These discrepancies were even more obvious in adults with moderate intellectual disability: the mean level of emotional development was 3.9 in those with just an intellectual disability, and 3.0 in those with an intellectual disability and ASD. In individuals with severe to profound intellectual disability, those with only an intellectual disability showed significantly ($p < .003$) more advanced levels of emotional development (mean SED = 3.1) than those with an intellectual disability and ASD (mean SED = 2.4). To understand a given behaviour, adjust expectations accordingly and fulfil the emotional needs of an individual with developmental disabilities, knowledge of the level of emotional development is pivotal and cannot be deduced from the level of intellectual disability only.

A second study assessed the level of emotional development with the Scale of Emotional Development – Short (SED-S) and compared emotional development in 327 adults with an intellectual disability with (N = 83) and without (N = 244) ASD (Sappok *et al.*, submitted; Sappok *et al.*, 2016). Persons with additional ASD showed lower levels of emotional development compared to those with an intellectual disability only (mean reference ages 7–18 v. 19–36 months). For mild to moderate intellectual disability, the level of emotional development within the SED-S domains 'differentiating emotions', 'relating to peers', 'engaging with the material world' and 'communication' was lower in persons with ASD compared to persons without ASD. For persons with severe/profound intellectual disability, the level of emotional development of the SED-S domains 'dealing with change – object permanence', 'differentiating emotions', 'relating to peers', 'engaging with the material world' and 'regulating affect' were lower in the ASD than in the non-ASD group.

From birth, ASD influences social development in various ways, which results in different behaviours from those seen in persons with an intellectual disability only. In ASD, emotional needs are even more complex, because the emotional process seems to develop from day one, but it influences social development in other ways, which also creates different behaviours (Došen, 2013).

3 The profile of emotional development is more uneven in adults with an intellectual disability/ASD combined compared to adults with an intellectual disability only

In the study from 2013, specific deficits in certain domains of the emotional developmental profile could be observed in individuals with an intellectual disability and ASD when compared to individuals with an intellectual disability alone (Sappok *et al.*, 2013). In fact, differences in the level of emotional development could be observed in all domains except for 'dealing with change – object permanence'. The most prominent delays in emotional development in the ASD group could be observed in the domains 'interaction with peers', 'interaction with caregivers' and 'communication'. These delays in emotional development are consistent with the diagnostic criteria of ASD. Substantial reductions could also be observed with regard to 'anxieties' and 'differentiating emotions'. Individuals with ASD but without an intellectual disability appear to be relatively competent in dealing with basic emotions, such as joy and sadness, but have more difficulty with complex emotions such as pride and shame, whereas in individuals with ASD and an intellectual disability, emotional difficulties are more widespread. These difficulties could be partly explained by the delays in 'differentiating emotions' that were observed in this study. Initiation of a maturing process of emotional development could be an alternative approach to laying the developmental foundations for emotion recognition and regulation in a population with learning difficulties (Bergmann *et al.*, 2011; Schuengel *et al.*, 2009).

The improvement of emotion recognition skills is of particular importance because reduced emotional knowledge is associated with enhanced aggression and anger, reduced school success and reduced prosocial behaviour (Denham *et al.*, 2002; Denham *et al.*, 2012). The SED domain 'anxieties' was delayed in ASD individuals compared to non-ASD individuals. According to the developmental approach, causes of anxiety vary over the different developmental levels: anxiety due to intense or unknown stimuli (level one), separation anxiety (level two), anxiety due to loss of autonomy (level three), anxiety due to fear of failure (level four) and social anxiety i.e. not being accepted (level five). A broad body of literature describes an increased occurrence of anxiety disorders in ASD individuals (for a review, see: Howlin, 2004). This increased susceptibility to anxiety disorders could in part be caused by the observed developmental delays; that is, the type of anxiety may be related to the level of emotional development. Thus, recognition of basic emotional needs associated with a certain level of emotional development could further prevent mental health problems from emerging.

In addition to social impairments and impairments in individuals' relation to the self, delays in the 'dealing of material objects' can be observed in our study. These deficits could lead to the previously described impairments in executive functions in ASD (Barnard *et al.*, 2008). Thus, belonging to the pervasive developmental disorders, ASD not only affects contact with the social world but also affects the relation to the self and to material objects.

Interestingly, the significant differences within the emotional development profiles could not be replicated in the second study from 2020 (Sappok *et al.*, submitted). In this study, persons with ASD did not exhibit more heterogeneous developmental profiles than those with an intellectual disability only. This may be explained by distinct differences in the assessment instruments, as the Scheme for Appraisal of Emotional Development (SAED) consists of 10 domains, while the SED-S comprises only eight domains (Sappok *et al.* 2013; Sappok *et al.* 2016). The chance of differences between the domains increases with the number of domains. Furthermore, the items of the SED-S are based on expert judgements about appropriateness for a certain reference age. Therefore, the items contained in the SAED and SED-S differ and may lead to different results. The current results indicate that the SED-S items describe the emotional developmental stage of a person more uniformly – independently of the presence or absence of an additional ASD.

4 The case of Ben

4.1 Description

Ben is a man of 22 with a mild intellectual disability (intelligence quotient = 52) and severe ASD. Ben seems to be apathetic, shows only very little initiative and communicates very little, although he talks a lot. There is some social contact with others, provided that this can be controlled by him and that he can determine what others say or do. If he looks at something, he can start laughing uproariously. This laughter is often not context appropriate. He recognises the basic emotions in others as long as they are very clear. However, he does not pay attention to others, even if it seems that he has noticed them. He can name feelings by himself. He also argues that, even if something has gone wrong, he has done everything right.

Ben needs a lot of predictability and structure. He has his own cutlery; he dines at set times, in a specific order, and he will not deviate from this routine. Ben keeps a number of small screws with him, and he wants the same holiday, to the same destination, every year. If things do not go the way he had in mind, he becomes angry and runs away. He seems to manage himself; he comes back and repeats 'run away isn't good'. However, it takes hours before he can become quiet. On the other hand, the prospect of loss does not alter his behaviour very much.

People who know him very well find it difficult that he can say a lot, and even sometimes become somewhat pedantic, but actually does not do much. In addition, he has become increasingly stubborn.

4.2 Results

On the Mini PAS-ADD (Psychiatric Assessment Schedules for Adults with Developmental Disabilities), he scores 7 (threshold value = 4) for social behaviour, 1 (threshold value = 1) for communication and 4 (threshold value = 3) for repetitive behaviour. These scores indicate ASD. The Mini PAS-ADD is a screening instrument that helps carers to detect mental health problems in people with intellectual disabilities (Taylor *et al.*, 2004). On a 2 to 4 point scale, severity must be indicated for 66 items. The Mini PAS-ADD detects symptoms of depression, anxiety disorder, mania, obsessive compulsive disorder, psychotic disorder, ASD or any disorder not otherwise specified. He has also been tested on the *Autisme- en verwante stoornissenschaal* (AVZ). This is a validated Dutch screening scale for ASD for the population of people with intellectual disabilities (Kraijer, 1999). On the AVZ he gets a score of 12.

Ben has an general level of emotional development reaching not higher than the third phase (table 7.1). He also has lower levels for 'interaction with peers' and 'interaction with emotionally important others'. His verbal communication only reaches the third phase of emotional development. A substantial reduction could also be observed for 'anxieties'.

The results as shown in table 7.2 were included in the algorithm that was developed around the profile of the Scale of Emotional Development (Sappok *et al.*, 2013). The result was a total score of -1.70, which in the algorithm indicates the possible presence of autism. The lowest scores were used in this algorithm, as mentioned in the guidelines of the SED-R^2. We only used domains 1–10, as indicated in the algorithm. In this case the algorithm follows the prediction.

Table 7.1 Scale of Emotional Development – Revised[2] (SED-R[2]) profile

Domain	Phase 1 Adaptation Months 0–6	Phase 2 First socialisation Months 7–18	Phase 3 First individualisation Months 19–36	Phase 4 Identification Years 4–7	Phase 5 Reality consciousness Years 8–12
1. Dealing with own body		x			
2. Dealing with emotionally important others		x			
3. Self-image in interaction with the environment		x	x		
4. Dealing with a changing environment – object permanence		x	x		
5. Anxieties	x			x	
6. Dealing with peers		x	x		
7. Dealing with materials			x		
8. Communication			x		
9. Emotion differentiation			x		
10. Aggression regulation			x		
11. Day activity – play development		x	x		
12. Moral development			x		
13. Emotion regulation		x			

Table 7.2 Interpretation of the ASD score from SED assessment

SED domain	Developmental phase
1. Dealing with own body	2
2. Dealing with emotionally important others	2
3. Self-image in interaction with the environment	2
4. Dealing with a changing environment – object permanence	2
5. Anxieties	4
6. Dealing with peers	3
7. Dealing with materials	3
8. Communication	3
9. Emotion differentiation	3
10. Aggression regulation	3
Mean of 10 domains	3.50
ASD score	**-1.70**

NB: Interpretation of ASD score: > 1 = no ASD, < 1 or > -1 = ASD possible, < -1 = ASD probable

4.3 Interpretation of behaviour against the background of emotional development

Looking at his ASD and emotional development, it becomes clear that Ben needs a lot of predictability, but also that he often just tries things, without regard for others. This is not something that he does on purpose because he wants to hurt others, but something that he does as part of his own experimental phase, just as people in the first individuation phase are often busy with themselves. Of course, this is also behaviour typical of a lack of 'theory of mind' in autism.

Given his emotional development it is appropriate to create sufficient learning opportunities with sufficient variation. This demands more time than people familiar with other people with an intellectual disability (without ASD) might expect, and will probably be linked less to people than to objects.

The problem behaviour that Ben exhibits is rather peculiar to his emotional development, and is annoying, but at the same time it is typical for his level of emotional development. It requires no additional measures beyond those that have already been implemented in the environment in response to his autism. Of course, it will take time and effort to find out how to stimulate him in the right ways.

Way of proceedings can be found in the way Ben becomes aware of experiences of success and learns to deal with things that do not work for him. As supervisors we can reflect on the resilience that Ben has, and can regard his quick relapse into physical unease as a signal of fear. The creation of moments and places of rest is important. He already provides this himself in being punctual (e.g. precise dining hours).

Because of his autism, Ben will approach a number of things differently from others. Making these things concrete by means of visualisation and predictability will be an issue. This means that supervisors have to learn how to provide this predictability, but they also have to offer consolation and security very quickly when he gets anxious. Rigidity on Ben's part demands flexibility on the part of the supervisors.

5 Classification of ASD group membership using the SAED

The differences in the various domains of the SED – between adults with and without ASD – can be used to support the diagnostic clarification of ASD. The classification using a selection of SAED domains revealed a sensitivity of 78% and a specificity of 76%. ASD risk increased 2.7-fold with every level of the SED.

Like the SAED, the SED-S is supportive in the diagnostic assessment of ASD (Sappok *et al.*, submitted). In order to enhance the prediction accuracy and interpretability of the statistical model it produces, Lasso (least absolute shrinkage and selection operator), a regression analysis method that performs both variable selection and regularisation, was used. The Lasso regression revealed that the domains 'differentiating emotions', 'relating to peers' and 'regulating affect' can form an algorithm for ASD group membership. These domains relate to ASD-defining behaviours. However, the SED-S is not specifically designed for diagnosing ASD and does not directly refer to the current diagnostic criteria described in the diagnostic manuals ICD-11 and the *Diagnostic and Statistical Manual of Mental Disorders* (fifth edition). Consequently, the diagnostic accuracy was lower than in other ASD-specific assessment instruments (sensitivity 80%, specificity 62%, AUC of .74.).

A number of studies have shown a disharmonious profile of intelligence in ASD individuals with and without an intellectual disability at different ages (Soulières *et al.*, 2011). These specific cognitive patterns are to be considered as a possible diagnostic aid. In addition to these distinctive cognitive profiles, the emotional profile was also uneven in adults with ASD when compared to adults with an intellectual disability only (Pessoa, 2010). However, this approach is not a tool that is specifically designed for this purpose, and it is not oriented towards the ASD diagnostic criteria. The algorithm is not expected to substitute for a specific ASD measure; instead, it can add a further perspective, especially in individuals with profound or multiple disabilities. The algorithm can be useful as a supplement to the Mini PAS-ADD or the AVZ.

6 The missing link: emotional development predicts the severity of challenging behaviour

The ability to adapt to everyday life is pivotal for an individual to live up to their personal and professional potential and to lead a contented life. Depending on the level of emotional development, certain capacities or difficulties in self-regulation, behavioural control and executive functions emerge. Indeed, the severity of challenging behaviour increases with lower levels of emotional development, and individuals display specific types of problem behaviours according to the developmental level (Sappok *et al.*, 2013; Sappok *et al.*, 2014). Therefore, the level of emotional development results in a distinct pattern of *adaptive* or *maladaptive behaviour* that proceeds along a developmental trajectory.

ASD was associated with developmental delays in 'aggression regulation'. An increase in aggression, especially in self-injurious behaviour, is known in ASD individuals (Howlin, 2004). The analysis of the causes of aggressive behaviour is complex. In individuals with an intellectual disability and ASD, besides physical disorders, functional analysis of aggressive behaviour and alterations in sensory perceptions are the most common approaches to the understanding and treatment of aggression. The developmental approach could help us further to understand this dysfunctional behaviour because certain developmental levels are associated with distinct processes of self-organisation and action systems. From the developmental viewpoint, aggression in phase one is often due to discomfort, pain or auto-stimulation. Aggression in phase two arises because of insecure attachment and separation anxiety, while in phase three aggression derives from autonomic efforts.

The impact of cognitive and emotional functioning on challenging behaviour could be replicated in a second sample (N = 262) using the SED-S (Böhm *et al.*, 2018). Despite the high correlation between intellectual disability and emotional development, cognitive-emotional developmental discrepancies were found in every second patient. The severity of challenging behaviour was associated with a lower level of emotional development, especially in the domain of 'aggression regulation'.

Further research is needed to analyse the influence of these uneven emotional developmental profiles on the rates and severity of challenging behaviour or psychiatric diseases.

7 Conclusion

The level of emotional development is reduced and more uneven in adults with an intellectual disability and ASD compared to adults with an intellectual disability only. The distinct developmental profile in ASD individuals could serve as a diagnostic aid when evaluating ASD in adults with intellectual and multiple disabilities. Maladaptive behaviour can be understood as an expression of unmet needs due to discrepancies between emotional and mental ages or within the developmental profile. Thus, accounting for these discrepancies could become a starting point for additional treatment options (Sappok *et al.*, 2012; Sappok *et al.*, 2014). The level of emotional development could be the missing link that, alongside deficiencies in cognitive function, may account for reduced adaptive functions in ASD. Aligning the support provided to persons with ASD and an intellectual disability with the respective level of emotional development may reduce challenging behaviours and stimulate the maturation of personality.

References

Barnard L, Muldoon K, Hasan R, O'Brien G, Stewart M (2008) Profiling executive dysfunction in adults with autism and comorbid learning disability. *Autism* **12** 125–141.

Baron-Cohen S, Leslie AM, Frith U (1985) Does the autistic child have a 'theory of mind'? *Cognition* **21** 37–46.

Bergmann T, Dziobek I, Reimer S, Schumacher K, Diefenbacher A, et al. (2011) Jenseits des Dialogs – Beziehungsqualität in der Musiktherapie bei Menschen mit Autismus und Intelligenzminderung. *Med Mensch Geist Mehrf Beh* **8** 14–20.

Böhm J, Diefenbacher A, Heinrich M, Sappok T (2019) Autismusspektrumstörungen bei Erwachsenen mit Intelligenzminderung – Häufigkeit und Charakteristika. *Der Nervenarzt* **90** 490–496.

Böhm J, Dziobek I, & Sappok T (2019) Emotionale Entwicklung, Aggressionsregulation und herausforderndes Verhalten bei Menschen mit Intelligenzminderung. *Fortschritte Neurologische Praxis* **87** 437–443.

Denham SA, Caverly S, Schmidt M, Blair K, DeMulder E, et al. (2002) Preschool understanding of emotions: contributions to classroom anger and aggression. *J Child Psychol Psychiatry* **43** 901–916.

Denham SA, Bassett HH, Thayer SK, Mincic MS, Sirotkin YS, et al. (2012) Observing preschoolers' social-emotional behavior: structure, foundations, and prediction of early school success. *J Genet Psychol* **173** 246–278.

Došen, A (2013) Vragenvuur met Anton Došen [online]. Available at: http://hollandsemeesters.cce.nl (accessed January 2016).

Dosen, A & De Groef, J (2015) What is normal behaviour in persons with developmental disabilities? *Advances in Mental Health and Intellectual Disabilities* **9** (5) 284–294.

Happé F & Frith U (2006) The weak coherence account: detail-focused cognitive style in autism spectrum disorders. *J Autism Dev Disord* **36** 5–25.

Hobson RP (1986) The autistic child's appraisal of expressions of emotion. *J Child Psychol Psychiatry* **27** 321–342.

Howlin, P (2004) Psychiatric disturbances in adulthood. In: Howlin, P (Ed) *Autism and Asperger Syndrome – preparing for adulthood* (pp270–299). London: Routledge.

Kanner L (1943) Autistic disturbances of affective contact. Nervous Child 2 217–250.

Kraijer, DW (1999) *AVZ–R, Autisme– en verwante stoornissenschaal –Z–Revisie. Handleiding. Derde, sterk herziene en uitgebreide uitgave*. Lisse: Swets & Zeitlinger.

Pessoa L (2010) Emergent processes in cognitive–emotional interactions. *Dialogues Clin Neurosci* **12** 433–448.

Rieffe, C, Oosterveld, P, Terwogt, MM, Mootz, S, Van Leeuwen, E & Stockmann, L (2011) Emotion regulation and internalizing symptoms in children with autism spectrum disorders. *Autism* doi: 1362361310366571.

Ronsse, E (2015) Een blik op de emotionele ontwikkeling. *Sterk in Autisme!* **1** 32–34 and 2 31–34.

Sappok T, Heinrich M, Böhm J (submitted) *Autism Spectrum Disorder, Intellectual Developmental Disabilities, and Emotional Development: Relatedness and diagnostic impact.*

Sappok T, Barrett BF, Vandevelde S, Heinrich M, Poppe L, Sterkenburg P et al. (2016) Scale of emotional development – Short. *Research in Developmental Disabilities* **59** 166–175.

Sappok T, Budczies J, Bölte S, Dziobek I, Došen A, (2013) Emotional development in adults with autism and intellectual disabilities: a retrospective, clinical analysis. *PLoS ONE* **8** (9) e74036.

Sappok T, Budczies J, Dziobek I, Bölte S, Došen A, Diefenbacher A (2014) The missing link: Delayed emotional development predicts challenging behavior in adults with intellectual disability. *Journal of Autism and Developmental Disorders* **44** 786–800.

Sappok T, Diefenbacher A, Bergmann T, Zepperitz S & Dosen A (2012) Emotionale Entwicklungsstörungen bei Menschen mit Intelligenzminderung: Eine Fallkontrollstudie. *Psychiatrische praxis* **39** (5) 228–238.

Schuengel C, Sterkenburg PS, Jeczynski P, Janssen CG, Jongbloed G (2009) Supporting affect regulation in children with multiple disabilities during psychotherapy: a multiple case design study of therapeutic attachment. *J Consult Clin Psychol* **77** 291–301.

Soulières I, Dawson M, Gernsbacher MA, Mottron L (2011) The level and nature of autistic intelligence II: what about Asperger syndrome? *PLoS One* **6** e25372.

Taylor, JL, Hatton, C, Dixon, L & Douglas, C.(2004) Screening for psychiatric symptoms: PAS–ADD Checklist norms for adults with intellectual disabilities. *Journal of Intellectual Disability Research* **48** 37–41 doi: 10.1111/j.1365–2788.2004.00585.x.

Chapter 8
Sexual and emotional development in people with intellectual disabilities

Welmoed Visser-Korevaar and Jolanda Vonk

Summary

Like people of average ability, in people with intellectual disabilities, sexual development and emotional development are inextricably linked. In the current approach to sexuality and sexual development, biopsychosocial aspects play a role in sexual need, perception and behaviour.

Paying attention to emotional development leads to awareness of the importance of reflecting on the needs and resilience of people with intellectual disabilities. Emotional functioning is a dynamic feature and is influenced by experiences in context. Insufficient insight into and a lack of knowledge of emotional development are among the factors that have a negative influence on the personality development of people with disabilities (Vonk & Hosmar, 2009).

This chapter describes the relationship between emotions and sexuality, as well as between emotional and sexual development. Subsequently, sexuality, intimacy and sexual problems in general, and more specifically in people with intellectual disabilities, are discussed.

Knowledge of emotional development can provide an appropriate foundation and guidelines for social interaction, support and treatment of people with intellectual disabilities when it comes to sexuality. To make this more concrete, the first three stages of emotional development are elaborated and linked to sexological support.

Case: Frank

Frank is a young man with a mild intellectual disability. For four years he has lived under supervision in a house for people with intellectual disabilities. He has never had sex education before. Frank likes young, blonde girls. He fantasises about them, talks a lot about it to the caregiver and really wants a girlfriend. If the staff do not respond to this, he loses himself, gets excited and feels a great urge to masturbate. When this happens, he is sent to his own room. His caregiver is not sure how to deal with this.

1 Introduction: emotions and sexuality

When it comes to the combination of emotions and sexuality, we often think of terms such as lust, sense, desire, pleasure, infatuation, curiosity and feeling loved or fulfilled, but also shame, shyness, hurt, taboo, fear and frustration. Emotions and sexuality are both expressions of deep-seated needs; they are basic drivers that become visible in expression and behaviour and that are set in motion and controlled by biological factors such as the senses, brain and hormone balance.

Emotions represent 'acute, short-lived reactions associated with confusion and physical changes' (Vonk & Hosmar, 2009). The term refers to the experience of being moved or touched (we also speak of 'mood movements'). Emotions arise from the estimation of stimuli. If something has a sexual connotation, it can lead to sex-related emotions. Willingness to act, arousal and affect then play important roles (Frijda, 2008).

Feelings come from 'to feel', and the latter starts very concretely: all senses, especially the sense of touch, play a role. For example, newborn babies display an urge to be held, moved and touched because of their dependence on the caregiver. A feeling leads to an experience of what the environment does to us and how we give meaning to it. Frijda (2016) indicates that a feeling assesses the meaning of the stimuli. A feeling is therefore the conscious experience of this assessment process and the resulting willingness to act, arousal and affect (Hermans, *et al.*, 2013). When we express our feelings, we are vulnerable because we reveal what has touched us. Learning to deal with our own feelings is an important task for every one of us.

There is a distinction between needs, feelings and emotions. There are always needs, although we are not always aware of them: they are demanding in nature and do not need to have a direct connection to our actions. Examples include hunger (the need for food) or fatigue (the need for sleep). Feelings are like a process guard: they warn us and make us aware of our needs. Emotions are much stronger than feelings: emotions create an urge to act, such as screaming to express your anger. People can learn to deal with their emotions in a targeted way: one can learn to reflect on emotions and try to turn them into feelings. This leads to awareness and prevents interests from expressing themselves through impulsive emotions, which may frighten or hurt others.

As a child develops, it becomes important to regulate emotions and put them into words (emotion regulation). Nowadays much attention is paid to the concept of mentalising, in which these skills play an important role. Adults play a crucial role in this by helping their children to name and regulate emotions and to talk about pleasant, unpleasant or violent events with these words. In this way, children become aware of the meaning of stimuli. They get to know and learn to express their emotions and feelings.

According to Ekman (1992), central characteristics of emotions are their own importance (weight and usefulness) and their specificity. Over the course of evolution, emotions have been developed to deal with fundamental life tasks. There is a connection between physiological responses on the one hand and a subjective, conscious interpretation of specific emotional situations on the other.
Everaerd (1998) argues that these characteristics also apply to sexuality and/or sexual arousal. 'Sexuality has evolved over the course of evolution in order to deal with reproduction as a life task in the most appropriate way,' he writes (1998). There is a specific physiological response (such as genital arousal) and its interpretation in the brain.

The circular model (based on Basson, 2001 and Singer 1987; taken from Leusink and Ramakers, 2014) shows this schematically (see figure 8.1).

This is a contemporary model that describes the stages of sexual response. The circular model (such as that of Bancroft) is supplemented by the incentive motivation model (Basson 2001; Singer 1987).

In their *Handboek seksuele gezondheid (Handbook of Sexual Health),* Leusink and Ramakers (2014, p. 10-11) summarise this model as follows:

- This is a context in which people are receptive to receiving sexual stimuli from a sexually neutral situation or to engaging in sexual activities.
- Furthermore, there should be adequate sexual stimuli. These can be visual, tactile or auditory stimuli, but also memories or fantasies. Whether a stimulus has a sexual meaning differs from individual to individual and depends on experiences, gender and age.

- Finally, there must be an intact sexual system that can process these stimuli. This sexual system contains psychological and physical processes.

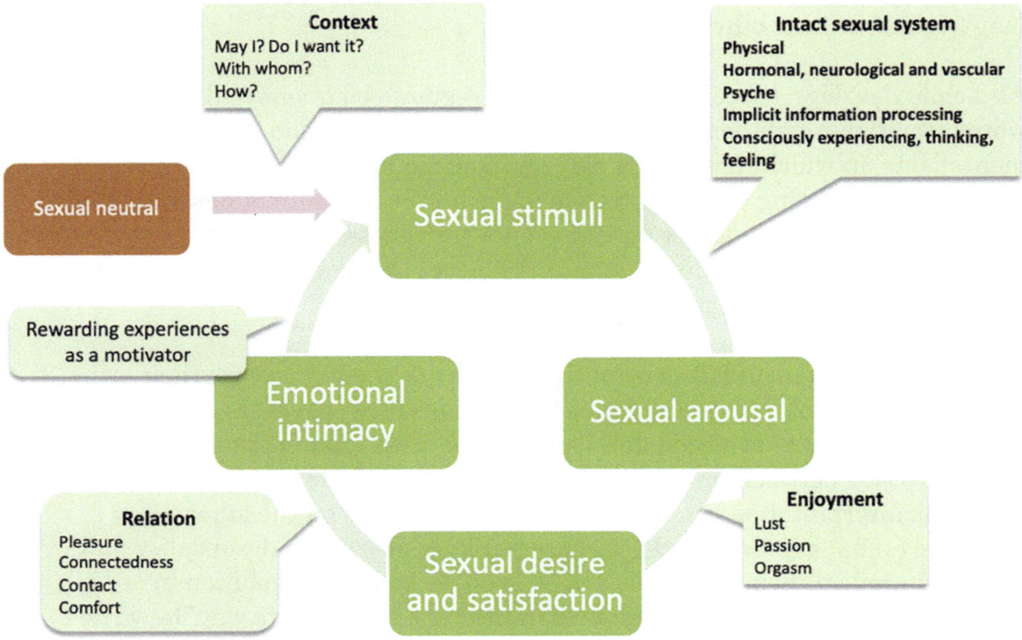

Circular model sexual response
(among others from Basson 2001, Singer 1987; derived from Leusink and Ramakers, Handbook sexual health [2014])

Figure 8.1 The circular model

Leusink and Ramakers (2014) indicate that if sexual arousal is valued as positive, for example through emotional and physical satisfaction (e.g. intimacy and orgasm), then a learning effect arises. A rewarding experience through positive appreciation of sexual stimuli then leads to sexual motivation (incentive motivation). Desire and excitement then coincide and reinforce each other. Sexual desire is thus aroused by the anticipation of expected physiological (orgasm) and emotional rewards (relaxation/arousal). Negative experiences can slow down the process.

Basic survival needs (such as food and protection, but also reproduction) lead to emotions that are activated by subcortical and cortical brain systems (LeDoux, 2002). Stimulation of these systems results in motivations for certain behaviours (Kernberg, 2012; LeDoux, 2002; Panksepp & Biven, 2012), including sexual behaviour. When environmental conditions (the context in the circular model in figure 8.1) do not meet those basic needs, disturbed motivational conditions arise, which can lead to maladaptive behaviour or problem behaviour (Sappok *et al.*, 2012). Sexual problems can also arise in this way. An example of this is the emergence of an inadequate pattern of masturbation in a young man with an intellectual disability who, because of a repressive attitude in his environment, did not receive sufficient sex education, as outlined in the case at the beginning of this chapter.

2 Emotional development and sexual development

Emotional development is described as 'a dynamic process in which the basic primary emotions will develop into a differentiated emotional life and thus make a major contribution to the formation of personality. Emotional development plays an essential role in the perception and behaviour of the individual throughout life' (Vonk & Hosmar, 2009, p. 24).

Connecting with emotional development has increasingly become a guiding principle in the treatment of people with intellectual disabilities in European countries that are familiar with the developmental dynamic model of Anton Došen and the scales that map emotional development (the Scale of Emotional Development – Revised[2] and Scale of Emotional Development – Short).

Sexual development already begins in the womb and continues into childhood, puberty and adulthood. This consists of an interplay between physical, cognitive, emotional, social, relational, ethical, religious and cultural factors. Children and young people themselves play an active role in this by responding to the environment, by giving meaning to ideas, emotions and behaviours and by making their own choices (Netherlands Centre for Youth Health, 2012). Emotional development contributes to sexual development and both are domains of normal development. These and other domains interlock and contribute to the formation of personality. Sexual behaviour and the experience of sexual feelings are not linked to a specific physical, cognitive, social or emotional development level: everyone develops sexually regardless the presence of a disability. A delay in emotional development certainly influences the way in which sexual feelings and behaviours are experienced and expressed. The body usually matures according to chronological age. People with intellectual disabilities will therefore usually develop 'adult' physical sexual behaviour. In these people, however, the relevant knowledge and emotional and social skills may not be sufficiently developed to deal with their sexuality in an adult and socially responsible manner (www.begrensdeliefde.nl).

3 Overview of sexuality

Views on sexuality have changed over the years, influenced by scientific insights and social changes. In the early 20th century, sexual desire was mainly seen as a biologically determined drive. Sigmund Freud, the founder of psychoanalysis, called the sexual drive 'libido'. This drive had to be controlled as much as possible. The influence of this view declined in the late 1920s, under the influence of sexual reforms. In the 1960s, with the introduction of birth control pills, there was a growing insight into the fact that sex is more than a biological fact aimed only at reproduction. People could now consciously look for pleasant stimuli without worrying about a possible pregnancy. The 'sexual revolution' was a fact in Western society. The word 'libido' therefore gave way to 'sexual arousal', which can be seen as something positive that you can also influence. At the same time it was recognised that negative experiences may inhibit sexual functioning.

In the 1970s and 1980s, the biopsychosocial model (IJff, 2006) was introduced, bringing with it an increased focus on non-biological aspects of sexuality. In this approach there is room for physical, psychological and social aspects to be involved in sexual need, perception and behaviour. This model expresses a sexual liberalisation. In addition to this model, still used in sexology, other trends have also been observed in recent years. For example, there is an increasing interest in somatic explanations as a result of advancing insights into neuroscience. Growth can also be observed in pharmacological therapies, such as the use of Viagra as a pleasure pill for men (IJff, 2006).

4 Definition of sexuality

The World Health Organization (WHO) defines sexuality as:

> A central aspect of human life. It includes sex, gender identity and roles, sexual orientation, eroticism, pleasure, intimacy and reproduction. It is experienced and shaped in thoughts, fantasies, desires, beliefs, attitudes, values, behaviour, actions, roles and relationships. Although sexuality can encompass all of these dimensions, they are not always experienced or shaped. Sexuality is influenced by the interaction of biological, psychological, social, economic, political, ethical, legal, historical, religious and spiritual factors.

In their sexual health handbook, Leusink and Ramakers (2014) describe three dimensions of sexuality:

- sexual behaviour as expression of visible sexuality (psychological and somatic processes)
- the sexual relationship: what happens between two people (such as the balance of power within in the relationship, gender roles, expectations and communication)
- sexual identity: the meaning of sexual behaviour and the sexual relationship between two people (self-image, uniqueness, being part of a group).

5 Intimacy in relation to sexuality

In this section we take a closer look at the concept of intimacy. As we saw in the definitions above, intimacy is closely linked to sexuality.

According to Van Ussel (1975), intimacy is a broader concept than sexuality: it is about the structure of the contact. For Delfos (1994), intimacy is central to human development. It is the degree to which a person makes personal contact with another, whereby the boundaries of each other's bodies and minds can come to be intertwined. Delfos describes 13 stages of the role of intimacy in a human life. The interactional poles of 'give and take' continuously play a role in this. In intimacy, a connection is made between physicality, experienced emotions and sexuality. If one does not have unpleasant sexual experiences, this is a great positive factor in human well-being (Delfos, 1994). Paul Verhaeghe recently wrote about this concept in his book *Intimacy* (2019). Where Ussel and Delfos describe the concept of intimacy in relation to the other, Verhaeghe indicates that the development of intimacy starts with the relationship you have with your own body. In a lecture for the Dutch organisation of family and relation therapy (NVRG) in 2019 Dr. P. Verhaeghe, a well known Belgian clinical psychologist mentioned that, he says:

> From birth we have developed an intimate relationship towards our own body, more broadly towards ourselves, containing all possible shades that intimacy can entail. As a relationship, it is the result of interactions with our parents and the environment in which we grow up. Our intimacy as an adult will therefore be strongly determined.

In our words that means that 'The relationship with yourself, your own body and the "zeitgeist" in which you grow up influences your relationship with the other and how intimacy is formed'. As a result, skin hunger, where you lose contact with your own body and yourself, is what matters. Restoring intimacy with yourself and your own body leads to the restoration of intimacy and/or sexuality with the other. So intimacy and sexuality are closely linked.

6 Sexual problems

Sexual problems arise when someone does not experience sex as they wish, in their perception, competencies or identity. For example, a sexual problem may arise out of differences in desire between two partners or a gender identity problem.
Sexual dysfunctions are disorders that impede the ability to be sexually active or experience sexual pleasure. According to the *Diagnostic and Statistical Manual of Mental Disorders* (fifth edition) (DSM-5), the complaints must be present for at least six months and there must be clinically significant suffering in order to speak of a disorder. Eight sexual dysfunctions are described, four in men, three in women and one in both men and women. Sexual dysfunctions occur in the sexual response cycle. This is the process of sense, excitement, orgasm and relaxation. Problems can arise in all of these stages.

Both people with and people without disabilities go through the same cycle of desire, arousal, orgasm and relaxation, in which one alternately focuses on oneself and the other, the so-called sexual response cycle (figure 8.2).

Sexual tension, which is evoked by desire, arousal and orgasm, leads to a greater focus on oneself, which is necessary to properly complete the response cycle. In the plateau stage (the preliminary stage of the orgasm; see figure 8.2), one is temporarily completely self-focused in order to have an orgasm. For example, one is less able to say 'stop' during this stage, even if the sex hurts, despite the skills one has learned. This is due to a lack of positive and focused sexual experiences and/or low cognitive, but also social and emotional, functioning. People with intellectual disabilities are therefore more vulnerable to sexual and relational problems. Sexologists can provide excellent help with these problems.

Incidentally, if according to the criteria of the DSM-5 there is no question of a sexual disorder or dysfunction, this does not mean that people cannot have a problem with sex.

When people come to their doctors or care providers with complaints, problems or questions related to sex, patients usually do not describe these as sexual dysfunctions or disorders. The DSM-5 criteria for sexual dysfunction are not always met. However, there is still a sexual problem that may hinder the client. Both men and women may have complaints that are not described in the DSM-5 but are described elsewhere in the literature. In men, these can be, for example, complaints about no ejaculation, or premature or painful ejaculation, as well as about orgasm. In women, there may be unwanted genital arousal, where orgasm does not cause pleasure but pain, or orgasm may cause long-term physical and mental complaints.

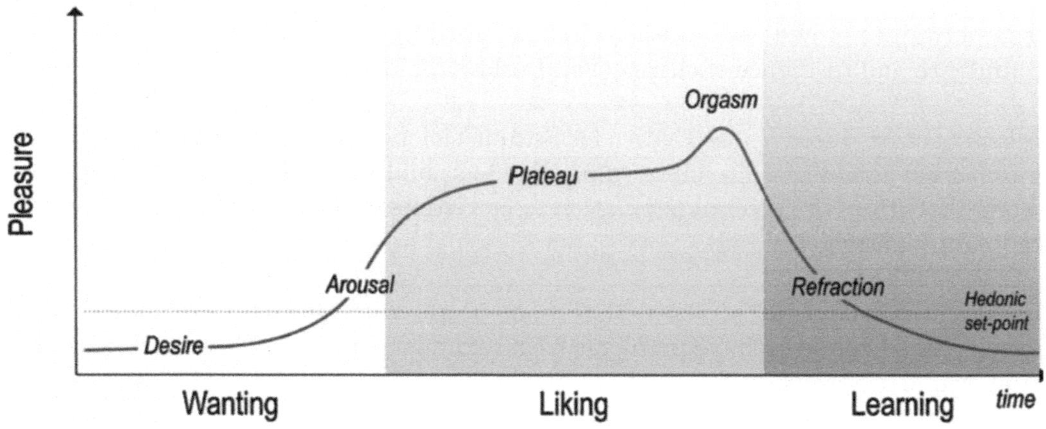

Figure 8.2: A graphical depiction of the human sexual response cycle (Georgiadis & Kringelbach, 2012)

6.1 Sexual problems in people with intellectual disabilities

Every year, the Special Interest Group (SIG) Mild or Moderate Intellectual Disablity, part of the Netherlands Scientific Association for Sexology (NVVS), provides an overview of the most common sexual problems in people with intellectual disabilities, in collaboration with the Rutgers Foundation. The following picture emerges from the 2018 survey.

In women with an intellectual disability, the main problems are being a victim of sexual violence, reduced resilience and orgasm problems (delayed or no orgasm). In addition, inappropriate verbal behaviour and relationship problems also occur. In men there is more diversity in problems, namely being a perpetrator, inappropriate touching of others, inappropriate language and paraphilia. Paraphilia is an unusual, atypical sexual interest or preference for certain activities or certain erotic goals in relation to objects. The sexual arousal is intense and comes back repeatedly, manifested in fantasies, urges or actions. The lack of a partner, arousal problems and gender identity problems also occur (PPT Rutgers SHVB survey, 2018). It is harrowing, but not surprising, that a lot of problems are the result of sexual violence.

People with intellectual disabilities are more likely to become victims of sexual violence as a result of problems in early childhood, their upbringing or increased vulnerability. Rutgers Nisso WPF's report *Restricted Resilience* shows that 61% of women and 23% of men have experienced sexual violence, ranging from a hurtful touch to rape. Parents/relatives and professionals report significantly lower rates, but they are often unaware. Compared to the general Dutch population, people with intellectual disabilities have experienced sexual violence more often than people without disabilities. For the prevention and reduction of sexual violence it is important to provide information (from an early age) and to increase the self-confidence and resilience of clients (Van Berlo *et al.*, 2011).

A factsheet produced by the Centre for Sexual Violence also shows that people with intellectual disabilities are more vulnerable to sexual abuse. They are four times more likely than the general population to be victims of sexual abuse (source: www.centrumseksueelgeweld.nl).

Research (Kok *et al.*, 2009) shows that many people with moderate and mild intellectual disabilities have problems with sexual experiences. These problems are often complex because of a lack of knowledge, experience and support. Educators and carers are often reluctant to talk to someone with intellectual disabilities about their 'complex' sexual experiences.

This fact is also reflected in a Rutgers study of sex in people under 25 at cluster three and four schools. Children and young people at special needs education schools in particular indicate that they lack information about sexuality, sexually transmitted diseases and contraception. Young people at special needs education schools also say they receive little information about relationships and sexuality in people with a disability (source: www.seksonderje25e.nl).

7 Sexual health

Attention to sexual health is therefore important: preventive measures can help to raise awareness of sexual violence and possibly decrease rates of abuse. The aim of counselling, treatment and sexual and relational training around sexological care questions is therefore to improve the sexual health of people with intellectual disabilities. The WHO (2010) describes sexual health as follows:

> Sexual health is a state of physical, emotional and mental well-being related to sexuality. It is more than the absence of illness, dysfunction or deficiency and requires a positive and respectful approach to sexuality and relationships. It requires the ability to have pleasant and safe sexual experiences free from coercion, discrimination and violence. To achieve this, the sexual rights of all people must be respected and fulfilled.

The focus on sexual health in the Netherlands has increased over the years, resulting in a policy letter by Jet Bussemaker in 2009 in which autonomy, resilience, the awareness of reciprocity, respect for the wishes and boundaries of the other and the right to sexual and relational training and good assistance were central. Vulnerable groups were specifically mentioned in this policy letter.

However, the right to enjoyable sexual experiences is still rarely mentioned. Fun is still an underexposed theme in the Netherlands and beyond (Lunsen & Laan, 2017). It is therefore noteworthy that at a meeting of the World Association for Sexual Health (WAS) in October 2019, a 'declaration on sexual pleasure' was signed by representatives from a large number of countries (source: www.worldsexualhealth.net)

A recent article by Ten Hag (2020) argues that attention to sexual health is even necessary in the treatment of sexual offenders. In his view, sexuality is fluid and flexible and therefore may be influenced, and this is important as a theme for treatment.

7.1 Sexual health in people with intellectual disabilities: working within an integrative model

Attention and guidance in maintaining sexual health is therefore certainly a part of the care of people with intellectual disabilities. It requires a holistic or integrative approach, which means that key development areas are identified and linked to provide co-ordinated guidance and treatment. This ties in with the biopsychosocial model within sexology, in which an integrative thinking framework is central. This includes a sexological history, possibly supplemented with diagnostic research in which biological, psychological, relational and social aspects of the person's request for help and/or perceived problem are examined (Van Doorn *et al.*, 2014).

As early as the 1980s, Došen (2014) developed a multidimensional model of personality development, known as the developmental dynamic model. Emotional development plays an important role in this model. The model was translated by Došen into seven stages of emotional development, described in chapter 3 of this handbook.
Other colleagues in the field have also worked with this integrative working method. For example, Bosch and Suykerbuyk (2006) use the hermeneutic circle to map out the information needed to start sex education. Derived from hermeneutics, this circle is an aid to a holistic view on the human being. By adapting sex education to the different developmental ages, the person in question has the opportunity to gain experiences of success and thereby take control of their life, which promotes growth and development. The different development stages not only include qualitatively different behaviours but also characteristic basic needs (Vugts-de Groot, 2009).

In order to gain a better understanding of what is going on in this area among people with intellectual disabilities, the next section links sexual need to the stages of emotional development.

8 The stages of emotional development linked to sexual development

Many people with intellectual disabilities have basic needs that are appropriate for the first three stages of emotional development. At each stage, these basic needs are different and are expressed in particular behaviours. This requires co-ordinated behaviour on the part of the professional in the treatment of these people. The characteristic sexual behaviours and feelings of the relevant stages listed below may be present.

8.1 Stage 1: homeostasis

In the first stage of emotional development, emotional needs are linked to physiological needs. The person in question is focused on themselves. Next comes the integration of sensory stimuli; the structure of place, time, persons and activities; constancy of the environment; and the stimulation of attachment behaviour.

Karin has regular sexual intercourse with different men, at different times. Actually it happens every day. Boredom, restlessness or frustration often play a role, but sometimes the reason for sexual intercourse cannot be traced back to a cause. When asked, Karin often reports abdominal pain, pain during sex and painful cramps after penetration. She does not really care with whom she has sex. She fulfils the need for satiety at that particular moment.

Sexual behaviours and sexual feelings that characterise this stage are:

- The whole body is a pleasure organ: skin contact is very important. Discovery with the proximal senses (smell, taste, mouth and touch) is primary.
- The sensory experience, in particular merging with that experience, is central.
- The client is not consciously in contact with their own sexuality or body. The focus is on their own experience. When sexuality is experienced with the other, the person is of secondary importance. Sexuality can be used to numb oneself, for example.
- The emotions are basically focused on lust and discomfort, exertion and relaxation.
- The responsibility for physical contact lies with the other person and contact takes place on the initiative of the other person. The client does not experience any direct influence.

- The client has many varying sexual contacts with random persons, with the sexual behaviour being aimed at themselves and the other being used as an object. There is no empathy for how the other person experiences it. (The sensory experience/action is central: there is often no concrete awareness of feelings associated with sense, excitement and orgasm.)
- Sexuality is all about obtaining comfort, as a counterpart to frustration and/or pain.
- The client's attention to their own and other people's bodies is undifferentiated, taking place especially through sensory experiences.
- Sexual arousal is not a conscious process: there is no targeted, intentional self-gratification yet.

In this first stage, sexuality support focuses on:

- gaining positive body experiences (e.g. the environment offers them to gain positive body experiences)
- creating a safe, shielded space where sexuality can be appropriately expressed and experienced, for the purpose of the client discovering their own body
- touching (comforting, cradling, physical care) between the client and the educator/caregiver, which is often about relieving helplessness
- ensuring safety (a desirable, pleasant, non-damaging situation) and organising preconditions (e.g. purchasing and preparing contraception in advance, regularly checking for venereal diseases at the mental health clinic), whether with regard to sexuality alone or with someone else
- providing psychoeducation, giving words to body parts, which aims at sensing specific parts of the body and pleasant/unpleasant sensations, and any sexual feelings or desires, when touching the body part concerned
- organising and structuring experiences in body awareness and sexual body experience (the difference between 'ordinary' touches and touches that lead to sexual arousal and possibly orgasm) so that the client can interpret sexual acts in context, which can be related to sensory stimulus processing (over- and understimulation) or can also be a form of interaction with physical excitement (not linked to a sexual fantasy) that is not intentional
- making decisions that transcend the client's 'ability to cope' (for example, decisions about whether to be sexually active, end a courtship, regulate social media use).

8.2 Stage 2: the attachment or first socialisation stage

In this stage, physical contact is central, as are reciprocity, attachment to the important other, the creation of safety and basic trust, and handling material. The person in question is very focused on the (important) other.

John indicates that he likes to be 'in' (penetrate) his girlfriend; only then does he feel connected to her. He likes this, and it makes him feel appreciated.

Sexual behaviours and sexual feelings that characterise this stage are:

- Touching and being touched play a major role. This means making a distinction between the person and the other person. This also creates the awareness that there is a body that you can control with regard to sexuality (such as stroking the breast or squeezing the breast or feeling the buttocks of another).
- The person begins to discover their own body in a targeted manner and to link it to a feeling/experience (anger, happiness, fear or sadness).
- There is the start of bonding, love or attachment in the form of reciprocity (give and take).
- There is a need for fully blending in with another person, for symbiosis, which is expressed in the beginnings of intimacy aimed at the other.
- The experience of sense, arousal, orgasm and relaxation are central: more focused stimulation and auto-erotic behaviour for the purpose of obtaining sexual arousal and orgasm arise from previous positive learning experiences (action–reaction). Repetitive behaviour, sometimes side by side (together with the other), to seek out the pleasant sensation may occur, similar to young children playing side by side during this stage.
- The body's own fluid is experienced as pleasant, and there is no restraint in this regard. Because of the need for experimentation and the lack of shame in this stage, it may be used in the course of sexual acts (involving stools, urine or semen).
- Emotional expressions can be seen as an action reaction.
- There can be unboundaried and grasping behaviour ('sticking' to a specific important other/partner).

In this second stage, sexuality support focuses on:

- emphasising the body image/experience for the benefit of the sexual body experience, for example in the form of body-oriented exercises in which the client experiences what feels pleasant

- talking about shaping sexuality with the permanent and reliable caregiver
- making it clear that physical pleasure, intimacy and sexuality take place with someone you want to share this with, within a built-up bond between two people, which both want
- emphasising that two persons can have sexual contact side by side, where this sexual contact consists of interconnectedness and of mutual satisfaction on the basis of mutual consent, the purpose of which is to share sexual arousal and orgasm
- if relevant, indicating the desirable behaviour (always putting in frames) when using social media and dating sites
- if the client is in a relationship, continuously linking psychoeducation and interventions to the partner, emphasising jointness and behavioural agreements (how it should be and how it should not be in a relationship)
- in addition to experiencing and sharing physical pleasure together with a partner, signalling boundaries: 'This is fine for you, but it may be different for someone else.'

8.3 Stage 3: autonomy or first individuation stage

Central to the third stage are discovering one's own will, fighting for autonomy, wanting to do things oneself (which also means saying 'no') and enlarging the world. Egocentric behaviour and not being able to control all kinds of feelings are characteristic of this stage. People at this stage are mainly focused on themselves.

This requires the caregiver or important other to be present at a visible distance, to emphasise 'me and you', to stay out of the battle and to be distracted without making this obvious.

John wondered afterwards whether he should have asked Nadia if she also liked the first time they went to bed together. He liked it.
Sexual behaviours and sexual feelings that characterise this third stage are:

- The client develops their own autonomy and self-determination (doing it themselves, not wanting anyone to pry into their sexual behaviour, sexual contact or relationship).
- The client is mainly focused on fulfilling their own sexual needs/wishes.
- Holding and letting go are central (attention to the relaxation and tightening of the pelvic floor may be necessary: control mechanisms around arousal and orgasm can cause problems).

- The anus can be a source of pleasant feelings (anal fixations and sexual needs aimed at the anus), but there is also a risk of injury and the like. This behaviour is separate from sexual preference; it is behaviour that suits this development stage in normal child development.
- The client discovers targeted masturbation and associated (pleasant and/or unpleasant) feelings. This is not only a repetition of sexual behaviour (auto-erotic behaviour) but also a targeted manipulation and experimentation with masturbation in different ways.
- There is no sense of shame yet. Public masturbation can also occur at this stage.
- The client begins to consciously discover the differences between men and women. Gender identity is developing. The differences are seen/experienced as a constant: 'I am a girl and will remain a girl.'
- Cuddling and walking are experienced as pleasant.

In this third stage, sexuality support focuses on:

- emphasising 'me and you' and presenting concrete choices within an established framework of accepted manifestations of sexuality
- giving room to physical sensations (nothing is crazy or strange) and making the link with sexual stimulation (body experience is linked to the sexual experience)
- strengthening the 'I' identity for the purpose of strengthening the sexual identity, for example by using an 'I book', a workbook which helps create and enhance an I-identity by collecting information about themselves. This information can be in words, pictures, photos and its about their life.
- offering/advising body-oriented exercises for the purpose of discovering one's own body and/or other people's bodies, experimenting with it and relieving any fear of touch
- continuing to indicate a framework and boundary for safe, pleasant and desired behaviour.

8.4 Stage 4 and beyond

From the fourth stage, guidance in the sexuality of a client will deal with aspects that increasingly affect the sexuality of people with normal development. The person in question increasingly takes the other person into their choices and considerations.

This could include:

- making a script/manual with the client for use in sexual contact with themselves and/or someone else
- regulating sexual behaviour, feelings and desires, in order for the client to gain more insight and control over their own sexuality
- mapping out the sexual response cycle and interventions (e.g. how to develop and maintain a sense of purpose) in consultation with the client
- exploring wishes and boundaries and making them conscious and concrete
- clarifying and shaping the framework (social-sexual rules and agreements and discrimination skills)
- clarifying concepts around sexuality, intimacy and relationship formation
- providing information about cognitions and inhibitions, distinguishing real from unreal and erroneous cognitions
- normalising questions, thoughts and feelings about sexuality, intimacy and relationship formation
- paying attention to sexual identity and sexual preference
- paying attention to sexuality and perception of sexuality in the social, religious and cultural context.

9 Talking about sexuality in people with intellectual disabilities

It is important to discuss the sexuality of people with intellectual disabilities and to have an understanding of the sexual development of members of this group. Sex is also an ordinary part of the lives of people with intellectual disabilities.

Bender (2008) says that talking about sexuality within care relationships is still far from common. Many well-trained professionals do not know how to deal with this subject, even if the client brings it up. It hardly receives any attention in training, and there is a lack of knowledge about solutions.

Policy in this area is often insufficient. There may be a fear of the emotions it evokes, or making sexuality open to discussion may be perceived as expressing an inappropriate curiosity about the client. In caring for people with intellectual disabilities, people are often reluctant to name things concretely and to ask concrete questions. There is also sometimes the old idea that it is better to let sleeping dogs lie. The risk of all this is that sexuality will only be discussed if there are sexual problems, or if the client exhibits sexually transgressive behaviour or is a victim of sexually transgressive behaviour.

Attention to sexuality can be realised in various ways within the care for people with an intellectual disability. The Rutgers Foundation (1998) talks about 'living up to life': everything you do or do not do sends a message about sexuality, intimacy and relationships. 'Ad hoc' attention to sexuality (a short conversation during dinner or following a television programme, or chat sparked by the pregnancy of a colleague or the relationship of group members) is necessary. In addition, it is important to pay attention to sexuality in a structured and planned manner. There should be a vision and policy about sexuality, and there should be a support plan for an employee who discusses this. In addition, talking about sex can also just be disarming and funny. Various materials can be used to start the conversation. The use of visual aids in the conversation is recommended. At the end of this chapter some sexual education materials are mentioned.

Case: how did things go with Frank?

Frank's cognitive functioning is higher than his emotional functioning. In Frank we see many characteristic behaviours of the third stage of emotional development. He is mainly focused on his own experience of lust, despite talking a lot about blonde girlfriends. In concrete questioning it turns out that he is imitating remarks made by his brother, who pursues his many sexual conquests during nights on the town. Frank's sexual identity is in full development. He copies and imitates others in order to master the desired behaviour. Frank receives customised sexological support, which focuses on arousal and orgasm and creates clarity and frameworks around his sexual behaviour. Frank is not yet looking for a real relationship or friendship with a blonde girl. However, he would like to have more pictures or DVDs of blonde girls in his room: they stimulate his sexual excitement. It is important that Frank knows where he can and cannot masturbate. It is discussed with Frank that sex drive and the expression of sexual behaviour are normal. It is agreed that he can watch and masturbate to these DVDs in his own room at night. Frank can talk to his regular contact person about sexuality, what his wishes are and how he can fulfil them in an appropriate and healthy way. With some simple humour, Frank can talk about his experience of sexuality in a lighthearted and relaxed but clear way. Frank is sensitive not only to what is said but especially to the way in which it is said.

10 Conclusion

Emotional development is inextricably linked to sexual development. Knowledge of the emotional development of people with an intellectual disability provides a good basis for understanding and guiding their requests for sexological help. This contributes to the sexual health of these people, who are usually very vulnerable. Connecting with their emotional and sexual development means step-by-step growth and development at their own pace, according to their own wishes and needs.

11 Finally

In recent years, there has been increasing attention paid to the sexual feelings of people with intellectual disabilities. More education has been offered in the field of sexuality education, and there is a strong focus on increasing knowledge. More methods have become available, and there are more websites and dating sites especially for people with disabilities. This is a positive trend.

In the Netherlands, we see evidence of this positive trend in the establishment of a national platform for sexologists in this sector, the SIG of the NVVS, mentioned above, which represents an advance for sexologists in dealing with problems related to sexuality. We also see an increase in the number of symposia on this topic in the country.

Both in clinical practice and in scientific research it is important to make sexuality and sexology more visible as a discipline in the care for people with intellectual disabilities. Structural research is already being carried out into sexuality among people with intellectual disabilities at Maastricht University, in collaboration with the Gouverneur Kremers Centre, and scientific research is also taking place in Tilburg and Groningen.

For everyday practice, it is desirable that emotional development be even more embedded and implemented in the approach to requests for sexological help from people with intellectual disabilities. We hope this chapter offers an inspiring invitation to this.

References

Berlo, W van, Haas, S de, Oosten, N van, Dijk, L van, Brants, L, Tonnon, S, & Storms, O (2011) *Beperkt weerbaar Een onderzoek naar seksueel geweld bij mensen met een lichamelijke, zintuiglijke of verstandelijke beperking*. Utrecht: Rutgers wpf/Movisie.

Bender (2008). De faciliterende rol van het instituut. In: WL Gianotten, MJ Meihuizen-de Regt, N van Son-choones (Eds) 2008 *Seksualiteit bij ziekte en lichamelijke beperking* (pp 606–616). Assen: van Gorcum.

Bosch, E, & Suykerbuyk, E (2006) *Seksuele voorlichting aan mensen met een verstandelijke handicap De kunst van het verstaan*. Soest: Nelissen.

Centrum seksueel geweld. Factsheet [online]. Available at: www.centrumseksueelgeweld.nl/wp-content/uploads/2020/01/FIER005-Flyers-factsheet-NL.jpg (accessed March 2021).

Doef, S van der (1994) *Kleine mensen, grote gevoelens Kinderen en hun seksualiteit*. Amsterdam: Ploegsma.

Delfos, MF (1994) De ontwikkeling van intimiteit Een ontwikkelings–psychologisch model gekoppeld aan een model van de gevolgen van seksueel misbruik. *Tijdschrift voor Seksuologie* **18** (4) 282–292.

Doorn, P van et al (2014). Seks hoort bij mij. In: Leusink, P & Ramakers, M (Eds) *Handboek seksuele gezondheid: Probleemgeoriënteerd denken en handelen* (pp240–260). Assen: Koninklijke Van Gorcum.

Došen, A (2014) *Psychische stoornissen, probleemgedrag en verstandelijke beperking Een integratieve benadering bij kinderen en volwassenen* (5th edition). Assen: Van Gorcum.

Ebbers, S (2002) Seksualiteit en seksueel misbruik Werkboek voor agogische en zorgverlenende beroepen. Amersfoort: Thieme Meulenhoff bv.

Ekman, P (1992) An argument for basic emotions. *Cognition and emotion* **6** (3-4) 169–200.

Everaerd, W (1998) Commentary on sex research: Sex as an emotion. *Journal of Psychology & Human Sexuality* **1** 3–15.

Hag, ten B. (2020). Seksuele scriptanalyse bij cliënten met seksueel delictgedrag. *Tijdschrift voor Seksuologie,1*, 10-21.

IJff, M (2006) *Sexcounseling Handleiding voor seksuologische hulpverlening* (3rd edition). Assen: Van Gorcum.

Kernberg, O (2012) Exploring the interface of neurobehaviourally linked personality dimensions and personality organization in borderline personality disorder: the Multidimensional Personality Questionnaire and Inventory of Personality Organization. *Journal of Personality Disorder* **26** (6) 902–18.

LeDoux, JE (2002) *Synaptic Self: How our brains become who we are*. New York: Macmillan.

Nederlands Centrum Jeugdgezondheid (NCJ) (2012) *richtlijn; JGZ richtlijn seksuele ontwikkeling* [online]. Available at: http://www.ncj.nl (accessed March 2021).

Panksepp, J & Biven, L (2012) *The Archaeology of Mind: Neuroevolutionary origins of human emotions*. New York: Norton.

Hehenkamp, L & van Zenderen, K (2015) *SHVB registratie 2011–2014*. Utrecht: Rutgersstichting.

Kok et al (2009) Zorgverleners over seksualiteit van mensen met een verstandelijke beperking; een kwalitatief onderzoek *Tijdschrift voor seksuologie (TvS)* **33** (3) 199–206.

Sappok, T, Diefenbacher, A, Bergmann, T, Zepperitz, S & Došen, A (2012) Emotional developmental disorders in individuals with intellectual disabilities (ID): A case–control–study *Psychiatrische Praxis* **39** (5) 228–238.

Spanier, GB (1977) Seksual socialisation: a conceptual review *International Journal of Sociology and the Family* **6** 121–146.

Rutgersstichting (1998) Rutgers [online]. Available at: www.seksonderje25e.nl/files/uploads/Samenvatting%20Seks%20onder%20je%2025e%20VSO.pdf (accessed April 2020).

Salemink E & van Lankveld, JJ (2006) The effects of increasing neutral distraction on sexual responding in women with and without sexual problems. *Archives of sexual behaviour* **35** 179–190 doi: 101007/s10508–005–901450–2.

Ussel, JMW van (1975) *Intimiteit*. Deventer: Van Loghum Slaterus.

van Lankveld, JJ DM & van den Hout, MA (2004) Increasing neutral distraction inhibits genital but not subjective sexual arousal of sexually functional and dysfunctional men. *Archives of Sexual Behaviour* **33** 549–558 doi:101023/b:aseb00000447392911373.

Vonk, J & Hosmar, A (2009) *Emotionele ontwikkeling bij mensen met een beperking Een denk- en handelingskader voor de praktijk*. Leuven: Acco.

Vugts-de Groot, B (2009) *Werken met ontwikkelingsleeftijden Afstemmen op mensen met een verstandelijke beperking*. Baarn: Nelissen.

World Health Organization (WHO) Sexual and reproductive health [online]. Available at: https://www.who.int/teams/sexual-and-reproductive-health-and-research/key-areas-of-work/sexual-health/defining-sexual-health (accessed May 2020).

World Sexual Health (2019). Declaration on sexual pleasure [online]. Available at: www.worldsexualhealth.net/declaration-on-sexual-pleasure/ (accessed March 2021).

Websites:

www.begrensdeliefde.nl
www.rutgers.nl
www.seksindepraktijk.nl
www.seksualiteit.nl
www.steffie.nl
www.sclera.be

Materials used in the Netherlands:

- Vrienden en vrijers (Edugarant)
- Lief, lijf en leven (klos tv)

Chapter 9 The developmental concept of social brain functions: intellectual disability and mental health

Tanja Sappok and Marco O Bertelli

Summary

Intellectual disability is a neurodevelopmental disorder. The complex relationship between structural and functional brain connectivity during development may provide a crucial background for a better understanding of health and illness in persons with developmental delays. The developmental concept of social brain functions links the levels of circuit organisation of the emerging limbic system (structure) to the associated mental and behavioural capacities of a person (function). The developmental dynamics of mental health in persons with intellectual disability may add a dimensional perspective to psychiatric diagnostics, treatment and care.

1 Background

To date, the conceptualisation of psychopathology and mental disorders has relied on the grouping of defined symptoms into syndromes that yield psychiatric diagnoses. The benefits of this categorial approach have been overestimated, not only in the way these categories have been taken to reflect real divisions between diseases in nature but also in the clinical utility claimed for these psychiatric diagnoses. Insights into the connection between alterations of structural and functional brain development and psychopathological vulnerability may provide a more dynamic understanding of psychopathology. This link seems to be expressed more in people with intellectual disabilities, autism or other developmental disabilities than in other population subgroups. In fact, intellectual disability or disorders of intellectual development, according to the most recent International Classification of Diseases (11th revision) (ICD-11) terminology (WHO, 2018), constitute a group of neurodevelopmental conditions associated with a high vulnerability to psychological distress, psychopathological features, and challenging behaviours (World Health Organization, 2018; Bertelli *et al.*, 2012; Pessoa, 2010; Bertelli *et al.*, 2016; Bowring *et al.*, 2019). According to the ICD-11 definition, disorders of intellectual development are encountered in the group of *neurodevelopmental disorders* that 'arise during the developmental period' and 'involve significant difficulties in the acquisition and execution of specific intellectual, motor, language, or social functions' (World Health Organization, 2018). As such, in addition to pure cognitive functions, social, affective and adaptive functions are also affected. Considering the evidence on the complexity of cognitive-emotional network interactions during brain development, and the association between social competencies (located in the limbic system) and other intellectual, motor, language, emotional and adaptive functions, intellectual disability can be considered much more than a pure learning disorder, and this fact has to be acknowledged, especially in those with additional mental health problems. (Pessoa, 2010).

This chapter will address the impact of this *developmental concept of social brain functions* on the understanding of the behaviour and mental health issues of persons with intellectual disabilities and/or other developmental disabilities and, through this, will provide some more general indications of a useful approach to psychopathology that is alternative or complementary to the categorial one.

2 Impact of the developmental level on problem behaviour and mental health

The developmental pattern in relation to behavioural and mental functioning may have relevant implications for the psychopathological diagnosis. The most important of these implications is the identification of the causal role that a certain developmental level may have in those behavioural and mental-functioning alterations that are commonly referred to as psychopathological symptoms. For instance, the definition of the developmental level may help in defining the extent to which a repeated and unusual problem behaviour of a person with intellectual disability may be attributed to a specific stage of personal growth, a co-occurrent psychiatric disorder or a combination of the two.

Another relevant positive implication of the developmental approach is the introduction of a dimensional interpretation of psychopathological symptoms as an alternative or complement to the categorial one. The dimensional interpretation focuses on the degree (intensity, pervasiveness) of every single symptom or abnormal behaviour that a person with intellectual disability may exhibit rather than on how many symptoms there are and how they are clustered. For instance, a person with an intellectual disability who is actually depressed may not exhibit an abundance of depressive symptoms, and another who displays several symptoms may not actually be depressed.

A third advantage of the developmental approach is the focus on antecedents and contextual factors. This point considers the 'what came before?' and 'when and where?' of the symptom or problem behaviour and the response of the social environment to it. Many problem behaviours are progressive and go from being 'annoying' in mild forms to destructive and dangerous in severe forms.

The identification of the developmental level has relevant implications for a comprehensive diagnosis of the condition of intellectual disability and the possible co-occurrence of psychiatric disorders. As the first World Health Organization working group on the re-classification of 'mental retardation' in ICD-11 stated (Bertelli *et al.*, 2016): 'At any given cross-sectional encounter point with convergence of the various possible trajectories it is difficult for a clinician to make an informed decision about the developmental course of [an intellectual disability or intellectual developmental disorder].'

2.1 Challenging behaviours

Problem behaviours may be caused by various biological factors, such as somatic diseases or genetic syndromes, and psychosocial factors, such as communication problems, negative life events or a lack of social support (Bowring *et al.*, 2019). When conceptualised as invariably linked to the person's social environment, these behaviours are defined as 'challenging behaviours' (Emerson & Bromley, 1995).

In persons with more severe cognitive impairment, challenging behaviours are frequently reported to be associated with psychiatric disorders (Felce *et al.* 2009; Bowring *et al.*, 2019). However, there is an ongoing discussion about the conceptualisation of challenging behaviours (Bowring *et al.*, 2019), and additional dimensions, such as the developmental perspective, have been addressed (Sappok *et al.*, 2014). Melville *et al.* (2016), for example, found an underlying emotional dysregulation dimension for problem behaviours that differed from psychiatric symptomatology. The authors suggest the use of a dimensional model for the analysis of problem behaviours and point out the limitations of the current categorial diagnostic system. Rojahn *et al.* (2004) found an association of aggressive and self-injurious behaviours with impulse-control and conduct problems, indicating the developmental approach as fundamental to a comprehensive individualised diagnosis. This is supported by other findings of high correlations between the severity of the challenging behaviours and lower developmental and emotional stages, especially the levels of affect regulation (Sappok *et al.*, 2014; Böhm *et al.*, 2019). The level of emotional development has been reported to have even more of an impact on the onset and severity of challenging behaviours than does the level of intellectual disability (Sappok *et al.*, 2014; Böhm *et al.*, 2019). Otsuka *et al.* (2017) found that 'emotional perception' mediates the relationship between levels of cognitive functioning and adaptive skills.

To conclude, in addition to well-known causes of challenging behaviours, such as somatic disorders and environmental factors, developmental neuroscience may add another perspective and should be considered in the diagnostic workup of challenging behaviours, especially in the case of an incongruence between the individual's level of social brain functions and a given social setting.

2.2 Mental disorders

As mentioned above, developmental neuroscience, which focuses on developmental age-related and life-event-related emotional patterns and motives, and their co-regulation in a social context, may provide an alternative or complementary perspective to the current assessment and diagnosis of psychiatric disorders, which relies on given symptoms and their grouping into syndromes (World Health Organization, 2018), especially in persons with intellectual disability. An understanding of the interdependence of developmental changes and variations in psychopathology may result in a more dimensional understanding of psychopathological features (Hofer *et al.*, 2009; Di Martino *et al.*, 2014), and the developmental miswiring at sensitive periods may be associated with certain mental disorders (Di Martino *et al.*, 2014). For example, in autism spectrum disorders (ASD), which often co-occur with intellectual disability, core symptoms are related with emotion dysregulation (Samson *et al.*, 2014), which, in turn, may be rooted in developmental delays of the brain circuits related to social cognition (Sappok *et al.*, 2013). Attachment disorders are highly prevalent among clinically suspicious children with intellectual disability, and even more prevalent in those with additional ASD (Giltaij *et al.*, 2015; Teague *et al.*, 2020). Insecure bonding is linked to social experiences occurring during critical periods of development, which imprint on the brain architecture and contribute to behavioural and emotional problems later in life (Teague *et al.*, 2020). Clinical disorders that develop prenatally or early in life, such as ASD or attachment disorders, and also certain behavioural equivalents of psychopathology, such as pica, self-injury or rumination, may be seen more frequently in persons with disturbances of high-order neural circuits, such as the theory of mind network or the attachment system (Happé & Frith, 2014; Di Martino *et al.*, 2014; Matson & Shoemaker, 2011). In contrast, other disorders, such as body image disturbances or social phobia, seem to require that the affected person has a theory of mind or good mindreading skills and therefore can be diagnosed only in persons with a rather regular formation and activation of the respective neural circuits. In post-traumatic stress disorder (PTSD), for example, Plana *et al.* found significant deficits in mentalisation and emotion recognition, which could not be observed in social anxiety (Plana *et al.*, 2014). In a small longitudinal study, Battaglia *et al.* found that specific cerebral reactivities to angry faces at the age of around eight to nine years could predict the development of a social anxiety disorder in adolescence (Battaglia *et al.*, 2012). Other findings connected psychotic experiences during childhood and adolescence with cognitive impairments and emotional and behavioural problems at the age of around five years (Polanczyk *et al.*, 2010; Zammit *et al.*, 2013). Magnetic resonance imaging studies pointed out that these psychotic experiences can be associated with abnormalities in the local gyrification index but not in the underlying white matter, indicating a possible causality for an atypical cortical development rather than a progressive disorder (Fonville *et al.*, 2019).

In summary, it seems probable that certain developmental delays may increase the susceptibility to certain mental disorders, and this effect is attributable not only to the maturation of the social brain functions but also to a number of correlated alterations of the immunological and endocrine systems (Champagne, de Kloet & Joëls, 2009; Bilbo & Schwarz, 2012; Procaccini *et al.*, 2014). Lewis *et al.* (2020), for example, describe an increased risk of depression in girls at more advanced stages of breast development at age 14 compared to girls at lower stages of breast development, irrespective of age at pubertal onset, which may be due to higher oestradiol levels.

Understanding the developmental trajectories of psychopathological features of certain mental or genetic disorders may also help to characterise associated changes in cognitive, emotional and behavioural functioning (Mollon *et al.*, 2018; Keysor & Mazzocco, 2002). For instance, in a population-based longitudinal study, Mollon *et al.* (2018) identified specific dynamic processes of working memory, visuospatial abilities and other cognitive functions throughout the first two decades of life of those with psychotic disorder that did not appear in those with depression or psychotic depression (Lewis *et al.*, 2018). Detailed knowledge of the neuropsychological changes that underlie psychological symptoms and clusters of symptoms may increase our understanding of the nature and origin of psychiatric disorders as well as help us to produce more effective and timely interventions (figure 9.1).

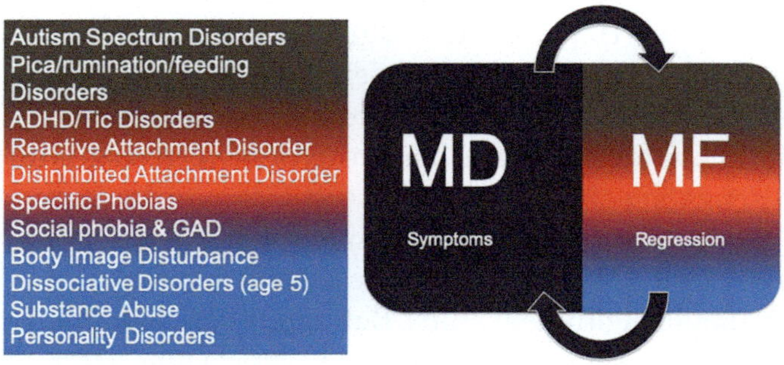

Figure 9.1: The socio-emotional brain functions are decisive for the development of certain mental disorders. However, some mental disorders, such as dementia or PTSD, seem to occur somewhat more independently from the level of brain development and associated social brain functions.

To conclude, in persons with an intellectual disability, psychopathology should be interpreted according to the background of the developmental dynamics of social brain functions. The developmental perspective expands the biopsychosocial model of mental disorders by adding a continuous dimension, namely, time (figure 9.2).

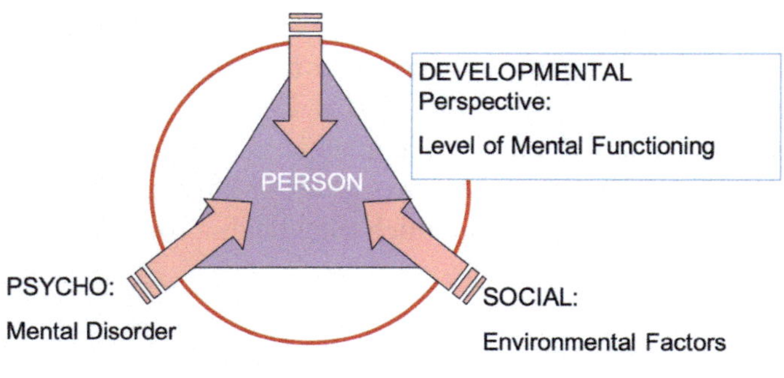

Figure 9.2: The biopsychosocial model of mental disorders is complemented by the developmental perspective on social brain functions.

Deficits in emotion regulation, which are associated with dysfunctions in the social brain networks, have also been suggested as a common factor for psychopathology in the general population (Aldao, Nolen-Hoeksema & Schweizer, 2010). As deficits in emotion regulation are also linked to social cognition networks in persons without intellectual disability, the developmental concept of social brain functions may be of value for the understanding and treatment of disorders such as chronic depression, borderline personality disorder or PTSD (Visted *et al.*, 2018; Austin, Riniolob & Porges, 2007; Fitzgerald *et al.*, 2018).

3 Impact of the level of social brain functions on treatment and support

The quantity and quality of studies evaluating the efficacy of therapies in persons with intellectual disability are still limited, and the findings produced to date 'are inconclusive at best' (Ali *et al.*, 2015; Koslowski *et al.*, 2016), especially in those with severe to profound intellectual disability (Vereenooghe & Langdon, 2013; Ali *et al.*, 2015; Vereenooghe *et al.*, 2018). Neither in mild to moderate intellectual disability nor in severe to profound intellectual disability is there a clear recommendation for a certain treatment method for mental health problems. Interestingly, the type of intervention is chosen according to the type of disorder and not according to the level of functioning of the person who needs the treatment. Sometimes, distinct study populations are recruited depending on the level of intellectual disability or verbal abilities, but even these basic parameters are often not described properly, or mixed study samples are used (Koslowski *et al.*, 2016; Vereenooghe & Langdon, 2013; Ali *et al.*, 2015).

When it comes to treatment and support, the maturation of the social brain and the associated mental state may suggest a decision for or against a certain method. Good perspective-taking skills, for example, may increase the probability of an individual benefiting from cognitive interventions, while people without theory of mind abilities may profit from bodily and experience-based treatment methods. Attachment-based behavioural therapy, for example, may be helpful in persons with insecure bonding and associated externalising behavioural problems (Mohamed & Mkabile, 2015; Sterkenburg *et al.*, 2008). Dance and movement therapy fosters empathy and perspective-taking skills in persons with pervasive developmental disorders and associated delays in social brain functions (Mastrominico *et al.*, 2018; Koehne *et al.*, 2016). In contrast, cognitive behavioural therapy is promising in persons with borderline to mild intellectual disability who are able to mentalise (Nicoll *et al.*, 2013; Taylor *et al.*, 2016).

Targeting effective treatment programmes according to individual abilities is pivotal in persons with intellectual disabilities (Ali *et al.*, 2015). The *social information processing model*, for example, aims to choose the type of intervention according to the mental state of a person during a social interaction (Larkin *et al.*, 2013). In their review, Larkin *et al.* found a difference in patterns of social information processing in adults with intellectual disability with and without aggressive behaviours and concluded that treatment and support should be aligned accordingly (Ali *et al.*, 2015). Besides the verbal abilities and the severity of intellectual disability, elements of social cognition, such as perspective-taking skills, self-regulating skills and social abilities, may also suggest that a certain type of therapy would be beneficial.

4 Conclusion

In persons with intellectual disabilities, the identification of the developmental level has relevant implications for a comprehensive diagnosis of the condition of intellectual disability itself and co-occurrent mental disorders. The most important of these implications are as follows: a) the identification of the causal role of the level of emotional development, as the associated behaviours may be typical for the respective reference age and may not necessarily be understood as psychopathological symptoms; b) the introduction of a dimensional interpretation of psychopathological symptoms as alternative or complementary to the categorial one; c) the consideration of antecedents and contextual factors of psychopathological symptoms; and d) the consideration of social brain development in the identification of maladaptive behaviours. However, these implications seem not to be applicable to all mental disorders in the same way. Some mental disorders, such as dementia or PTSD, seem to occur somewhat more independently from the level of brain development and associated social brain functions.

The developmental perspective may also represent a useful framework for therapeutic interventions in terms of both choosing between currently available treatment options and developing future strategies.

Individually tailored interventions acting at specific levels of mental development and functioning may increase the treatment effectiveness in this highly vulnerable population.

Despite the great importance for psychiatric diagnostics and treatment in persons with intellectual disabilities, findings to date from developmental neuroscience appear to be limited and to have few immediate implications for practice or policy. Research is urgently needed to remedy this shortcoming. Further research is also needed to assess how emotional development and mental disorders are intertwined and especially the effects of mental disorders on the level of emotional development and vice versa. The effects of the level of emotional development on the prevalence of certain disorders should also be assessed in detail.

References

Aldao, A, Nolen-Hoeksema, S, Schweizer, S (2010) Emotion regulation strategies across psychopathology: A meta-analysis. *Clinical Psychology Review* **30** (2) 217–237.

Ali, A, Hall, I, Blickwedel, J, Hassiotis, A (2015) Behavioural and cognitive-behavioural interventions for outwardly-directed aggressive behaviour in people with intellectual disabilities. *Cochrane Database Syst Rev* 2015.

Austin, MA, Riniolob, TC, Porges, SW (2007) Borderline personality disorder and emotion regulation: Insights from the polyvagal theory. *Brain Cognit* **65** (1) 69–76.

Battaglia, M, Zanoni, A, Taddei, M, Giorda, R, Bertoletti, E, Lampis, V, et al. (2012) Cerebral responses to emotional expressions and the development of social anxiety disorder: A preliminary longitudinal study. *Depress Anxiety* **29** (1) 54–61.

Bertelli, M, Scuticchio, D, Ferrandi, A, Lassi, S, Mango, F, Ciavatta, C, Porcelli, C, Bianco, A, Monchieri, S (2012) Reliability and validity of the SPAID-G checklist for detecting psychiatric disorders in adults with intellectual disability. *Res Dev Disabil* **33** (2) 382–90 doi: 10.1016/j.ridd.2011.08.020.

Bertelli, MO, Munir, K, Harris, J, Salvador-Carulla, L (2016) 'Intellectual developmental disorders': Reflections on the international consensus document for redefining 'mental retardation-intellectual disability' in ICD-11. *Advances in Mental Health and Intellectual Disabilities* **10** (1) 36–58.

Bilbo, SD & Schwarz, JM (2012) The immune system and developmental programming of brain and behavior. *Frontiers in neuroendocrinology* **33** (3) 267–286.

Böhm, J, Dziobek, I, Sappok, T (2019) Emotionale Entwicklung, Aggressionsregulation und herausforderndes Verhalten bei Menschen mit Intelligenzminderung. *Fortschr Neurol Psychiatr* **87** (8).

Bowring DL, Painter, J, Hastings, RP (2019) Prevalence of Challenging Behaviour in Adults with Intellectual Disabilities, Correlates, and Association with Mental Health. *Curr Dev Disord Rep* **6** 173–181.

Champagne, DL, de Kloet, ER, Joëls, M (2009). Fundamental aspects of the impact of glucocorticoids on the (immature) brain. *Seminars in Fetal and Neonatal Medicine* **14** (3) 136–142 https://doi.org/10.1016/j.siny.2008.11.006.

Di Martino, A, Fair, DA, Kelly, C, Satterthwaite, TD, Castellanos, FX, Thomason, ME, et al. (2014) Unraveling the miswired connectome: a developmental perspective. *Neuron* **83** 1335–1353.

Emerson E, Bromley, J (1995) The form and function of challenging behaviours. *Journal of Intellectual Disability Research* **39** 388–98.

Felce, D, Kerr, M, Hastings, RP (2009) A general practice-based study of the relationship between indicators of mental illness and challenging behaviour among adults with intellectual disabilities. *J Intellect Disabil Res* **53** (3) 243–54.

Fitzgerald, JM, DiGangi, JA, Phan, KL (2018) Functional neuroanatomy of emotion and its regulation in PTSD. *Harv Rev Psychiatry* **26** (3) 116–128.

Fonville, L, Drakesmith, M, Zammit, S, Lewis, G, Jones, DK, David, AS (2019) MRI indices of cortical development in young people with psychotic experiences: Influence of genetic risk and persistence of symptoms. *Schizophr Bull* **45** (1) 169–179.

Giltaij, HP, Sterkenburg, PS, Schuengel, C (2015) Psychiatric diagnostic screening of social maladaptive behaviour in children with mild intellectual disability: Differentiating disordered attachment and pervasive developmental disorder behaviour. *J Intellect Disabil Res* **59** (2) 138–49.

Happé, F, Frith, U (2014) Annual research review: Towards a developmental neuroscience of atypical social cognition. *J Child Psychol Psychiatry* **55** (6) 553–557.

Hofer, SM, Gray, KM, Piccinin, AM, Mackinnon, A, Bontempo, DE, Einfeld, SL, et al. (2009) Correlated and coupled within-person change in emotional and behavior disturbance in individuals with intellectual disability. *Am J Intellect Dev Disabil* **114** (5) 307–321.

Keysor, CS, Mazzocco, MM (2002) A developmental approach to understanding Fragile X syndrome in females. *Microsc Res Tech* **57** (3) 179–86.

Koehne, S, Behrends, A, Fairhurst, MT, Dziobek, I (2016) Fostering social cognition through an imitation- and synchronization-based dance/movement intervention in adults with autism spectrum disorder: A controlled proof-of-concept study. *Psychother Psychosom* **85** (1) 27–35.

Koslowski, N, Klein, K, Arnold, K, Kösters, M, Schützwohl, M, Salize, HJ, Puschner, B (2016) Effectiveness of interventions for adults with mild to moderate intellectual disabilities and mental health problems: Systematic review and meta-analysis. *Br J Psychiatry* **209** (6) 469–474.

Larkin, P, Jahoda, A, MacMahon, K (2013) The Social Information Processing model as a framework for explaining frequent aggression in adults with mild to moderate intellectual disabilities: A systematic review of the evidence. *J Appl Res Intellect Disabil* **26** (5) 447–65.

Lewis, G, Ioannidis, K, van Harmelen, AL, Neufeld, S, Stochl, J, Lewis, G, Jones, PB & Goodyer, I (2018) The association between pubertal status and depressive symptoms and diagnoses in adolescent females: A population-based cohort study. *PloS one* **13** (6) e0198804 https://doi.org/10.1371/journal.pone.0198804.

Mastrominico, A, Fuchs, T, Manders, E, Steffinger, L, Hirjak, D, Sieber, M, et al. (2018) Effects of dance movement therapy on adult patients with autism spectrum disorder: A randomized controlled trial. *Behav Sci (Basel)* **8** (7) ppi 61.

Matson, JL, Shoemaker, ME (2011) Psychopathology and intellectual disability. *Curr Opin Psychiatry* **24** (5) 367–71.

Melville, CA, Johnson, PC, Smiley, E, Simpson, N, Purves, D, McConnachie, A, Cooper, SA (2016) Problem behaviours and symptom dimensions of psychiatric disorders in adults with intellectual disabilities: An exploratory and confirmatory factor analysis. *Res Dev Disabil* **55** 1–13.

Mohamed, AR, Mkabile, S (2015) An attachment-focused parent-child intervention for biting behaviour in a child with intellectual disability: A clinical case study. *J Intellect Disabil* **19** (3) 251–65.

Mollon, J, David, AS, Zammit, S, Lewis, G, Reichenberg, A (2018) Course of cognitive development from infancy to early adulthood in the psychosis spectrum. *JAMA Psychiatry* **75** (3) 270–279.

Nicoll, M, Beail, N, Saxon, D (2013) Cognitive behavioural treatment for anger in adults with intellectual disabilities: A systematic review and meta-analysis. *J Appl Res Intellect Disabil* **26** (1) 47–62.

Otsuka, S, Uono, S, Yoshimura, S, Zhao, S, Toichi, M (2017) Emotion Perception Mediates the Predictive Relationship Between Verbal Ability and Functional Outcome in High-Functioning Adults with Autism Spectrum Disorder. *J Autism Dev Disord* **47** 1166–1182.

Pessoa, L (2010) Emergent processes in cognitive-emotional Interactions. *Dialogues Clin Neurosci* **12** (4) 433–448.

Plana, I, Lavoie, MA, Battaglia, M, Achim, AM (2014) A meta-analysis and scoping review of social cognition performance in social phobia, posttraumatic stress disorder and other anxiety disorders. *J Anxiety Disord* **28** (2) 169–77.

Polanczyk, G, Moffitt, TE, Arseneault, L, Cannon, M, Ambler, A, Keefe, RS, et al. (2010) Etiological and clinical features of childhood psychotic symptoms: Results from a birth cohort. *Arch Gen Psychiatry* **67** (4) 328–38.

Procaccini, C, Pucino, V, De Rosa, V, Marone, G and Matarese, G (2014) Neuro-endocrine networks controlling immune system in health and disease. *Front Immunol* **5** 143.

Rojahn, J, Matson, JL, Naglieri, JA, Mayville, E (2004) Relationships between psychiatric conditions and behavior problems among adults with mental retardation. *Am J Ment Retard* **109** (1) 21–33.

Samson, AC, Phillips, JM, Parker, KJ, Shah, S, Gross, JJ, Hardan, AY (2014) Emotion dysregulation and the core features of autism spectrum disorder. *J Autism Dev Disord* **44** (7) 1766–1772.

Sappok, T, Budczies, J, Bölte, S, Dziobek, I, Dosen, A, Diefenbacher, A (2013) Emotional development in adults with autism and intellectual disabilities: A retrospective, clinical analysis. *PLoS One* **8** (9) e74036.

Sappok, T, Budczies, J, Dziobek, I, Bölte, S, Došen, A, Diefenbacher, A (2014) The missing link: Delayed emotional development predicts challenging behavior in adults with intellectual disability. *J Autism Dev Disord* **44** 786–800.

Sterkenburg, P, Schuengel, C, Janssen, C (2008) Developing a therapeutic relationship with a blind client with a severe intellectual disability and persistent challenging behaviour. *Disabil Rehabil* **30** (17) 1318–27.

Taylor, JL, Novaco, RW, Brown, T (2016) Reductions in aggression and violence following cognitive behavioural anger treatment for detained patients with intellectual disabilities. *J Intellect Disabil Res* **60** (2) 126–33.

Teague, SJ, Newman, LK, Tonge, BJ, Gray, KM, MHYPEDD Team (2020) Attachment and child behaviour and emotional problems in autism spectrum disorder with intellectual disability. *J Appl Res Intellect Disabil* **33** (3) 475–487.

Vereenooghe, L, Flynn, S, Hastings, RP, Adams, D, Chauhan, U, Cooper, SA, et al. (2018) Interventions for mental health problems in children and adults with severe intellectual disabilities: A systematic review. *BMJ Open* **8** (6) e021911.

Vereenooghe, L, Langdon, PE (2013) Psychological therapies for people with intellectual disabilities: A systematic review and meta-analysis. *Res Dev Disabil* **34** (11) 4085–102.

Visted, E, Vøllestad, J, Nielsen, MB, Schanche, E (2018) Emotion regulation in current and remitted depression: A systematic review and meta-analysis. *Front Psychol* **9** 756.

World Health Organization (2018) International Classification of Diseases for Mortality and Morbidity statistics (11th revision) WHO 2018 (l.a. 19/2/2021).

Zammit, S, Kounali, D, Cannon, M, David, AS, Gunnell, D, Heron, J, et al. (2013) Psychotic experiences and psychotic disorders at age 18 in relation to psychotic experiences at age 12 in a longitudinal population-based cohort study. *Am J Psychiatry* **170** 742–750.

Chapter 10
The systemic and family approach in relation to emotional development and intellectual disability

Rita Erlewein

Summary
The view of socio-emotional development that was made possible by the SED-S, lances new connections between behaviour and emotional needs from people with ID. These systems of connections, in which each individual is involved, paves the way to make a primarily challenging behaviour more understandable and also provides concrete indications of pedagogical approaches. In relation to these more external systems, the intra-individual system reflects a state of maturation of the brain to its degree of functioning. If the care system is able to engage in suitable pedagogical approaches, all together can become a learning system and an enriched cooperation can develop in the sense of reciprocal interactivity. This chapter emphasizes this approach.

1 Introduction
What does a systemic and family-oriented approach mean when we look at emotional development in people with an intellectual disability? The systemic perspective refers to the interaction between the I (a self) and a you. This 'system' brings three aspects into the process, 'I', 'you' and the 'interaction', as determining factors. Understanding the I and you only as senders of information or messages corresponds to a more antiquated linear model of information exchange. Regarding the interaction as a factor in itself brings us closer towards a constructivist model. What I mean by this is that it is possible that some

independent 'third' or new factor can arise. This new factor is, to put it in the language of wave physics, amplification and reduction, depending on which moment during the wave people meet each other (figure 10.1).

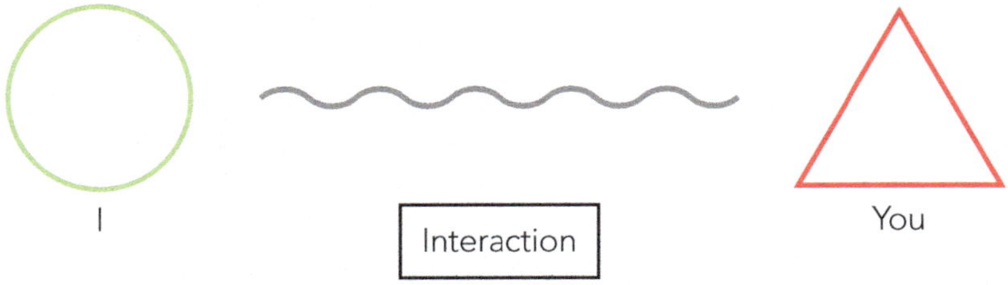

Figure 10.1 The interaction between I and you

Systemic aspects can be understood as either a) the social interaction skills the participants bring into the system or b) the process-related interaction design, which depends on the preconditions that system partners bring to bear. Both aspects are addressed in this chapter.

2 Interaction in systems

Family aspects in this context mainly refer to families who have children or adolescents with intellectual disabilities. From these perspectives, knowledge of the socio-emotional developmental stage should be viewed as providing support for more understanding and enriched relationships between parents and children. This is especially the case where the developmental period is one in which the child is shaped by attachment and bonding that significantly influences further development (including the brain, the nervous system and physiological processes generally) (Kain & Terell, 2020).

There is no doubt that family aspects play a role in adults with intellectual disabilities throughout their lives, so an understanding of the emotional developmental stage can lead to an improvement in relationships, even if the person no longer lives in the parents' household. The importance of the family care environment then often becomes the responsibility of the institutions or care teams that are necessary to meet the basic needs of adults with intellectual disabilities. Family and systemic relationships are shaped by, among other things, the nature and extent of the intellectual developmental disorder, how the disability came about, the course of the disability and the prognosis of the disability (Retzlaff, 2010).

We are all parts of different systems into which we are integrated: those we were born into, those we are assigned to by social conditions or traditions and those we have chosen voluntarily. Every human being is integrated into different systems from an early age. These systems change over the course of one's life. The transitions from one system to the next (kindergarten, school, education, etc.) present special challenges. Bronfenbrenner describes this, in his ecosystem approach, as the 'dynamic adaptation of interaction' (Bronfenbrenner, 1983). Any system in which children, adolescents and adults are involved results in further system affiliations and requirements.

Children, adolescents and adults with intellectual development deficits are embedded in various relationships and specific care systems that are important for both satisfying basic needs (e.g. protection and security) and helping them to explore the world for themselves (Hoffman *et al.*, 2016).

Children and young people with intellectual disabilities have the same basic emotional needs as those without intellectual disabilities (Porges, 2018). However, because of the diverse physical, socio-emotional and intellectual challenges people with intellectual disabilities face, they require additional measures and have additional needs, for example 1) special conditions for communication (more time, more awareness), 2) more expertise (about special needs and particular conditions) from caregivers and 3) more self-awareness on the part of caregivers. These additional needs broadly characterise the axis of interaction between them and their system partners (Retzlaff, 2010).

In a nutshell, these interactions include aspects that relate to a) bonding, b) communication and the possibility of sharing and being understood, c) a variety of environmental conditions, such as the coping behaviour of caregivers, living and housing conditions and resources available to caregiving systems and d) the individual developmental range (Ainsworth, Bell & Stayton, 1974; Retzlaff, 2010). Delayed emotional development combined with a below-average intellectual development in children/adolescents always affects their being together with others and their attachment. Whether this proceeds in a positive or negative direction depends on the resources of the relationship partners (Sappok, 2019).

Any of the attachment styles and attachment qualities described by Ainsworth may be exhibited, depending on the different capabilities of the child and parents or primary care systems (Ainsworth *et al.*, 1978). They often persist throughout adolescence and adulthood unless specific therapeutic or educational interventions can be offered to change the interaction style.

During the survey of levels of socio-emotional development, indications of insecure or disorganised attachment should prompt an additional assessment (Giltaij, Sterkenburg & Schuengel, 2016).

3 Basic needs

People with disabilities' need to be understood in order to have their essential emotional needs met corresponds to an evolutionarily basic human need. This basic need also provides the basis for the feeling of belonging and unconscious as well as conscious feelings of security (Porges, 2018). The basic needs can be disturbed by stress and elements of role attribution.

A disability in children or adolescents can trigger or maintain particular stress in the parents: parental or family stress, overload (pressure on the system), restriction of quality of life and a negative spiral in interaction caused by misinterpretation (defensiveness, fighting or feeling provoked) (Kain, Terell & Marvin, 2016; Retslaff, 2010).

From the point of view of the children and adolescents concerned, role attribution can be the result of an unconscious factor, like the unconscious feeling of a polluter who causes to much pollution. As such it can lead to a basic feeling of being misunderstood (Kain *et al.*, 2016).

Stress and role attribution can create significant problems. Between the poles of systems breaking apart through overload and systems being strengthened through the resilience acquired in the process of problem solving, all things are possible.

Another essential and system-related task of professional care is to make clear where the care system and its resources are located (Sappok, 2019).

4 Assessment of systemic elements

The way in which a diagnostic process, like that using the Scale of Emotional Development – Short (SED-S), takes place, namely as a semi-structured interview, offers the chance to obtain both individual information about the child/adolescent or adult and information about the system, which is part of the interaction and provides a basic attitude. It thus provides information about how the person is anchored in their specific systems. The process during the interview is to be seen as a circular process in which both the types of questions and the outcome can trigger new questions or suggestions. This can ultimately lead to an expanded assessment and deepened understanding of the person concerned.

Assessing emotional and social levels of development rather than only physical factors such as size, shape, etc. or cognitive function levels (e.g. intelligence quotient testing) opens up new possibilities for understanding behaviour, behavioural variations and underlying emotional needs (Huber, 2018). We should bear in mind the motto: 'All behaviour is a form of communication and all communication contains a message that needs to be understood.'

Reaching an understanding of a seemingly incomprehensible message requires motivation, professional information and, in particular, the assistance of specially trained experts (Sappok & Zepperitz, 2019).

5 Consequences of the assessment

Children/adolescents and adults whose emotional developmental stage is delayed have the typical emotional needs of their developmental stage. Because these needs are often not recognised before the emotional developmental age is assessed, the emotional distress often remains hidden. This is frequently a reason why the same maladaptive behaviour patterns are exhibited again and again in crisis situations (Sappok *et al.*, 2019).

The assessment of emotional development can be a decoding aid that provides the appropriate means for a counterpart to help bring the affected person back to a sense of security and a feeling of being understood. This will help the person avoid defensive strategies and instead adopt open interaction patterns (Giltaij, Sterkenburg & Schuengel, 2016). It thus creates the possibility of a change, which can manifest itself both in a relaxation or reduction of overwhelming states and in the expansion of possibilities.

Reaching fundamental milestones of emotional development, such as adaptation, attachment, object and person permanence and the complex ability of mentalising (Sappok *et al.*, 2019; Sappok, 2019), enables biologically and chronologically expanding abilities to shape social life in an open, nurturing and creative way. Normal emotional development is based both on typical brain development (Staudt *et al.*, 2000) and on a safe, enriched, development-enhancing environment (Bentzen & Hart, 2016).

In order to do justice to the ability of the environment to enhance the development of affected children, it is of fundamental importance for parents, educators, therapists, etc. to calibrate the perspective of the person with an intellectual disability to where they are in their emotional stage of development. In this way, overstraining and insecurity can be avoided. To make this possible, there is a need for assessment aids and appropriate tools, such as those offered by the pedagogical approaches described by Sappok and Zepperitz (2019).

6 Systemic support

There are several aspects essential to the interaction wave that are to be taken into account in systemic support. The first of these is the developmental concept of learning steps. We know that these are an intrinsic and complex combination of nature and nurture.

Insisting on learning steps that are predetermined from the outside and do not start where the children and adolescents can take the next step for themselves often leads to stress and subsequently to defensive behaviour, to devaluation and often to the isolation of the child/adolescent, an escalation spiral that can develop into severe behavioural problems and psychiatric symptoms (Sappok *et al.*, 2019).

This brings us to another systemic aspect, namely the responsibility of the professionals who carry out the socio-emotional assessment to pass on and explain the resulting insights to all other essential care systems, and in any case to the parents of the children and adolescents with intellectual disabilities.
It can be irritating for parents and care teams when the gap between cognitive and emotional development is wide. People with cognitive impairment and maladaptive behaviour often have an even lower level of development in the emotional sphere than in the cognitive sphere. It requires a good instinct on the part of the person conveying the benefits of such a view of emotional development if they are to do so in such a way that the benefit for the child or adolescent becomes recognisable.

Within the systemic perspective, special attention should be paid to the SED-S domains 'differentiating emotions', 'regulating affect' and 'communication'. Perceiving these aspects in relation not only to the child but also to the whole systemic field can be very enriching and can help to support concrete next steps in development.

If a system is aware of its possibilities and abilities in the areas of emotion differentiation, affect regulation and communication, in the sense of perception and regulation possibilities, then the child/adolescent concerned can be embedded in a nourishing environment, and aspects of interaction that promote resilience can be strengthened.

A challenge that can arise systemically in the stage-based view of development is that it can generate a certain expectation regarding the dynamics of development: that, if enough has been done at the assessed emotional developmental stage, the next stage will automatically be reached. This is based on a misunderstanding: the pace of individual emotional development is also essentially determined by various intrinsic aspects of people with intellectual disabilities and is related to the causal background of the developmental delay (e.g. illness, disability, attachment disorder, trauma, etc.). Better opportunities for care by enrichment of the interaction levels with the 'socio-emotional developmental view' arise after an initial reorientation phase which implies a significant relief for both sides in the interaction (Sappok *et al.*, 2019).

7 Experiences

In my own history with socio-emotional developmental assessment, which spans the last six to eight years, I have witnessed a significant expansion of the perspective and have seen the possibilities this has opened up in my concrete work with disabled children and adolescents (degree of severity ranging from mild to multiple disabilities).

Previously, the only possibility in my psychiatric field of work was to 'translate' challenging behaviour into child psychiatric diagnoses. This approach ignored developmental aspects, especially a lag of emotional development as a cause.

These diagnoses often did not cover the specific aspects of intellectual developmental delay very well, and thus did not always prove to be appropriate. Further, unfortunately they often led to the prescription of psychopharmacological medication that, although it could dampen the physiological arousal level of the affected person, did not meet their actual needs.

Since our team has regularly conducted assessments using the SED-S, and trained teams of special schools in the SED-S, many more problems in the behaviour of children and adolescents with disabilities have been solved with educational means without the need for additional medication.

8 Stage assignment

With the group of children diagnosed, using the Scale of Emotional Development – Revised, as being at emotional developmental stage one, it often proved to be particularly helpful to point out the *lack of adaptation* of basic needs, such as the fact that providing food can help to de-escalate by satisfying the person's hunger. Insistence on fixed mealtimes can be a trigger for crises. In this stage of development, the regulation of states of tension is only possible with the help of another (well-regulated) person. And rules cannot be understood verbally or with the help of a caregiver (even if repeated a hundred times). Interactive conflicts need the guidance of a regulating caregiver. This knowledge is often an eye-opener for many parents and teams.

Children and adolescents at SED developmental stage two still need the external regulation of a caregiver for stress and interactive conflicts. They primarily use the feeling of security to orient themselves. In concrete terms, we teach the parents and caregivers of children in this stage of development how important it is not to interrupt physical and emotional contact with the children during a crisis situation.

There is often a mistaken belief that in a crisis these people should be 'isolated' so that they can calm down. This triggers the opposite and often leads to a resigned withdrawal and numbness, which in turn is misinterpreted as reassurance.

People in SED developmental stage three are often described by the support teams as the most difficult to care for. It seems one can 'do nothing right' for these people. At this stage, children and adolescents are often perceived as provocative, as if they want to deliberately annoy the other person to get attention. This is a significant misunderstanding that puts a strain on the axis of interaction, to the detriment of the person concerned. We like to pay special attention to this aspect in our education about socio-emotional knowledge and explain to parents and care teams the developmental need for autonomy.

In some domains, children and adolescents are still in the previous stage, where safety is the issue, and in others they are already striving for autonomy. This can mean that on the one hand the protective and regulating proximity of a caregiver is still being sought, while on the other hand this caregiver is already felt to be restrictive. This requires a special and generous understanding of these two aspects on the part of the caregivers in order to maintain the relationship in the face of this partly contradictory behaviour. We emphasise again and again that, when these autonomy efforts can be observed, it is important to promote autonomy as a motor for further development.

The parents of disabled children and adolescents, who sometimes take it for granted that their children need special protection for a long time, are occasionally surprised by newly emerging autonomy efforts and sometimes misinterpret them as maladaptive behaviour.

The SED developmental stages four, five and six are not the causes of maladaptive behaviour to the same extent as the first three, which is why I have not given examples relating to them.

9 Conclusion

The actual emotional needs of a person with intellectual disabilities in everyday life, and especially in a crisis, can be met by development-adapted pedagogical behaviour. By paying more attention to the systemic wave and the determining aspects of I and you, we can establish a better understanding and support. This leads to a fundamental and lasting relaxation of the situation both for the individual and for the systems in which the person lives and works.

References

Ainsworth, M, Bell, SM & Stayton, DJ (1974) Infant-mother attachment and social development: 'Socialisation' as a product of reciprocal responsiveness to signals. In: M Richards (Ed) *The Integration of a Child into a Social World* (pp9–135). London: Cambridge University Press.

Ainsworth, M, Blehar, MC, Water, E & Wall, S (1978) *Patterns of Attachment: A psychological study of the strange situation*. Hills-Dale: Lawrence Earlbaum Associates.

Bentzen,M & Hart, S (2016) *Neuroaffektive Therapie mit Kindern und Jugendlichen*. Lichtenau: GPProbst Verlag.

Bronfenbrenner, U & Crouter, A (1983) The evolution of environmental models in developmental research. In: P-H Mussen (Ed) *Handbook of Child Psychology, Volume I: History, Theory and Methods* (pp357–414). New York: John Wiley & Sons.

Giltaij, H, Sterkenburg, PS & Schuengel, C (2016) *Diagnosis of disordered attachment behaviour* IASSIDD: 15th World Congress, Melbourne, Australia.

Hentrich J & Huber, M (2018) *Emotionale Entwicklung und Verhaltensauffälligkeiten bei Kindern und Jugendlichen mit geistiger Behinderung, Masterarbeit*. Zürcher Hochschule für angewandte Wissenschaften, Angewandte Psychologie Zürich.

Hoffmann, Cooper, Powell and Marvin (2016) *Circle of security* [online]. Available at: www.circleofsecurity.net (accessed March 2021).

Kain, KL & Terell, SJ (2020) *Bindung, Regulation und Resilienz*. Paderborn: Jungfermann Verlag.

Porges, SW (2018) *Die Polyvagaltheorie und die Suche nach Sicherheit*. Lichtenau: GPProbst Verlag.

Retzlaff, R. (2010). *Familien-Stärken. Behinderung, Resilienz und systemische Therapie*. Stuttgart: Klett-Cotta.

Sappok,T (2019) *Psychische Gesundheit und intellektuelle Entwicklungsstörung*. Stuttgart: W Kohlhammer GmbH.

Sappok, T & Zepperitz,S (2019) *Das Alter der Gefühle*. Hogrefe Verlag: Bern.

Staudt, M, Krägeloh-Mann, I & Grodd, W (2000) Die normale Myelinisierung des kindlichen Gehirns in der MRT *RöFö* **172** (10) 802–811.

Part III Diagnostics and support

Chapter 11
Emotional development and assessment in persons with an intellectual disability

Stijn Vandevelde and Angelique Peters

Summary

This chapter describes an integrative approach to the assessment of persons with intellectual disabilities. It expands the 'classic' biopsychosocial approach with a developmental dimension, focusing on emotional development, based on the work of Anton Došen. (Challenging) behaviour is described as the result of the interaction between a person and the environment. Assessment takes these different aspects into consideration, which leads to a comprehensive description of what causes challenging behaviour and how this behaviour is maintained. This description can be used in order to develop an integrative support and treatment plan, including biological, psychological, social and developmental dimensions. This creates space for an approach that goes beyond treating symptoms situated in the person.
A case example illustrates the different steps in the integrative assessment of (challenging) behaviour.

1 Introduction

1.1 Screening in persons with an intellectual disability

Several authors refer to the importance of emotional development in the assessment (and support/treatment) of mental health problems (used here as an umbrella term for behaviour problems and psychiatric disorders; Morisse, Vandevelde & Došen, 2014) in persons with an intellectual disability. Emotional development is considered as an essential aspect complementing the 'classic' biopsychosocial assessment (Došen, 2014; Wieland *et al.*, 2014). Emotional development is not static, but dynamic: a healthy emotional development is possible under the right circumstances, and in regular conditions it coincides with cognitive development. Under less favourable conditions, we often see that emotional development falls behind other developmental areas. Emotional development is an indicator of one's strength/resilience. If one's load is too heavy for one's capacities (is 'over-demanding'), emotional development stagnates, and in severe cases we may see a drop in the developmental level. Anton Došen's theory of emotional development (Došen, 2005a, 2005b, 2014) offers an integrative framework that focuses not on mental health problems as characteristics of a person but instead on the interaction between the biological, medical, psychological and developmental characteristics of the person and the environment (Došen *et al.*, 2008). This links well with the social-ecological model that underpins the concept of intellectual disability developed by the American Association on Intellectual and Developmental Disabilities (AAIDD) (Schalock *et al.*, 2010). This model refers to the attunement of strengths and disabilities on five dimensions, the expectations of the environment and support (Van Hove, Van Loon & Vandevelde, 2010).

In this model, an analysis of strengths and possible weaknesses is carried out along five dimensions: intellectual functioning; adaptive behaviour; participation; interaction; and social roles, health and context. This analysis is supported by the use of standardised instruments. Intellectual functioning is – preferably – assessed by means of an intelligence test (although the AAIDD is also critical of narrowing intelligence down to an intelligence quotient (IQ) figure). Furthermore, a broad assessment of functioning in the other dimensions is performed. This is often based on observations in different environments, contexts and situations. This comprehensive assessment leads to the identification of support strategies to decrease the 'mismatch' between personal competencies and environmental expectations (Schalock *et al.*, 2010; Thompson *et al.*, 2009). In this way, a distinction could be made between classifying assessment, which focuses on applying a label based on specific criteria (Schalock *et al.*, 2010; Van Hove *et al.*, 2010), and action-oriented assessment. The latter pays attention to assessing both strengths and weaknesses on different dimensions (see the dimensions of the AAIDD and those of Došen (2007)). This is always embedded in the relationship between the support worker and the client.

The difference between classification (diagnosis) and assessment is linked to the distinction, made by De Bruyn and colleagues (De Bruyn *et al.*, 2005), between 'identifying', 'explanatory' and 'advisory' assessments. (In some cases, they also refer to 'clarifying' assessment that aims at investigating whether a support worker has correctly understood the support needs of the client.)

Identifying assessment is focused on describing behaviour. It is linked to internationally used classification systems such as the Diagnostic and Statistical Manual of Mental Disorders (fifth edition) (DSM-5) or the International Classification of Diseases (10th revision) (ICD-10). These systems are valuable because of their capacity to define and classify disorders; yet these systems do not explain how disorders are caused or maintained.

Explanatory (or functional) assessment is focused on the causes of behaviour: how does it originate and how is it maintained? This kind of assessment makes use of theoretical models that map underlying (biological, psychological or social) processes.

Advisory assessment leads to suggestions for interventions. It is linked with the concept of action-oriented assessment, as developed by Pameijer and Van Laar-Bijman (2007, p. 12):

> *The model of action-oriented assessment delivers guidelines for support workers and is aimed at fostering demand-driven, effective and result-oriented working. It focuses on the support needs of a client (what does this client need?) and what this means for the support provided by the client system and the support workers (which approach is desirable?).*

Pameijer and colleagues (2007) refer to a number of important aspects when carrying out action-oriented assessment in persons with an intellectual disability. The assessment should (1) be systematic and transparent, (2) be goal oriented, (3) be based on a transactional framework, (4) rely on co-operation between client and context and (5) take into account the strengths of the client.

1.2 Assessment of mental health problems in persons with intellectual disabilities

Several of these elements from action-oriented assessment are also found in the guidelines for the assessment and support of persons with intellectual disabilities and mental health problems that were developed by Došen and colleagues (2008, p. 51) (see box 11.1). In the text below, we will primarily focus on step one and step two, as these are focused specifically on assessment. We will also briefly go into step three, integrative treatment. The case example in section 2 illustrates these steps.

Guidelines for the assessment, diagnosis and treatment of persons with an intellectual disability and mental health problems (from Došen *et al.*, 2008, p. 51)

Step 1: Assessment: identification of explanatory factors, central processing characteristics and maintaining conditions in the originating triangle

a. in the interaction between person and environment

b. in the person

c. in the environment

Step 2: Integrative/multimodal case formulation/diagnosis

a. biopsychosocial and developmental factors that are involved in challenging behaviour

b. origination mechanism

c. diagnostical formulation of challenging behaviour

Step 3: Treatment

a. a holistic approach to the recovery of the person's mental well-being

b. integrative treatment of conditions that lead to challenging behaviour

1.2.1 Step one: assessment of factors in relation to the challenging behaviour, the person and the environment

Step one of the guidelines (see box 11.1) focuses on aspects that are related to the challenging behaviour, the person and the environment. Došen and colleagues (2008) provide an overview of important themes and activities that relate to each of these levels. Challenging behaviour, that is, behaviour that disrupts the interaction between person and environment, is assessed by means of conversations with the different stakeholders (the client, support staff and parents), observations and standardised instruments and procedures. In relation to the person, different dimensions are taken into account: biological characteristics (e.g. genetic disorders), psychosocial aspects (including cognitive, social and emotional development), physical and mental health and functional/adaptive skills (Došen *et al.*, 2008). In relation to the environment, there is a focus on school, work, home, daily activities and pedagogical, social and cultural factors, among other things. It is essential, as the guidelines of the AAIDD also make clear, that strengths as well as weaknesses are assessed. In the past, the assessment of the (challenging) behaviour of persons with intellectual disabilities was often limited to cognitive abilities (often only focused on IQ scores). Nowadays, with the influence of the AAIDD and Došen's developmental approach, there is more attention paid to integrative assessment. Assessing emotional and social development (alongside cognitive development) provides a more holistic view of a person's total personality development. This leads to more and better knowledge of the basic needs of clients and their importance in relation to further development (see chapter 3 of this manual). For the assessment of cognitive development, several standardised, valid and reliable instruments are available (e.g. the Wechsler Adult Intelligence Scale). In relation to the assessment of emotional development, a limited number of instruments are available, including the Infant-Toddler Social and Emotional Assessment (ITSEA), developed by Carter and Briggs-Gowan (2000); the Functional Emotional Assessment Scale (FEAS), developed by Greenspan, DeGangi and Wieder (2001); the Frankish Tool, based on the theory of Mahler (Frankish, 2013); the Levels of Emotional Awareness Scale (LEAS) (Lane *et al.*, 1990); the *Experimentele Schaal voor de beoordeling van het Sociaal Emotionele Ontwikkelingsniveau* (ESSEON-R), developed by Hoekman and colleagues (2014); and the *Schaal voor Emotionele Ontwikkeling bij mensen met een verstandelijke beperking* – revised^2 (SEO-R^2) (also available in other languages, including German, Italian and English: the Scale of Emotional Development – Revised^2 (SED-R^2)) (Morisse & Došen, 2016) and its short version, the Scale of Emotional Development – Short (Sappok *et al.*, 2016; Vandevelde *et al.*, 2016).

The ITSEA, FEAS and ESSEON-R are focused on children and adolescents, and the LEAS on adults, but none of these instruments are specifically developed for persons with intellectual disabilities (Sappok *et al.*, 2016). The SED-R^2 scale was developed for persons with an intellectual disability, and it is suitable for both children and adults. The purpose, design and use of the SED-R^2 is extensively described in chapter 13, so this instrument is not described in this chapter.

In relation to the assessment of functioning and of psychiatric disorders, several methods and systems have been developed. Instruments such as the Vineland Adaptive Behavior Scales (VABS) (Sparrow *et al.*, 2008) or the Diagnostic Adaptive Behavior Scale (DABS), developed by the AAIDD in 2015, can be used for the assessment of adaptive behaviour. The National Association for the Dually Diagnosed developed an adapted version of the DSM-4, the Diagnostic Manual – Intellectual Disability (DM-ID) (Fletcher *et al.*, 2007), and DSM-5, the Diagnostic Manual – Intellectual Disability 2 (DM-ID2) (Fletcher *et al.*, 2017) for the assessment of psychiatric disorders.

The assessment of the environment is another essential aspect of assessment and focuses on investigating the influence of living and work situations and the roles of persons in society (Došen *et al.*, 2008; Van Hove *et al.*, 2010).

1.2.2 Step two: integrative diagnosis

In this step, we follow the approach of Došen, who makes a plea in several publications for people to recognise the importance of integrative assessment (see e.g. Došen, 2005b, 2007; Došen *et al.*, 2008) instead of only using adapted classification systems, such as the DM-ID2 (Fletcher *et al.*, 2017). Exclusively relying on DM-ID and other classification systems carries the risk that challenging behaviour or mental health problems will be attributed to psychiatric diagnoses. An integrative assessment, on the other hand, looks for the underlying factors of challenging behaviour. If these different factors have been assessed, they can be integrated into a description of how challenging behaviour originated and how it is maintained (Došen *et al.*, 2008). This leads to a diagnostical formulation that, in its turn, leads to an integrated treatment plan.

1.2.3 Step three: integrative treatment

Došen (2007) refers to four dimensions of integrative treatment: (1) the developmental dimension, (2) the social dimension, (3) the psychological dimension and (4) the biological dimension. In relation to the developmental dimension, it is important to take into account a person's emotional development alongside their cognitive development. The social dimension refers to activities focused on adapting the environment in order to address a client's basic emotional needs (Došen *et al.*, 2008). The psychological dimension can refer to psychotherapy or skill training, while the biological dimension can include pharmaceutical and other treatments. Because this chapter is focused on assessment, treatment is not discussed further, even though assessment and treatment should not be seen as different parts.

Case: Hakan

'Dear colleague, can we please consult about Hakan? He asks so many questions we conclude that he might understand less than we expected based upon his file. Maybe you can consult a speech therapist if we need to help him to understand us in some way?'

By sending this message, Hakan's mentor asks for help. Hakan is a twenty-eight-year-old Dutch-Turkish man. From a young age, he has been living in healthcare institutions. After attending schools for children with special needs, he now works in a sheltered workplace. In his group, housed next to his institution, he shares an apartment with Arie, a boy with mild intellectual disabilities and autism. Besides them, the group consists of nine other persons. All of them receive individual support. Hakan participates very little in society; he pursues activities that are specifically organised for people with disabilities. Support staff in both his living environment and work environment report him asking more questions than usual on a daily basis and are asking themselves whether he is understanding all the verbal communication addressed to him.

In his file, we read that Hakan has a mild intellectual disability (total IQ 49, verbal IQ 55 and performance IQ <55 on the Wechsler Intelligence Scale for Children III). His social competencies are comparable with a normal developmental age of six to eight years. The file does not mention his emotional development. In the file are descriptions of him feeling unsafe. This is explained by the divorce of his parents and the cultural ➔

and environmental differences between his Turkish and his Dutch families. In the past, Hakan suffered from epilepsy, for which he was treated. He sometimes resists authority. Hakan wants to succeed in what he does and has a fear of failure. He is uncertain of his own skills and wants to dominate and have control over situations. Part of his poor social functioning can be explained by his hemiparesis: the left side of his body is weak and he is deaf in his left ear.

After talking to support staff and studying his file, the remedial educationalist consults the speech therapist as to whether there may be more information about his speech comprehension in his file and whether someone has already done some work on this specific subject. The file mentions that Hakan is continuously asking questions and that he wanders from caregiver to caregiver until he gets an answer. To increase his awareness of time, a TimeTimer[12] is used. This does not help him. Hakan seems to be overestimated on several aspects (for example social functioning and communication). On the one hand, he seems to understand much information; on the other hand he does not seem to be able to stop asking questions regarding very simple topics. The speech therapist will observe and test Hakan to produce an analysis of his language and time comprehension. At the same time the behavioural scientist will interview his caregivers in order to understand the function of the questions he asks them.

2.1 Contact/language – speech therapy examination

For Hakan, eye contact is difficult at the beginning of the test. He sometimes actively avoids eye contact, and when he makes eye contact, he quickly looks away. As the test progresses, he increasingly makes eye contact. This eye contact is functional: he uses it to support communication. Hakan speaks in full but short sentences and has a reasonable vocabulary. Word-finding difficulties stand out at various points. Hakan speaks spontaneously and can make himself sufficiently clear verbally. He is generally easy to understand and follow, and it is noticeable that he speaks very softly.

In consultation with the behavioural expert, it was decided that the domain of communication would be included in the speech therapy assessment. In 2012, Hakan's level of supportive communication was assessed with ComFor (Forerunners in Communication),[13] which led to the conclusion that Hakan observes at a representation level. This means that he is also able to understand concrete language or objects outside of context. The conclusion is that Hakan's continuously asking many questions can be interpreted in several ways, and thus it is decided to conduct broad research.

---

12 TimeTimer is a device like a clock or stopwatch. It works like an hourglass; time visually 'disappears' as the clock counts down.

13 ComFor is a diagnostic test, performed by trained speech therapists, that identifies a person's communication level. It provides an indication of communication interventions.

Using the Reynell test for word comprehension, it was shown that Hakan's word comprehension is significantly higher than his sentence comprehension. He often needs a lot of time to process information. Adding more structure during a conversation, if possible, preferably with the support of visualisation, seems to help. This allows Hakan to focus better and remain in the here and now, albeit with the help of the other person. Hakan's ability to take into account the context or the (mis)understanding of his interlocutor in a conversation is poorly developed. He experiences difficulty when putting his thoughts into words. Hakan likes to give the impression that he knows a lot: he sometimes uses words that you do not immediately expect from him. In this way he may overestimate himself, but at the same time there is also the danger of overestimation by people in his environment. It is important to adjust to his emotional level and his experience world.

Hakan sometimes confuses fantasy and reality. Nonverbal language is not always properly interpreted. This makes having a conversation a complex activity for him. To make sure that one is talking about the same thing as Hakan, it is essential to keep asking questions until certain – not to fill in the gaps but to remain curious. This is particularly important when assessing social situations and interpreting emotions. Hakan is vulnerable in communication. It is important to take him seriously; this strengthens his sense of self-worth. With this basis in the conversation, Hakan can be more forthcoming.

2.2 Social self-assurance and emotional development

To gain insight into Hakan's resilience, supervisors fill in the standardised resilience scales (*Sociale Redzaamheidsschaal voor Zwakzinnigen* (SRZ) and SRZ Plus, a Dutch scale for measuring social resilience) for Hakan. He scores in accordance with other people with an intellectual disability and a severe to moderate intellectual disability when it comes to social components. Practical skills are, taking into account his physical disability, appropriate to his level of thinking.

In addition, Hakan's level of emotional development, and consequently the way he adapts to social demands, was examined. To gain insight into the emotional development level, the SED-R^2 interview was conducted with two supervisors who know Hakan well. It is striking that, when filling out the scale, it is particularly difficult for Hakan to answer questions aimed at the relationship with (important) others. Hakan does not seem to attach himself to anyone and seemingly draws his role models from fantasy figures, caricatures or characters from films, TV series and comics.

In domains to do with attuning to his environment (SED-R^2 domains 3, 5, 6, 9, 12, 13), Hakan's development level is not higher than the second phase. Hakan mainly seems to want to be in his own 'cocoon', and his ability and willingness to approach the world is limited. His certainty consists of the stable environment (phase one) and the search for an attachment figure. He pays little or no attention to other clients and displays a fear of unpredictability (especially when it comes to people). Hakan does not really join any group; he quickly feels rejected and infers that he does not belong anywhere. This is what he always heard in his early childhood, and he has integrated it into his self-image.

From an emotional point of view, Hakan's communication is mainly aimed at making and maintaining contact; this is comparable to the very young child (phase two). Functional communication has developed to a limited extent. Hakan cannot distinguish the basic emotions; he exhibits comfort and discomfort but never to an extreme extent. He does not recognise what emotions he himself has, and he cannot read them in others. Hakan exhibits very easy-to-read emotions that are expressed in a quite straightforward way. A capacity to reflect on emotions, the causes of situations and the results of his own actions has not been developed.

2.3 Conclusion

Applied to this case description, the integrative diagnosis (step two in the model of Došen *et al.*, 2008; see also Došen, 2005b) could look like this:

2.3.1 Relevant findings regarding the biopsychosocial and developmental elements that may play a role in problem behaviour

Organic:
Hakan has congenital left hemiparesis. Further reference is made to epilepsy, for which Hakan is receiving medication.

Cognitive factors:
Hakan has a mild to moderate intellectual disability.

Neuropsychological:
No data are available on this subject.

Personality development:
In domains of the SED-R[2] to do with alignment with his environment (3, 5, 6, 9, 12, 13) we see that the development level is not higher than the second phase. Hakan mainly seems to want to be in his own 'cocoon', and is able and willing to approach the world only to a very limited extent.

Personality traits:
Hakan is fearful of failure and often insecure. He would like to control what happens. Hakan does not seem to attach himself to anyone and seemingly draws his role models from fantasy figures, caricatures or characters from films, TV series and comic strips. He does not pay attention, or hardly pays attention, to other clients, and he exhibits a fear of unpredictability (especially when it concerns people).

Basic needs:
Hakan struggles to feel safe. He continuously seeks proximity to his supervisors or other important others.

Communication/language:
Hakan often takes a long time to process information. Hakan's perception is situated at the level of representation.

Interaction patterns:
Hakan's communication is mainly aimed at making and maintaining contact; it is comparable to that of a very young child (phase two) and he has only limited functional communication. Hakan does not really join social situations; he quickly feels rejected and infers that he does not belong.

Environmental factors:
Hakan's parents are divorced and there are cultural and social differences between his Turkish family and his Dutch family. Hakan's Turkish family does not see his impairments: they expect him to lead a normal life. His Dutch mother has very irregular contact: sometimes she demands his full attention, but sometimes she does not make contact for months. Hakan has decided to break off contact with her. A professional mentor has been appointed.

Psychiatric findings:
There is no psychiatric diagnosis.

Developmental psychiatric findings:
Disturbances can be identified with regard to both the development of (psychophysiological) homeostasis and the development of basic safety. The congenital half-sided paralysis with half-sided deafness limits interaction with his environment. The (cultural) differences between his parents caused confusion and ambiguity. In addition, there was aggression between his parents, which left him in a continuously tense environment.

2.3.2 Origination mechanism

Hakan predominantly functions in the first two emotional development stages. He may have functioned at a higher development level in the past (the file refers to toddler behaviour), but at this moment he no longer exhibits this level, with the exception of more function-oriented areas.

Because of his complex childhood (cultural influences, the insufficient parenting capacities of parents, problems accepting his limitations) it is concluded that Hakan is insecurely attached.

2.3.3 Diagnostic formulation of the problem behaviour

Because of the very limited ego development, insecure attachment and the delayed emotional development, Hakan requires almost continuous closeness.

This case study makes it clear that 'problem behaviour' can be related to basic emotional needs that are strongly linked to the need for closeness (phase one) and basic security (phase two). The key words in the first development phase are sensory integration; individual approach; body language; physical care and body contact; rest and relaxation; stimulus regulation; constancy in the environment; and simple structures of space, time (regularity), persons and activities. Key words in the second development phase are physical contact, attachment person, trust, predictability (structure and security), individual approach and proximity, limitation and active intervention, and social stimulation (see chapter 3). These key words collectively indicate why Hakan continuously asks questions: these are an expression of an insufficient perception of safety and a call for proximity and the simplification of the world, as was also outlined by the speech therapist.

By incorporating preventive contact moments in the way his programme is immediately structured, his support needs could be met. As the caregivers started to offer more closeness, the number of questions Hakan asked immediately decreased drastically. This makes clear that Hakan's questioning is not related to his level of understanding but is the result of his level of emotional development and the insufficient satisfaction of his need for proximity. In terms of the above, we could say that in this case mainly explanatory and advisory diagnostics were used (see section 1).

3 Conclusion

It is very important for integrative assessments to pay attention to emotional development alongside other factors, as illustrated in the case of Hakan. This approach starts from a more holistic perspective, in which attention is paid to the interaction between the person and their environment. It thus creates space to go further than simply 'treating' symptoms or problems situated in a person. Context also comes into play, and changes in a person's environment can often help to reduce problem behaviour and, perhaps more importantly, to increase the quality of life of persons with disabilities and improve the contexts in which they live (Vandevelde *et al.*, 2016).

Future challenges in this area will include the further development of diagnostic tools to validly and reliably map emotional development (see e.g. Sappok *et al.*, 2016). In addition, the diagnostic cycle should include the assessment of emotional development in children, adolescents and adults.

Finally, care professionals, parents and other members of the social network should be supported in transferring the collected knowledge about emotional development into daily practice (see for example Morisse *et al.*, 2014).

References

Carter, AS & Briggs-Gowan, MJ (2000) *Infant-Toddler Social and Emotional Assessment (ITSEA) Manual*. New Haven, CT: Yale University.

De Bruyn, E, Ruijssenaars, A, Pameijer, N & Van Aarle, E (2005) *De diagnostische cyclus: een praktijklee.* Leuven, Voorburg: Acco.

Došen, A (2005a) Applying the developmental perspective in the psychiatric assessment and diagnosis of persons with intellectual disability: part I – assessment. *Journal of Intellectual Disability Research* **49** 1–8 doi: 101111/j1365-2788200500656x.

Došen, A (2005b) Applying the developmental perspective in the psychiatric assessment and diagnosis of persons with intellectual disability: part II - diagnosis *Journal of Intellectual Disability Research* **49** 9–15 doi: 101111/j1365-2788200500657x.

Došen, A (2007) Integrative treatment in persons with intellectual disability and mental health problems. *Journal of Intellectual Disability Research* **51** 66–74.

Došen, A (2014) *Psychische stoornissen, probleemgedrag en verstandelijke beperking*. Assen: Van Gorcum.

Došen, A, Gardner, WI, Griffiths, DM, King, R, & Lapointe, A (2008) *Richtlijnen en principes voor de praktijk: Beoordeling, diagnose, behandeling en bijbehorende ondersteuning voor mensen met verstandelijke beperkingen en probleemgedrag*. Utrecht: Vilans/LKNG.

Fletcher, R, Loschen, E, Stavrakaki, C, & First, M (2007) *Diagnostic Manual -Intellectual Disability (DM-ID): A Textbook of Diagnosis of Mental Disorders in Persons with Intellectual Disability*. Kingston, NY NADD Press.

Fletcher, RJ, Barnhill, J & Cooper, SA (2017) *Diagnostic Manual--Intellectual Disability 2 (DM-ID): A textbook of diagnosis of mental disorders in persons with intellectual disability* (2nd edition). New York: National Association for the Dually Diagnosed.

Frankish, P (2013) Measuring the emotional development of adults with ID. *Advances in Mental Health and Intellectual Disabilities* **7** 272–276.

Greenspan, S, DeGangi, G, & Wieder, S (Eds) (2001) *The Functional emotional assessment scale (FEAS) for infancy and early childhood clinical and research applications Interdisciplinary council on developmental and learning disorders* [online]. Available at: http://wwwicdlcom/research/functional-emotional-assessment-scale (accessed February 2016).

Hoekman, J, Miedema, A, Otten, B, & Gielen, JO (2014) *ESSEON-R Schaal voor het sociaal-emotioneel ontwikkelingsniveau* [online]. Available at: http://wwwhogrefenl/producten/producten-single/esseon-r-schaal-voor-sociaal-emotioneel-ontwikkelingsniveauhtml (accessed February 2016).

Lane, RD, Quinlan, DM, Schwartz, GE, Walker, PA, & Zeitlin, SB (1990) The levels of emotional awareness scale: A cognitive-developmental measure of emotion. *Journal of Personality Assessment* **55** (1&2) 124–134.

Morisse, F, & Došen, A (Eds) (2015) *Schaal voor Emotionele Ontwikkeling bij mensen met een verstandelijke beperking – Revised[2]: Een instrument voor assessment.* Antwerpen/Apeldoorn: Garant.

Morisse, F, Vandevelde, S & Došen, A (2014) Mensen met een verstandelijke beperking en geestelijke gezondheidsproblemen: een praktijkdefinitie *Vlaams Tijdschrift voor Orthopedagogiek* **33** (4) 21–33.

Pameijer, N & van Laar-Bijman, E (2007) *Handelingsgerichte diagnostiek Een handreiking voor orthopedagogen en psychologen werkzaam in de zorg voor mensen met een verstandelijke beperking*: LKNG / Vilans / Uitgeverij LEMMA [online]. Available at: http://wwwkennispleingehandicaptensectornl/docs/producten/HandelingsgerichteDiagnostiekpdf (accessed February 2016).

Sappok, T, Barrett, BF, Vandevelde, S, Heinrich, M, Poppe, L, Sterkenburg, P, … Morisse, F (2016) Scale of emotional development – Short. *Research in Developmental Disabilities* **59** 166–175.

Schalock, RL, Borthwick-Duffy, SA, Bradley, VJ, Buntinx, WHE, Coulter, DL, Craig, EM, Yeager, MH (2010) *Intellectual Disability: Definition, classification, and systems of supports*. Washington, DC: American Association on Intellectual and Developmental Disabilities.

Sparrow, S, Balla, D & Cichetti, D (2008) *Vineland Adaptive Behavior Scales* (2nd edition). *Expanded Interview Form Manual* UK: Pearson.

Thompson, JR, Bradley, VJ, Buntinx, WH, Schalock, RL, Shogren, KA, Snell, ME, Yeager, MH (2009) Conceptualizing supports and the support needs of people with intellectual disability. *Intellectual and Developmental Disabilities* **47** (2) 135–146 doi: 101352/1934-9556-472135.

Van Hove, G, van Loon, J, & Vandevelde, S (2010) Personen met een verstandelijke beperking. In: E Broekaert, G Van Hove, S Vandevelde, V Soyez & W Vanderplasschen (Eds) *Handboek bijzondere orthopedagogiek* (pp. 19-63). Antwerpen/Apeldoorn: Garant.

Vandevelde, S, Morisse, F, Došen, A, Poppe, L, Jonckheere, B, Van Hove, G, Claes, C (2016) The scale for emotional development – revised (sed-r) for persons with intellectual disabilities and mental health problems: Development, description, and reliability *International Journal of Developmental Disabilities* **62** (1) 11–23.

Wieland, J, Kapitein, S, Otter, M & Baas, RWJ (2014) Diagnostiek van psychiatrische stoornissen bij mensen met een (zeer) lichte verstandelijke beperking. *Tijdschrift voor Psychiatrie* **56** (7) 463–470.

Chapter 12
The Scale of Emotional Development – Short

Tanja Sappok and Marieke Conty

Summary

The Scale of Emotional Development – Short (SED-S) is an instrument for the assessment of a person's level of emotional functioning. It is based on Anton Došen's dynamic model of emotional development and describes the emotional reference age from birth to twelve years within eight different domains. Every domain is characterised by certain developmental milestones for each developmental level and is described by five items per domain and stage. The SED-S is applied by an expert in developmental psychology who conducts a structured interview with close caregivers about the characteristic behaviours of the person being examined. The scale's validity has been shown to be in high agreement with the biological age of the children (81% exact agreement) and to have a kappa value of .95. The internal consistency and the inter-rater reliability were high (Cronbach's alpha .99, kappa 1.0).

The identification of the developmental reference age of a person will give further insight into their motivations and needs, thus stimulating new ideas and approaches for support and intervention.

1 Introduction

People with an intellectual developmental disability frequently develop mental health problems or display challenging behaviours (Cooper *et al.*, 2007). The severity of the behavioural problems depends on the severity of the intellectual developmental disability (Tsakanikos *et al.*, 2007; McCarthy *et al.*, 2010). People with an intellectual disability basically go through the same stages of emotional development as others; however, the risk of delayed or incomplete development is increased. Because of the high correlation of cognitive and emotional functioning, eg. easuring similar issues, recent studies have shown that, like the degree of cognitive impairment, the level of emotional development is crucial in determining the severity of the problem behaviour (Sappok *et al.*, 2014). At present, functional behavioural analysis is the basic diagnostic tool for gaining an understanding of the external causes of behavioural disorders (Beail, 2003). Considering the emotional state of development may contribute to an understanding of the inner mechanisms that lead to certain challenging behaviours (Begeer *et al.*, 2008; Sappok *et al.*, 2014). Therefore, a proper assessment of the level of emotional functioning is a central element in the diagnostic process for challenging behaviour. The assessment instrument should be scientifically sound in terms of its objectivity, reliability and validity. Therefore, the 'SED scheme' delineated by Anton Došen (2005) has been further developed by an international working group (the Network of Europeans on Emotional Development (NEED)) to meet the requirements of scientific validity and to incorporate new developmental psychological findings and concepts. This led to the creation of the Scale of Emotional Development – Short (SED-S) (Sappok *et al.*, 2016), which will be described in the following chapter.

2 Scale description

The SED-S (Sappok *et al.*, 2016) is based on Anton Došen's stage model of emotional development (2005) and determines the level of emotional development according to the emotional reference age of typically developed children in successive stages:

1. adaptation stage: 0–6 months
2. first socialisation stage: 7–18 months
3. first individuation stage: 19–36 months
4. identification stage: 37–84 months (4–7 years of age)
5. reality awareness stage: 85–144 months (8–12 years of age)

---

6. social individuation stage: 145–204 months (13–17 years of age)
7. social responsibility stage: 205–300 months (18–25 years of age).

The SED-S comprises stages one to five (Sappok *et al*, 2016); work on stages six and seven is currently in preparation.

The SED-S in its current form consists of a total of 200 yes/no questions and describes the emotional state of development using five items (observation points) per stage in a total of eight development domains:

- domain 1: relating to own body (short: body)
- domain 2: relating to important others (short: important others; originally SED domains 2 and 3)
- domain 3: dealing with change – object permanence (short: object permanence)
- domain 4: differentiating emotions (short: emotions; originally SED domains 4 and 9)
- domain 5: relating to peers (short: peers)
- domain 6: engaging with the material world (short: materials)
- domain 7: communication (short: communication)
- domain 8: regulating affect (short: affect regulation).

Every domain is characterised by certain developmental milestones for each developmental level and is described by five items.

3 Development of the SED-S

The SED-S was developed on the basis of the SED-R[2] (in Dutch the SEO-R2, *Schaal voor Emotionele Ontwikkeling bij mensen met een verstandelijke beperking* – revised[2]; Morisse and Došen, 2016). First, all items of the SED-R[2] were assessed with regard to their validity and observability by a total of 30 experts from Germany, the Netherlands and Belgium. In a subsequent consensus process, the final items were selected and the structure of the questionnaire was defined (Sappok *et al.*, 2016). The resulting scale, SED-S, was published in three languages, German, English and Dutch, in a scientific journal (Sappok *et al.*, 2016). Moreover, the application of the scale and the instructions for the appraisal and interpretation of the SED-S were described in a manual, which was published in German and Dutch (Sappok *et al.*, 2018; Morisse *et al.*, 2018).

4 Psychometric properties

Validity: the scale was validated against a group of 160 typically developed children, with at least 30 children for each developmental stage (Sappok *et al.*, 2019). The degree of agreement with the biological age of the children was 81% (exact agreement). Taking into account the closeness to the exact value, a kappa value of 95% was found. Thus, the high degree of agreement between the chronological age of the children and the reference age assigned in the SED-S confirmed that the SED-S addresses appropriate behaviours and characteristics alongside the developmental trajectory and measures these correctly.

Internal consistency: the internal consistency measured with Cronbach's alpha was .99 (Sappok *et al.*, 2019).

Inter-rater reliability: the inter-rater reliability was determined at N = 25 typically developed children. For this purpose, the parent interview was assessed by a second psychologist. There was complete agreement between the results of the two psychologists (Cohen's kappa 1.0; Sappok *et al.*, 2019).

Validation in children: in a sample of 118 children from Switzerland and the Netherlands (Sterkenburg *et al.*, 2020), the internal consistency of the SED-S was high (Cronbach's alpha = .94) and suggested a one-factor solution in the principle component analysis (PCA). The reliability was good as the domains were highly yet not perfectly intercorrelated. The convergent validity with the severity of intellectual disability was good as well (G = –.69, p < .001). The divergent validity was shown by a non-significant correlation with the chronological age (H = 9.25, p = .055) and for adaptive functioning, as the emotional reference ages of the lower SED-S levels (SED-S-1 to SED-S-3) did not correspond to the age equivalents observed by the Vineland Adaptive Behavior Scales.

Further test psychometric examinations of the SED-S are currently being carried out in the different study centres (Belgium, Netherlands, Switzerland, Germany and the UK) of the NEED group. These examinations are being conducted with adults and children with different levels of cognitive impairment and with and without additional mental disorders or challenging behaviours.

5 Application of the scale

The SED-S is applied by an expert in developmental psychology who conducts a structured interview with close caregivers about the characteristic behaviours of the person being examined and assigns them to particular developmental stages.

The behaviour of the person being examined is assessed in various everyday situations (e.g. when eating, washing or getting dressed), in interaction with caregivers or peers and in handling objects. In order to obtain a comprehensive picture, different caregivers or relatives from different areas of life and professions should be included in the assessment. If the interviewer does not know the client personally, video recordings, for example, can be helpful in order to evaluate the behaviour appropriately. In order to ensure an effective discussion, it can be useful to hand out the questionnaire and the developmental milestones beforehand. The individual results are then discussed during the assessment process. The different items of the SED-S questionnaire should be formulated as questions during the interview. The assessor assigns the statements of the interviewees to the items. In order to assign the correct developmental age, it is often necessary to take into account not only overt behaviour but also the intention behind the behaviour. Therefore, the assessment should only be carried out by somebody who is experienced in developmental psychology. A brief summary of the milestones of the emotional developmental steps can be helpful.

When assessing the emotional development of adults, their level of life experience and increased cognitive learning must be taken into account. For example, an adult may have learned and mentally practised how to shake hands as a greeting, but they may do so mechanically e.g. without making eye contact or without registering the other person's feeling of joy. It is therefore important not only to evaluate a certain behaviour functionally but also to consider the motive for the behaviour. For example, if someone paints pictures only when invited to do so (domain 6, 'engaging with the material world'), and otherwise tends to sit passively, then the behaviour is probably not associated with their own motivation and joy. Moreover, the behaviour should be seen against the background of the basic and developmental needs associated with a certain stage.

In an inpatient setting, an observation period of at least two weeks prior to the assessment is necessary. This allows for the observations of creative therapists, nursing staff, doctors, remedial educationalists, behavioural therapists and physiotherapists to complement each other and leads to a more accurate assessment. For the person concerned, however, an inpatient stay is likely to represent an exceptional situation, either because they are suffering an illness or because of environmental factors. The assessments made in this context must be interpreted in the light of the person's unfamiliar surroundings.

In the case of an outpatient assessment in the person's familiar living environment, the SED-S interview should, if possible, include informants from all areas of life, such as work, leisure, therapy and family. As certain people's level of emotional functioning may differ depending on time and location (e.g. between home and the workplace or between a relaxed period and a stressful period), the SED-S may be applied in different environments and at different times.

The assessment takes about 30–60 minutes.

6 Appraisal of the scale

Domain level: at the domain level, the stage with the most 'yes' responses is defined as the result. The behavioural pattern characteristics that the client has confidently mastered thus determine the emotional developmental stage. It can be difficult to determine the developmental stage if behaviours from different stages are observed simultaneously. If the person shows the same number of behaviours from two adjacent developmental stages, the lower stage should be assumed as the result, in order to avoid overestimation.

Scale level: the individual results of the eight domains are sorted in ascending order of size, with the fourth value in the series marking the overall result. In addition to the overall result, however, it is also important to take a differentiated view of the developmental profile. Particularly if there are large discrepancies between the different areas of development, an overall result should be dispensed with and the differentiated profile should be used. A graphic presentation of the results of the individual development domains is particularly helpful here.

7 Case example

Mrs F is a 42-year-old woman with a moderate intellectual disability who lives in a group setting with five other adults. She cannot independently perform activities of daily living and needs staff support in all areas of life.

Mrs F constantly seeks to contact her staff and follows them around. She enjoys physical contact as well as short conversations in plain, simple language. She uses a lot of stereotypic language to gain the staff's attention and asks the same questions repeatedly. When interacting with staff, she is very friendly and laughs a lot. She especially loves singing with them.

She is very interested in the weather and fearful when it comes to thunderstorms. She checks weather conditions by looking out of the window several times in an hour, asks staff about the latest weather reports and needs a lot of reassurance.

She shows no great interest in her fellow flatmates, but is rather interested in their belongings. If possible, she goes into their rooms, lies in their beds or takes objects that are of interest to her, which she plays with, relocates and sometimes breaks.

She likes simple colouring books and mandalas but has difficulties concentrating for more than a few minutes. She does not keep pieces of art that she finishes. She has difficulties postponing needs and wishes, and urges staff to instantly respond to her requests. When caregivers are engaged with other clients, leave the room or close doors between them and Mrs F, she is often distressed, and she screams and cries. If she continues to be upset, she throws objects and grabs staff by their clothes.

8 Practical implementation of the SED-S in the example

The main goal of the staff when initiating the SED-S assessment was to gain a better understanding of Mrs F's emotional developmental functioning and needs overall (Sappok *et al.*, 2016; Sappok *et al.*, 2021; Došen, 2005). The purpose of the assessment was to generate ideas on how to comfort her and find activities that she could perform independently in situations when she is distressed.

In this example, a psychologist who provides consultant work for the group home carried out the assessment. Three of the main caregivers, as well as Mrs F's family, provided information in the interview.

In the SED-S, Mrs F was found to have an overall result of stage two, 'first socialisation', with an emotional reference age of a typically developed child of seven to eighteen months. The differentiated emotional profile of Mrs F is presented in figure 12.1.

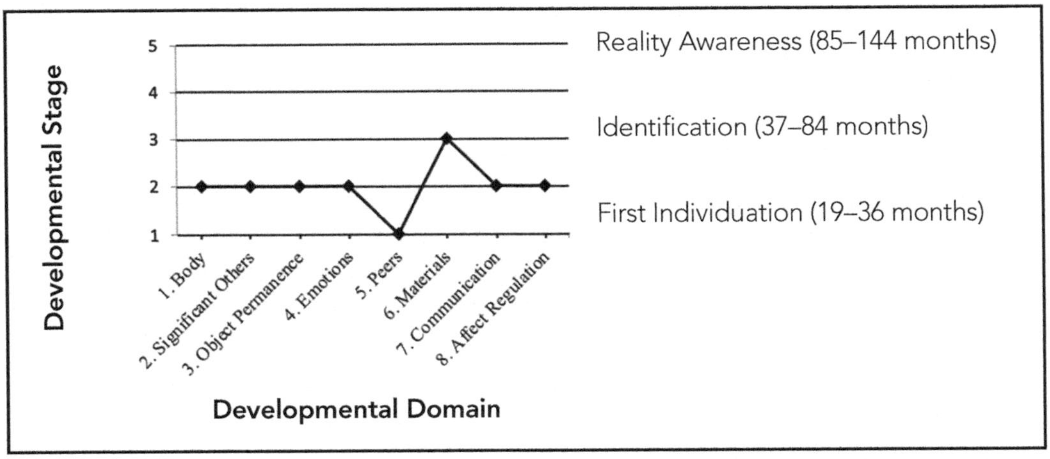

Figure 12.1 Case example: SED-S profile with the developmental stages for each developmental domain

The interpretation of Mrs F's profile is based on the understanding of emotional needs and development in stage two: socialisation describes the developmental process of disengaging from the symbiosis with the closest caregivers, being able to discriminate between 'self' and 'others' and developing social attachment. Developmental tasks also cover the mastering of object permanence, the practice of skills, the purposeful use of one's own body and exploration of the surroundings.

At this developmental stage, the person's main orientation is still towards the attachment figure. A separation from that attachment figure is the main fear (Sappok *et al.*, 2021).

Applying this knowledge to Mrs F changes the interpretation of her behaviour from possibly being *annoying*, *attention seeking*, *egoistic*, *greedy* and *impatient* to being that of a person who loses all orientation and security whenever caregivers leave the room.

In the case example, staff and family developed several individualised adaptations to Mrs F's support that ranged from environmental adaptions, alteration of staff behaviour and implementation of specific pedagogical activities and interventions. The development of such adaptions is always predicated on an in-depth understanding of developmental psychology. Suggestions for interventions for each developmental stage in every domain can be found in the literature (Sappok *et al.*, 2021), but must always be individualised for the particular person.

Environmental adaptations aimed to reduce stress, make the environment more accessible for Mrs F and promote independent engagement in activities:

- Staff began to identify small changes to the environment that made it easier for Mrs F to stay on her own for some time (e.g. putting on her favourite music or recordings of stories read by familiar voices).
- Knowing that Mrs F cannot reliably discriminate between her own possessions, others' possessions and materials that belong to everybody in the household, the caregivers shifted that responsibility. They installed doorknobs on the rooms of peers who are able to handle them and made sure they supported others to close their rooms and redirect Mrs F.
- As Mrs F cannot concentrate on activities for very long, the caregivers now put out different objects and materials for her to engage with in her favourite places.
- Acknowledging Mrs F's significant need to stay close to caregivers, the caregivers ensured that non-private rooms (such as the office) were fitted with glass doors and/or windows. This enabled Mrs F and other clients to see caregivers even when they were not in the same room.

With the increased understanding of Mrs F's developmental needs, a significant alteration of staff behaviour occurred naturally. Nevertheless, a shared set of actions, as well as the implementation of specific pedagogical activities and interventions, was agreed on:

- As Mrs F depends on close contact to attachment figures, staff agreed on a schedule of reliable, brief contacts initiated by caregivers.
- Staff changed their routines so that they can be within Mrs F's field of vision as much as possible.
- Whenever a separation is necessary, the caregivers hand Mrs F something to hold on to while they are gone (e.g. a scarf or a picture of themselves). This procedure aims to give her some security while practising the use of transitional objects.
- Whenever possible, staff involve Mrs F in daily tasks, she accompanies them and they share activities (such as cooking and setting the table).
- In order to build on her strengths and interests, staff initiate the colouring of mandalas and pictures and increasingly distance themselves from Mrs F and spend longer periods of time away from her while she engages in these activities.
- Mrs F has been provided with new materials and encouraged to explore different textures and functions (e.g. amorphous material like sand).
- Visual aids indicating the weather forecast have been provided. These aim to give her some security whenever staff are not able to reassure her personally.
- Caregivers accept that thunderstorms are a big fear of Mrs F's and that their occurrence means that Mrs F might panic and need extra support. Staff are developing comforting and distracting (shared) activities that help her through these times (e.g. singing or taking a bath).
- Staff see the moderation and supervision of group interaction and contact with peers as their responsibility, as Mrs F is not at a developmental level where she can handle such interaction independently.
- Mrs F's needs have to be met in a timely fashion. Staff can prepare by providing snacks, contact, etc. before going into situations that are demanding for Mrs F. Carrying objects to distract Mrs F or changing rooms in times of distress can be helpful.
- Whenever Mrs F experiences outbursts it is vital not to leave her alone but to stay within her field of vision and provide comfort and safety.

The NEED group developed a description of five index cases for SED-S stage one to stage five to support the alignment of the scale in different languages and sites (Sappok *et al.*, 2020).

9 Conclusion

The SED-S is a valid and reliable instrument for the assessment of the level of emotional functioning; further validation is needed in different populations and languages. The SED-S gives insights into the level of emotional development, which is crucial for understanding the mechanisms within the person that lead to behaviours of concern. Understanding a person's emotional development will help to alter and broaden interpretations of challenging behaviour and will therefore often lead to a better acceptance and toleration of behaviours that might be experienced as difficult. Developing support plans and interventions based on the emotional developmental level of a person might create new initiatives and ideas.

References

Beail, N (2003) What works for people with mental retardation? Critical commentary on cognitive-behavioral and psychodynamic psychotherapy research. *Mental Retardation* **41** 468–472.

Begeer, S, Gevers, C, Clifford, P, Verhoeve, M, Kat, K, Hoddenbach, E & Boer, F (2011) Theory of Mind training in children with autism: a randomized controlled trial. *Journal of Autism and Developmental Disorders* **41** 997–1006.

Cooper, SA, Smiley, E, Morrison, J, Williamson, A & Allan, L (2007). Mental ill-health in adults with intellectual disabilities: prevalence and associated factors. *British Journal of Psychiatry* **190** 27–35.

Došen, A (2005) Applying the developmental perspective in the psychiatric assessment and diagnosis of persons with intellectual disability: part I-assessment. *Journal of Intellectual Disability Research* **49** 1–8.

Morisse, F, Sappok, T, De Neve, L, Došen, A (2018) *Handleiding bij de Schaal voor Emotionele Ontwikkeling – Verkort: SEO-V.* Antwerpen/Apeldoorn: Garant.

Morisse, F, Došen, A (2016) *SEO-R2 Schaal voor Emotionele Ontwikkeling van mensen met een verstandelijke beperking – revised 2.* Antwerpen/Apeldoorn: Garant.

McCarthy, J, Hemmings, C, Kravariti, E, Dworzynski, K, Holt, G, Bouras, N et al. (2010) Challenging behavior and co-morbid psychopathology in adults with intellectual disability and autism spectrum disorders. *Research in Developmental Disabilities* **31** 362–366.

Sappok, T, Budczies, J, Dziobek, I, Bölte, S, Došen, A & Diefenbacher, A (2014) The missing link: Delayed emotional development predicts challenging behavior in adults with intellectual disability. *Journal of Autism and Developmental Disorders* **44** 786–800.

Sappok, T, Barrett, BF, Vandevelde, S et al. (2016) Scale of emotional development – Short. *Research in Developmental Disabilities* **7** 166–175.

Sappok, T, Böhm, J, Birkner, J, Roth, G, & Heinrich, M (2019) How is your mind-set? Proof of concept for the measurement of the level of emotional development. *PloS one* **14** (4) e0215474.

Sappok, T, Došen, A, Zepperitz, S, Barrett, B, Vonk, J, Schanze, C, Ilic, M, Bergmann, T, De Neve, L, Birkner, J, Zaal, S, Bertelli, MO, Hudson, M, Morisse, F & Sterkenburg, P (2020) Standardizing the assessment of emotional development in adults with intellectual and developmental disability. *Journal of Applied Research in Intellectual Disabilities:* JARID **33** (3) 542–551 https://doi.org/101111/jar12697.

Sappok, T, Zepperitz, S, Barrett, B F & Došen, A (2018) *Die Skala der emotionalen Entwicklung – Diagnostik (SED-S).* Bern: Hogrefe.

Sappok, T, Zepperitz, S, Hudson, M (2021) *Meeting Emotional Needs in Intellectual Disability: The developmental approach.* Bern: Hogrefe.

Sterkenburg, PS, Kempelmann, GEM, Hentrich, J, Vonk, J, Zaal S, Erlewein, R, Hudson, M (2021) Scale of emotional development – short: reliability and validity in two samples of children with an intellectual disability. *Research in Developmental Disabilities* **108** doi.org/101016/jridd2020103821.

Tsakanikos, E (2010) Challenging behavior and co-morbid psychopathology in adults with intellectual disability and autism spectrum disorders. *Research in Developmental Disabilities* **31** 362–366.

Chapter 13
The Scale of Emotional Development – Revised² for people with intellectual disabilities and its translation into (treatment and) support

Filip Morisse, Soetkin Roskam, Leen De Neve and Anton Došen

Summary

Anton Došen's Scheme for Appraisal of Emotional Development (SED) (Došen, 1990) evolved over the course of 25 years into a fully fledged, reliable and validated Scale of Emotional Development – Revised² (SED-R²) for people with intellectual disabilities (Morisse & Došen, 2017). It has become an indispensable assessment tool in the imaging, diagnostics and support of people with intellectual disabilities. In cases of comorbidity between intellectual disabilities and additional psychiatric vulnerabilities, including behavioural problems and/or psychiatric disorders, the SED-R² helps us to better understand certain behaviours and to adapt the environment to the client's basic emotional needs. This chapter provides advice based on 25 years of clinical use of this scale in the Netherlands and Belgium. It mentions a number of pitfalls that may arise from an overly isolated and oversimplified use of the scale and of the developmental dynamic model. And although the idea of scaling the level of emotional development is increasingly popular, there are still major challenges in translating this scaling into support. To this end, a concrete methodology of reflective questions is suggested.

1 The history and development of the SED-R²

In 1990, Anton Došen published the SED (Došen, 1990, p. 93). This questionnaire contained seven domains. In 2007 it was extended to 10 domains. Normal emotional development was divided into five stages. In each domain, three specific characteristics were given for each stage (Došen, 2007). Each stage was further characterised by associated types of support needs.

Table 13.1 shows the five stages of emotional development and their corresponding types of support needs.

Table 13.1 Stages of emotional development and types of support needs

	Stage of emotional development	Type of support needs
1.	Adaptation (0–6 months)	Homeostasis versus dysregulation
2.	First socialisation (6–18 months)	Trust versus distrust
3.	First individuation (18–36 months)	Autonomy versus dependency
4.	Identification (3–7 years)	Initiative versus inhibition
5.	Awareness of reality (7–12 years)	Self-confidence versus inferiority

Based on this questionnaire, the Scale of Emotional Development – Revised (SED-R) for persons with intellectual disabilities was developed (Claes & Verduyn, 2012). The aim of the SED-R was to strive for a more accessible and user-friendly discussion tool for estimating the level of emotional development of people with intellectual disabilities. As part of the Belgian project 'Steunpunt Expertise Netwerk Sociaal Emotionele Ontwikkeling'(SEN-SEO), there was an intensive collaboration with a core group of 15 experts with extensive theoretical background and practical experience in the use of the SED-R.

In the SED-R, the five stages of emotional development were retained, but the 10 domains of the questionnaire were thoroughly edited and supplemented. The stage-specific properties in each domain were replaced with a larger number of statements on stage-specific behaviour, divided into three sections: the 'core', the 'development' and 'examples'. In addition, three new domains were added, namely 'day activity – play development', 'moral development' and 'emotion regulation'.

Although SED-R mainly maps emotional development, certain domains also have a cognitive and social dimension (Morisse & Došen, 2017, p. 17). Table 13.2 gives an overview.

The SED-R comprises the following 13 domains:

1. dealing with own body
2. dealing with emotionally important others
3. self-image in interaction with the environment
4. dealing with changing environment – object permanence
5. anxieties
6. dealing with peers
7. dealing with materials
8. communication
9. emotion differentiation
10. aggression regulation
11. day activity – play development
12. moral development
13. emotion regulation.

Table 13.2 Which domains of SED-R relate to which development dimensions

Dimension	Domains
Emotional development	1, 3, 5, 9, 13
Integration of cognitive and emotional systems	4, 8, 11
Social development	2, 6, 7, 10, 12

In principle, it can be said that in more or less all domains of the first two stages the characteristics of emotional development are recognisable, while in later stages cognitive and social aspects increase in importance.

As a result of scientific research into the inter-rater reliability of the SED-R in 2011–2012, domains 9 (emotion differentiation), 10 (aggression regulation) and 13 (emotion regulation) were thoroughly revised. In addition, an expert group of users in Flanders and the Netherlands were asked about the use of SED-R. Psychologists and remedial educationalists with clinical expertise with SED-R provided rigorous feedback. The revision of the SED-R led to the SED-R², which was examined for validity in 2015 (Morisse & Došen, 2017).

The main differences between SED-R and SED-R^2:

- Domains 9, 10 and 13 were revised.
- The scale was completely revised based on the experience of clinicians.
- Efforts were made to make it more user friendly by revising and extending the manual in relation to the scoring and interpretation of various profiles.
- The results of the scientific research into the psychometric properties of the SED-R (reliability) and the SED-R^2 (validity) were added to the manual.

An online version is available at www.sen-seo.be.

The developers of the SED-R^2 are also involved in a promising European research project (the Network of Europeans on Emotional Development (NEED) project) related to the SED-S (Scale of Emotional Development – Short; Sappok *et al.*, 2016; see chapter 12), an abridged version of the SED-R^2. This instrument, which is even more focused on objective grading, classification, diagnostics and scientific research, complements the SED-R^2 in certain situations.

2 Objectives, use and interpretation of the scale

An assessment with SED-R^2 can be helpful when one wants to gain insight into the client's emotional development. A qualitative and intersubjective classification of a client is made, based on a semi-structured interview of at least two persons (informants) who have been able to observe the client for at least six months. During an extensive interview, the assessor will acquire information in order to estimate emotional development in the different domains. This information will be gathered on the basis of the recognisability of the different items in each domain and the search for concrete examples that are specific to this person. The dialogues with and possible differences in experiences between at least two informants provide many opportunities for exchange and for searching for and identifying the appropriate levels.

In assessments using the SED-R^2, the underlying needs and motivations of the client's behaviour are extensively considered. After all, the same symptoms can hide very different needs. For example, a client's screaming may be caused by fear, incomprehension and the fear of being left alone, but the client may just as well scream because they want to be able to decide what happens for themselves rather than just agreeing with what is expected of them at that moment. Undoubtedly there are other possible explanations for this behaviour. Table 13.3 presents an example.

Table 13.3 Same behaviour with different underlying emotional meanings		
Perceived behaviour	Tom is in the pool. After an hour of swimming and having fun, Tom's daddy says: 'It's over. Now get out of the water; it's time to go home.' Daddy swims to the edge and gets out of the water. Tom throws a tantrum. He doesn't come out of the pool.	
Motivations	Swimming and the many stimuli in the pool demand a lot from Tom. Daddy's close proximity is very important, especially when the activity has lasted for a while. When suddenly an appeal is made to him, this creates too much excitement. He doesn't know what comes next; he wants to get a grip.	Tom doesn't want to lose control and wants to put his own will above the will of the others. Tom wants to be able to decide for himself when he gets out of the pool. He can't suddenly interrupt his beloved activity.
Basic emotions	Despair – Tom has completely lost it, feels the ground beneath his feet slipping away.	Anger
Needs	Feeling safe – Tom wants to be 'carried' figuratively; he wants grip, predictability.	The desire to determine, need for autonomy
	STAGE 1	STAGE 3

In finding the appropriate support, the assessment can also be seen as a very valuable moment. In addition to examples, a lot of interpretations are often exchanged. Frequently, informants implicitly or explicitly exchange elements of the current support style. In this dialogue, aspects of the support style are discussed and therefore also influenced.

When going through the items, the recognisability of the items for the client is assessed. It is up to the assessor to ask adequate questions in order to collect sufficient information to score the various domains. A pleasant side effect of the assessment with a team is that the discussion and insights not only positively influence the alignment with the emotional needs of the client involved but also get transferred to other support domains. Therefore, in this process there are many opportunities to work on a good alignment of the support style with the current needs of the client.

The result of an assessment is reflected in an emotional development profile (table 13.4).

Table 13.4 Emotional development profile

		Stage 1	Stage 2	Stage 3	Stage 4	Stage 5
1.	Dealing with own body	X				
2.	Dealing with emotionally important others		X			
3.	Self-image in interaction with the environment	X				
4.	Dealing with changing environment – object permanence		X			
5.	Anxieties	X				
6.	Dealing with peers		X			
7.	Dealing with materials	X				
8.	Communication		X			
9.	Emotion differentiation	X				
10.	Aggression regulation		X			
11.	Day activity – play development	X				
12.	Moral development	X				
13.	Emotion regulation	X				
Conclusion: the level of emotional development of this person at the time of this assessment is not higher than the stage of first socialisation (= the emotional level of a 18-month-old child)						

It is important to 'read' the profile. Is there a harmonious picture (for instance, at least eight out of 13 domains are scored at the same stage, or at least five domains are scored at the same stage and the other domains are scored at an adjoining stage; Sappok *et al.*, 2013) or rather a disharmonious profile (domains are scored at very different stages)? It may be useful to zoom in on the domains that are 'outliers'. Since there are domains with specific cognitive or social aspects, this can provide more information and provide insight into the needs of the client concerned.

In addition, it is also desirable to look at emotional development as part of a broad picture, in addition to, for example, cognitive development, the development of general daily life skills and verbality. When a person functions on a much lower level emotionally than they do cognitively, this is described as a discrepant profile.

Sometimes it is not possible to score a domain because behaviour is not observed. In that case the domain may be omitted; assessors should not make assumptions. This is then taken into account when scoring. Informants also often describe different functioning in different situations, and it may also be the case that someone exhibits different functioning depending on their level of tension. If, during an assessment, it turns out that it makes sense to take into account the effects of different 'states of mind', this can be done by, for example, scoring with different colours (green: top level, red: level in a stressful situation). This information can help assessors to learn to look more closely at the support needs of the client when later developing a support style. This not only contributes to better observation but also makes the supporter more sensitive to the client's needs.

3 From assessment to support

Thanks to the widespread use of the SED-R², insight into the emotional needs of individual clients is increasing. However, the translation of this insight into support needs and appropriate support does not appear to be evident. The SEN-SEO project tried to translate insights into emotional development into useful tools for the daily support of clients. In the chapter 'From assessment to support' (Claes *et al.*, 2012, pp. 67–181) Claes and colleagues give ideas and tips for practice. They do not give 'ready-made solutions for every problem' but inspiring examples, illustrations of good practice and critical questions that encourage (even better) alignment of the support of individual clients with their basic emotional needs.

Nevertheless, there is a great risk of getting seduced by ready-made manuals and tips and tricks. We do understand the demand for concrete solutions, and it is very tempting for experts to dive straight into this material and formulate concrete answers. However, we want to put the usefulness of these recipes, prescriptions and tips into perspective: it is always slightly different for this particular client, in this particular situation, in these particular circumstances. This is not only because every client is unique but also because, as supporters, we are always involved in the circumstances (De Belie & Van Hove, 2013). Our own strengths and weaknesses partly determine how we attune to the client's needs.

For these reasons, a 'reflection brochure' was designed (De Neve, 2015). The underlying thought of this brochure is that, when we have an idea of a client's emotional development, we can use reflective questions to take a closer look at which aspects of daily support can be adjusted. The questions in the brochure invite us to discuss, to further explore the client's needs (for example, does the client have a safe place?) and to explore our own roles as caregivers in meeting those needs (for example, is there a particular behaviour of the client's that can really irritate? What helps to deal with that irritation?).

The aim of these reflective questions is to provide opportunities to (further) attune one's own actions to the needs of the client and in this way increase the quality of life of this client. The focus is exclusively on the role of the facilitator/supporter: 'what can I do to ...?' and not 'what should the client do?' The brochure is built on the basis of the five stages of emotional development. For each stage, the questions are grouped according to the following themes (Claes *et al.*, 2012): distance and proximity, relationships, structure and boundaries, and activities and communication.

The reflective questions are an accessible way to reflect on support and to initiate or support mentalisation (De Belie & Van Hove, 2013). However, in using these questions, one will have to look for ways to hold on to this process of mentalisation and turn it into action agreements for concrete support. The challenge may lie in allowing this process to culminate in concrete agreements that are shared within the team.

4 The toll of fame: pitfalls in the use of SED-R²

Partly thanks to the activities of SEN-SEO in Flanders and FORTIOR (organisation for training) and the LNEO (the National Network Emotional Development) in the Netherlands, the idea of emotional development spread like wildfire. Numerous training sessions and coaching programmes were organised and accessible publications were published. The activities and developments of what can now be called a 'movement' were followed by hundreds of professionals. In most services and organisations for people with intellectual disabilities, the assessment of emotional development and its translation into support plans were given a permanent place.

However, there was also a downside to this popularity. There were increasingly peculiar interpretations of the model, such as: 'this client is a Došen two,' 'you have to deal with a resident in stage one like a baby,' 'someone in stage two will never be able to live alone,' or 'from stage three on, punishment and reward are good.' Gradually it became clear that the model of emotional development was increasingly being applied as a new system of classification.

Although this chapter emphasises the importance of a proper assessment of clients' emotional development, it should never be an isolated exercise, and this developmental dimension should always be included within a broader perspective. A holistic assessment, with emphasis on biopsychosocial and developmental aspects, in addition to investigating relevant influences from the environment, should serve as the basis for supporting the client (Došen, 2014). There is a general agreement in the literature on the need for a methodical, interdisciplinary and integrative approach, as opposed to the often still monodisciplinary approach prevalent today. In addition to the biopsychosocial and existential needs of persons with intellectual disabilities and mental health problems, particular attention to the developmental perspective is required (Došen, 2014). In other words, at what stage of development is the person located cognitively, socially and emotionally? (Early) developmental history and life events are also important. After all, we know that many mental health problems are rooted in early childhood development, before the age of five. Paying attention to developmental history is not only important for assessment and diagnostics; it also leads to a better understanding of the way in which the problems are created and maintained. In this way, individual elements and symptoms become a meaningful (life) story (De Belie & Van Hove, 2013).

The following remarks from Anton Došen respond to the gradual narrowing of the philosophy that has taken place, as described above:

> Stage-thinking is a simplification of reality. Development is an irregular continuum with decelerations, accelerations, lags and jumps. It is important to be able to read typical characteristics (e.g. social behaviour) that belong to certain levels of development, so that the underlying needs of the person can be recognised. Other authors speak of personality structures or personality layers, which are applied at a certain stage of development. Some researchers consider emotional development to be the core of the personality. Development starts with the formation of a biological core in which basic life processes take place, including the formation of basic survival needs. Emotions are seen as expressions of basic survival needs. The development of different emotions is seen as the formation of different layers that grow around the biological core, just as an onion is formed. The layers of emotional development alternate with cognitive layers, which together with the emotional layers become overgrown in social behaviour. According to this model, it is difficult to speak of one stage of development through which the personality is determined. Usually characteristics of two or even more stages are found. In that case we say: the level of this aspect, this dimension is 'not higher than …'. This emphasises the need to discuss the findings with other researchers. (Anton Došen, 4 December 2015)

Emotional development has everything to do with dynamics, with ambivalence, with dialectics: trust versus distrust, autonomy versus dependency. It is advisable to return to the core of the model, to the types of support needs, which pertain to basic emotional needs and motivations, rather than just focusing on behaviour. It is not about separating categories or scores; it is not the case that stage three stops somewhere and stage four starts there. The development is a continuum, a process.

This reasoning is confirmed by what Gerrit Vignero writes about his concept of 'de draad' ('the thread') (Vignero, 2011; 2015; see also chapter 19 in this book). The thread is a metaphor for how the connection between people grows through the different development steps. This concept is a way of responding to questions such as 'with whom and in what way is the client connected?' 'Which are the intense contacts and which are the superficial, interchangeable contacts?' 'How does the client gradually enter into a relationship with new people?' Most people have a 'strong thread' and a 'vulnerable thread' (Vignero, 2015). There is often a kind of superstructure that clients are happy to reveal (with self-overestimation, but also learned helplessness, imitation and talking along), but apart from this level we also have to work with the substructure. In that respect, what is interesting is not always the average emotional functioning but rather the spread in the development profile.

5 Psychometric properties

In table 13.5 we give an overview of the psychometric research conducted on scales for emotional development based on Došen's model of emotional development.

First, there was psychometric research on the SED-R that focused on inter-rater reliability (N = 67) in 2013 (Vandevelde *et al.*, 2014). For all 13 domains significant correlations were found, ascertaining mostly moderate correlations between interviewers for most domains (and high correlations for one domain, 'dealing with peers'). Nevertheless, some correlations were weak, in particular domain 9 (emotion differentiation), domain 10 (aggression regulation) and domain 13 (emotion regulation), as these scores fell in the range of the cut-off value for a 'low' correlation.

The total score here can be regarded as a substantial level of agreement. The same can be said about the average score (intraclass correlation coefficient (ICC) = 50.76). In about 10 of 13 domains a moderate to substantial level of agreement was found. Compared to the correlation indicators, the ICC scores were weaker for domains 9, 10 and 13, as these scores fell in the range of the cut-off value for a 'fair' agreement.

Table 13.5 Overview of psychometric research

Scale name	Author	Year of publication	Psychometric research by	Aspect of psychometric research
SAED	Došen	2005	La Malfa et al., 2009	Correlation between SAED and Vineland Adaptive Behavior Scales
SED-R	Claes & Verduyn	2012	Vandevelde et al., 2014	Inter-rater reliability and internal consistency
SED-R²	Morisse & Došen	2016	Morisse et al., submitted	Correlation between SED-R² and Vineland 2 and experts
SED-S	Sappok et al.	2016	Sappok et al., 2016	Consensus process to design abbreviated version of the SED-R²
SED-S	Sappok et al.	2016	Sterkenburg et al., 2021	Reliability and validity in two samples of children with an intellectual disability

A second, practice-based scientific study (by Hogeschool Gent/Expertisecentrum E-QUAL in collaboration with SENvzw, Tranzo – Tilburg University and Ghent University) into the SED-R² was carried out (Morisse *et al.*, submitted) in line with the research of La Malfa and colleagues (2009) and the master's thesis of Lore Riské (2014). More specifically, the convergent validity of a first version of the SED-R² with the Vineland 2 scale and the criterion validity (expert judgement) of the SED-R² in a sample of 62 clients were investigated. Of these clients, 64.5% had additional psychiatric or behavioural problems. This study also addressed the lack of empirical research – based on reliable and valid instruments – into the level of emotional development in individuals with intellectual disability. Using the most recent SED-R² (Morisse & Došen, 2017) and the most recent Vineland 2 scale on a larger and more heterogeneous sample, previous results for reliability and validity (La Malfa *et al.*, 2009; Vandevelde *et al.*, 2016) were confirmed. Our psychometric analysis indicated that the SED-R² displays a high internal consistency (Cronbach's alpha = .98). There is a relatively high correlation between the total score of the SED-R² and the scores for the Vineland 2 total score (Spearman's rho .768).

As in the La Malfa study (2009), correlations were calculated between the SED-R² total score and the subdomains communication, socialisation, daily skills and motor skills, all of which were found to be statistically significant. The correlation between the SED-R² total score and the clinical expert judgement was only moderately positive (Spearman's rho .58). This could possibly be explained by the fact that the 'inner side' (people's basic emotional needs) is difficult to measure, and the fact that we still do not know how this 'inner side' can (best) be assessed: through clinical assessment, behavioural indicators or a combination of both. The present study indicates that more research on this topic is recommended.

An important challenge that remains is the difficulty of quantifying emotional development accurately. Observable behaviour can easily be discerned, but similar behaviours of individuals with intellectual disabilities can depend on different emotions and varying levels of emotional development. Moreover, an individual's level of emotional development is not isolated but depends on relationships and on the sensitive responsiveness and relational attunement of others. Furthermore, emotional development is dynamic and ambivalent, especially in vulnerable individuals with intellectual disabilities. The goal of the SED-R² is not only to classify individuals according to stages of emotional development but also to 'read out' a unique and individual developmental profile in accordance with support needs (including correlation with other developmental domains).

It would be interesting for future research to empirically test a number of hypotheses from clinical practice with a matched sample. For instance, it would be useful to align the level of emotional development with the level of intellectual disability and comorbidity and to analyse discrepant profiles and compare them to harmonious profiles. Finally, future reliability and validity scores will benefit from the further development of the SED-R² through sustained research efforts. Finally, there are a few studies in which the SED-R² was used alongside other scales, for example the correlation studies between SED-R², the AVVB (*Adaptieve Vragenlijst Verstandelijke Beperking*) and risk taxation scores (Nijman *et al.*, 2017), and the correlation studies between SED-R² and SED-V (SED for Adults) (Vandeputte, 2018; Niehoff, 2018).

6 Case study

6.1 Description of Lisa

Lisa is 24 years old, has a moderate intellectual disability and lives in a group home. She is very social, spontaneous and helpful, both towards her fellow residents and towards the people who support her. She can be very sweet and has clear affection for certain people. Lisa has a very strong will, and when she has set her mind on something, it is hard to change it. She is aware of the weaknesses of certain people, and from time to time she will test/explore/seek out these weaknesses. Lisa likes to joke, but she uses the same phrases she has been repeating for years. Lisa frequently asks for the next support worker. As the hour of arrival approaches, one can observe tension building up inside of her.

Lisa can choose for herself, although this is not easy for her. She is very receptive to suggestion and seems to want to make socially desirable choices. Because of this, she can sometimes neglect her own needs. She aspires to be the 'good client' and will do anything to obtain this status. Sometimes the support worker really has to insist in order to get Lisa to make her own choice. It helps if she is allowed to choose between specific options and is reassured that her choice will not affect her relationship with the caregiver.

Lisa has a number of fixed rituals. She will always tidy up the same things in the group home. She organises fellow clients' possessions while leaving her own possessions lying around. Sometimes it is necessary to point out to her that some things are not expected of her. When Lisa is confronted with criticism, she can react emotionally. Either she gets excited and indicates that she is not well, or she cries when she is addressed. Sometimes, when she talks to herself, she will use the same words used by the caregiver in order to comfort herself.

Lisa washes herself independently and asks for help when needed, for example to wash her hair. Usually she puts on clean clothes on her own, although she needs some support in this. Especially when she has new clothes, she prefers to wear them for days on end. When Lisa is alone in the bathroom in front of the mirror, she will have all sorts of fantasies about herself and her aspirations. During dinner, Lisa will make sure it all goes well. She will verbally correct her fellow clients. She focuses on those clients who receive more support from the support workers. On Sunday evening Lisa will choose what she wants to eat next week. When there is a thunderstorm Lisa, who is afraid of thunderstorms, will actively look for someone to talk to about her inability to sleep. Lisa usually shows her emotions easily and clearly, but sometimes via a detour. You can see how Lisa feels from the expression on her face. When she is in pain or sad, she cries. She can burst into tears all of a sudden, but most of the time this emotion quickly fades away. When experiencing pleasure or joy, she laughs loudly. When Lisa is really worried about something, she paces and talks to herself. When a caregiver wants to talk to her, she is not very accessible, and it is necessary to be insistent. Because this has happened regularly lately and because Lisa really did not know what to do with her feelings, she has been advised to write down what she is struggling with in a notebook or make a drawing about it. However, this proved to be too difficult and needed to be simplified. As an alternative the caregivers provided stickers that she could put in her notebook. She can also do this in between activities; she seems to find it soothing. Every now and then she shows her notebook to caregivers, as a means of communicating about her difficulties. However, it is difficult to talk with her about what has happened. She can only focus her attention on something for a short time. Lisa asks for affection by giving a hug or asking for a kiss. Physical care seems to be a way of seeking closeness. She likes her blood pressure to be measured, her hair washed, a wound taken care of and so on. It seems she is aware that physical complaints ensure that people will pay attention to her. Lisa likes to receive compliments. Lisa is a very caring person. She is helpful and enjoys being close to others. A while ago Lisa had rabbits to take care of, but she sometimes cuddled them so forcefully that she almost suffocated them.

Lisa occasionally falls in love with a male caregiver. She then will actively look for him, ask when he is coming into work and not stop talking about him. In these periods she can find it difficult to accept support from anyone other than the person she has a crush on. Lisa's contact with support workers is usually positive. She is helpful, uses humour and laughs a lot. When she needs support, it is not always easy to offer it in an appropriate way because the root cause of the problem she is facing is not always clear. Sometimes it seems as if she is stuck in a certain train of thought. At these moments she is not open to reasoning. This stubbornness is difficult to overcome. Sometimes Lisa can claim her 'personal' caregiver and does not want the caregiver to interact with the other clients. Working with this behaviour can be difficult. If an activity gets cancelled, she can be very negative towards the person who gave her this message. Lisa really enjoys a chat with the caregivers. She asks questions about their private lives and will often return to these topics on her own initiative. When new support workers start work, Lisa first observes them for a while. Only when she is used to them will she initiate contact, and after a while she will allow physical contact. Lisa makes the beds of some fellow clients every morning. She does this very quickly, but not very carefully. She initiates this task herself and verbalises the success of the accomplished task to the person whose bed it is. After her afternoon nap, she collects the leftover food from the other groups and, together with a support worker, feeds it to the chickens. She also collects the eggs, and afterwards she washes out the buckets. In the group community Lisa sets the table, makes the coffee, occasionally sweeps and helps to clear the tables. Lisa waters the plants in the group. Sometimes she does not want to understand that no more watering is necessary and that the plants are in danger of drowning. At those moments it is necessary to clarify what is expected, but even then it is necessary to keep an eye on her; as mentioned above, when she has something in mind, she tends to push on. Lisa also likes to draw and paint. In the evening she watches TV and likes to sit with people. This is why it would be nice for her to have a table in the living room of the group home as a craft corner. She has a limited ability to deal with work and has difficulty concentrating. However, when she is driven to do something, she can succeed at it. She seems to have the most difficulty concentrating in conversations. Sometimes it seems as though she is afraid of what will be discussed. If she is asked to sit down at that specific moment, she will sit down, although not for long. When she has a problem, she will communicate this clearly. With guidance she is able to look for a solution. Lisa has a positive self-image, and it does not seem as if she is aware of, or disturbed by, her intellectual disability.

6.2 Assessment with the SED-R²

The SED-R² assessment was conducted in collaboration with the whole team. During the assessment there were several discussions about the way Lisa seeks to be close to her supporters. This showed that Lisa is primarily and almost exclusively focused on her caregivers, and much less on her co-residents. It is clear that great tension builds up during changes and transitional moments, despite a fairly stable living climate. Because of this, in domain 4 (dealing with changing environment – object permanence), stage two was chosen instead of stage three, even though elements of the individualisation stage can certainly be recognised. There was also a discussion about the 'no' one sometimes gets from her when a new caregiver comes on the scene. Gradually it became clear that the motivation behind the 'no' is predominantly based on a need for security and support and is less based on a need for autonomy. Further, in many other ways it is clear that Lisa wants to create an environment that is as safe and reliable as possible (preferably known caregivers, fixed habits and rituals, stubbornness, fear of losing). Because she has been living in the same place for years – even though there have been changes in personnel – her life has increased in stability in comparison to the past. Currently, when she experiences strong emotions, her behaviour can also be adjusted fairly quickly. However, incidents involving self-mutilation and aggression did occur in periods of intense tension and stress, and these periods were often accompanied by feelings of uncertainty and involved changes in daily routine. Table 13.6 presents Lisa's emotional development profile.

Table 13.6 Lisa's emotional development profile

		Stage 1	Stage 2	Stage 3	Stage 4	Stage 5
1.	Dealing with own body				X	
2.	Dealing with emotionally important others		X			
3.	Self-image in interaction with the environment		X			
4.	Dealing with changing environment – object permanence		X			
5.	Anxieties		X			
6.	Dealing with peers			X		
7.	Dealing with materials			X		
8.	Communication		X			
9.	Emotion differentiation			X		
10.	Aggression regulation		X			
11.	Day activity – play development			X		
12.	Moral development			X		
13.	Emotion regulation		X			
Conclusion: we do not see any emotional development higher than stage two. When 'reading' the profile, it becomes clear that many domains were also scored at stage three. Lisa seems to score at stage three in domains with a more cognitive angle. This has to be taken into account when developing the support style.						

6.3 Translation to support

Lisa exhibits a harmonic profile, with many domains at the second and third stages and one peak in stage four. In converting her basic emotional needs into support needs – and thus into very concrete advice for how to support Lisa – stages two and three are most important. The reflection questions serve as an approach to getting started with the team.

A difficult theme in Lisa's support is distance and proximity. In the profile the domains that have a higher score on this (e.g. dealing with emotionally important others) are more likely to be classified as stage two. That is why we start with the reflective questions for stage two for that theme. The following are some of the questions that were discussed:

- How does the caregiver bridge gaps of time or space when it is not possible to be close to the client immediately? Can one give examples where and when a reliable other connects with the client in situations where physical proximity is not possible, but still helps the client in a positive way? (eg. words, objects – like transitional objects, referring to another time and place where one can meet).
- Do caregivers have a relationship of trust with this client? How is this acquired? What are pointers for new caregivers in gaining the trust of this client?
- Is it clear to the client who to turn to if an individual caregiver is not present? Is a 'replacement' caregiver appointed? How does the client notice that the individual support workers and the replacing support workers are transferring care responsibilities to each other?
- How can one be helpful to this client? What can be done to be meaningful/ reliable for this client?
- How can one prevent the client from 'splitting' the team (splitting up the team into 'good' and 'bad' caregivers)?
- Are there moments during the day when the support worker can really be there for the client, without interference from outside (e.g. telephone, questions from other clients)? If not, is it possible to create these moments?

This ensured a good discussion among the team in which differences between the team members were confronted. The advice formulated by the team is as follows:

- It is clear that Lisa is often still very uncertain about the reliable proximity of her caregivers (a proximity that she needs in any case). The support workers should try to put more effort into this by:
  - inserting a fixed moment of care in her agenda (which will also have a preventive function), without Lisa having to 'ask' for this through physical complaints
  - having fewer 'real' conversations with her, but more 'refuelling moments' in between, by doing something with her that makes her feel safe and reassured instead of having face-to-face conversations. (Occasionally we make the link to stage three: doing something together might also mean doing it in a discreet way, without her feeling patronised.)

- Occasionally Lisa seems to prefer one caregiver to the other. How can we – almost literally – continue to pass on the thread (see also Gerrit Vignero in chapter 19) to each other, in the sense that a 'disconnection' from one caregiver goes hand in hand with a 'connection' to the other one?

7 Conclusion

When it comes to assessing emotional development, we continue to advocate in favour of a dualistic approach. On the one hand, scaling will always remain an intersubjective act of discussion, expectations, dynamics and fluctuating functioning ('assessing'). On the other hand, it is our duty to further scientificise and optimise existing instruments and methodologies in terms of psychometric robustness ('scaling'). Depending on the objective of the assessment of emotional development (in order to tune one's own support style and that of the team, or to carry out more categorial diagnostics or scientific research), we should vary which instruments are used and how they are used.

In addition, a number of exciting challenges concerning this theme remain. We previously mentioned the toll of fame: another consequence of success seems to be that the emotional level of development gets used as a standalone, comprehensive framework. In addition to the further implementation of this model in daily practice, it seems important to us that this theme simultaneously remains well connected to other valuable themes, frameworks, practices and methodologies.

References

Belie, E De, & Hove, G Van (Eds) (2013) *Wederzijdse emotionele beschikbaarheid Mensen met een verstandelijke beperking, hun context en begeleiders samen op weg*. Antwerpen: Garant.

Claes, L, Declercq, K, Neve, L De, Jonckheere B, Marrecau J, Morisse, F … Vangansbeke, T (Eds) (2012) *Emotionele ontwikkeling bij mensen met een verstandelijke beperking*. Antwerpen/Apeldoorn: Garant.

Claes, L & Verduyn, A (Eds) (2012) *SEO-R Schaal voor Emotionele ontwikkeling bij mensen met een verstandelijke beperking – Revised*. Antwerpen/Apeldoorn: Garant.

Došen, A (1990) *Psychische en gedragsstoornissen bij zwakzinnigen Een ontwikkelingsdynamische benadering*. Amsterdam: Boom.

Došen, A (2007) Psychische stoornissen, gedragsproblemen en verstandelijke handicap Een integratieve benadering bij kinderen en volwassenen. *Tijdschrift voor Psychiatrie* **49** (7) 456–457.

Došen, A (2014) *Psychische stoornissen, probleemgedrag en verstandelijke beperking: Een integratieve benadering bij kinderen en volwassenen* (5th edition). Assen: Van Gorcum.

La Malfa, G, Lassi, S, Bertelli, M, Albertini, G, & Došen, A (2009) Emotional development and adaptive abilities in adults with intellectual disability: A correlation study between the Scheme of Appraisal of Emotional Development (SAED) and Vineland Adaptive Behaviour Scale (VABS). *Research in Developmental Disabilities* **30** (6) 1406–1412.

Morisse, F & Došen, A (Eds) (2017) *SEO-R² Schaal voor Emotionele Ontwikkeling bij mensen met een verstandelijke beperking – Revised²*. Antwerpen/Apeldoorn: Garant.

Morisse, F, Vandevelde, S, Claes, C, De Ruysscher, C, Poppe, L, Verleysen, G, Embregts, P, Hendriks, L, Vonk, J, Dijkxhoorn, Y, Sappok, T & Došen, A (submitted) Emotional development and adaptive behaviour of persons with intellectual disabilities: A correlational study.

De Neve, L (Eds) (2015) *De juiste vraag?* SEO-brochure SENvzw, Antwerpen.

Niehoff, I (2018) *Een onderzoek naar de Schaal Emotionele Ontwikkeling – verkort ' Kan de SEO-V ingezet worden ter vervanging van de SEO-R2 om het emotionele ontwikkelingsniveau van mensen met een verstandelijke beperking te beoordelen binnen de Twentse Zorgcentra?'.* Saxion Hogeschool Deventer.

Nijman, H, Didden, R & Hesper, B (2017) *Handreiking Risicomanagement LVB.* Kwaliteit Forensische Zorg.

Riské, L (2014) De validiteit van de Schaal voor Emotionele Ontwikkeling bij mensen met een

verstandelijke beperking – Revised (SEO-R) Onderzoek naar de soortgenootvaliditeit en de gelijktijdige criteriumvaliditeit van de SEO-R (master's thesis). Universiteit Gent.

Sappok, T, Zepperitz, S, Barrett, B, Vonk, J, Schanze, C, Ilic, M, Bergmann, T, De Neve L, Birkner, J, Zaal, S, Bertelli, M, Hudson, M, Morisse, F, Sterkenburg, P (2020) Standardizing the assessment of emotional development in adults with intellectual and developmental disability. *Journal of Applied Research in Intellectual Disabilities* **33** (3) 542–551.

Sappok, T, Budczies, J, Bölte, S, Dziobek, I, Došen, A, & Diefenbacher, A (2013) Emotional development in adults with autism and intellectual disabilities: A retrospective, clinical analysis. *PLoS ONE* **8** (9) e74036.

Sappok, T, Barrett, B, Vandevelde, S, Heinrich, M, Poppe, L, Sterkenburg, P, Vonk, J, Kolb, J, Claes, C, Došen, A & Morisse, F (2016) Scale of emotional development – short. *Research in Developmental Disabilities* **59** 166–175.

Sterkenburg, PS, Kempelmann, G E M, Hentrich, J, Vonk, J, Zaal S, Erlewein, R, Hudson, M (2021) Scale of emotional development – short: Reliability and validity in two samples of children with an intellectual disability. *Research in Developmental Disabilities* **108** doi.org/101016/jridd2020103821.

Vandeputte, E (2018) *Onderzoek naar psychometrische kenmerken en bruikbaarheid van de Schaal voor Emotionele Ontwikkeling-Verkort (SEO-V).* Universiteit Gent.

Vandevelde, S, Morisse, F, Došen, A, Poppe, L, Jonckheere, B, Van Hove, G, Maes, B, van Loon, J & Claes, C (2016). The Scale for Emotional Development-Revised (SED-R) for persons with intellectual disabilities and mental health problems: Development, description, and reliability. I*nternational Journal of Developmental Disabilities* **62** (1) 11–23.

Vignero, G (2011) *De draad tussen cliënt en begeleider.* Antwerpen/Apeldoorn: Garant.

Vignero, G (2015) *De draad tussen ouder en kind Voor een gewone en buitengewone opvoeding.* Antwerpen/Apeldoorn: Garant.

Chapter 14
The SED-R^2 colour profile

Rachel de Groot

Summary
The SED-R^2 colour profile is an interactive tool based on the Scale of Emotional Development – Revised^2 (SED-R^2) for people with intellectual disabilities. The tool uses colours to support the process of estimating developmental levels. The working method is useful for groups. It promotes team discussions, care conferences, multidisciplinary consultations and so on. This chapter explains the practical use of the colour profile. By means of a case example, pitfalls in interpretation will be discussed.

1 Introduction
The development of the colour profile can be derived from an inspiring but often frustrating quest, which many colleagues will recognise. After estimating the emotional development level with the Scale of Emotional Development (SED), it often proves to be difficult for the environment to adapt to the basic emotional needs of the client. When they have not been involved in the estimation process, people find it difficult to grasp these emotional needs and what is necessary to meet these needs. Involving them in this process by using a colour profile leads to more knowledge of emotional development overall and of the needs of their client specifically.

The colour profile has been adjusted to the different versions of the SED over the years, from the Scheme for Appraisal of Emotional Development (Došen, 1990) to the current SED-R^2 (Morisse & Došen, 2016).

The colour profile makes it possible to involve the entire environment of the person whose emotional development is being explored in the process of discovering the basic emotional needs. Preferably, everyone in the daily life of a person with an intellectual disability participates in the estimation: parents, support staff in housing and work, therapists and so on. Experience in recent years has shown that participating in the estimation process helps people to understand the basic emotional needs and to recognise the function of the behaviour the client exhibits: to see the 'question behind the question'. This understanding is crucial for bringing about the (often needed) behavioural change within the environment, and so for meeting the emotional needs of the client.

2 Description and procedure of the SED-R² colour profile

2.1 Description

The SED-R² colour profile consists of a suitcase with a manual, images of the developmental phases, 13 domain cards and 13 trays containing the item cards for each domain. The different phases of Došen's developmental dynamic model are given their own colours in this method. The colour serves to visualise the phases in each domain. The colours are arbitrary and have no specific significance.

Table 14.1 Phases of the developmental dynamic model with associated colours

Phase	Type of support question	Colour
1 Adaptation	Homeostasis versus dysregulation	Pink
2 First socialisation	Trust versus mistrust	Green
3 First individuation	Autonomy versus dependence	Blue
4 Identification	Initiative versus inhibition	Purple
5 Reality awareness	Self-confidence versus inferiority	Yellow

Within the SED-R^2 (Morisse & Došen, 2016), a structure is applied to each domain such that the central theme of the development is first identified for each phase. Then the items that describe the development are listed, and finally examples are given of behaviour that is characteristic of the determined phase. Box 14.1 presents an example of the design (Morisse & Došen, 2016, p. 55).

Example of the construction of a phase

SED-R^2 domain 1: dealing with own body — Phase one: 0–6 months

CENTRAL THEME: Discovering own body and processing stimuli

DEVELOPMENT

a. He is constantly confronted with all kinds of *stimuli and sensations* from his own body (e.g. hunger, thirst, fatigue, pain, etc.) and from the environment. The main task is to receive these stimuli through the senses, to recognise, to select and to respond.
b. In the beginning, he is still sensitive to sensory stimuli. These can easily flood and *overstimulate* him. He then gets excited or anxious. Gradually he can find rest by directing the senses to the world. In this way, he learns to deal with discomfort and pleasure. He records observations, processes them into experiences and learns to give meaning to stimuli, items and persons.
c. ...

EXAMPLES

a. He *passively enjoys* sensory stimuli, care, skin contact.
b. The degree of physical reaction varies from underreacting (= passive) to overreacting.
c. An *insatiable* physical *urge* can occur for food or drink, for mirror image, for sexual pleasure, etc.
d. Short, momentary *physical outbursts* can occur, or the movement of the body is sometimes stereotyped: tics, fluttering, shouting, banging, rocking.
e. …

The colour profile uses the same domains, central themes and development items as the SED-R². However, to limit the number of item cards, specific examples are not used in the colour profile. There are larger cards for the domains, with compartments in which item cards can be placed. There are item cards for each domain consisting of core cards (in bold) and cards with the developmental items. All item cards are coded in the colour of the phase to which the item belongs. All parts of the colour profile, together with the manual, are stored in a box so that it is easy to carry.

2.2 Procedure

The colour profile is suitable for various purposes. It can be used to transfer knowledge about emotional development or to discuss subthemes of emotional development. However, it is often used to assess people with intellectual disabilities. Ideally, such assessments should involve as many people who are involved in the care and support of the person being examined as possible.

The participants, divided into small groups, produce an estimation of the level of emotional development by using the item cards. The chosen item cards, those which are most appropriate to the person, are placed on domain cards. These domain cards can be collected in a central part of the room. When all domain cards are assessed, the behavioural expert[14] invites the subgroups to show and tell which items have been chosen for each domain and why. This requires a lot of flexible knowledge of emotional development on the part of the behavioural expert, who supports the group with supportive questions that are central to the various phases. Together with the group, the behavioural expert produces the final assessment for each domain, using for each domain the colour of the phase or phases that are most apparent.
The result of the estimation is a colour profile across 13 domains. At a glance it can be seen which domains have matching colours (phases) and which domains differ in that respect (i.e. are graded higher or lower).

14 In the Netherlands, 'behavioural expert' is usually used as a general description for a psychologist or remedial educationalist.

The behavioural expert invites participants to look at the profile together and also stimulates them to reflect on and explain what the profile means. Which basic emotional needs are presented? This conversation will form the basis for a follow-up discussion to discover how the environment can best adjust to the basic emotional needs of the person.

3 Using the colour profile

It is recommended to use the colour profile in combination with the SED-R^2. The colour profile has not been developed for diagnostic use and has not been tested for reliability and validity.

The concrete material of the colour profile is often experienced as pleasant. By literally holding the cards, putting them side by side and shuffling them, the grading becomes an active working method or procedure. The items are weighed against each other, and the use of cards stimulates the conversation. Why does a particular item suit a particular person? These are precisely the sorts of considerations that are important in order to raise awareness of emotional functioning.

The colours of the different stages of development help us to analyse and interpret the final emotional development profile. At a glance it becomes clear which developmental phase is most apparent for each domain. By looking at the profile together, the interpretation can also be arrived at together. This could be a great basis for further reflection: what does this profile mean for us as supporters? Where do we already connect? What can be improved and how? And what do we need to do?

During the meetings participants usually have a lot of fun. They often ask: 'when are we going to do this for the other clients?' The procedure invites people to behave in a different way, using emotional development as a guideline. It provides insight into the perception of the client and their own functioning and actions. In practice, the colours also appear to act as an 'anchor' for the information that is generated during the estimation process. The visualisation keeps the profile in the forefront of people's minds. At a later time, it is easy to refer to the colours to refresh the information.

4 The role of the moderator

The role of the test co-ordinator, usually a behavioural expert, is crucial in using the colour profile to achieve the most appropriate assessment. Usually a lot of people are involved when using the colour profile. This is a great strength of the procedure; a shared image arises, which serves as a shared starting point for optimising the care of people with intellectual disabilities.

At the same time, working with groups can create pitfalls for the estimation process. Added to the substantive role of the behavioural expert are tasks such as dividing groups into subgroups, assigning different tasks to the subgroups, monitoring time and addressing different views of the domain. Being able to manage the group and achieve the best possible estimation at the same time demands a lot of the behavioural scientist. The knowledge of emotional development should be internalised so well that it can be deployed quickly and flexibly in order to support the groups. When this is not the case, the outcome of the colour profile becomes less specific and reliable.

The phase in which the subgroups tell each other how they view a domain is crucial. At that time, a great deal of knowledge and expertise is required of the behavioural expert. Different views will emerge, and the behavioural scientist will have to help the group return to the central points over and over again: which behaviour do you see? In which situation? Which basic needs are at the core of that behaviour? What kind of request for help is appropriate to this level? It is the responsibility of the behavioural expert to continue asking questions until the developmental dynamics have been clarified.

Example of detecting misinterpretation of item cards

Test administration of Anne's colour profile: domain 3, self-image in interaction with the environment.

The subgroup has chosen the following cards:

- uses the word 'I'
- says 'no', originating from the will to decide for themselves
- becomes more aware of who they are, have their own will and think in a 'self-centred' way.

All these cards derive from phase three: autonomy versus dependence.

It is explained that Anne is often very stubborn, angry and rebellious. She cannot relate to the other and wants to see her own needs met quickly.

When asked further questions, it turns out that Anne is especially stubborn when support staff leave her. She uses all kinds of behaviour (positive and negative) to prevent them from leaving her room: from offering another cup of coffee to literally hanging on their legs. Her stubbornness and rebelliousness do not arise from the needs of phase three, the need for autonomy and to determine her own will. The motivation for her behaviour stems from separation anxiety, from the need to experience safety. These are needs placed in phase two: trust versus mistrust.

This conversation eventually leads to an adjustment of the original classification. The item cards of phase three (blue) are removed and cards of phase two (green) are inserted in the domain cards, so the colour of phase two becomes visible within the profile.

Tips for those leading the classification process using the colour profile

Make sure you have in-depth knowledge of the different development phases.

- Take into account the pitfalls that may exist in the interpretation.
- Make a clear timetable and stick to it.
- Reserve enough time for the plenary part of the meeting, when the classification, under your guidance, actually becomes final.
- Keep the original SED-R² nearby for inspiration (to ask questions) and for making notes.
- Make notes for each domain. Recording the conversation can help. Do not forget to ask the group's permission.

An emotional development level is not something static. It is a flexible, dynamic continuum that fluctuates throughout the day. It would therefore be misguided to strive for an outcome in the classification in which all domains are scored at the same development phase and adapt the guidance style accordingly. Often, needs from multiple stages of development intermingle, depending on the context in which the client is situated. With stressors, the client usually falls back on one or two preceding developmental phases (stress activates the emotional systems). This is seen as the basis of the ability to cope. During the classification, it is therefore important to be clear about whether what is at issue is a stressful moment or a stress-free moment.

The environment in which the client functions can mask the basic emotional developmental level. When the client is in an environment that matches their basic emotional needs, they will experience more relaxation and higher levels of well-being, and they will be able to exhibit behaviour appropriate to a higher developmental phase. If stress factors are not taken into account during the estimation and one only looks at the behaviour that occurs most often, the client may be classified too highly.

The story of Jarno illustrates this.

5 Jarno

Jarno is 23 years old and has a mild intellectual disability. He has lived in a facility for people with challenging and risky behaviour for a number of years. He has a problematic life history marked by mistreatment and abuse. He has shown a lot of dangerous behaviour in the years that he has stayed in residential care. His strong physical aggression has created a lot of trouble in this environment. He has received various treatments over the years, unfortunately without result. More and more freedom-restricting measures were deployed to keep him and his environment (people included) safe. The door of his room was often locked, and when he left his room he was guided by an attendant.

When there is no stress, Jarno is a cheerful, happy young man who loves playing his guitar. He idolises a certain pop group and does everything he can to look like them. His hair is cut the same way, nails painted the same colour and so on. Jarno shows a lot of creativity: he makes bags from old jeans and initiates his own activities during daycare. He can discuss the news and ask adequate questions in relation to it.

Jarno attaches great importance to his personal supervisor, who organises everything for him. He often asks when he will be on duty again; only then they will decide which groceries will be bought and Jarno will receive his pocket money. Sometimes he demands or claims his supervisor completely for himself and can hardly bear it when someone else is getting his attention. Jarno then gets unruly and becomes disinhibited.

Jarno talks with everyone, both supervisors and fellow residents. He shows an interest in others by asking questions but is often unable to wait for the answer when more than two people are present. He then hops from one heel to the other and his tension increases.

Jarno has a signalling plan that describes what behaviour he exhibits when his tension is increasing and what he can do to reduce the tension: listening to music, smoking a cigarette and having a hot shower help him to relax. The plan also describes what the supervisors can do to help Jarno unwind. Once a week, Jarno has a meeting with the psychologist; she discusses difficult situations with him by using a scheme of five central behaviour items (event, thought, feeling, behaviour and effect). Jarno can easily name and fill in the forms.

At night, Jarno finds support in the stuffed animals on his bed; he cannot sleep without them. He is afraid of loud noises and people who are angry with him or shout loudly. This makes him feel restless and get angry more quickly. Jarno has a clear idea of the future: he would like to have a rocking chair and a cat and to live somewhere quiet. He would also like to have a boyfriend.

5.1 Working with the colour profile for Jarno

The colour profile session was attended by the team that supports Jarno in everyday life, both at home and at work. His social worker was also present. The treatment/support team had been struggling for some time with the perspective of Jarno's future. Every attempt at stimulating growth seemed to overload his capabilities.

The colour profile initially contained a lot of purple cards, matching the dynamic of initiative versus inhibition (phase four). His identification behaviour was mentioned in particular, and Jarno was seen as a happy and creative man. However, further enquiries revealed that Jarno's support staff had rated him based on the behaviour that had occurred most often in the past six months within the support situation, in which stimuli were offered in a dosed manner and Jarno's environment was made very small. Because of that situation, Jarno's life contained relatively few stressful moments. A lot of discussion was triggered when it was asked how Jarno would behave under stressful conditions. For Jarno, stress occurred when he received too many stimuli without a supervisor nearby. At these moments, Jarno was not able to carry out his creative activities and the identification behaviour completely disappeared. He became stubborn and was frequently verbally and physically aggressive, which requires intervention to ensure the safety of Jarno and others. His stubbornness and aggressive behaviour did not arise through him imposing his own will but through overstimulation and dysregulation.

During the discussion, it emerged that Jarno's basic emotional needs derived from the first phase, which is marked by the dynamic of homeostasis and dysregulation. The environment had been designed in such a way that few moments of dysregulation occurred. In the discussion, it became clear that during the years that Jarno had stayed in this institution, numerous attempts had been made to give him more freedom and to allow him to participate in the group process. Each time, however, this led to more agitation and aggression, after which it was decided to dose the stimuli again. Within a context adapted to the basic needs of the first phase – the need for perceived safety, stimuli that can be handled and 'peace, cleanliness and regularity' – Jarno was able to grow on a cognitive level, but also on an emotional level. Within that context, behaviour emerged that matched the identification phase (phase four, purple). The weekly meetings with the psychologist turned out to have the function of allowing Jarno to experience positive and safe contact: 'Exclusive attention, a nice cup of coffee, I like that.' Although he was able to answer questions about his behaviour, it was the contact that regulated him, not his new cognitive insights.

But how should this fact be dealt with? Both stages of development are important in Jarno's life. His personal strength and capacity was mainly in phase one, the adaptation phase. But when the needs that characterise this phase are met, Jarno appears to have needs at the identification level.

It was decided that a double profile would be created for Jarno: Jarno's basic request for support lies in experiencing homeostasis, phase one – pink, in the colour profile. When these needs are sufficiently met, there is room for needs from phase four, the identification phase (purple), for example the need to be able and allowed to take the initiative and make use of his creativity.

5.2 Pitfalls in interpretation

There are several problems that may arise in interpreting Jarno's case:

- The environment had already been partially adapted to Jarno's basic emotional needs (phase one) because of the need to ensure the physical safety of him and the people around him. Because he experienced few stress moments in his daily functioning, these basic emotional needs no longer seemed to play a role. However, in times of stress (when those needs are not met), he dysregulates, which reveals his actual needs. So, when using the colour profile, it is important to look at how he functions under stress, because these are the moments our emotional systems are most activated and emotional needs need to be met.
- Jarno's cognitive capabilities mask his emotional level of development. He can participate relatively well in conversations, which leads to high expectations from those in his environment. 'When he is able to talk about it, he must be able to act like [it].' When disrupted, it is quickly thought that Jarno 'acts out on purpose': 'he knows what the rules are, right?!' Yes, Jarno knows very well about the rules, but this knowledge is not what guides his behaviour. He remains dependent on a well-designed environment and guidance to prevent a build-up of tension. Over the years, Jarno has received many treatments. He knows all the techniques on a cognitive level. He can name the five items of the behaviour scheme flawlessly. However, he cannot convert them into behaviour. The therapy sessions have the function of providing safe and predictable contact with another person.
- Jarno's skills mask his emotional level of development. Jarno has many practical and creative skills. When he is relaxed, he can apply them perfectly. This also leads people to expect too much from him: if he can keep his room in order, should he not be able to perform his household duties within the group? Yes and no. Yes, he can perform these duties, but only if there are few other people in the group and the supervisor is with him to regulate his tension.

6 From estimation to support

Once the basic emotional needs have been mapped out, matching and subsequent support can be put in place. In recent years, on the basis of VINO (Van Inzicht Naar Ondersteuning) (Claes *et al.*, 2012), various working methods and lists have been developed to formulate guidance styles based on the dominant developmental phase. It is wonderful that these resources are available, but they also have a downside. They provide general advice and guidelines. It cannot be stressed enough that each person's emotional needs are met in particular ways. Guidelines must always be tailor-made for every person.

After using the colour profile to produce the estimate, it remains important to incorporate the information and specific needs in the holistic and overall developmental profile when formulating the style of guidance. How can these needs be met by this client, with this overall developmental profile? This in turn requires knowledge and flexibility on the part of the behavioural expert, who must suggest ways of supporting the environment surrounding the person in the search for an appropriate style and environment. Gerrit Vignero's metaphors, described in his book *De draad tussen ouder en kind (The Wire between Parent and Child)* (2015), can be helpful in this. In addition, the reflection questions that are included in the book *Emotionele ontwikkeling bij mensen met een verstandelijke beperking* (*Emotional Development in People with Intellectual Disabilities* (Claes *et al.*, 2012) are a nice way of helping teams evaluate the existing guidance and environment structure in relation to emotional needs.

6.1 The use of images

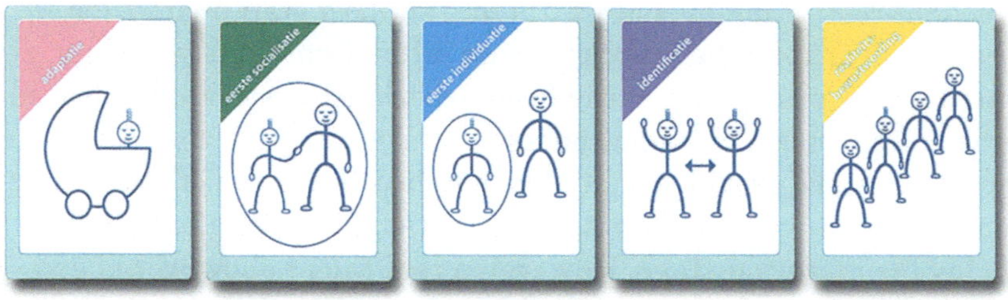

The colour profile suitcase contains images that represent the different developmental phases. They can be used to initiate the conversation about emotional needs. The images refer to normal early childhood development and can be used as a prompt to reflect on the needs of each developmental phase.

The images can sometimes provoke outrage: 'Thomas is 38t; you cannot think of him as a baby!' And this is true. The basic emotional needs might be comparable, but the person is physically mature and often has more life experience. The necessity of meeting the basic needs takes on a different form and content. In thinking about emotional development, it may be helpful to fall back on childhood stages, but it is necessary to adapt to the specific person.

For example, in phase one, a baby who is constantly restless and upset can be reassured by taking them firmly on your lap or swaddling them. In an adult, we must look for a tool that gives that same reassurance, perhaps something that exerts the pressure of sitting on someone's lap or being swaddled, but is more suited to the calendar age – an extra heavy blanket in bed, for example.

6.2 Back to Jarno: from estimation to support

Jarno's basic needs were located in phase one. He needs a tailored environment to experience balance (homeostasis) and not be overrun by the stimuli around him. Before the estimation this was achieved (by trial and error) by keeping the world small for Jarno. Many freedom-restricting measures were used to keep his world uncomplicated: his room became, as it were, his playpen. However, these measures meant that his future prospects were very limited. To improve his quality of life, it was therefore important for the team to look for other ways to ensure that Jarno's basic safety needs were met and to allow him to experience homeostasis.

The treatment team realised that it was particularly important to look for a way to enrich his living environment, without putting too much pressure on the basic needs deriving from the first phase. By focusing on basic needs, efforts could gradually be made to make adjustments to the environment that would reduce the need for the freedom-restricting measures. Having support staff nearby, for example, meant that his door could be unlocked more often. Consciously dealing with stimuli and proactively preventing Jarno from experiencing stressors ensured that he could handle a little more. Within a context that continued to connect to phase one, more activities were provided that also matched the needs of phase four. For example, Jarno thought it would be fantastic to participate in a talent show in which he could play his guitar on stage. However, a real talent show would give him too many stimuli and lead to fear, resulting in derangement. Jarno eventually gave a performance for a two-person audience, which he enjoyed a lot. Eventually, freedom-limiting measures were no longer needed, and Jarno moved to a regular care facility, where they continue to meet his phase-one emotional needs while enjoying his phase-four creativity.

7 Finally

Over the past decade, developments around Anton Došen's developmental dynamic framework have accelerated, thanks in particular to the efforts of our Flemish colleagues, who have embraced and further developed this framework within the 'Steunpunt Expertise Netwerk Schaal voor Emorionele Ontwikkeling' (SEN-SEO) project. In the care for people with intellectual disabilities, the framework is crucial. However, the developmental dynamic framework appears to be universal and applicable to a wider target group. It is to be hoped that more people, for example in psychiatry or the forensic field, will benefit from new developments in the coming years. At this time, the emotional development level is mainly assessed by questioning people who support the person. How wonderful it would be if there were a method for exploring emotional needs with clients themselves! That is a nice future challenge.

References

Claes, L, Declercq, K, Neve, L De, Jonckheere B, Marrecau J, Morisse, F ... Vangansbeke, T (Eds) (2012) *Emotionele ontwikkeling bij mensen met een verstandelijke beperking*. Antwerpen/Apeldoorn: Garant.

Došen, A (1990) *Psychische en gedragsstoornissen bij zwakzinnigen Een ontwikkelingsdynamische benadering*. Amsterdam: Boom.

Došen, A (2014) *Psychische stoornissen, probleemgedrag en verstandelijke beperking*. Assen: Van Gorcum.

Groot, R de (2011) *SEO-R kleurenprofiel – Revised Handleiding*. Doetinchem: Graviant.

Morisse, F, & Došen, A (Eds) (2016) *SEO-R² Schaal voor Emotionele Ontwikkeling bij mensen met een verstandelijke beperking – Revised²*. Antwerpen/Apeldoorn: Garant.

Vignero, G (2015) *De draad tussen ouder en kind Voor een gewone en buitengewone opvoeding*. Antwerpen/Apeldoorn: Garant.

Chapter 15
What works? Cross-fertilisation between forensic psychiatry and care for people with mild intellectual disabilities

Bren Hesper, Rachel de Groot, Robert Didden and Henk Nijman

Summary

Treatment of people with a mild intellectual disability (MID) and high-risk (criminal offending) behaviour often falls short because their emotional development is not sufficiently taken into account. In this chapter, we reason that a treatment will be more effective if it is focused not only on risk factors but also on the emotional needs of people with MID. This can be achieved by integrating knowledge in a cross-fertilisation between the fields of forensic psychiatry and care for people with intellectual disabilities. This will lead not only to a reduction in high-risk behaviour and recidivism but also to a better quality of life for people with MID. In this chapter we illustrate this integrative approach by means of a case study.

1 Introduction

People with MID or borderline intellectual functioning (intelligence quotient (IQ) 50–85) relatively often engage in some kind of high-risk behaviour or criminal offending, such as aggression, addiction and problematic sexual behaviour. They are over-represented in forensic care and prisons (Kaal *et al.*, 2015; van Esch *et al.*, 2020) and mental health care (Nieuwenhuis *et al.*, 2017; Seelen *et al.*, 2019). It is estimated that between 10% and 40% of people in the criminal justice system in the Netherlands have MID (Kaal, 2014). The reason for this over-representation is that people with MID have more risk factors for criminal behaviour and mental disorders than people with average intellectual functioning. In addition, low IQ is a risk factor of criminal behaviour in itself (Kaal, 2014).

Forensic psychiatry treatment aims to reduce the risk of recidivism. A reduction in recidivism can be achieved by following the 'what works' treatment principles: risk, need and responsivity. In the context of this chapter, the principle of responsivity is of crucial importance. Responsivity means that treatment should be tailored to the needs and learning style of the patients, in our case people with MID. The specific needs of patients with MID make forensic treatment complicated. Best practice in both forensic care and care for people with intellectual disabilities have to be combined, and care providers should be able to integrate different perspectives and different (legal) frameworks.

Patients with MID form a heterogeneous and complex patient group that requires specific treatment and care. Despite the increased attention paid to people with MID, all too often forensic care is still inadequate because the MID is simply not recognised. Even if the MID is identified, there is a lack of knowledge about treatment for intellectual disability. Counsellors in forensic psychiatry are trained to focus on high-risk behaviour and/or mental disorders and much less on the implications of MID. As a result, patients with MID often become subjected to significant demands that they cannot meet. This has a negative effect on treatment effectiveness and hence on the risk of recidivism.

On the other hand, those who care for people with intellectual disabilities often have a lack of knowledge about risk factors for high-risk (criminal) behaviour. Risk factors for criminal recidivism, such as hostility or a lack of insight into one's problem, may not be recognised as such or may be seen as a symptom or consequence of the MID. As a result, treatment and prevention of high-risk behaviour remains ineffective.

Effective treatment requires the integration of knowledge and skills from both perspectives (Didden, 2014). In our experience treatment will be more effective in reducing recidivism if the assessment of risk factors is combined with an assessment of the person's intellectual and emotional levels of development. Assessment of patients' emotional development and needs may change our interpretation of their high-risk behaviour, our thinking about how professionals should deal with high-risk behaviour and thus also our beliefs about what kind of interventions are needed to ensure effective risk management in patients with MID.

2 What works?

The treatment of offenders has received a great deal of attention in scientific research for decades. As early as 1990, Andrews, Bonta and Hoge formulated three principles for effective treatment, which have now become the most important principles in forensic psychiatry: risk, need and responsivity. These principles are also described as the 'what works' principles because a large number of studies and meta-analyses have shown that the application of these principles leads to lower recidivism rates and greater treatment effectiveness. Although it has not been specifically investigated, it is assumed that this also applies to the treatment of people with MID, as they make up a large part of the population in forensic psychiatry and therefore of the participants in this type of research. The three principles will be briefly explained here.

The risk principle states that offenders with a high risk of recidivism should receive intensive or clinical treatment, while offenders with a low risk can be given less intensive or outpatient treatment. This decision about the level of risk should be based on the results of a valid risk assessment instrument and procedure.

The need principle states that a treatment should focus on risk factors that are known to be associated with criminal or high-risk behaviour, again as assessed by a risk assessment instrument. Researchers agree that patients with MID have additional risk factors that are related to their intellectual disability and limited adaptive skills. For example, a deficiency in adaptive skills can lead to high-risk behaviour, as it did in the case of a man who lived alone and could barely read or write. This man missed out on important letters, as a result of which he got into trouble with the authorities. Because of his deficient coping skills, he relapsed into high-risk behaviour. We regularly come across cases like these. We can observe that a patient's willingness to be supported in these kinds of situations is an essential protective factor that reduces the chance that they will run into problems again.

The third principle, the responsivity principle, states that a treatment can only be effective if it considers the characteristics, needs and learning style of the patient. A number of responsivity factors are common to people with MID, as all of these patients have limitations in intellectual and adaptive functioning and emotional development. Below, we will elaborate on which responsivity factors specifically should be taken into account in the treatment and risk management of (violent) offenders with MID.

3 Responsivity factors for people with MID

With respect to intellectual functioning, we often encounter the following problems (Snell *et al.*, 2009). Patients with MID usually function at a lower language and communicational level: they understand concrete concepts but are often unable to master abstract ones. Many patients have a slower processing speed, and they experience stress when multiple questions are asked within a short time. Patients also find it difficult to combine different types of information, as a result of which they often have trouble interpreting social situations. Because of this they easily feel stressed or powerless when they get involved in a conflict or another challenging social situation. They also find it difficult to come up with strategies for solving problems. However, many patients have learned to hide their limitations because they have had to cope for years in situations where too much is asked of them. Their use of 'streetwise language', however, can make it harder to recognise the MID. Caregivers should provide patients with MID with ample time to process and answer a question before asking a new question, offer information in an orderly manner and in small pieces and only use concrete concepts and language. Otherwise, the patient will not understand and stress will increase, as a result of which the patient will no longer absorb even simple information. Staff members and therapists are often not aware of their own use of difficult words and abstract language, like sayings, proverbs and metaphors. After an important issue has been addressed, patients should be asked to repeat what has been discussed in their own words.

Because of a combination of intellectual disability and unfavourable family factors or psychological problems, patients also often function at a low level of emotional development. The way they regulate their emotions is similar to that of children. They have difficulty processing negative emotions, which is an obstacle to both successful treatment and the acceptance of support. Moreover, emotional development is related to the development of conscience, impulse control and the regulation of aggression. Because of a low level of emotional development, stress is more likely to lead to (reactive) aggression or other externalising problem behaviour. A low level of emotional development is a risk factor for overall challenging behaviour in patients with intellectual disabilities (Sappok *et al.*, 2014). Taking into account the emotional development level is therefore a prerequisite for successful treatment and recidivism risk management.

It is assumed that people with intellectual disabilities have a higher chance of developing psychopathology because of their vulnerability to deficiencies within the various dimensions of emotion regulation (McClure *et al*.e, 2009). This is in line with our experience: in a large number of patients, especially in those who also have psychological problems, we observe a disharmonious functioning profile. In those cases their intellectual functioning level does not match (i.e. is higher than) the expected emotional level. This discrepancy makes it harder to tailor the treatment to the needs of the patient. The patient is potentially able to display more skills than they can handle emotionally, just as a child might already know the way to the store but not really dare to go alone. If the child goes to the store alone, they will panic when an unexpected event occurs. In the same way, when the patient's intellectual and adaptive abilities are called on but they are not able to handle this emotionally, the treatment will lead to stress and possibly to high-risk behaviour.

Although responsivity factors are essential to effective treatment, even if responsivity factors are taken into account high-risk behaviour can still occur because of the presence of all kinds of risk factors. If counsellors do not pay attention to such risk factors, the safety of themselves, co-residents and society is at stake. Where risk factors indicate the subjects for which treatment and risk management is needed, responsivity factors indicate how that treatment should be provided to match the patient's intellectual, adaptive and emotional developmental levels. One cannot provide effective treatment without paying attention to responsivity factors, as we illustrate in the following case study.

4 Case study: Pete

Pete was convicted eight years ago of multiple assaults on women in his neighbourhood. He wandered through the city and assaulted women while under the influence of alcohol. When he was arrested, he resisted arrest and fought with the police.

Pete's treatment was based on the diagnosis 'antisocial personality disorder'. A risk assessment revealed the following risk factors: alcohol abuse, antisocial views, limited coping skills, sexual preoccupation, non-cooperation in treatment and unrealistic plans for the future. Different kinds of therapies were offered to treat these risk factors, without positive results. Pete continued to exhibit aggressive and sexually problematic behaviour. The clinic where Pete was initially treated described him as a man whose emotions and intentions were not easy to read. He was compulsive and often aggressive, and he refused therapy. The aggression was considered to stem from the antisocial personality disorder and turned out to be difficult to influence. Eventually, his MID came to light. His total IQ score was assessed to be 65, as a result of which Pete was moved to Trajectum, a forensic psychiatric centre that specialises in the treatment of offenders with MID.

After being admitted to Trajectum, Pete's background and personality were studied from an integrative perspective. The developmental history showed that Pete could not keep up at school. As an adult he worked in the factory where his father worked, and he lived in an apartment next to his parents' home. He functioned reasonably well, and at that time he did not get into trouble with the police. After his parents moved to another city, however, things quickly went downhill. Pete could not cope without the emotional support of his parents and developed a habit of consuming large quantities of alcohol and watching porn. He no longer had any control over his impulses, and he proceeded to develop assaultive and aggressive behaviour. The diagnosis of the previous clinic was found to be correct, but incomplete. Pete functioned at the level of a mild intellectual disability, and his practical adaptive skills were insufficient for him to live on his own without the support of his parents. Pete also appeared to function on a low emotional developmental level, the so-called identification level as measured by the Scheme of Appraisal of Emotional Development (Došen, 1997). His desire for autonomy often clashed with a need for emotional support to cope with everyday social challenges. As a result, Pete got upset easily, and this manifested in inflexible and offensive behaviour. The clinic where Pete was initially admitted failed to see that the aggression and antisocial coping was a result of significant contextual demands. Pete did not understand several things that he needed to understand to be able to live independently, which made him anxious and angry. This stress led to antisocial coping and sexual disinhibition. Because Pete was supported on both an intellectual level and an emotional level during his hospitalisation in Trajectum, he visibly calmed down. By giving him choices about things he understands, his need for autonomy was met and there was no more aggression. The treatment modules that focused on risk factors (problem awareness and coping skills) turned out to be too complicated for Pete, even though they were adjusted for patients with MID. However, over time Pete gained a more realistic perspective on his future, which was considered important progress in his treatment.

By looking at Pete from a different angle, a new explanation for the high-risk behaviour emerged. Pete was functioning on a low emotional development level, where he craved autonomy even though he often could not cope with too much responsibility. The risk factors (needs) turned out to be difficult to treat, and because of the severity of his behavioural problems an involuntary admission to the clinic was necessary (risk). By adapting the style of support to his emotional level (responsivity), the risks could eventually be controlled within a more open environment. By this he will be able to lead a relatively independent life. However, if the environment is not adapted to his emotional development level, the chance of high-risk or antisocial behaviour would also increase again.

5 An integrative perspective on risk management

With Pete's case we have tried to illustrate the value of an integrative perspective. Pete's case shows the importance of taking responsivity factors fully into account, in particular in offenders with MID, and the importance of diagnosing the emotional development level of forensic patients in general. Especially for patients with MID the forensic treatment should not focus solely on the risk factors (needs). This is not to say that risk management should not be based on risk factors. These risk factors are still central to risk management. But a strictly forensic view of risk management might for example focus solely on prohibiting Pete from drinking alcohol, watching porn and going to town by himself. An integrative view on risk management will add the function of behaviour: Pete needs support in daily tasks to prevent him from feeling anxious and stressed, which heightens the chance he will drink alcohol or watch porn excessively. To prevent Pete from getting (verbally) aggressive, he needs room to make decisions and have control over his life, but this can only be done within the safe boundaries of the support system of his care institution.

A large number of people in the justice system have MID, but the methods of diagnosis and treatment for patients with MID often still seem to be insufficient and therefore ineffective. As a result, we have developed guidelines for an integrative view of risk management for patients with MID that aim to create a cross-fertilisation between forensic psychiatry and the care for people with intellectual disabilities. We want to make professionals in forensic care, but also in other domains, more aware of the emotional functioning of people with MID. When the treatment of risk factors is ineffective, patients like Pete tend to be subjected to highly repressive measures to reduce and prevent high-risk behaviour. An integrative perspective (diagnosing the intellectual level, adaptive and social skills, and the emotional development level) makes it possible to apply measures that reflect the patient's need for support. As a result, fewer repressive measures may be needed.

References

Andrews, D, Bonta, J & Hoge, R (1990) Classification for effective rehabilitation: Rediscovering psychology. *Criminal Justice and Behavior* **17** 19–52.

Didden, R (2014) Forensische zorg voor mensen met een lichte verstandelijke beperking: Inleiding tot het themanummer. *Nederlands Tijdschrift voor de Zorg aan Verstandelijk Gehandicapten* **4** 283–287.

Došen, A (1997) *Psychische Störungen bei geistig behinderten Menschen*. Stuttgart: Gustav Fischer Verlag.

Esch, AYM van, Vries de, J & Masthof, EDM (2020, in press) Screening for intellectual disability in Dutch psychiatrically disturbed detainees: Assessing the psychometric properties of the Screener for

Intelligence and Learning Disability (SCIL). *Journal of Applied Research in Intellectual Disabilities* https://doiorg/101111/jar12769.

Kaal, H (2014) Licht verstandelijke beperking en crimineel gedrag: samenhang en prevalentie. In: H Kaal, N Overvest & M Boertjes (Eds) *Beperkt in de keten Mensen met een licht verstandelijke beperking in de strafrechtsketen* (pp53–63). Den Haag: Boom Lemma Uitgevers.

Kaal, H, Nijman, H & Moonen, X (2015) Identifying offenders with an intellectual disability in detention in The Netherlands. *Journal of Intellectual Disabilities and Offending Behaviour* **6** (2) 94–101.

McClure, KS, Halpern, J, Wolper, PA & Donahue, JJ (2009) Emotion regulation and intellectual disability. *Journal on Developmental Disabilities* **15** (2) 38–44.

Nieuwenhuis, JG, Noorthoorn, EO, Nijman, HLI, Naarding, P & Mulder, CL (2017) A blind spot? Screening for mild intellectual disability and borderline intellectual functioning in admitted psychiatric patients: Prevalence and associations with coercive measures. *Plos One* **12** (2) e0168847.

Sappok, T, Budczies, J, Dziobek, I, Bölte, S, Došen, A & Diefenbacher, A (2014) The missing link: Delayed emotional development predicts challenging behavior in adults with intellectual disability. *Journal of Autism and Developmental Disorders* **44** (4) 786-800.

Seelen-de Lang, BL, Smits, HJH, Penterman, BJM, Noorthoorn, EO, Nieuwenhuis, JG & Nijman, HLI (2019) Screening for intellectual disabilities and borderline intelligence in Dutch outpatients with severe mental illness. *Journal of Applied Research in Intellectual Disabilities* **32** 1096–1102.

Snell, M, Luckasson, R, Bortwick-Duffy, S, Bradley, V, Buntinx, W, Coulter, D & Yeager, M (2009) Characteristics and needs of people with intellectual disability who have higher IQs. *Intellectual and Developmental Disabilities* **47** 220–233.

Chapter 16 Emotional development and methodical support for people with intellectual disabilities[15]

Ad van den Broek

Summary

In this chapter, a first step is taken towards the realisation of methodical support for people with intellectual disabilities that is tailored to their emotional development. Preferably, the method used should have two important basic characteristics: (i) it should correspond to the client's basic emotional needs and contribute to positive experiences and (ii) it should be based on making contact and building a relationship. The developmental dynamic model (Došen, 2014, 2018; Sappok & Zepperitz, 2016) forms the basis for this approach, in which each stage has specific basic emotional needs. It is possible to identify matching methods of support for these basic emotional needs.

1 Introduction

Guided by Anton Došen's developmental dynamic approach (Došen, 2014; 2018), professionals involved in the care of people with intellectual disabilities can gain insight into the emotional needs of their clients. In translating this insight into concrete practical advice, the question arises as to how the support of clients can be tailored to their emotional developmental level. More specifically, this may involve questions such as: how can the imaging and diagnosis be translated into concrete advice? How can professionals in daily practice be coached? How can the support

15 Thanks to Jac de Bruijn, Anton Došen, Max Feltzer, Filip Morisse, Paula Sterkenburg and Jolanda Vonk for their feedback on earlier versions of this chapter.

meet the client's needs? This chapter seeks to answer the following question: can existing methods be used by professionals to support their clients more adequately and purposefully in the field of emotional and personal development?

There are only three known methods that are specifically designed with the developmental dynamics model as a starting point: the developmental dynamic relationship therapy of Anton Došen himself (Došen, 2014), the Integrative Therapy for Attachment and Behaviour (ITAB) of Paula Sterkenburg (Sterkenburg *et al.*, 2008) and 'the thread' approach of Gerrit Vignero (chapter 19 of this manual). Among the methods and techniques that are not designed with emotional development in mind, there are surely methods that can be used to support emotional development, or elements thereof. So it is useful to explore the relevance and usefulness of these methods.

In this chapter, the term 'method' is used as an umbrella term for interventions, programmes, etc. This term is preferable to other possible terms because it refers to methodical work (De Bruijn & Twint, 2019).

The term 'support' is used to indicate that the developmental approach is ultimately aimed at creating optimal conditions for promoting the autonomy, self-determination and quality of life of the client. Developmental ages are used as a tool to respond to the client's needs and to give the client a chance to pursue developmental opportunities. In this way, the interests of the client and their environment are served in a respectful manner.

The method chosen for emotional development support should have two basic characteristics:

1. It should correspond to the client's basic emotional needs and contribute to positive experiences.
2. It should be based on making contact and building a relationship.

These two basic characteristics are discussed in the next section (2). Then, in section 3, the corresponding methods are discussed. The chapter concludes with a final review (4).

2 Description of the basic characteristics

2.1 Basic emotional needs and positive experiences

Došen (2014; 2018) distinguishes between basic needs and basic emotional needs, saying that basic emotional needs are part of basic needs. Basic needs are needs that are 'essential to the existence of the individual and involve subjective biological and objective environmental aspects' (Došen, 2014, p. 74). For each of the first five stages in the developmental dynamics model (the complete model consists of seven stages of development; see chapter 3 of this manual), six basic needs can be described: physiological needs, territory, mobility, sensory input, material environment and social interaction (Došen, 2014; 2018). Each of these needs changes depending on the stage of development. For example, social interaction involves bonding behaviour in stage one and changes into attachment in stage two because of intensive interaction with the parent.

Basic emotional needs relate to 'psychosocial development, social behaviour and the subjective mental state of the individual' (Došen, 2014, p. 74). For each stage of development a number of basic emotional needs can be identified, as the first column of table 16.1 shows. The psychosocial development of an individual is determined by the satisfaction of basic emotional needs. This satisfaction depends to a large extent on the way in which the environment meets the basic emotional needs of the person with an intellectual disability. This means it is essential for the development of a person with an intellectual disability that parents and professional counsellors are aware of the person's basic emotional needs. Meeting basic emotional needs in an appropriate way can be considered the most important basic characteristic of the method of support.

In the first stage of development on the developmental dynamic model, meeting basic emotional needs coincides for the most part with meeting basic needs, such as, for example, the need for structure. In the following stages of development, the satisfaction of basic emotional needs lies more in the psychosocial and personality development of the individual (Došen, 2014; 2018).

Meeting basic emotional needs is also a necessary stimulus for the reward system, as Došen mentions in chapter 2 of this manual. The reward system is built on the importance of pleasure (*liking*) and creates motivations and incentive salience. The reward system stimulates the learning process, which is related to the will (*wanting*) or wish (*desire*) to obtain a positive reinforcement.

This relates to the basic emotion of 'seeking' (Panksepp & Biven, 2012), which has to do with the great value of searching for means of survival: the pleasure of searching, finding and eventually getting hold of something. Methods used to promote development should therefore stimulate the process of learning and the motivation behind it.

Pleasure thus reinforces motivations to pursue paths that lead to positive experiences and promote relaxation. This makes pleasure and positive experiences good counterparts to negative emotions and to tension and stress. Positive experiences, fun and rewards create a healthy sense of well-being and play an important role in adapting to given circumstances (Berridge & Kringelbach, 2013; Došen, 2016).

2.2 Contact and building a good relationship

In the scientific literature, a good relationship is described as a fundamental factor in supporting people with intellectual disabilities. A good relationship with the counsellor has a positive effect on the regulation of stress (Sterkenburg in chapter 6 of this manual), on the client's well-being and on the prevention of problem behaviour (Roeden *et al.*, 2010; Willems, 2016). With his developmental dynamic relationship therapy, Došen demonstrated that a relationship of trust enables emotional growth in children (Došen, 2001; 2014; 2018). Sterkenburg *et al.* (2008) showed in her study of the effects of the attachment relationship in therapy that a client, Roy, learned more from the 'attachment therapist' than from the control therapist. A good relationship therefore creates opportunities for the growth and development of the client. The client is given the opportunity to build up self-confidence, to make choices and to work on their place in society. As a result, the quality of life increases.

What is a good relationship? This question is answered differently by different authors, although their views sometimes overlap. A good relationship may involve sensitive responsiveness in the context of the attachment relationship, denote a connection with the client or refer to a basic attitude. De Belie and Morisse (2007) point to emotional availability as the basic attitude of parents and social workers. This basic attitude has sensitive responsiveness at its core, complemented by structuring (providing support) and respecting the limits of the person with an intellectual disability. Dekker-van der Sande and Sterkenburg (2016) also refer to a basic attitude for mentalisation.

3 Methods

3.1 Introduction

There are many methods and interventions that can be used in the care of people with intellectual disabilities (in the Netherlands there are about 30 known methods). In addition to these methods, there are also all kinds of specific methods in the field of e.g. sensory information processing, communication and locomotion. This section deals with the elaboration of the characteristics previously described in section 2.

3.2 Methodical support of basic emotional needs and the need for positive experiences

3.2.1 Basic emotional needs

Ways of responding to basic emotional needs have been discussed in more detail by various authors. Došen himself has specified the basic emotional needs for each level of emotional development (Došen, 2014; 2018). He has also formulated a number of concrete guidelines under the heading of 'interventions' (Došen, 2016). See table 16.1.

Table 16.1 Basic emotional needs and associated interventions[16]

Stage of development	Basic emotional needs	Interventions
1. Adaptation	■ basic emotional needs (fun, relaxation) are linked to the regulation of physiological need ■ integration of sensory stimuli ■ structure of place, time, persons and activities ■ constancy in the environment ■ stimulation of bonding behaviour	■ regulation of physiological functions ■ regulation of emotional charge ■ social intervention: proximity, responsiveness, 'reciprocal stimulation' (facial expression and eye contact) ■ structure in space, time, activity–inactivity and persons ■ dosage of sensory stimuli ■ communication using available sensory channels ➔

16 Note: the table is based on a handout from a seminar on emotional development in people with intellectual disabilities (Došen, 2016). The column 'basic emotional needs' corresponds to table 8 from the manual *Psychische stoornissen, probleemgedrag en verstandelijke beperking (Psychological Disorders, Problem Behaviour and Intellectual Disability)* (Došen, 2014; 2018).

2. First socialisation	■ physical contact, attachment ■ Important other ■ social stimulation ■ security ■ handling material	■ 'affective synchrony' between mother and child: attention, play, verbal dialogue, regulation of affect and arousal, reactions to signals, tempo, rhythm of activity–passivity, symbolic play ('transitional object') ■ social interaction: emotional availability of a person, proximity, limits and clarity (structuring of activities), predictability, acting together, unconditional acceptance
3. First individuation	■ distance from other ■ confirmation of certain degree of autonomy ■ reward for social behaviour	■ relationship of trust with one or two persons, structure of space, time and activities ■ determining necessary distance in communication and interaction (communication via vision and hearing) ■ ignoring undesirable behaviour, keeping initiative in your own hands (limiting) and paying sufficient attention to children's needs ■ ensuring pleasant moments of interaction ■ helping the child to regulate their own behaviour and emotions (guidance and support instead of control) ■ ensuring there are situations where positive behaviour can be expressed ■ confirming competence and autonomy (within the necessary limits) ➔

4. Identification	■ identification figure ■ social acceptance ■ social competence	■ caregiver serves as an example (role model) ■ positive feedback, success experiences strengthen self-confidence ■ facing own behaviour with caution ■ encouraging responsibility, avoiding conflict with authority ■ stimulating creativity ■ supporting competence
5. Awareness of reality	■ recognition of own achievements ■ fully-fledged awareness ■ productivity and creativity in dealing with the material world ■ fixed rules of social behaviour ('golden rules')	■ remote assistance (appointment) ■ developing a supportive and insightful relationship of trust ■ attention to 'golden rules' and social behaviour ■ social competence ■ promoting productivity and creativity ■ promoting friendship and group activities

Marrecau and De Neve (2012) have also produced an overview of basic emotional needs. Together with a large number of colleagues, they drew up a schedule within the framework of the VINO (*Van Inzicht Naar Ondersteuning*, or From Insight to Support) trajectory that used five themes to formulate points of departure for each level of development in order to offer the best possible tailored support. The five themes are the result of the practical experiences of the professionals who helped draw up the programme: distance and proximity, structure and borders, activities, communication, and problem behaviour. In this way, the authors provide an extensive hands-on guide for parents and supporters seeking to offer concrete support for particular individuals.

Finally, Vonk and Visser-Korevaar have also described the first three stages of the developmental dynamic model to support clients in the sexual field (see chapter 8 of this book).

In the light of the purpose of this chapter, the discussion of stage one will cover aspects drawn from the publications of Došen and of Marrecau and De Neve. For practical reasons, the discussion will be limited to stage one. This is an example that can provide more insight into the match between support and emotional needs.

This first stage of development stresses the aspects of dosage of sensory stimuli, regulation of emotional charge, structure, communication and social intervention.

3.2.2 Dosage of sensory stimuli

It is important to start with the use of stimulus dosage and, in a broader sense, sensory information processing, because biological conditions strongly influence the child's development. The core of this development is the baby learning to deal with all kinds of sensory stimuli. At the same time, the baby learns to regulate themselves and, later, to let their body do what it wants (Greenspan *et al.*, 1998). Experts in sensory information processing can help identify strengths and weaknesses in this area and set up a sensory activity programme (SAP) (Dun, 2007).

3.2.3 Regulation of emotional charge

Regulation of emotional charge (in short, emotion regulation) is also referred to as affect regulation, stress regulation or regulation of arousal (Došen, 2014; 2018). According to various authors, emotion regulation is decisive for adapted and goal-oriented behaviour, optimal attention and motivation for learning (see also various chapters in this manual). A lot of information can be found in the literature about emotion regulation and the support it requires. In any case, the methodical approach includes the handling of the relationship and is otherwise related to remedying the cause of the tension and arousal.

The methodical approach to emotion regulation includes, to begin with, the well-considered commitment of the parent or professional to the relationship with their child or client. The Gentle Teaching method provides tools for using the support relationship in this context (Gentle Teaching website; Start, 2008).

Sterkenburg (Sterkenburg *et al.*, 2008; Sterkenburg *et al.*, 2008) emphasises the functional value of the relationship as a buffer for tension and stress and for establishing a psychophysiological homeostasis (see chapter 6 of this manual). Information and communication technology (ICT) can support this function of relationships. The application de *Slimme Sok* (the Smart Sock) and the accompanying Flower app are designed to help parents and support staff to react sensitively to (physiological) signals of stress (Sterkenburg, 2020) and to the pain of the client (Korving *et al.*, 2020).

Mentalisation helps counsellors to regulate themselves and remain calm so they are able to support clients in regulating tension (Dekker-van der Sande & Sterkenburg, 2016) and in dealing with difficulties in living (De Belie, 2017; chapter 16 in this manual). Mentalisation means the ability to think about the thoughts or emotions that determine one's own behaviour or the behaviour of others.

In addition to consciously using the relationship to support the client, a treatment may be needed that addresses the causes of stress. If the cause is sensory, then sensory information processing must be considered as part of an adequate response. In other cases, it may be necessary to provide clarity by means of limitation, or to allow the client to take a break until they can find peace of mind (Marrecau & De Neve, 2012).

3.2.4 Structure

Methods developed to support people with autism spectrum disorder (ASD), such as TEACCH (Treatment and Education of Autistic and Communication-related handicapped Children) and The Essential 5 (de Bruin, 2012), are often used. It is important to check whether these methods are suitable for the client in the first stage of emotional development. The idea of clarifying, organising and making predictable is useful, but above all making the structure visible and concrete should fit within this stage.

However, people who cannot use these methods may need the parent or caregiver to offer structure and verbally announce which activity is about to happen instead of using an object or a picture. Offering structure is closely linked to limiting and setting boundaries. Groot (Groot & Saris, 2016) indicates how to set boundaries: they should be firm, clear and considered.

3.2.5 Communication

A great deal of knowledge and practical advice on communication and supporting communication can be found in the literature. ComFor-2 (Forerunners in Communication) (Verpoorten *et al.*, 2016; Noens *et al.*, 2006) can be of great use in determining which aspects of this knowledge and advice are suitable for communication in the initial development stage. ComFor-2 measures the level of meaningfulness. This level indicates how someone perceives and interprets incoming stimuli (Maljaars *et al.*, 2012). There are three levels: sensation, presentation, representation. At the sensation level, communication consists of various sensory experiences (Maljaars *et al.*, 2012). In principle, this level corresponds well with the basic emotional needs of development stage one. This applies not only to people who have ASD in addition to an intellectual disability but also to people with an intellectual disability only.

Encouraging and stimulating active communication among people with intellectual disabilities is of fundamental importance. The Floortime method, for example, can be used for this purpose. This method aims to stimulate communication by creating as many 'communication circles' as possible (Greenspan *et al.*, 1998).

3.2.6 Social intervention

Social intervention is aimed at stimulating bonding behaviour. This section looks at how to work on this methodically, while section 2.2 deals with how to work on the contact and the relationship itself. This distinction is artificial and only useful for describing the two sides of the coin. In practice, each one is inseparable from the other.

Here, Floortime offers practical opportunities to work on the contact with the child. The first two structural development levels described by Greenspan in the DIR (development, individual, relationship) model, self-regulation and shared attention (milestone one) and attachment and involvement (milestone two) (Greenspan *et al.*, 1998), are in line with the first stage of the Došen model of emotional development. Floortime shows how important playing and activities aimed at action–reaction or 'doing it together' are as means of making contact (Vignero, 2011). Table 16.2 summarises the methodological support discussed.

Table 16.2 Summary of methodological support appropriate for stage one

Development stage	Aspects	Possibilities for methodical support
1. Adaptation	■ dosage of sensory stimuli	sensory information processing
	■ regulation of emotional charge	the relationship: Gentle Teaching, ITAB, mentalisation
	■ structure	TEACCH, the Essential 5
	■ communication	means of communication (ComFor-2), supported communication (the parent or supervisor themselves, objects, pictures), Floortime
	■ social intervention	Floortime

3.2.7 Offering positive experiences

Stimulating the reward system is, in part, stage specific. Table 16.3 provides an overview of useful interventions.

By meeting basic (emotional) needs, one can adequately offer positive and enjoyable experiences in the first stage of development. In practical terms this means, among other things, responding to clients' initiatives, following them in their play and doing fun movement activities together according to a method such as FloorPlay. Connecting to the sensopathic level of play, for example by snoozing (Sappok & Zepperitz, 2016), is also very appropriate in this context.

Table 16.3 Stimulating the reward system

Development stage	Fun and reward
1 Adaptation	pleasant sensory and motor stimulation
2 First socialisation	fun social play
3 First individuation	fun social play
4 Identification	material and social rewards, and rewards that contribute to self-actualisation
5 Awareness of reality	material and social rewards, and rewards that contribute to self-actualisation
Any level	■ sensory stimuli: taste, smell, touch, hearing (e.g. voice, singing, music), face (e.g. colours, images, space) ■ meet basic emotional needs

3.3 Methodical support for relationship building

How can contact making and relationship building be put into practice? Various methods are available to help caregivers in this.

The Heijkoop method helps professionals to look at their client in a new, broader way and to develop a positive and trusting relationship with them (Heijkoop, 2015; Webb, 2017).

Gentle Teaching is a method that is entirely focused on developing a relationship with a client in which the client feels safe and secure. The aim (or goal) is that the client becomes able to receive counselling and can be supported in a warm, personal way. This method also provides means to work towards new goals (Gentle Teaching website; Start, 2008).

Begeleiders in Beeld (Spotlight on Support Staff) is a programme that helps counsellors to improve their actions towards their clients, so that the relationship and interaction with those clients improve (Zijlmans, 2014; Embregts & Zijlmans, 2016).

Using attachment theory, Sterkenburg (2011) describes the elements needed to build a relationship of trust with children or adults with a severe intellectual disability or multiple disabilities. Furthermore, Sterkenburg and her research group explore the added value of ICT for the support of parents and carers in making contact and building a relationship. Three of their applications are the EMB Hi Sense App, the Hi Sense App MVB+LVB (EMB: severe intellectual disability, MVB/LVB: mild and borderline intellectual disability) and *de wereld van Empa* (The World of Empa). These are e-learning tools for parents and caregivers that aim to improve their sensitivity and responsivity (Sterkenburg, 2020).

In coaching and supporting counsellors, it is useful to map and set out objectively the relationship between client and professional. The STRS (Student Teacher Relationship Scale) (Pianta, 2001) offers a way to do this. The STRS is designed to measure the teacher–student relationship; the LLRV (the Dutch version of the STRS) can also be used to measure the client–supporter relationship (Roeden *et al.*, 2011).

4 Conclusion

The question from the introduction was whether existing methods can be used by professionals to provide their clients with adequate and targeted support in the field of emotional and personal development. It can certainly be answered in the affirmative. The two typical basic characteristics with which the selected methods should comply have been described. The exploration carried out in this chapter indicates that there is much to be gained from various existing methods that have been developed for other purposes.

Usually, the existing methods are working methods that have shown their value in practice (good practice). Some have been theoretically substantiated or had their effectiveness investigated. Ideally, systematic case descriptions and single case studies should be used to investigate the effectiveness of these methods in providing emotional support. In order to understand how the methodical support works, it is important to look at process factors: what works and what does not.

The inventory in this chapter shows that in stage one, the adaptation stage, there are more methodical interventions available for certain aspects than for others. For example, with regard to emotion regulation several forms of methodical support are available. The question is whether this is good in view of the freedom of choice of supporters or undesirable because this multiplicity makes it difficult to see what works and what does not.

This chapter has mentioned two measuring instruments, the ComFor-2 and the STRS. It would be good if the methodical element in the support were strengthened by the use of measuring instruments, both to establish a baseline and to evaluate progress and impact.

This chapter does not explicitly discuss co-operation between different disciplines, but it will be clear that the contributions of professional therapists, speech therapists and sensory information processing therapists are indispensable in certain areas.

References

Berridge, KC & Kringelbach, ML (2013) Towards a neuroscience of well-being: implications of insights from pleasure research. In: H Brockmann & J Delhey (Eds) *Human Happiness and the Pursuit of Maximization: Is More Always Better?* (pp81–100). Dordrecht: Springer Science+Business Media BV.

Bruin, C de (2012) *The Essential 5: A practical guide to raising children with autism*. Doetinchem: Graviant.

Bruijn, J de & Twint, B (Eds) (2019) *Handboek verstandelijke beperking: 25 succesvolle methoden*. Amsterdam: Boom Publishers.

Claes, L , Declercq, K, De Neve, L, Jonckheere, B, Marrecau, J, Morisse, F, Ronse, E & Vangansbeke, T (Eds) (2012) *Emotionele ontwikkeling bij mensen met een verstandelijke beperking*. Antwerpen/Apeldoorn: Garant.

De Belie, E (2017) Mentaliseren als leidraad bij coaching. In: Morisse, F, De Belie, E, Blontrock, M, Verhasselt, J & Claes, C (Eds) *Emotionele ontwikkeling in verbinding Coachingsmethodiek voor begeleiders van cliënten met probleemgedrag* (pp113-158) Antwerpen/Apeldoorn: Garant.

Dekker-van der Sande, F & Sterkenburg, P (2016) *Mentalization Can Be Learned: Introduction to Mentalization Based Support* (MBS). Bartiméus Series Webedu.

Došen, A (2014) *Psychische stoornissen, probleemgedrag en verstandelijke beperking Een integratieve benadering bij kinderen en volwassenen* (5th edition). Assen: Koninklijke Van Gorcum BV.

Došen, A (2016) *Emotionele ontwikkeling bij mensen met een verstandelijke beperking*. Seminar in Den Bosch on 19 February 2016, organised by FORTIOR.

Došen, A (2018) *Psychische Störungen und Verhaltensauffälligkeiten bei Menschen mit intellektueller Beeinträchtigung: Ein integrativer Ansatz für Kinder und Erwachsene*. Gottingen: Hogrefe.

Dunn, W (2007) Living Sensationally: *Understanding your senses*. London: Jessica Kingsley Publishers.

Embregts, P J C M, & Zijlmans, L (2016) *Begeleiders in beeld Een werkboek voor begeleiders*. Gennep: Dichterbij Kennisn@.

Gentle Teaching Website. Available at: https://gentleteachingnl/gentle/en/method/intro-meth) (accessed September 2020).

Greenspan, SI, Wieder, S, & Simons, R (1998) *The Child With Special Needs: Encouraging intellectual and emotional growth*. Reading, Massachusetts: Perseus Manuals.

Groot, A & Saris, J (2016) *Grenzen*. Seminar in Utrecht on 10 June 2016, organised by FORTIOR.

Heijkoop, J (2015) *Ontdekkend Kijken, Basisboek Methode Heijkoop* [online]. Available at: https://www.heijkoop-academy.nu/english/ (accessed March 2021).

Korving, H, Peters,P, Barakova, E, Feijs, L, & Sterkenburg, P (2020) Pain signaling with physiological data for persons with communication difficulties: A pilot study of the Pain App *11th IEEE International Conference on Cognitive Infocommunications (CogInfoCom)* 1–5 doi: 101109/CogInfoCom5076520209237900.

Maljaars, J, Noens, I, Scholte, E, & van Berckelaar-Onnes, I (2012) Level of sense-making in children with autistic disorder and intellectual disability: Patterns of delay and deviance in development. *Research in Autism Spectrum Disorders* **6** 808–814.

Marrecau, J & De Neve, L (2012) Van inschatting naar ondersteuning. In: L Claes et al. (Eds) *Emotionele ontwikkeling bij mensen met een verstandelijke beperking* (pp69–181). Antwerpen/Apeldoorn: Garant.

Noens, I, van Berckelaer-Onnes, I, Verpoorten, R, & van Duijn, G (2006) The ComFor: An instrument for the indication of augmentative communication. *Journal of Intellectual Disability Research* **50** 621–632.

Panksepp, J & Biven, L (2012) *The Archaeology of Mind Neuroevolutionary Origins of Human Emotions*. New York/London: WW Norton & Company.

Pianta, RC (2001) *STRS: Student-teacher Relationship Scale: Professional manual*. Odessa, Fl: Psychological Assessment Resources, Inc.

Roeden, JM, Maaskant, MA, Koomen, HMY, Candel, MJJM & Curfs, LMG (2011) Assessing client-caregiver relatioships and the applicability of the 'student-teacher relationship scale' for people with intellectueal disabilities. *Research in Developmental Disabilities* **33** 104–110.

Sappok, T & Zepperitz, P (2016) *Das Alter der Gefühle. Über die Bedeutung der emotionalen Entwicklung bei geistiger Behinderung*. Bern: Hogrefe Publishing House.

Start, T (2008) *Practicing unconditional love: the experience of applying gentle teaching principles with individuals diagnosed with developmental disorders* [online]. Available at: https://gentleteaching.nl/gentle/images/downloads/toni%20start.pdf (accessed September 2020).

Sterkenburg, PS (2020) Ontwikkelen in Sociale Relaties: hoe technologie sociale relaties kan bevorderen van mensen met een visuele of visuele-en-verstandelijke beperking *NTZ* **46** (2) 73–83.

Sterkenburg, PS, Janssen, CGC, & Schuengel, C (2008) The effect of an attachment-based behavior therapy for children with visual and severe intellectual disabilities. *Journal of Applied Research in Intellectual Disabilities* **21** (2) 126–135.

Sterkenburg, PS, Schuengel, C & Janssen, CGC (2008) Developing a therapeutic relationship with a blind client with a severe intellectual disability and persistent challenging behavior. *Disability and Rehabilitation* **30** (17) 1318–27.

Sterkenburg, PS (2011) *Vertrouwensrelatie voor ontwikkeling Een werkboek voor het opbouwen van een vertrouwensrelatie met kinderen en volwassenen met een ernstig verstandelijke of een meervoudige beperking*. Doorn: Bartiméus.

Verpoorten, R, Noens, I, Maljaars, J & Berckelaer-Onnes, I (2016) Forerunners in Communication - renewed edition [online]. Available at: https://www.kuleuven.be/pserg/comfor (accessed September 2020).

Webb, JC (2017) *The use of discovery awareness in intellectual disability services: examining a European approach to challenging behaviour in a UK setting* (PhD thesis). University of Nottingham. Available at: https://www.heijkoop-academy.nu/english/ (accessed September 2020).

Willems, APAM (2016) *Challenging relationships Staff interactions in supporting persons with intellectual disabilities and challenging behaviour* (doctoral thesis). Tilburg University.

Zijlmans, LJM (2014) *Knowing me, knowing you: On staff supporting people with intellectual disabilities and challenging behaviour* (doctoral thesis). Tilburg University.

Websites

EMB Hi Sense app: www.embinbeeld.nlwww.vbinbeeld.nl
Hi Sense app MVB+LVB: www.vbinbeeld.nl
De wereld van Empa: https://www.dewereldvanempa.nl

Chapter 17 The importance of social relationships for persons with an intellectual disability: emotion regulation and how ICT can support parents and caregivers

Paula Sterkenburg and Vernandi Dyzel

1 'What makes you happy?'

The pursuit of happiness is one of the most significant quests that people embark on in life. In 2012, a UN resolution identified the pursuit of happiness as 'a fundamental human goal' (General Assembly, 2012). This is evident in various self-help books and philosophical, religious, sociological and social science studies. Franklin (2010) highlighted that various people and institutions have created the perception that money brings happiness. This dominant perception of money is seen in the increased amount of time and energy that people invest in earning more (Aknin *et al.*, 2009). Even though money plays an important role in meeting essential needs such as security, food, shelter and the freedom to fulfil various desires, it has also been shown that any additional income has little effect on happiness (King & Napa, 1998). From this it can be concluded that money is not the answer to the pursuit of happiness.

Harvard conducted a longitudinal study following men over a period of 80 years and found that close relationships, more than money or fame, influence people's happiness (Mineo, 2017). Robert Waldinger, the director of the study, stated during his TED talk the following: 'Those who kept warm relationships got to live longer and happier, and the loners often died earlier.' He equated the power of loneliness to that of smoking and alcoholism (Mineo, 2017). The importance of relationships for people with intellectual disabilities has been emphasised by Shalock (2004), who reports that relationships are the most frequently referenced quality of life indicator. Trusting, warm relationships safeguard people from life's challenges, assist in delaying any physical and mental decline and are in general a better predictor of long and happy lives (Mineo, 2017).

2 The importance of social relationships: social baseline theory

The importance of significant relationships was highlighted in an experiment conducted by Coan *et al.* (2006). During this experiment, women received a magnetic resonance imaging (MRI) scan while being confronted with a threat of an electric shock under three different conditions: while alone, while holding the hand of a stranger and while holding the hand of a caring partner. The results of the MRI scans showed that in the presence of a caring partner the women experienced less stress activation within the brain than in the presence of a stranger. The results also showed that the most stress activation within the brain was evoked when the women were alone (Coan *et al.*, 2006). The increase in the stress response while alone suggests that being alone requires additional vigilance and self-regulation efforts (Coan, 2011).

In a threatening situation, according to Coan's 'social baseline theory', you experience the baseline (lowest amount of stress) when important others are present and you move away from this baseline (higher levels of stress and anxiety) when strangers are around or when you are alone (highest levels of stress and anxiety).

In non-threatening circumstances the proximity of another person does not play a significant role. However, when threatening circumstances arise, the presence of an important other becomes more significant. This may be due to our limited capacity to cope on our own. Furthermore, the ability to self-regulate emotions diminishes during prolonged periods of self-regulation, as metabolic resources required for regulation are depleted (Coan, 2011). In order to preserve the limited ability to self-regulate their emotions, individuals tend to rely on a social resource. Thus, by relying on important others the individual experiences the lowest amount of stress.

There are two ways in which the presence of another person can help. The first is risk distribution: in groups the amount of risk an individual bears becomes significantly less. The second and more important is load sharing: another person can be relied upon for safety and care behaviour (Coan, 2008). Thus, in the presence of a trusted other person, the person under threat can attend to the most urgent and threatening aspects of the situation without having to cope with or focus on other stressors or problems that are related to the threatening situation. If these most urgent aspects are attended to, the person under threat remains at their baseline. In conclusion, the presence of another person allows for less anxiety and a decreased need for hypervigilance, and in turn fewer metabolic resources are used during the threatening situation. However, there are three ways in which the other (social resources) can be categorised: secure important other, well-known other and unknown other.

2.1 Secure important other

A secure important other is described as a person who is trustworthy and reliable in terms of assisting with emotional regulation and providing adequate support that will enable the person to cope with the situation. The person who relies on this secure important other will experience less arousal and stress, as they will trust the secure important other to cope with various additional problems that may occur in the threatening situation and will only need to cope with their own threat burden. Figure 17.1 depicts the outsourcing to the secure important other of various other stressors (see figure 17.1, stressors A–C) and the baseline.

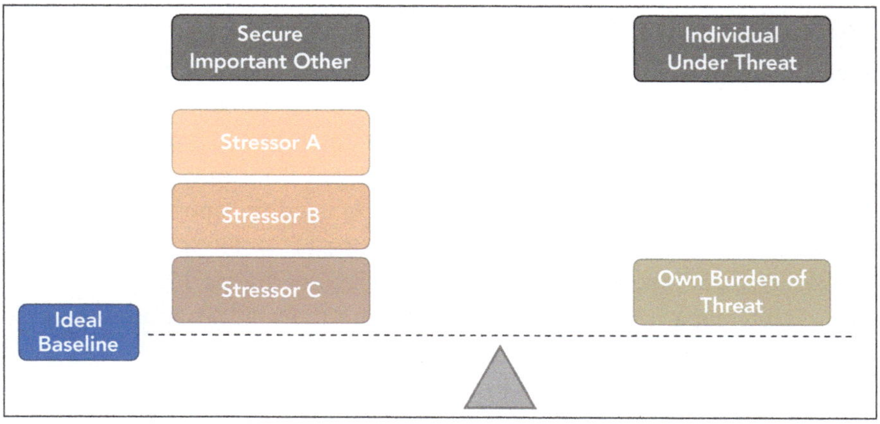

Figure 17.1 The role of the secure important other in outsourcing stress

2.2 Well-known other

People in this category are described as persons who are familiar and will be alert, supportive and helpful. On the other hand, it is also assumed that the well-known other will not be able to fulfil this role in relation to potentially dangerous and unpredictable aspects of the threatening situation. There is some expectation that this person will be able to solve some problems presented, but they will be able to solve fewer than the secure important other. As such, less stress is eliminated (see figure 17.2, purple line) and more arousal is experienced compared with the presence of a secure important other; the person can outsource some of their stress and anxiety (see figure 17.2, stressors B and C) but will need to cope with an additional stressor (see figure 17.2, stressor A) and their own burden.

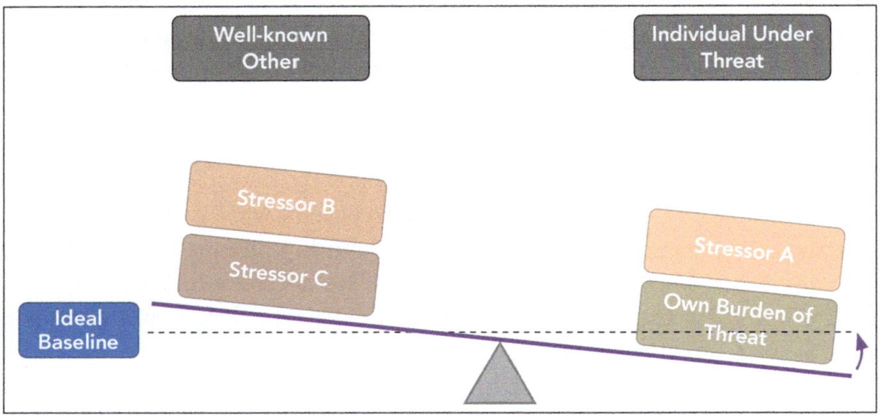

Figure 17.2 The role of the well-known other in outsourcing stress

2.3 Unknown other

In threatening circumstances in which the important other is not known, the individual under threat may expect that the other person will be alert and supportive. Notwithstanding this, the person under threat relies less on the other person, as they are not trusted to respond to all the dangers that may arise. As a result even less stress is alleviated and more energy is used to cope with the threatening situation (as seen in the orange line in figure 17.3). Thus, only a small part of the person's stress and anxiety can be outsourced (see figure 17.3, stressor C), and they will need to cope with their own burden and more additional stressors (see figure 17.3, stressors A and B).

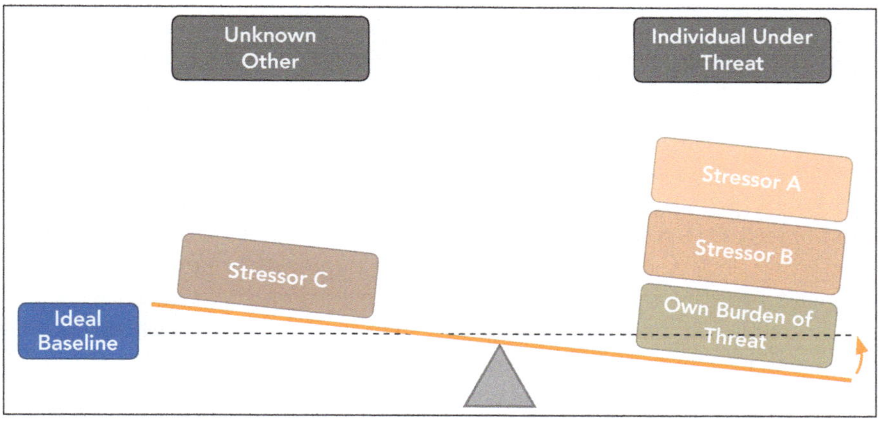

Figure 17.3 The role of the unknown other in outsourcing stress

In the three situations mentioned, some relief is experienced by the individual under stress. On the other hand, experiencing a threatening experience alone creates a situation in which there is no one to rely on and stress cannot be outsourced. Coping with this situation alone will lead to very high levels of stress, as the person feels they cannot 'outsource' additional stressors. They have to cope with the situation all by themselves and rely on themselves. The consequence is that the person has very high levels of stress as they have to cope with all the stress on their own (see figure 17.4, stressors A, B and C and red arrow).

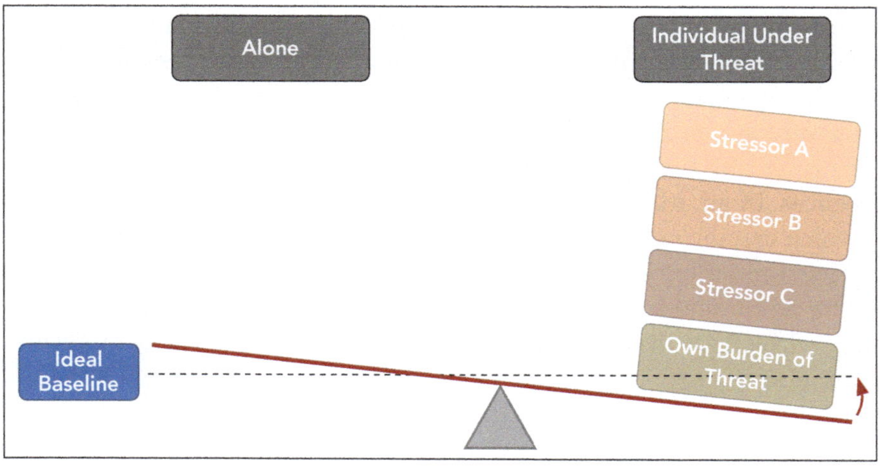

Figure 17.4 Coping alone with a threatening situation

Case study: Roy

Roy is blind, 17 years of age, with a diagnosis of Down's syndrome and severe intellectual disability. He is unable to complete any of his activities of daily living e.g. dressing himself and using the toilet. Furthermore he presented with a history of persistent and severe self-injurious behaviour and aggressive and disruptive behaviour towards caregivers. In an attempt to protect Roy and others, Roy had been mechanically restrained and had limited contact with others. He was completely isolated from the world and, when he did not react in an aggressive manner, appeared disengaged. In fact it could be said that Roy did not have any important others who he could rely on and to whom he could outsource his stress. Roy lived in a group home for children with intellectual disabilities. This placement was made because it offered special medical care and a complex home environment. Throughout his life he experienced various disruptions as he moved from various group homes and encountered numerous caregivers. As such he experienced the persistent neglect of his basic emotional needs for comfort and affection, as well as of his physical needs. Various treatment interventions, such as behaviour modifications, medical interventions and special diets, were unsuccessful. His case is also described by Sterkenburg, Schuengel and Janssen (2008).

3 Chronic stress and intellectual disability

Prolonged periods of chronic stress (not having the possibility to outsource stress) have been shown to lead to physical and mental health problems (Anisman, 2015). These prolonged periods can place the biological response system into a continuous state of 'fight, flight or freeze'. As a result, individuals are more prone to maladaptive responses even during less threatening situations (Janssen *et al.*, 2002). This maladaptive response due to chronic stress is particularly relevant for people with severe and profound intellectual disability, as they have fewer coping skills for regulating their emotions by themselves (self-regulation) during stressful experiences. In an attempt to manage this stress, maladaptive responses are employed, which can include challenging and self-injurious behaviour such as spitting, scratching, screaming and physical harm to others, themselves or objects. There is a need for additional support for people with intellectual disabilities with regards to coping with stress (having the ability to outsource stress) in an adaptive and healthy manner.

4 Framework: stress management and social baseline theory for people with intellectual disabilities

In the past persons with intellectual disabilities who engaged in challenging and self-injurious behaviour were either isolated or restrained in order to protect them and others present (Webber *et al.*, 2011). However, the maladaptive behaviour continued and these persons remained restrained or isolated, often for many years (Bonner *et al.*, 2002). Since the beginning of 2020 a new act, the Care and Coercion Act, came into effect in the Netherlands. It prohibits the use of any restraints unless there is no other way of preventing challenging and self-injurious behaviour. Furthermore, the use of restrictions needs to be revised and reassessed every four months (De Staatssecretaris van Volksgezondheid, Welzijn en Sport, 2020). This new act has created an opportunity to re-evaluate the manner in which persons with intellectual disabilities who present with challenging and self-injurious behaviour can be supported during stressful situations.

A secure attachment relationship has been identified as key in affect regulation, with the secure important other functioning as a buffer against stress (Schuengel *et al.*, 2009). Without these relationships, persons with intellectual disabilities are more likely to develop maladaptive coping strategies for regulating stress (Sterkenburg *et al.*, 2008b). The importance of forming a secure attachment relationship is key in the revision of measures for supporting people with intellectual disabilities who present with challenging and self-harming behaviour during stressful or threatening situations.

The social baseline theory can act as a framework in which the importance of secure and trusting relationships can be understood. This secure attachment relationship will allow persons with intellectual disabilities to outsource their stress and focus on working towards returning to a social baseline at which they can function effectively and adaptively. Furthermore, over time the relationship can assist persons with intellectual disabilities in learning how to effectively self-regulate (Sterkenburg *et al.*, 2008b). A secure attachment relationship should be with a parent or caregiver who is sensitive and responsive and spends high-quality time (being attuned and supportive and having the other in their mind) with the individual.

That being said, Sterkenburg *et al.* (2008a) have also indicated that forming a secure attachment relationship may be challenging, as people with intellectual disabilities appear insensitive to social cues and rewards. Furthermore, interpreting behaviour and reacting appropriately to this behaviour have also been identified as challenging, as people with intellectual disabilities are less reactive and clear in their signals (Frederiks *et al.*, 2015). Developing these secure attachment relationships requires more time and effort; it takes a lot of time to build up such a relationship with a specific person. The relationship building can be done by a sensitive and responsive person who keeps the high stress and arousal level of the person in mind, and then progresses through the various types of social resources: first becoming an unknown other, then a well-known other and finally a secure important other.

Becoming a secure important other requires time spent together. During this time the caregiver will need to work on gaining the trust of the person with the intellectual disability (Sterkenburg *et al.*, 2008a). This process will start with being present and sensitive to behaviour, wishes, thoughts and feelings. During this phase there usually needs to be enough physical distance between the two people in order to provide a sense of safety (Sterkenburg *et al.*, 2008a). Once familiarity is established, proximity will be sought out. Building this familiarity consists of playing games, having fun together and stimulating development. After familiarity is established the caregiver focuses on providing a safe haven when a challenging situation presents itself (Sterkenburg *et al.*, 2008a). This allows for stress to be outsourced to the caregiver. Once the caregiver becomes more meaningful, reliable and trustworthy, most of the stress will be outsourced to them. The presence of a secure important other helps the person with the intellectual disability to return to their social baseline and use adaptive behaviour to communicate their needs.

Case study: Roy

The use of restraints did not improve Roy's aggressive and self-injurious behaviour, and as he was isolated he found himself in a state of chronic stress. Behaviour therapy approaches were unsuccessful. Therefore, the treatment intervention chosen was the Integrative Therapy for Attachment and Behaviour. This intervention focuses on the development of a secure attachment in order to decrease challenging behaviour. It could be said that the goal was for the therapist to progress from being an unknown other to a well-known other and, finally, a secure important other.

In order to become an unknown other, some form of contact needed to be established. The therapist therefore spent time with Roy and responded in a sensitive and stimulating manner. Roy and the therapist got to know each other through enjoyable and positive experiences. The development of the relationship happened in a safe and predictable environment, and the therapist created physical distance that was comfortable for Roy. During these therapy sessions, the therapist mirrored Roy's behaviour and feelings, and remained present throughout the therapeutic session. Furthermore, instead of isolating Roy when he exhibited any challenging behaviour, the therapist acted in a soothing and caring manner. ➔

Over time Roy and the therapist started to get to know each other better. The therapist was able to predict Roy's behaviour and act accordingly in an empathic and sensitive manner. Furthermore, Roy was encouraged to initiate more contact with the therapist through having fun, playing games, moving together and enjoying music together. The therapist became a well-known other. Over time, the therapist was able to offer comfort during times of anxiety and anger. Roy became comfortable exploring and relying on the therapist for support during anxiety-provoking moments. The therapist became a secure important other, and it was noted that Roy's challenging behaviour decreased. After about four months of therapy Roy's restraints were removed, and it was clear that he was starting to physically grow again and gain weight. He was able to outsource his stress and focus on more adaptive coping strategies and learning. He could learn new positive behaviour: for example, asking for what he wanted instead of pinching him. He learned to more adequately ask for food or specific kinds of music (Sterkenburg *et al.*, 2008).

5 Additional resources and strategies for the development of secure, important and trusting relationships

The challenges related to developing secure, important and trusting relationships, as well as the difficulty of reading and reacting to emotional and behavioural cues, can be overcome with additional resources and strategies. These additional strategies include mirroring behaviour, supportive technology for accurate and sensitive responding and the enhancement of self-regulation (Sterkenburg, 2020).

5.1 Mirroring behaviour

At the core of building a secure attachment relationship is the ability to create a secure base and a safe haven (Powell *et al.*, 2016). Mirroring behaviour is the foundation of the former and latter. It can be described as observing and being sensitive to small signals and behaviours in order to understand the unique inner world of the person with the intellectual disability at a specific point in time. Additionally, caregivers must respond correctly to these signals and behaviours (Sterkenburg, 2012). This can mean accurately articulating in words emotions that may be experienced in the moment, or mimicking the person's behaviour. The former and latter should be done in such a way that it is very clear that mirroring is taking place. It is important to note that each person presents in a unique manner and this should be taken into account when mirroring takes place (Sterkenburg, 2019). For example, people with visual impairments may appear to be uninterested in activities because they turn their heads away or are less facially expressive, but this behaviour may be related to their attempts to hear better. Furthermore, some people with intellectual disabilities may use limited verbal communication because of the delays it involves, but they may use alternative ways of communicating their experiences, such as making noises or body movements, which could be easily misread. Lastly, stereotypical movements and physical impairments are also quite common. These make people more reliant on important others to meet basic needs, and focusing on basic needs may make caregivers less sensitive to emotional cues given. Sensitive and adequate mirroring of the emotional inner world of a person with an intellectual disability creates a safe and secure base, which fosters a secure relationship with parents and caregivers.

5.2 Supportive technology for accurate and sensitive responding

Teaching sensitive and accurate mirroring to caregivers can be challenging because of the difficulty involved in reading and responding to unique emotional and physical cues. The inability to understand and respond to cues creates stress within the parent and caregiver and in turn within the person with the intellectual disability (Frederiks *et al.*, 2015). Recently there has been a focus on overcoming these challenges through the use of technology. Frederiks *et al.* (2015) created an intelligent biofeedback system, the 'Smart Sock', which monitors arousal through galvanic skin response sensors. The sock is connected to a Shimmer device, which sends the measured skin conductance via a Wi-Fi connection to the Flower app, specifically developed for this project (see figure 17.5). The Flower app displays a flower that becomes bigger when the person wearing the sock experiences stress. This allows for caregivers to accurately and sensitively identify arousal.

Figure 17.5 The Smart Sock and the Flower App

In addition to reading cues more accurately, knowing how to respond sensitively to these cues can also be stressful. Developing parental and caregiver knowledge about attachment and how to respond effectively to the emotional needs of a person with an intellectual disability can increase a feeling of self-efficacy and decrease stress (Van Wingerden *et al.*, 2019). The availability of formal education about the mental and physical health of persons with intellectual disabilities is limited for parents and caregivers (Van Wingerden *et al.*, 2018). Recently there has been a focus on the application of e-learning and m-learning as means of psychoeducating parents and caregivers. The Hi Sense App-ID was developed to improve professional caregivers' knowledge of attachment through very short sessions of five minutes a day spaced over a long period of time, about 40 days. This app consists of 120 multiple-choice questions related to attachment theory and the experience of persons with intellectual disabilities (Van Wingerden *et al.*, 2018). The accessibility and flexibility of this app makes it possible to implement in various settings. The ability to read emotional and physical cues and to respond to these cues in an informed and appropriate manner will create the opportunity to mirror effectively and sensitively, which will allow for the development of a secure base and safe haven. Persons who experience sensitive mirroring will start to view their caregivers as trustworthy and meaningful.

5.3 Enhancement of self-regulation

Caregivers who can accurately mirror the behaviour of the person with the intellectual disability reassure the individual, help them to recognise emotions and play an important role in co-regulating emotions (Hoffman *et al.*, 2017). This role helps a person with an intellectual disability to expand and develop their window of tolerance. This refers to the amount of stress that the person can cope with. It suggests that between the extremes of hyperarousal and hypoarousal is a range of optimal arousal in which emotions can be experienced, tolerated and integrated (Ogden *et al.*, 2006). At both extremes the individual is unable to think calmly about the situation and act in an appropriate manner. This inability may lead to maladaptive coping strategies. The window of tolerance is a state in which the individual experiences adequate levels of alertness and concentration and is able to emotionally regulate (Ogden *et al.*, 2006). Furthermore, the optimal window of tolerance allows the individual to mentalise, that is, meaningfully reflect upon and interpret the actions of others and themselves on the basis of intentional mental states (Derks *et al.*, 2019). Mentalisation originates from mirroring that occurs within the secure relationship and dynamically develops over time. Mentalisation assists in the cultivation of self-regulation (Dekker-van der Sande & Sterkenburg, 2016).

As a result of developmental delays and limited executive functioning, persons with an intellectual disability may struggle to develop their mentalisation ability, even if adequate mirroring is provided (Derks *et al.*, 2019). That being said, with accurate and consistent mirroring and additional emphasis on developing mentalisation abilities, persons with an intellectual disability can develop some form of mentalisation. A game, 'You & I', has also been developed for persons with a mild or borderline intellectual disability (intelligence quotient (IQ) ranging between 50 and 85) to assist in improving mentalising abilities and emotional self-regulation (Derks *et al.*, 2019).

The aforementioned strategies and resources can assist in creating a secure and trustworthy relationship with a caregiver, which will in turn allow for the outsourcing of stress during threatening situations. It is important to note that not all of these resources may be applicable for each individual with an intellectual disability. The emphasis should still be placed on building a meaningful relationship in a manner that is tailored to the individual. Furthermore, a relationship takes place within an environment, and the environment plays a significant role in the lives of people with intellectual disabilities as it can create a scaffolding that provides predictability and safety (Mesibov *et al.*, 2002).

6 The environment

The subjective experience of the world around us varies from person to person. This is particularly the case for people with intellectual disabilities, as they are more prone to misinterpret social cues, become overstimulated by environmental cues and struggle with uncertainty (Janssen *et al.*, 2002). Managing the stressors mentioned requires additional energy to be expended in remaining alert and hypervigilant. As such people with intellectual disabilities often remain stressed for longer periods of time, and this limits their already limited capacity to regulate their affective state.

If the environment is predictable the person does not need to be alert and stressed. It is important to provide structure in their daily schedule that is safe and predictable but still allows for some level of autonomy so that they are continuously stimulated. These schedules should include the provision of a job or activity at the daycare centre. Providing day activities helps to regulate bedtimes and sleeping patterns. Furthermore, physical activities should also be included in the day programme as this assists with stress regulation. Lastly, as part of this routine, healthy meals should be scheduled.

This safe and predictable daily schedule should be implemented within an environment in which the person feels safe and secure, physically and emotionally, and in which there are different types of space: i.e. a space to be together, a space for the person to pursue their own activities (rest, make music, work on a computer) and a space to exercise. But there should be a way for them to stay connected in some way to their caregivers, as caregivers play such an important role in emotional regulation. If the environment succeeds in being perceived as safe and predictable, persons with intellectual disabilities can shift all their resources to forming meaningful relationships and developing their self-regulation abilities.

7 Conclusion

Some persons with intellectual disabilities experience high levels of stress and exhibit maladaptive coping strategies, which may result in self-injurious and challenging behaviour. Previous policies aimed at managing such behaviour in persons with intellectual disabilities and included the use of restraint and isolation. However, being isolated and restrained can cause extended periods of chronic stress, which has a negative impact on physical and mental health and can lead to the continued use of maladaptive coping strategies. The new Care and Coercion Act in the Netherlands prohibits the unnecessary use of isolation and restraints, and has created the opportunity to develop a new framework to support persons with intellectual disabilities who exhibit challenging and self-injurious behaviour. Secure social relationships play a significant role in emotional regulation for persons with intellectual disabilities, and these relationships are key to the creation of a revised framework of support.

The social baseline theory highlights the role that the presence of important others plays in threatening situations. An important other provides safety and care, which can enable a person under threat to outsource stressors and thereby experience less stress and anxiety. The amount of outsourcing depends on the type of relationship between the individual and the important other. The more secure, trustworthy and reliable the relationship is, the more stress can be outsourced. Developing a secure relationship is time consuming and requires a sensitive and responsive important other. Forming such a relationship may be difficult as behaviour is often hard to interpret, which makes it more difficult to respond to the person's needs. Nonetheless, developing a secure attachment relationship with a person with an intellectual disability is not impossible. But it may require additional strategies and resources.

The creation of a secure base and safe haven is the foundation of a secure attachment relationship. This foundation is created through sensitive and accurate mirroring, that is, observing and responding to small and unique signals and behaviours. Difficulty reading and reacting to emotional and physical cues can hinder the process of mirroring. Supportive technology, such as the Smart Sock, the Flower app and the Hi Sense App-ID, can help caregivers and parents to read and react more adequately and sensitively to such unique cues. Mirroring creates reassurance and assists with the recognition and co-regulation of emotions. This in turn creates the opportunity to expand and develop adaptive self-regulation skills.

An optimal window of tolerance and optimal stress level (not too high and not too low) can enable a person with an intellectual disability to mentalise, which in turn assists in the development of healthy emotional self-regulation strategies. As a result of limited executive functioning and other cognitive delays, mentalisation ability is often delayed in people with intellectual disabilities. Additional technological resources, such as the game 'You & I', can assist in the development of mentalisation and emotional regulation. It should be noted that the degree to which this ability develops might vary from individual to individual. Experiencing accurate and responsive mirroring and developing self-regulation skills allow for the development of a secure attachment relationship in which stress can be outsourced. Even though the attachment relationship is a core focus of this new framework, other potential stressors should also be considered and minimised. This can be done by making the environment more predictable and safe: e.g. by implementing a daily schedule, daily stimulation, sleep schedules and physical activities.

The reduction of environmental stressors and the use of technology to aid in accurate and responsive mirroring improves the chances of developing a healthy and secure social relationship and adaptive emotional regulation strategies. Trusting and warm relationships are critical for any individual's mental, physical and emotional life, but this is even more true of people with intellectual disabilities. It is important that organisations adopt the social baseline theory as a vision that informs daily practice. This will enable persons with intellectual disabilities to have more adaptive and healthy coping skills, less chronic stress and the opportunity to have longer, happier and more meaningful lives.

References

Aknin, LB, Norton, MI, & Dunn, EW (2009) From wealth to well-being? Money matters, but less than people think. *The Journal of Positive Psychology* **4** (6) 523–527 https://doi.org/10.1080/17439760903271421.

Anisman, H (2015) *Stress and Your Health: From vulnerability to resilience*. Wiley Blackwell.

Bonner, G, Lowe, T, Rawcliffe, D & Wellman, N (2002) Trauma for all: A pilot study of the subjective experience of physical restraint for mental health inpatients and staff in the UK. *Journal of psychiatric and mental health nursing* **9** 465–73 https://doi10.1046/j.1365-2850.2002.00504.x.

Coan, JA (2008) Towards a neuroscience of attachment. In: JC Cassidy & PR Shaver (Eds) *Handbook of Attachment: Theory, research and clinical implications* (pp241–265). The Guilford Press.

Coan, JA (2010) Adult attachment and the brain. *Journal of Social and Personal Relationships*, **27** (2) 210–217 doi: 10.1177/0265407509360900.

Dekker-van der Sande, F & Sterkenburg, P (2016) *Mentalisation Can Be Learned: Introduction to Mentalization Based Support* (MBS). Bartiméus Series. Webedu.

Derks, S, van Wijngaarden, S, Wouda, M, Schuengel, C & Sterkenburg, PS (2019) Effectiveness of the serious game 'You & I' in changing mentalizing abilities of adults with mild to borderline intellectual disabilities: A parallel superiority randomized controlled trial. *Trials* **20** (1) [500] https://doi.org/10.1186/s13063-019-3608-9.

Frederiks, K, Croes, M, Chen, W, Oetome, SB & Sterkenburg, P (2015) Sense – a biofeedback system to support the interaction between parents and their child with the Prader-Willi syndrome: A pilot study. *Journal of Ambient Intelligence and Smart Environments* **7** 449–459 doi: 10.3233/AIS-150327.

Franklin, SF (2010) *The Psychology of Happiness: A good human life*. Cambridge University Press.

General Assembly (2012) International day of happiness (A/66/L.48/Rev. 1). United Nations. https://undocs.org/A/RES/66/281.

Hoffman, K, Cooper, G & Powell, B (2017) *Raising a Secure Child: How circle of security parenting can help you nurture your child's attachment, emotional resilience and freedom to explore*. The Guilford Press.

Janssen, CGC, Scheungel, C. & Stolk, J (2002) Understanding challenging behaviour in people with severe and profound intellectual disability: A stress-attachment model. *Journal of Intellectual Disability Research* **46** (6) 445–453.

King, L A, & Napa, C K (1998) What makes a life good? *Journal of Personality and Social Psychology* **75** (1) 156–165 https://doi.org/101037/0022-3514751156.

Mesibov, GB, Browder, DM, Kirkland, C (2002) Using individualised schedules as a component of positive behavioural support for students with developmental disabilities. *Journal of Positive Behavioural Interventions* **4** (2) 73–79.

Mineo, L (2017) Good genes are nice, but joy is better: Harvard study, almost 80 years old, has proved that embracing community helps us live longer, and be happier. Available at: https://news.harvard.edu/gazette/story/2017/04/over-nearly-80-years-harvard-study-has-been-showing-how-to-live-a-healthy-and-happy-life/ (accessed March 2021).

Ogden, P, Minton, K & Pain, C (2006) *Trauma and the Body A sensorimotor approach to psychotherapy*. New York/London: WW Norton & Company.

Powell B, Cooper G, Hoffman K & Marvin B (2016) *The Circle of Security Intervention: Enhancing attachment in early parent-child relationships*. New York City: Guilford Publications.

Schuengel, C, Sterkenburg, PS, Jeczynski, P, Janssen, CGC, & Jongbloed, G (2009) Supporting affect regulation in children with multiple disabilities during psychotherapy: A multiple case design study of therapeutic attachment. *Journal of Consulting and Clinical Psychology* **77** (2) 291–301.

Shalock, RL (2004) The concepts of quality of life: what we know and do not know. *Journal of Intellectual Disability Research* **48** (3) 203–216.

Sterkenburg, P, Schuengel, C, & Janssen, C (2008a) Developing a therapeutic relationship with a blind client with a severe intellectual disability and persistent challenging behaviour. *Disability and Rehabilitation* **30** (17) 1318–1327 doi: 101080/09638280701482597.

Sterkenburg, PS, Janssen, CGC & Schuengel, C (2008b) The Effect of an Attachment-Based Behaviour Therapy for Children with Visual and Severe Intellectual Disabilities. *Journal of Applied Research in Intellectual Disabilities* **21** (2) 126–135.

Sterkenburg, PS (2012) *Developing Attachment: a workbook for building up a secure relationship with children or adults with severe intellectual or multiple disabilities*. Bartiméus Reeks Microweb Edu, Doorn.

Sterkenburg, PS (2020) *Ontwikkelen in Sociale Relaties Hoe technologie sociale relaties kan bevorderen van mensen met een visuele of visuele-en-verstandelijke beperking*. Bartiméus Reeks Microweb Edu, Zeist.

Van Wingerden, E, Sterkenburg, PS & Wouda, M (2018) Improving empathy and self-efficacy in caregivers of persons with intellectual disabilities, using m-learning (HiSense APP-ID): study protocol for a randomized controlled trial. *Trials* **19** 400 https://doi.org/101186/s13063-018-2772-7.

Van Wingerden, E, Wouda, M, & Sterkenburg, PS (2019) Effectiveness of m-learning HiSense APP-ID in enhancing knowledge, empathy, and self-efficacy in caregivers of persons with intellectual disabilities: a randomized controlled trial. *Health and Technology* **9** 893–901 https://doi.org/101007/s12553-019-00361-0.

Volksgezondheid, Welzijn en Sport (2020) *Wet zorg en dwang psychogeriatrische en verstandelijk gehandicapte cliënten* (BWBR0040632). De Rijksoverheid Voor Nederland. Available at: https://www.rijksoverheid.nl/documenten/rapporten/2019/07/05/wet-zorg-en-dwang-psychogeriatrische-en-verstandelijk-gehandicapte-clienten (accessed March 2021).

Webber, LS, McVilly, KR, & Chan, J (2011) Restrictive interventions for people with a disability exhibiting challenging behaviour: Analysis of a population database. *Journal of Applied Research in Intellectual Disabilities* **24** 495–507. doi: 101111/j1468-3148201100635x.

Chapter 18
Child psychotherapy embedded within a mentalising network: the importance of coaching the network of people with intellectual disabilities in relation to emotional development[17]

Erik De Belie and Nicole Vliegen

> *I think I'll go to the park*
> *Watch the children playing*
> *Perhaps I'll find in my head*
> *What my heart is saying*
> – 'Any World (That I'm Welcome To)'
> (Becker & Fagen, 1975)

17 This chapter is a translated and adapted version of: De Belie, E & Vliegen, N (2019) Gedesorganiseerde gehechtheid bewerken: individuele kindertherapie verankerd binnen een dragend netwerk. *Tijdschrift voor orthopedagogiek, kinderpsychiatrie en kinderpsychologie* **3-4** 171–180.

Summary

Children with an intellectual disability growing up in an unsafe family context are at heightened risk for a disorganised attachment development. These emotionally and socially vulnerable children are in high need for extra support from their primary caregivers whom they have grown to distrust. This history renders them less open to help and guidance and makes them 'harder to reach'. These double dynamics increase relational stress and can lead to severe behavioural problems, which subsequently puts the mentalisation capacities of parents and residential care workers under pressure. The road to recovery for these children starts at coaching the network and restoring this network's mentalising abilities in relation to the child's emotional development. Psychodynamic therapy with the child makes sense when embedded in and supported by such a mentalising and trauma-sensitive network.

1 Intellectual disability and vulnerable attachment development

> *Eight-year-old Jane is referred for hard-to-handle behaviour. There is a thin line between moments of aggressive and moments of regressive and chaotic behaviour, and sometimes she seems to lose sight of the distinction between fantasy and reality. Her life story has been characterised by neglect and suspected sexual abuse. Her father died in prison last year, and her mother is living in a psychiatric ward for people with intellectual disabilities. Jane, who has a mild intellectually disability, is in special education because her ability to learn is emotionally hindered.*

Having more vulnerable affect- and stress-regulation skills, which is an inherent part of growing up with an intellectual disability, leads to an increased risk of developing behavioural problems (Schuengel & Janssen, 2006). Therefore, children with intellectual disabilities have a great need for sensitive and responsive relationships with their caregivers (Ganiban *et al.*, 2000; Biringen *et al.*, 2005). At the same time, because they are more difficult to understand and to raise, these children put greater pressure on parental emotions and skills (De Belie & Morisse, 2007). Consequently they are at greater risk of developing an unsafe attachment relationship with their caregivers (Howe, 2006; Sullivan & Knutson, 2000).

When children with an intellectual disability, like Jane, grow up in an unsafe family context (Vliegen *et al.*, in prep.), there is a heightened risk of their attachment development becoming disorganised. When these children are in residential care, both they and residential care workers are faced with particular relational challenges. In this chapter, we will briefly outline the consequences of the disorganised attachment for the child and relate this to the residential living context, and then we will explain how to work therapeutically towards recovery with the child and the context.

1.1 Intellectual disability and disorganised attachment

Whereas an anxious-ambivalent or avoidant attachment style can be considered as a protective strategy to deal with the fear and arousal evoked in early unsafe or stressful situations (Powell *et al.*, 2014), a disorganised attachment style goes hand in hand with a loss of a clear strategy. Relationships mostly feel unsafe and frightening, whatever the closeness or distance that characterises the interaction. This 'lack of strategy' implies that the child cannot escape the high level of anxiety and arousal, and this heightens emotional and relational vulnerability. Fear and distrust become the building blocks of a 'script' for relationships and interactions within the social world (Vliegen *et al.*, in prep.). In a way that is not only paradoxical but almost cruel, fear and distrust become all the more palpable when these children cautiously start to desire to attach themselves to others. Along with the wish for being close and connected there arises the fear of both being engulfed in closeness or being abandoned and distanced. This makes it fairly difficult for caregivers to attune themselves to these children. In order to find some basis for a growth-promoting relationship with such a vulnerable child, we need to gain insight into their underlying emotional needs. As these needs are recognised and cautiously met, the relational stress may decrease somewhat. This increases the likelihood that the child will be able to experience a safe connection with a caregiver and will open up to a new attachment experience.

It is important to remember that an 'attachment style' is a script the child has developed, not a fixed and immutable way of engaging in relationships. There remains a certain amount of flexibility, which can be used in a therapeutic environment. Understanding the needs of these children and reflecting on how their particular needs influence relationships and on what these children evoke in the caregiver are prerequisites for the development of a more secure base and a safer haven. These processes can be summarised as 'mentalisation' (Allen *et al.*, 2008), a concept that refers to the psychological processes in caregivers or therapists that enable them to remain focused on the child as well as on their own 'inner world', on thoughts, feelings, desires and convictions. A mentalising stance helps us to 'interpret' both the meaning behind children's behaviour and the mutual relational influence. As such, mentalisation can function as the compass for finding the right relational wavelength.

1.2 Essential for recovery: an attachment-oriented context and a therapeutic space

In order to create a care context that enables recovery, two complementary pillars are needed. First and foremost, the child needs day-to-day growth-promoting relationships within an attachment-oriented and trauma-sensitive supportive network. A mentalising collaboration within and between caregiving contexts is essential in this regard. This collaboration focuses on how the context can help the child to regulate stress and to maintain safe relational images while respecting the child's boundaries, needs and desires.

Additionally, individual psychodynamic child psychotherapy functions as a 'safe testing room' or as a 'psychotherapeutic laboratory'. It offers a playful and 'stress-free' space in which the child can learn how to deal with vulnerabilities and strengths, and is in this regard of major added value. Both the daily interactions and the therapy are aimed at helping the child to feel a little more secure within existing and new relationships.

Relationships with caregivers who are able to take into account the child's underlying developmental needs offer the child the opportunity gradually to experience that relationships can be safe and reliable, and can lead to corrective positive emotional experiences. However, building up a trustworthy attachment relationship is a starting point and prerequisite for further development, and in that sense only part of the process (Fonagy & Allison, 2014). When caregivers empathically focus on the child's underlying thoughts, feelings and desires, seeing the child as a 'unique intentional being', this paves the way for the development of the child's emotional self-understanding, self-regulation and subsequent epistemic trust. The concept of 'epistemic trust' refers to 'an individual's willingness to consider new knowledge from another person as trustworthy, generalizable and relevant to the self' (Fonagy & Allison, 2014, p. 373).

It is the caregiver's attitude of interest in and mild curiosity about the inner world of the child (e.g. 'Oh dear, you seemed to look angry when I told you about the change of plans') that enables the child to 'open their mind' in order to learn about their inner and social world from the caregiver's mind (e.g. 'I was angry at first, and then felt sad because I was looking forward to going to the zoo.') During this process the child learns to rely on the knowledge the caregiver provides about how the child can understand themselves and their world and deal with thoughts and feelings. Epistemic trust is therefore an important building block for the development of mentalisation and paves the way for social learning. Hutsebaut (2017) puts it as follows:

> *As well as the fact that the therapeutic relationship itself generates new experiences, the therapeutic relationship becomes the vehicle for restoring the client's openness to social influences 'per se': the process of social learning recovers, allowing the client to continue learning from other relationships. In this way, the first steps are taken towards potentially experiencing the social world as benign again.*

In this chapter we first describe and illustrate how we develop a supportive and reflective network and then how a therapeutic process can be embedded in this contextual work. During this process a child receives opportunities to experience safe relationships and epistemic trust.

2 A supporting and reflective network

2.1 Restoring mentalising capabilities in context

Children with a relationship profile of disorganised attachment need a lot of relational support from their caregivers, while at the same time their intense feelings of distrust make them less willing to accept help and support from these caregivers. These complex dynamics put pressure on the relationships with – and sometimes also between – caregivers and result in increased relational stress. Consequently, working with these deeply hurt children burdens the mentalisation capacities of parents and professional caregivers. The path to recovery for the child is therefore created by the endless rediscovery and recovery of the mentalising abilities of all caregivers involved (Vliegen *et al.*, 2017, in prep.). Therefore, making mentalisation the theme of consultation among the different caregivers is part of the work that has to be done to create an attachment-oriented supportive network.

This process of change is characterised by a dynamic switching between implicit and explicit mentalisation. In 'good enough' circumstances, the caregivers' implicit mentalisation inspires the spontaneous, unconscious attunement to the child's developmental needs and creates an emotional connection. During these implicit mentalisation processes, caregivers use their experiential knowledge about the child, themselves and the relationship. In this context, De Groef (2017) has introduced the concept of 'impertise', referring to experiential knowledge that arises from being involved or implicated. The caregiver becomes aware of their 'impertise' by sharing it with other caregivers or within a team. However, when the stress in the relationship increases and the spontaneous relational dynamics are at risk, a coaching process that promotes 'explicit' mentalisation is needed in order to facilitate a predictable and safe emotional connection (De Belie, 2017).

2.2 Reflection with caregivers: fitting the cogs together

Caregivers often primarily focus on getting a clear image of the emotional needs of the child, but their view may be contaminated by negative or even dysregulating experiences they have had with this child. The thoughts and feelings these children evoke in their caregivers can intensely activate the caregivers' own stress and attachment systems (Bevington *et al.*, 2015). This dynamic therefore deserves our attention. It can be helpful to invite caregivers to reflect on the stress they experience as well as on the strengths and vulnerabilities of their own attachment and coping styles. This process is inspired by the concept of 'breathing space', which we borrow from the 'mindfulness literature' (Wallin, 2007, p. 351):

> *Mentalising and mindfulness are diverse, but at the same time complementary and intertwining, ways to get to know and respond to experiences – and each strengthens the other, because 'insight leads to calmness and calmness leads to insight'.*

Only when there is some 'breathing space' can the caregiver listen and look with an open mind and heart at the child they are working with, which can lead to the necessary understanding of the underlying needs of both the child and the caregiver themselves. In the process of losing each other and restoring the ability to listen and look with an open mind over and over again, the caregiver can start to be a secure base for the child, and a safer emotional connection with the child can grow. Furthermore, this process of 'reflecting together' promotes a more benign and open connection among the caregivers involved in the mentalising network, so much so that some caregivers have found this process of reflection a helpful way to prevent burnout.

The steps of this reflection process can be pictured as a series of cogs, in which each step implicates another one and in which processes interact spontaneously and dynamically. We apply this cog schema as a framework in our co-operation with caregivers who support children with attachment problems and feel challenged by their behavioural and relational problems. This process takes into account several closely connected topics that inspire the process of reflection (see figure 18.1).

The reflection process is a response to a *challenging situation* putting the 'good enough' relationship with the child at risk. This is often the case when a situation of 'challenging' or negative behaviour leads to relational stress and leaves the caregivers feeling that they are 'losing contact with the child', or when difficult behaviour in a group situation makes the attunement to multiple children a 'mission impossible' and interactions go wrong.

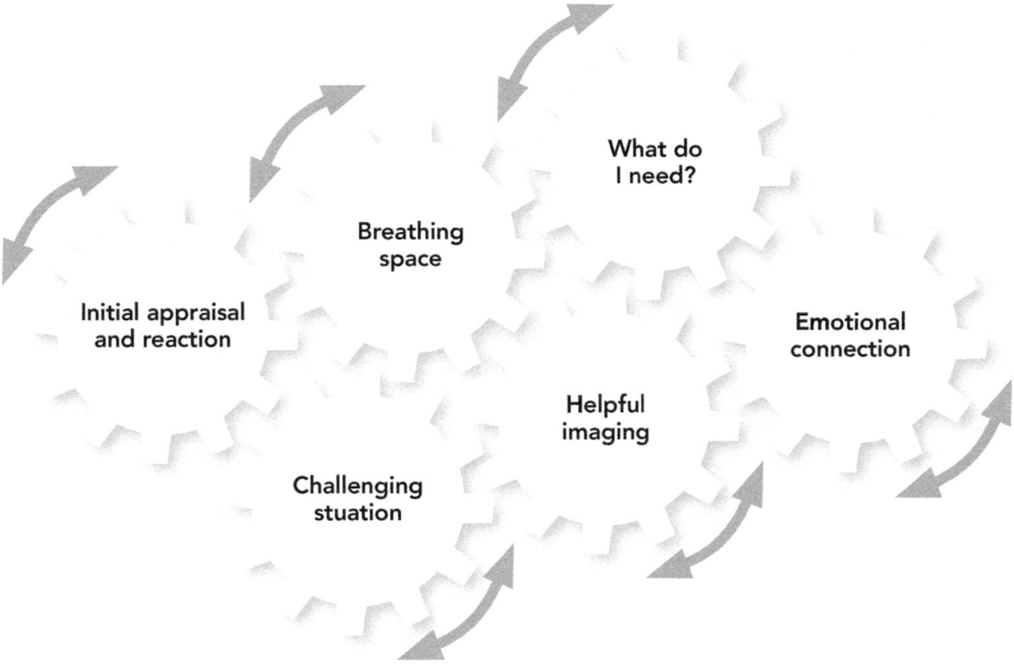

Figure 18.1 Process of reflection

In the *initial appraisal and reaction*, we talk about how caregivers spontaneously understand the behaviour of the child(ren): what thoughts and feelings are evoked by the situation? How did both child and caregiver react? How did the caregiver experience stress in their contact with the child? How did their feelings and thoughts evolve later on? Listening to these first impressions and interpretations in an empathetic and appreciative way leads caregivers to feel that what they are going through is being acknowledged. We invite them to 'mindfully' recognise and accept their thoughts, feelings and stress as 'normal reactions to a difficult situation' and to reflect on what they need to recover 'now the situation is quiet again'. This reflection creates *breathing space*: tension decreases and this facilitates recovery and emotional reconnection within themselves and with colleagues. Additionally, this initial listening process may provide important preliminary information on the issues involved. For example, when a caregiver feels particularly powerless or anxious, we might consider the idea that this may reflect the child's projections.

These first reflections form the stepping stone to *helpful imaging*, an assessment process that provides a way of taking into account the developmental needs of the child. During this assessment process, the child is seen as a unique person, living within a meaningful context, with their own life story and developmental issues. In the course of this process, the various emotional needs and domains can be classified using the Scale of Emotional Development – Revised[2] (Morisse & Došen, 2016; chapter 13 in this manual) in order to picture the child's strengths and vulnerabilities. During this assessment process, the observations of the child and the relationship are considered and reconsidered against the reflections of the caregivers: how does the child's behaviour effects the caregivers' thoughts and feelings? What do the caregivers need if they are to be able to attune themselves to the child's developmental needs? *Helpful imaging*, alongside paying attention to the *needs of caregivers*, therefore inspires a safe and reliable relational attunement. When the child is responsive to the caregiver's efforts to relate in an open and mentalising way, there is an *emotional connection*, and together they can move forward. If these efforts are rejected, something has probably been overlooked, and the reflection process starts again. We will illustrate the dynamic course of this process through the treatment of Jane and her context. Both in supporting the context and in the child therapy we kept the cog schema in mind. Since the processes of reflection are always fluid, the framework is followed in a flexible way.

2.3 A supporting and reflective network around Jane

2.3.1 Giving a place to Jane's mother

During the first exploratory interview, Mrs Sand, Jane's mother, was supported by her own individual social worker.[18] She comes across as tense and reticent. She herself was a victim of abuse and was unable to protect her young children from sexual abuse by their half-brother, after which the children were placed in a centre for child and family support.

> *Mrs Sand opens the conversation by explaining how she feels rejected by her daughter, who avoids her during visits. I indicate that I will mention this to the care workers at her residential care unit and ask them to support her contact with Jane during her visits. I suggest that this possibly has to do with Jane not knowing how to react when she sees her mother. I talk about my impression that Jane's mum is very important to her, and about how proud she can be that her mum does her laundry. Mrs Sand relaxes a little bit and goes on: 'Jane was a quiet baby who looked just like me.' She explains how happy Jane was when she went to visit Jane at the centre for child and family support.*

18 Jane is a pseudonym for a girl from the clinical practice of Erik De Belie, the first author of this chapter. The authors would like to express their thanks and appreciation to Jane, her mother, her uncle (foster carer) and the support team.

I tell Mrs Sand that I appreciate her telling me this, and for the second time she seems to relax a little bit. Then I talk about my therapeutic work with the children on our residential care unit, and ask her permission to start a psychotherapeutic process with Jane.

During this conversation, I try to create space for Jane's mother to talk and I listen to her perspectives on Jane. At first, she pictures a child who avoids and rejects her during visits. By taking her perspective seriously, acknowledging her care and underlining her importance as a mother to her child, I try to put a question mark over that first image of her daughter as a 'child who rejects her mother'. Moreover, in doing so, I hope to create space for other aspects of her perspective on her daughter. This brings her to how she used to feel welcome in previous periods – when Jane was staying at the centre for child and family support – and she can talk about Jane for a moment as the child who loves her and with whom she had a good bond.

2.3.2 Getting started with the residential care workers

In order to form a mentalising network around Jane, it is important to communicate with her daily residential care workers. By doing so, we ensure that a safe base in the residential care unit can be restored. During this conversation we invite caregivers to share their experiences, thoughts and feelings with regard to Jane as a starting point for a process of reflection.

A first conversation with the residential care workers about how they perceive Jane made me realise that two perspectives on her functioning exist alongside each other. There is the disobedient Jane who lies, hurts others and is helpless. This image goes hand in hand with feelings of irritation and powerlessness on the part of the residential care workers. On the other hand, there is the 'damaged' Jane who is still able to play. While talking about these care workers' experiences of their relationships with Jane, the compassion and connectedness they feel towards this girl is palpable. By explicitly naming and appreciating both perspectives and by recognising the commitment and involvement of her residential care workers, new 'breathing space' emerges.

During this first conversation with the residential care workers, I briefly related how affected I had felt when reading her history and said that the image of Jane strongly suggests developmental trauma (Vliegen et al., in prep). Because of this trauma Jane has serious problems in regulating her stress and emotions, which leads to her challenging and disruptive behaviour. Her serious difficulties in trusting caregivers prevent her from being open to relational support. So in working with children like Jane, the advice of Perry (2020), 'First regulate, then relate, then reason', is of major importance, as is helping the caregivers to be aware of their own (stress) responses, which can undermine their capacity to mentalise.

By appreciating the various perspectives in the *initial appraisal* of her residential care workers, as well as their spontaneous reactions, *breathing space* was created and residential care workers were invited to work towards a *helpful image* that could lead to *emotional connection*. The fact that after this conversation Jane became more open in the relationships with her residential care workers teaches us how small interventions lead to a more positive attitude on the part of residential care workers, which positively affects their emotional connection. The conversations with Jane's mother and the residential care workers laid a first safe basis for the development of a supporting and reflecting network, within which the child therapy can be embedded.

3 Jane: emerging safety and epistemic trust

3.1 First image based on the developmental assessment

Jane comes across as tense, hypervigilant and lacking in vitality. She is always looking for material fulfilment and the creation of order, and notices every shortcoming. She quickly gets 'disturbed': when something does not go as she had expected or if something does not work out, she reacts angrily and/or freezes up. In a story completion task (Emde *et al.*, 2003) she talks about a crocodile that threatens a lost pig. A little later, the mother of the little pig, who is apparently not aware of any danger, asks the crocodile to help her look for her child. Does this story reflect early experiences in which her mother was unable to recognise the danger and to offer her safety?

During the assessment, a worrisome switching between care and aggression is observable, for example in the following play sequence: at first Jane cares for a doll before suddenly throwing it to the ground, laughing. The therapist's attempts to mirror the doll's pain are ignored. The same thing happens with a cat: she takes care of the cat, only subsequently to hurt it by stabbing it violently with a pencil. Such unpredictable switching from care to aggression may reflect and actively repeat her earliest experiences, in which moments of care alternated with moments of neglect and transgression. Jane is not aware of this, but we assume an implicit blueprint of unpredictability that colours her relational perception (Ladan, 2013).

Jane seems primarily to focus on what goes wrong between her and the other children, and connects feelings of anger and sadness with frustration and a sense of being teased. Nevertheless, when she draws human figures, she draws both of her brothers 'so that she is not alone'.

Talking about her mother immediately brings her to the thought of wanting to go and live with her. She says without any emotion that her dad died. In the doll's house, she acts out a game in which two parents lovingly put their children to bed, after which they themselves go to sleep. Even though she does not really elaborate on the theme, she gives a first impression of 'good care' that does not immediately turn into aggression. By acting in this way, is she creating for herself a fantasy world of 'normal and good care' in order to survive (Ladan, 2013, p. 89)? Is she showing a longing for something that she never really knew? Is she avoiding what will inevitably have to be addressed: a reality in which care was at times inadequate? Does she want to give both of us some time to get used to being together before we start the 'real therapeutic work'?

3.2 A child in need for whom you cannot do anything

When the therapy starts and she realises that she can attend weekly, something changes in Jane's relational attitude. She increasingly controls the therapeutic relationship and makes the therapist 'the willing executor of her plans'. Jane blames me for every shortcoming and every failure. For example, she wants to draw a house and asks me to draw the roof because she says she 'can't do it well'. When I start, she is immediately unhappy with my drawing. She gets angry, throws the drawing away and cannot bear any closeness. I am not allowed to look; I cannot say anything. I have to leave her alone, and it is my fault that it has gone wrong!

During the next session, she asks me to lay a train track in a figure of eight, something we had been doing previously. While laying the track, I discover that a piece is missing, realising that I will fail in my task. I can already feel the storm brewing, and I expect anger in return. But at that moment, Jane freezes and stands for several minutes, tensed, with her arms above her head. Once again, she does not tolerate any reaction on my part. I experience this as an even more painful failure than when she gets angry. I see an abused, traumatised child, and I cannot reach her. It feels like every attempt to connect with her triggers her early blueprint of transgression, shortcoming and disruption, while I am doing my utmost to help this child in need.

In my reflections on these sessions afterwards, I see a number of evolving themes. There is her great need for a self-object – a 'good' father who, as an extension of herself, fully compensates for her shortcomings, as she wishes. However, this need goes hand in hand with the deep conviction that the other person will reject her and will clearly repeat what has caused her pain. Her fear leads to a controlling attitude, and she has a deep fear of failure, which may be linked to a fear of existence and expresses itself in anger and frustration with every shortcoming, for which she puts the blame on me. Jane has experienced a lot of harm, and now assigns me the role of the one who harms her.

Amid all of these dynamics, it is hard to remain in contact with the benign therapist in myself, and I become unsure about my therapeutic abilities. Sometimes I freeze in powerlessness, and I wonder whether I can actually help this child. These feelings are to some extent processed by my understanding of the underlying dynamics. Could it be that Jane is looking for herself by colliding with me (Vliegen *et al.*, 2017, p. 171), rather than finding herself through a growing organisation of her inner world? This reflection helps me to regulate myself, to find 'breathing space', to keep enough distance and to find patience again. I remain present and wait for her to regain her balance after she has regulated herself outside of the relationship.

To support her self-regulation, I make sure there are colouring pencils, because I know that drawing and colouring relax her. When her drawings are dark and chaotic, I am not allowed to say or ask anything about what she is drawing. At other moments, when she is more relaxed, she uses colours and the drawings are more detailed. These drawings depict recent positive experiences, with signs of hope: flowers, the sun and the dogs and house of her uncle, with whom she occasionally stays and who takes partial foster care of her and her brothers. Then she is open to my admiration and listens to what I say and ask about her drawing. For the first time, during these moments, I feel something of a deeper interaction.

3.3 The first steps to epistemic trust

During the first sessions, Jane asks a lot of questions about why things break and about whether something is 'real or a toy'. She is seldom satisfied with my answers, which she believes are incorrect: what she believes is how it is, and that is that. At the same time, it becomes noticeable that she is looking for a way to understand what is happening around her as a way of getting a grip on the outside world and possibly also on herself. Fonagy and Allison (2014, p. 374) call this 'epistemic hypervigilance', in which the child trusts neither their own knowledge nor the knowledge provided by a caring adult, and continues to wander around in search of understanding.

The relationship becomes a little more reciprocal during the next sessions, but the slowly growing sense of safety immediately brings the insecurity back to life. Jane seeks my care, relates fragments of what she has been through and is more open to my empathy. On one occasion, for instance, she tells me about a conflict with her best friend that made her very angry. By listening to her story and containing her anger, she feels comforted. Then she tells me that she is afraid of losing her friend, and she asks to be comforted. However, these moments of finding each other are interspersed with disorganisation: sudden and temporary disturbances and disruptions of the relationship, when Jane becomes very angry and/or shuts herself off.

After reducing her medication, a striking change is noticeable: Jane reacts in a more uninhibited fashion, but she is also more vital and authentic in the interactions. The next session (17) took place after her medication was adapted:

> *Jane comes in and says a bird peed on her hand. She asks for help washing her hands. Then she goes looking for a microphone she likes to talk through. On the way, she finds a note with a heart on it and says that her dad is dead. I ask her if she misses her dad and she says she played the guitar at his funeral. So, instead of answering my question, she starts fantasising about the funeral. I heard from her former caregivers that she attended the funeral but that she shut herself off and did not react at all.*
>
> *Jane then tells me that her mum took care of her clothes during the last visit, which is true. She lets me admire them and is really open to my admiration. She explains that she misses her mother and that she longs to be with her. At that moment she wants to leave immediately to go to her mother.*
>
> *Then she takes a stethoscope and listens first to her own breathing and heartbeat and then to mine. Doctor and patient find each other in a moment of physical proximity about signs of vitality. At that moment she tells me that her dad died because his heart stopped beating. She asks me if her heart can stop beating, revealing one of her deepest fears. I can reassure her by telling her that she is still a young girl and that her heart is strong.*
>
> *After that, she takes the guitar she loves playing. She plays and sings a nursery rhyme, but then forgets the words. So I continue to sing the song myself. Jane picks up on this and follows me for the very first time. I experience this as a special moment in which she is willing to open up and dares to learn something from me. We continue the nursery rhyme, to the part about 'flies rocking babies in the cradle'. Is it a coincidence that 'rocking babies in the cradle' makes her reach for the baby doll, which she immediately wants to toss back and forth? I wonder out loud if the doll is not scared, a question she ignores. She throws the doll hard at me, whereupon I speak for the baby and give words to the doll's fear. I ask on its behalf to be treated nicely. Jane does not listen to this, and she throws the doll again. After that, she reaches for a plaster to take care of the doll and soothes her kindly.*

> *Jane finishes this play sequence by hiding herself in the play tent: I have to look for her, but at first I am not allowed to find her. While playing hide-and-seek with her, I say out loud that I am looking for her. I ask a toy dog and a monkey where she might be, but they do not know. She stays very quiet and hides under a blanket. Then she calmly comes out clutching a plush dog. We have found each other: hidden and found! As Winnicott (1956, p. 186) once put it: 'It's a joy to be hidden, but a disaster not to be found.'*

This short episode during play therapy makes me hopeful. We look for and find each other more, and there are moments of openness to my input. Jane first asks for my help washing her hands. After being given this help, she tells me something about her parents. What she says about them is partly fantasy and partly true, but it reflects a deep desire to live with caring parents (Ladan, 2013).

I wonder whether the medical examination that follows, where we listen to each other's heartbeats and breathing, expresses her search for vitality within our relationship, while she tells me for the first time about her deep fears. First I showed empathy for her feelings, and expressed my appreciation for being taken into confidence. After that, she was open to learning something from me: her heart is strong and will not stop beating. But I understand her fear. This was a first sign of epistemic trust: she accepted my explanation, which reassured her at that moment. Afterwards Jane began to ask more questions in order to understand what was going on in her life. One of the central topics was the difference between what is real and what is not real, a search to learn to distinguish between reality and fantasy.

A few days after this session, a serious incident took place. Her residential care worker told me that Jane awoke at night, came out of her room and was panic stricken. At first, she would not tolerate any contact, so her care worker decided to stay in the room while respecting the distance she needed. Then, her care worker made up her bed and used a story book to tell a bedtime story. Jane calmed down by looking at the book with her care worker and by listening to the care worker's soothing voice. Only after a lot of reassurance could she go to sleep again.

During therapy Jane is open to music, rhythm and singing together. Because she cannot remember the lyrics of the song, she asks for my help, which indicates again that her basic trust is solid enough to allow her to learn from me. In her file, I read a passage about rare moments of good care by her father: he sang songs to her while she sat on his knee. However, this image is in danger of being lost as the switch between aggression and care rears its head again. Fortunately, she finishes by taking care of the doll for a moment, after which she calms down. This caregiving is very important for a child who was neglected and lacked care. Instead of repeating the trauma, she actively takes the role of a caregiver.

To my great surprise, she quietly retreats into the tent at the end of the session and is able to regulate her stress about being found again by me. In this tense moment, I felt uncertain about what was going to happen, and I feared derailment and disaster. Nonetheless, during this session, Jane can permit and tolerate the positive aspects within our relationship – a small step towards secure attachment.

The road we still need to travel is long, and there are many obstacles along the way. What reassures me is the information I receive from her residential care workers: Jane is beginning to understand that they are reacting to her behaviour and do not reject her as a person. She is more open to positive contact with her care workers and her mother, which enables her to learn from them in order to understand her experiences. Previously, she shut herself off, went into resistance mode and above all exhibited a fear of being rejected and/or punished. Despite all the positive developments, things can still get pretty intense from time to time.

4 Conclusion

The impact of the neglect and abuse of children with intellectual disabilities can lead to disorganised attachment. Moreover, on account of their intellectual disability, they are often marginalised in specialised mental health care institutions. Residential care workers do their utmost to provide a safe base for these children. However, they are often challenged by their behaviour problems, which lead to a lot of stress and uncertainty. These feelings undermine their capacity to mentalise with regard to the underlying emotional needs of both children and themselves. So we find it very important to form a mentalising network to support all the caregivers involved. Alongside this process we pay attention to the support of these children's parents. As psychotherapists we commit ourselves to a close co-operation with the caregivers in order to embed our psychotherapy in an attachment-oriented network. In close co-operation with residential care workers, parents or foster parents, we can support the child's first relational steps towards a safer attachment and epistemic trust. In this way, the developmental opportunities of the child are fostered, creating more hope.

References

Allen, J, Fonagy, P & Bateman, A (2008) *Mentalizing in Clinical Practice*. Washington & London: American Psychiatric Publishing Inc.

Bevington, D, Fuggle, P & Fonagy, P (2015) Applying attachment theory to effective practice with hard-to-reach youth: The AMBIT approach. *Attachment and Human Development* **17** (2) 157–174.

Biringen, Z, Fidler, DJ, Barrett, KC & Kubicek, L (2005) Applying the emotional availability scales to children with disabilities. *Infant Mental Health Journal* **26** (4) 369–391.

De Belie, E & Morisse F (Eds) (2007) *Gehechtheid en gehechtheidsproblemen bij personen met een verstandelijke beperking*. Antwerpen/Apeldoorn: Garant.

De Belie, E (2017) Mentaliseren als leidraad bij coaching. In: F Morisse, E De Belie, M Blontrock et al. (Eds) *Emotionele ontwikkeling in verbinding Coachingsmethodiek voor begeleiders van cliënten met probleemgedrag* (pp113–158). Antwerpen/Apeldoorn: Garant.

De Groef, J (2017) Nabeschouwing: Verbindende spiegelingen. In: F Morisse, E De Belie, M Blontrock, et al. (Eds) *Emotionele ontwikkeling in verbinding Coachingsmethodiek voor begeleiders van cliënten met probleemgedrag* (pp295–302). Antwerpen/Apeldoorn: Garant.

Emde, R, Wolf, D & Oppenheim, D (2003) *Revealing the Inner World of Young Children: The McArthur Story Stem Battery and parent child narratives*. Oxford: Oxford University Press.

Fonagy, P & Allison, E (2014) The role of mentalizing and epistemic trust in the therapeutic relationship. *Psychotherapy* **51** (3) 372–380.

Ganiban, J, Barnett, D & Chichetti, D (2000) Negative reactivity and attachment: Down's syndrome contribution to the attachment – temperament debate. *Development and psychopathology* **12** (1) 1–21.

Howe, D (2005) *Child Abuse and Neglect: Attachment, development and intervention* London: Palgrave/ Macmillan.

Hutsebaut, J (2017) Epistemic trust essentieel voor werkrelatie [online]. Available at: https://blikophulp.nl/epistemic-trust-joost-hutsebaut/ (accessed March 2021).

Ladan, A (2013) Berust overdracht op verdrongen herinneringen? *Tijdschrift voor Psychoanalyse* **2** 84–96.

Morisse, F & Došen, A (Eds) (2016) *SEO-R² Schaal voor Emotionele Ontwikkeling – Revised²*. Antwerpen-Apeldoorn: Garant.

Perry, B (2020) https://www.neurosequential.com/covid-19-resources

Powell, B, Cooper, G, Hoffman, K, Marvin, B (2014) *The Circle of Security Intervention – Enhancing Attachment in Early Parent-Child Relationships*. New York: The Guilford Press.

Schuengel, C & Janssen, C (2006) People with mental retardation and psychopathology: Stress, Affect Regulation and Attachment. *International Review of Research in Mental Retardation* **32** 229–260.

Sullivan, PM & Knutson, JF (2000) Maltreatment and disabilities: A population- based epidemiological study. *Child Abuse and Neglect* **24** 1257–1273.

Vliegen, N, Tang, E & Meurs, P (2017) *Van kwetsuur naar litteken Hulpverlening aan kinderen met complex trauma*. Pelckmans Pro.

Vliegen, N, Tang, E, Midgley, N, Luyten, P & Fonagy, P (in preparation) *Children recovering from complex trauma: A three-track contemporary psychodynamic treatment approach*. London: Routledge.

Wallin, D (2007) Attachment in Psychotherapy. New York: The Guilford Press.

Winnicott, DWW (1956) The antisocial tendency. In: DWW Winnicott (pp103–112). London/New York: Tavistock Publications.

Chapter 19
The thread: a source of inspiration for working with themes from emotional development

Gerrit Vignero

Summary
'The thread' is a metaphor that explaines and represents the different stages of emotional and social development. It is a translation of concepts and models from developmental psychology and was inspired by the work of Heijkoop and Dosen. Explaining the social and emotional development in a comprehensive and practical manner, the concept aims at facilitating the interaction between children/clients and parents/teachers/caregivers. It helps the professional to find a good alignment with the client.

1 Introduction
In the field of special education, developmental psychology has always been of great importance in situations of educational or developmental problems.

'The thread' is a metaphor that explains emotional development for professionals and parents and offers tools for education and support. Explaining social and emotional development in a comprehensive and practical manner, the model of the thread helps the professional to find a good alignment with the client and to develop a common language in conversations with parents. It translates 'what is known about development' into 'how to use developmental topics in (special) education'.

The thread represents the bond between parents and children that grows and evolves during the different stages of life. While at first the parent (literally) takes the child by the hand, later on, parents help their children to learn to move on without ever-present guidance and protection. Moreover, when dealing with everyday parenting problems with children falling back on earlier stages of emotional development, the thread can help to find solutions.

Based on developmental psychology and inspired by Heijkoop and Došen, the stages of emotional and social development have been translated using the metaphor of the thread. The model is linked to the application of the Scale of Emotional Development – Revised[2] and Scale of Emotional Development – Short. The different stages of emotional and social development are illustrated by using a thread during the development. Within the developmental stages each thread has its own characteristics relating to both the child and the parent. Concepts used in educational psychology, such as joint attention, attachment, emotional refuelling and exploration are integrated in the model. In addition, some new concepts are introduced (i.e. the track, the gate, the remote control and the network).

Education or support can become challenging because of different child-, parent- and environment-related aspects. The threads get tangled and parents or professionals are confronted with difficult educational questions. When education or counselling leads to stress and uncertainty, the thread may be 'under pressure', and one should look at the vulnerable spot in the thread for guidance. Parents, teachers and support staff should connect their threads to this fragile point in order to support the child or the client. When the parent or caregiver does not take into account these fragile parts of the thread, there is a risk that the social-emotional development of the child or the client is being overestimated.

The language used in this model is simple and allows for communication with parents and caregivers about development and education. The use of drawings and other tools makes the theory visual. The thread is also developed as a method to help professionals to analyse challenging behaviour and to suggest treatment.

The model was initially developed to facilitate the support of persons with intellectual disabilities. However, the implementation of the model demonstrated its applicability in different types of educational and counselling situations. There is experience with the method in residential care, in schools (special and mainstream), in outreaching support, with parents and in care for the elderly.

There is more than 10 years of good practice with the model in Flanders and the Netherlands. So far, the model has only been developed in Dutch in various articles and three books. There is a book for professional counsellors, a book for parents and a methodical handbook for team counsellors.

This article discusses:
1. the model of the thread
2. diagnosis: the vulnerable spot in the thread
3. treatment inspired by the thread.

2 The model

The different stages of emotional development are illustrated as different types of threads. Each thread has its own characteristics, relating to both the child and the caregiver. Figure 19.1 summarises the stages. For each thread, reference is made to the stages of the Scale of Emotional Development (SED) (Došen).

1. The first stage is *reaching for the thread* and refers to the first developmental tasks (stage one, adaptation) of a baby. The parent will bring regularity, regulate emotion and initiate interaction. The parent extends their thread and the child reaches for the thread. The bonding process is the basis for attachment.

   Through guidance, the professional will bring predictability into the life of the client and consider the signals the client gives about their basic needs. It is the professional who takes the initiative and offers a daily schedule such that the client follows the professional's track. There is predictability in time, in space and in basic experiences. The professional provides emotional comfort. By taking into account the client's sensitivities, the professional creates the conditions for the client to bond. The focus is on proximity and presence.

   This stage is often the first step in dealing with challenging behaviour. Because it is such a complex developmental task, the model distinguishes between a number of subtasks:

   - the *track*: predictability in time, space and activities – the daily schedule
   - the *gate*: emotional regulation in times of tension. Is the gate open or closed? How can it be opened?
   - *action and reaction*: the basic interaction between client and caregiver. The caregiver acts as centre of activity.
   - *joint attention*: doing things together as a condition for attachment. What does the client like to do with the caregiver?

2. Through all these experiences the newborn senses the thread and especially the predictable person behind it. *The thread is attached* (first part of stage two, first socialisation). The human, being preprogrammed to have relationships, becomes attached.

   We recognise this in clients as well. Who is the reliable person? Who picks up the thread? Who is the person who takes care of emotional refuelling and who provides comfort? Who is the person who can regulate emotions? The client experiences that there is someone who takes care of them. In cases involving clients with attachment trauma, the thread remains tangled and this developmental theme becomes a vulnerable spot in the thread.

3. To avoid the risk of symbiosis and to open the child up to others and to the exploration of the world, the parent puts a *loop in the thread* (second part of stage two, first socialisation).

   When the client always wants the caregiver to be close, the caregiver will vary the distance between them, elongating the thread. In this way, the professional consciously ensures that the client can transfer the thread to someone else. The professional circles around the client within feasible and safe limits. In this way the client learns to shape a clear image of the trustworthy person. Even when that person is gone for a while, the client can feel that the thread is still there. There is predictability in people. A transitional object, such as a stuffed animal, a toy or a sports bag that is taken everywhere, is a nice example of the loop in the thread.

   This theme is divided into three subthemes. The professional will alternate between *refuelling*, the *smooth transition* of the client to someone else and regulating *healthy boundaries*.

4. At a certain point in development, the child seeks to *draw the thread* themselves: the 'terrible twos' (stage three, first individuation).
   This client wants something from the caregiver, not only the attention of the caregiver. The caregiver feels that the thread is strong enough – even if it is pulled – to set limits and make demands. Boundaries are strengthened. Reward and punishment may work because there is the beginning of the formation of conscience.

5. For the toddler, the thread will become more and more like a *remote control* (stage four, identification).
   In the client, one recognises the first steps towards dealing with rules, social behaviour and a wider world. Punishment and reward pay off because they

are bound to the caregiver and the client does not want to lose the thread. The client learns to cope with rules even when the caregiver is not around. The self as a central part of the personality starts to fit into the surrounding world. Rules provided by important persons are internalised and can increasingly be followed from a distance. There is room for several others. The world grows. Social skills are learned. This developmental task of 'remote control' can be divided into three subthemes: remote control in *rules*, remote control in *others* and remote control in the wider *environment*.

6. At a primary-school age the thread evolves into a *contextual thread* (stage five, reality awareness). The child develops self-understanding and empathy towards others.

   This thread is aimed at the development of self functions. The child's actions start to be affected by what others may think. The child learns to attribute thoughts, intentions, feelings and ideas to themselves and others. Identity, an individual psychology and a pattern of interactions arise. At this stage one can work with contextual concepts, such as loyalty, give and take, etc.

7. In adolescence the thread turns into a *network* (stage six).

   Threads with peers emerge, making the world a bigger place. There are friends, girlfriends and boyfriends, new places and interests: a wider world. The client learns to organise their own life.

8. As an adult, all types of threads combine in a unique person who can themselves extend the thread to others: *the red thread in life* (stage seven).

   The themes discussed here are: future, meaning, perspective and quality of life. The caregiver is engaged in supporting the important further developmental tasks specific to the young adult and the adult. Being productive, building an identity, developing intimacy, integrity, usefulness, autonomy, emancipation, participation, etc. are the important life themes.

3 The thread and clients with intellectual disabilities

There is no difference in the developmental steps and the sequence of the stages between children with and without intellectual disabilities. The same themes are recognisable in members of each group. There are more similarities than differences between people with and without intellectual disabilities.

However, intellectual disability does determine to what extent a person becomes independent and what degree of support remains necessary in life. We can assume that there is an important connection between cognitive development, emotional development and social development, because certain cognitive processes are necessary for the realisation of certain threads.

This does not mean that later stages cannot be addressed, but it does mean that support is needed to shape the threads. The further a person has progressed in the development of the thread, the more language, independence and intellectual possibilities are called upon. The basic emotions of the first thread require little thinking. Socially capable behaviour and socially acceptable behaviour in the network require a lot of thinking.

The parents of children with intellectual disabilities are less able to draw on evidence from their own upbringing and education. As parents, they cannot simply look at other parents. Children with intellectual disabilities need more time, and each stage takes longer. It is important for parents to know what they can expect with regard to the intellectual disability so they do not overestimate or underestimate their child. The themes of emotional refuelling, transition and exploring – the loop in the thread – often remain very decisive in their child's life.

For a client with a *profound* intellectual disability, the themes of the first thread, 'reaching for the thread', will remain the most important. A daily schedule (the track), regulating tension (the gate) and regulating action and reaction are basic. It is important that parents are supported in organising daily life.

In the case of a person with a *severe* intellectual disability, the parent as an attachment figure will be able to loop to other people and teach the child to control themselves. Doing something and wanting things, learning skills for daily life and boundaries are important for both parent and child.

Someone with a *moderate* intellectual disability is capable of simple types of remote control. They can be trusted to follow rules and agreements, can make friends and are able to go to the convenience store independently.

> *Jack is twenty-seven. His network is the local soccer club, where he volunteers. He helps in the canteen, is responsible for overseeing the tombola, hands out the medals, cleans up the canteen, keeps track of the team's score, etc. In short, the club is his life. However, if you look closely, you can see that his father is never far away from him. His father is Jack's remote control and provides the necessary support to make Jack's network and social interaction possible.*

Someone with a *mild* intellectual disability is able to think about themselves and others in a contextual way, but needs help to adequately assess social situations and organise networks. After all, a network requires a lot of intellectual skills in terms of planning, reflection and organisation. The tension between dream and reality can lead to difficulties such as overestimation, acting tough and problems dealing with failure.

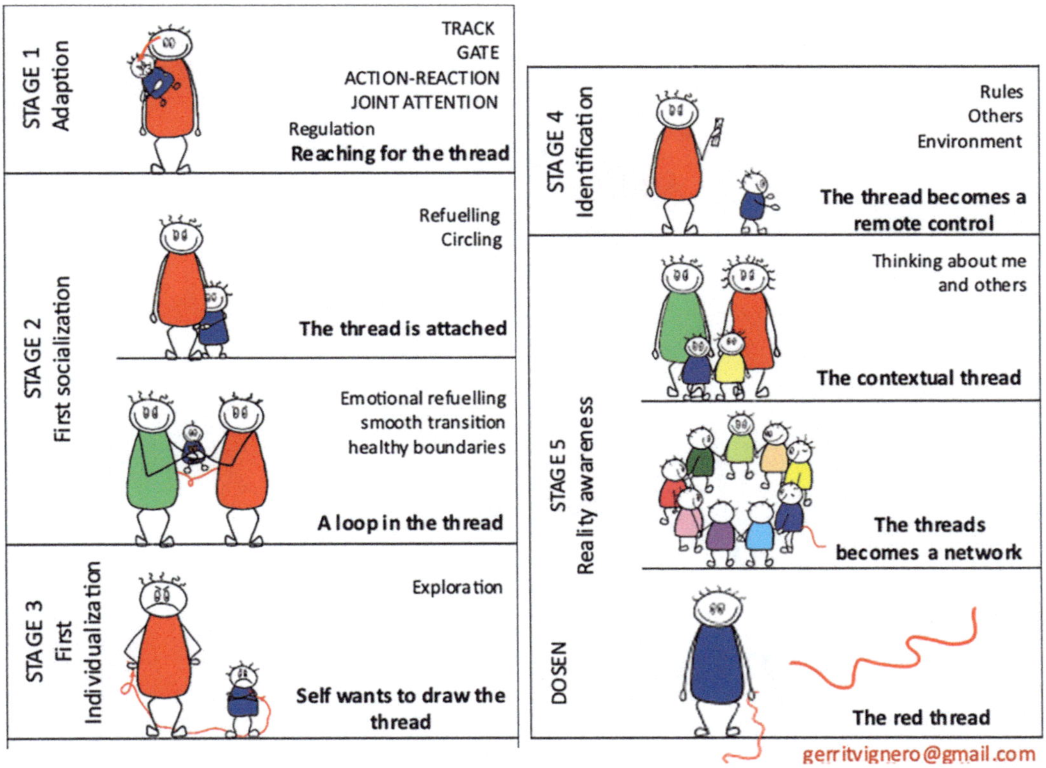

4 Diagnosis: the vulnerable spot in the thread

A person with an intellectual disability who develops harmoniously can be supported with regard to all types of thread despite the intellectual disability. The parent or companion can offer support to deal with cognitively more difficult types of thread and help to explore them.

The model does not focus on the search for the thread or the stage in which a client is situated but focuses on the dynamics (figure 19.2). How does the client deal with the various developmental themes, and what is the influence of the parent or caregiver? By using the diagnostic tool, professionals can create a diagnostic picture of the client.

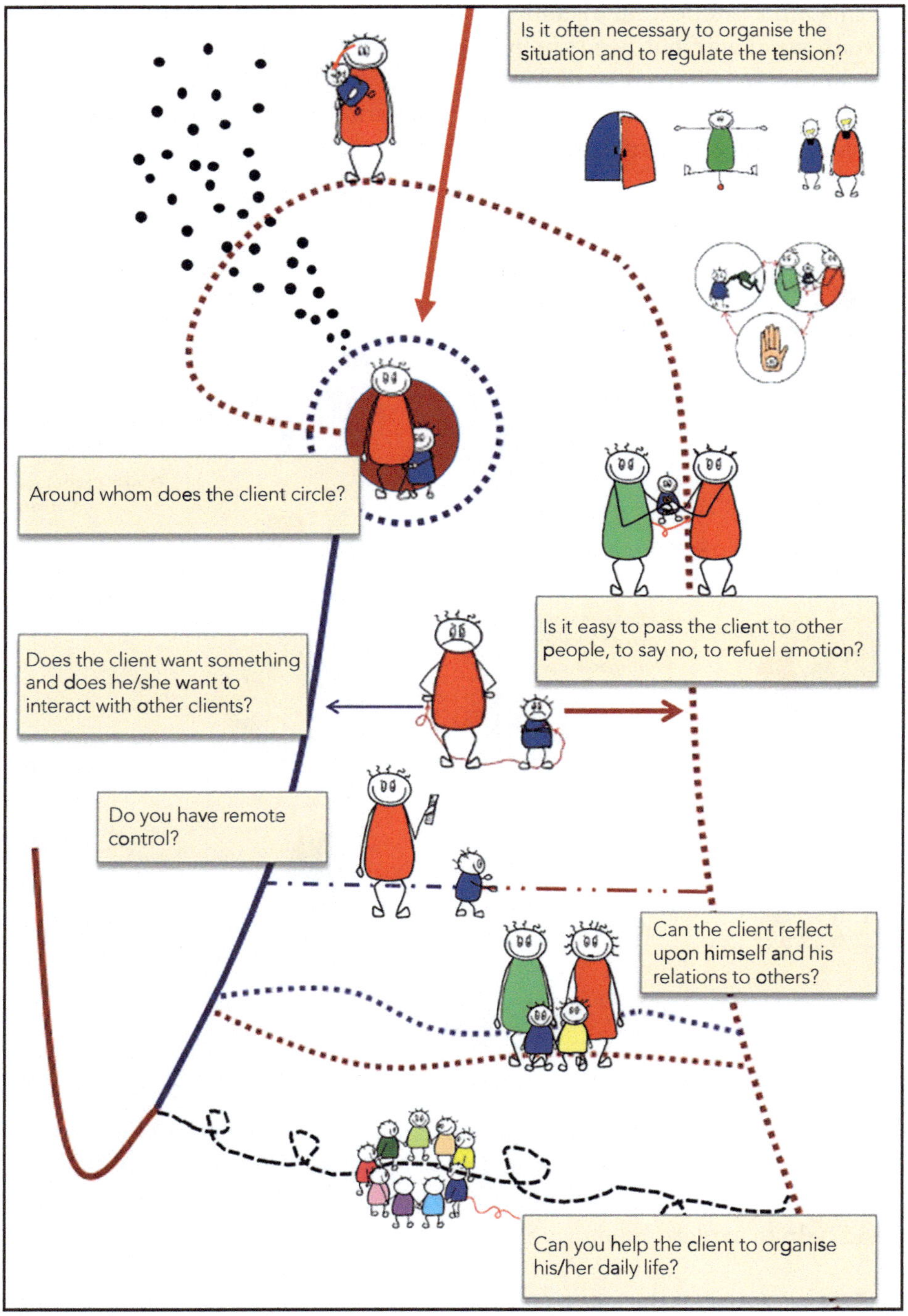

Figure 19.2 The dynamics of the thread

Jack's father dies unexpectedly. Jack is very sad. He retreats to his room, injures himself and cradles himself a lot. Because of the trauma of the death, he falls back on patterns that are characteristic of the first thread. He was very attached to his father, and now he has lost that thread. Jack has lost not only his dad as a thread but also the remote control that makes network and social interaction possible.

Luckily he also has a strong thread with his brother. His brother takes care of him and tries to pull the thread and comfort and support him. Jack's brother takes on a part of the role previously played by Jack's father but also tries to make a loop in the thread. Jack needs transport to go to football, and on the football pitch he constantly needs someone to take care of him. Jack's brother is not a soccer fan, but he can arrange for a number of daddy's soccer friends to become remote controls for Jack.

1. First one needs to analyse the basic attachment conditions and how they are organised in the setting where the client lives. How important is the track to the client? Is the daily schedule clear? How can you regulate the gate? How is the client's emotional self-regulation? What happens if there is problem behaviour? Is there action–reaction that is difficult to manage? Are there constructive forms of action–reaction? What themes lead to joint attention?
2. What is the quality of the attachment? Who is the thread for the client? Who are the most important persons for the client? Is the attachment constructive, or does the caregiver often lose their thread with the client? Can the caregiver regulate the emotions of the client? Are there signs of any attachment disorders?
3. How easy is it to make a loop in the thread? How well can the caregiver alternate between emotional refuelling, transition to other caregivers and the provision of boundaries?
4. Does a reward or a punishment have effects in the medium and long term? What does the client want? What are their interests? Can the thread be firm without the regression of the client to a previous thread? Is there regulation by rules?
5. Can you trust the client to a certain degree? How strong is the remote control of the caregiver? Can the client cope with simple rules, and is there the beginning of social interaction and theory of mind?
6. To what extent is the client capable of thinking about themselves in relation to others? What help do they need from professionals in mentalising? To what extent can the client align their action with their thinking? Is there a form of self-regulation?
7. How wide is the network of the client? Does it include family, friends, recreation, professional pursuits, hobbies? What kind of support is needed for the client to join a network?

Sometimes every tension, however little it may seem, causes a relapse into the first thread. Sometimes the client constantly claims the attention and attachment of the caregiver or the parent. Sometimes the caregiver or the parent feels that it takes a lot of energy to put a loop in the thread. Sometimes the problem behaviour is only seen at home but never at school or in the daycare centre.

In interaction with clients with challenging behaviour, it is helpful to use the diagnostic tool in combination with the SED in finding answers to cope with the behaviour. When parenting or counselling leads to tension, confusion and uncertainty, one should look for the vulnerable spot in the thread as a starting point for treatment. The thread method involves searching for the vulnerable thread and using it as a reference point in the relationship between client and caregiver.

It is my experience that, in the case of problem behaviour, the vulnerable spot often lies in the first types of thread, usually the first thread. When you do not take in account the vulnerable spot, there is a risk of overestimating the client and their socio-emotional development. That leads to an interaction in which the caregiver is not attuned to the client and to an increase in problem behaviour. Appropriate support that takes into account the emotional needs of the client will have a preventive effect on problem behaviour and increase the involvement and well-being of the client.

> *Henk, who has an autism spectrum disorder, becomes stressed when the programme is unpredictable. Recently a planned badminton activity could not take place: Henk froze. He stood at the edge of the field rocking back and forth violently. Luckily, his regular caregiver was present, who took Henk's behaviour as a sign: we will have to adjust the programme. Instead of badminton, we can schedule gaming on the iPad, something he really likes to do. Many people with autism are very attached to predictability in time, space and activities. The track is the vulnerable spot in the thread. As caregiver, you have to regulate the track. Is the situation predictable enough in time, space and activity?*
>
> *Luke is a boy from Afghanistan. He spent his early years in an orphanage. He was adopted when he was two. Pretty soon the adoptive family broke down. Luke is so unpredictable that the adoptive family had to be on their guard all the time. One day he's lovable; the next day there is one incident after another. The adoptive parents became exhausted. In the observational unit they found that it was important to take into account the topics relating to the first thread. When he was a baby, there was a lack of track, lack of rhythm and predictability and lack of a good daily schedule. He did not receive responsivity and sensitivity from the caregivers. There was*

no systematic action–reaction or joint attention. Trauma can have such an impact that the client easily falls back on the first thread, and caregivers feel that they cannot regulate emotions or the situation anymore. The attached thread stays tangled and is a vulnerable spot.

5 Treatment

Once there is a global picture of emotional and social development and of the vulnerable spot in the thread, the development themes become guidelines for treatment.

<table>
<tr><th>THE THREAD</th><th></th><th></th><th>Meaning for the CLIENT</th><th>Organising the SITUATION</th><th>Building up a wire by the CAREGIVER</th></tr>
<tr><td rowspan="6">Where is the vulnerable spot in the thread?</td><td rowspan="2">REACHING</td><td>TRACK</td><td></td><td></td><td></td></tr>
<tr><td>GATE</td><td></td><td></td><td></td></tr>
<tr><td rowspan="2">THE THREAD</td><td>ACTION–REACTION</td><td></td><td></td><td></td></tr>
<tr><td>JOINT ATTENTION</td><td></td><td></td><td></td></tr>
<tr><td colspan="2">ATTACHMENT</td><td></td><td></td><td></td></tr>
<tr><td colspan="2">THE LOOP</td><td></td><td></td><td></td></tr>
<tr><td rowspan="4">How can you help the client to explore?</td><td colspan="2">SELF</td><td></td><td></td><td></td></tr>
<tr><td colspan="2">REMOTE CONTROL</td><td></td><td></td><td></td></tr>
<tr><td colspan="2">CONTEXTUAL</td><td></td><td></td><td></td></tr>
<tr><td colspan="2">NETWORK</td><td></td><td></td><td></td></tr>
</table>

Table 19.1 Diagnostic tool

In my experience the vulnerable spot is often situated in the first three threads and has to do with emotion regulation and attachment. Once the thread is firm and attached, there is room for learning social skills and starting to explore the wider world.

The thread treatment schedule has first and foremost to do with the vulnerable spots in the thread.

As you can see in table 19.1, there are three subdivisions.

1. **The meaning for the client**. How can the meaning of the developmental task for the client be taken into account? How important is predictability for them? What kinds of self-protecting behaviour do they use to self-regulate their gate? Which signals do they give that the gate is closing? What are examples of positive action–reactions that are signs that the gate is opening again? What does the client like to do with the caregiver? What important things does the caregiver have to know about the client's preferences and interests? What are favourite locations for the client?
2. **Organising the situation**. How can the situation for the client be organised in a better way in order to meet the needs of the client? In team meetings and when offering guidance to parents, make mutual agreements about how to make the situation more predictable for the client. How can a safe place be created for the client? What do you do when there is aggression? What can be done or said in cases involving e.g. spitting or crying loudly as forms of action–reaction game on the part of the client? If you take something away from the client, what is put in its place? How can joint attention be fostered?
3. **Building up a thread by the caregiver**. How can the developmental themes be used to install or reinstall a thread with the client? How can a relationship be built up with the client? How can a programme for the caregiver be made with the client? How can professionals maintain self-control when there is aggression? How can the thread be picked up again after aggression? How might the things that the client likes to eat or to play with be used to establish joint attention?

Table 19.4 gives an overview of guidelines used in the method.

> *Charles is a ten-year-old with an attachment disorder. After a while, we noticed that the same process was taking place with new female caregivers over and over again. In the beginning Charles asks the new caregiver a lot of questions and wants to play with her, but after a while he starts claiming her. In the next stage he even stalks her. Charles wants her to take care of him exclusively. It is important for Charles and the facilitators to work on predictability in people. Instead of Charles deciding who is going to work with him, a turn-by-turn schedule is drawn up in blocks of two hours, so that it is clear which caregiver is the one who is offering the thread. A visual sign – a pin – serves as an aid, especially for the caregivers. Handing over the pin signals handing over responsibility for Charles.*

Kurt, 16 years old, can be very friendly, jovial and cheerful. He likes role play and participates in theatre. But after a period of fun and good cheer, you gradually see restlessness grow. A remark from someone is enough for him to flip. Kurt is so strong that several people sometimes have to hold him down, or the emergency services have to be called. The gate is his vulnerable spot, and when it closes, you lose your connection, your thread. In spite of Kurt's competencies, the caregiver has to focus strongly on safe situations and trying to hold the thread.

Tessa is a girl with a moderate intellectual disability and an attachment trauma. Nevertheless, she has come to fit in well in the home group. But caregivers have to remember that every new situation is exciting for her. Although it seems that she can handle much more, in new situations you have to accompany her very closely, refuelling her emotionally. Horseback riding was one of her dreams. The riding school arranged for her to do some riding. But the first time the caregiver came to the riding school with her, she did not want to get out of the car. She refused. The caregiver took a picture of the horse and agreed with the riding school to reschedule the appointment. After a while, Tessa managed to overcome her fear of the new situation. Now she even goes to the riding school on her own. With Tessa, you often see this process in new and exciting situations. If you do not take this into account, there is so much tension on the thread that problems arise. First you have to offer the thread to her. After a while you can make a loop in the thread, and eventually she can act with remote control.

6 Conclusion

The thread is a metaphor that explains emotional development for professionals and parents and offers tools for education and support. Explaining social and emotional development in a comprehensive and practical manner, the model of the thread helps the professional to find a good alignment with the client and to develop a common language in conversations with parents. It translates 'what is known about development' into 'how to use developmental topics in (special) education'. So far, the model has only been developed in Dutch. Professionals who are inspired by this article can contact the author to find out more about the model and the method.

UNTANGLING THE THREAD		CLIENT/STUDENT/CHILD	SITUATION How to manage the situation	CAREGIVER/TEACHER/PARENT Installing the thread
Reaching the thread	TRACK	How important is the daily schedule for the client? Is there a difference between organised and non-organised time? Is the daily schedule rich enough? What can the client decide in the daily schedule? What influence does the client have on the daily schedule? How does the client deal with transitions and changes? What are favourite locations for the client?	What is the daily schedule of the group? What is the daily schedule for the individual client? Is it different from that of the group? Are there major differences in different settings? How are transitions or changes in daily schedule, time, place and activity made clear to the client? What are the rules about place, time and space? Is there space for the client to nest themselves? Are 'triggers' on the end of the track used as reinforcers?	Do you have control over the daily schedule? Are there moments of encounter between client and caregiver? Which rituals help to meet the client? Do you yourself make changes and switches in the daily schedule? What is contact like, and how long can you have contact with the client?
	GATE	Draw the course of problem behaviour. Is it flight or fight? Or freeze? Which self-protective behaviours can you recognise? How many times does 'the gate close'? How does the client show that their gate is closing? How many times is there a total loss of self-control? What is relaxing for the client? What feels like a good restorative practice for the client?	What are the rules for the different stages of problem behaviour? What helps if you feel that the gate of the client is closing? Do you see differences in different settings? Are there situations that create tension?? Which activities in the daily schedule are relaxing? Are trauma-sensitive activities part of the programme? How is the situation adjusted in case of emerging tension? What is the effect on other clients? Which restraints, such as isolation, locking doors, etc., are used? Does the client take medication? What is the protocol concerning restorative practice?	Draw the course of your own tension. How do you lower your tension when you see that the gate is starting to close? What do you do when the gate is closed? How do you maintain your calmness as a caregiver? At which moment do you step out of the situation, seek help or use time out? How do you work on tension with the client? Do you take restoration to be your responsibility and not the responsibility of the client in this emotional stage?

Reaching the thread	ACTION REACTION	Is there too much or too little action–reaction? What are amusing action–reactions the client uses? Which rituals does the client use? Can you recognise challenging behaviour in negative action–reaction? What helps in taking time in action–reaction? Which action–reactions have to do with anxiety? Is action–reaction compulsive? Is action–reaction linked to a person or a situation? Is there sensory hypersensitivity? Is the client very sensitive to stimuli? Which stimuli?	Is positive action–reaction part of the daily schedule? Are there activities in the daily schedule that are based on action–reaction? How are negative action–reactions conditioned? How are situations with tensions reorganised? Which rules help to take time negative action–reaction? Are there team procedures concerning action–reaction? Do other clients have an effect on action–reaction? If you take something away from the client, are you aware that you need to give something else in its place? Are there too many or too few stimuli?	Do you use positive action–reaction in your contact with the client? Words, music, handshakes, etc.? Do different caregivers use different rituals? Is action–reaction an opportunity to build up 'contact circles'? Do you use positive action as a sign of restoration in the relation between the client and the caregiver? Do you use a 'yes message' rather than a 'no, stop'? Do you say what you expect from the client rather than what you do not expect? Does the client trigger you? Are you able to control action–reaction?
	JOINT ATTENTION	Is the client interested in daily routines? What does the client like to do with the caregiver? What are the important things you have to know: objects that they like, food, activities, pets, etc.? What is a good 'attention approach' with the client? Does the client experience doing together as emotional refuelling? Is there a risk that doing together leads to an obsession or overdemanding behaviour?	Is doing together and joint attention part of the programme? Is doing together and joint attention embedded in the daily routine activities? Is it clear that it is a matter of involvement and shared attention and not of result, output or performance? Are there activities in the programme that are 'the way is the goal' and that do away with the goal? Is doing together part of the restorative practice? What are the rules when the client becomes overdemanding? Do you use 'the attention approach' as regulation?	Which activities do you like to do with the client? How do you refuel the client emotionally? How do you involve the client in daily routine activities? Can you hold direction in 'doing together'? What do you grant to the client? What do you do or give them so they feel happy? Doing something together is a beautiful form of restoration. How do you use another track or a detour when doing together becomes claiming behaviour?

	ATTACHMENT	Has the attachment disorder to do with congenital or acquired factors? Are there signals of disruptive attachment behaviour? Who are the persons to which the client is attached? Is there difference in attachment in different environments or contexts? Is it 'flight' safety or 'attachment' safety? Does the client often fall back on topics of the first thread: action–reaction, the gate that closes? Is attachment activated in times of stress or separation? Is the client always searching for attention? Is attachment active, passive or rather symbiotic?	How many times does the system use elements of the first thread to regulate attachment? How do you deal with claiming behaviour? Are changes or transitions in the programme organised? Is predictability in persons organised? Does the system rather than a person function as a thread? Is 'together (the client and the caregiver) make it work' a slogan? What are 'the rules of the house'?	Who in the team is the real thread for the client? What do you do if the client keeps circling around you, claims you? Can you regulate the symbiosis? How do you mentalise for the client? How do you work on distance and proximity? Can you switch easily between refuelling and regulation? Do you think that you can refuel the client emotionally? How do you provide attention? How do you circle around them? What are the different attachment styles in the team, or at home? Do you see yourself as a locomotive that regulates the thread and as something the client can lean on?
	The LOOP	Draw the emotional hierarchy. Is there a difference between different settings? Is it easy for the client to switch between caregivers? What are transitional objects or rituals that refer to important persons (thread)? Is the client's type of attachment refuelling or exploring? Can the client control themselves when boundaries are provided or when they do not receive attention? Is there regression to the first thread? Is the attachment type avoidant or anxious?	Does the system make attachment constructive? How do you switch in the programme between refuelling, passing on and giving opportunities to explore? Are changes of personnel or activities organised? Are there rituals for greeting and saying goodbye? Is there a link between different settings? Are there 'loop' activities in the programme? Is there a trajectory for new caregivers? Does the client fall back on the system or on the caregiver as a person? Is 'no' or 'no attention' deliberately used in the programme?	How do you make a loop in the thread? How do you manage attention? How do you switch between refuelling and helping the client to explore? What is your position in the emotional hierarchy? Is your attachment style refuelling or exploring? How do you provide helpful boundaries? Do you mentalise about the process of the loop for the client? Do you use a transitional object as a symbol for connection? Can you maintain direction in passing the client on? How do you work together with parents and natural networks?

Table 19.4 Overview of guidelines used in the method

References

Bowlby, J (1969) *Attachment and Loss, Vol I: Attachment*. New York: Basic Books.

Bowlby, J (1969) *Attachment and Loss, Vol II: Separation, anxiety and anger*. New York: Basic Books.

Claes, L, Declercq, K, Neve, L De, Jonckheere, B, Marrecau, J, Morisse, F , Vangansbeke, T (Eds) (2012), *Emotionele ontwikkeling bij mensen met een verstandelijke beperking*. Antwerpen/Apeldoorn: Garant.

Došen, A (1990) Psychische en gedragsstoornissen bij zwakzinnigen Een ontwikkelingsdynamische benadering. Amsterdam: Boom.

Došen, A (2005a) Applying the developmental perspective in the psychiatric assesment and diagnosis of persons with intellectual disability: Part I – assessment. *Journal of Intellectual Disability Research* **49** (1) 1–8.

Došen, A (2005b) Applying the developmental perspective in the psychiatric assesment and diagnosis of persons with intellectual disability: Part II – diagnosis. *Journal of Intellectual Disability Research* **49** (1) 9–15.

Došen, A (2008) *Psychische stoornissen, gedragsproblemen en verstandelijke handicap*. Assen: Van Gorcum.

Buckwalter, K D & Reed, D (Eds) (2017) *Attachment Theory in Action Building Connections Between Children and Parents*. Laham: Rowman & Littlefield.

Fletcher, H K et al. (Eds) (2016) *Attachment in Intellectual and Developmental Disability: A clinician's guide to practice and research*. Hoboken: John Wiley & Sons Inc.

Heijkoop, J (1995) *Vastgelopen Anders kijken naar begeleiding van mensen met een verstandelijke handicap met ernstige gedragsproblemen*. Baarn: Nelissen.

Heijkoop, J (2015) *Ontdekkend kijken Basisboek Methode Heijkoop*. Heusden: Heijkoop-Academy.

Mahler, M, Pine, F & Bergman, A (1975) *The Psychological Birth of the Human Infant: Symbiosis and individuation*. New York: Basic Books.

Morisse, F & Došen, A (Eds) (2015) *SEO-R^2 Schaal voor emotionele ontwikkeling bij mensen met een verstandelijke beperking – Revised^2*. Antwerpen/Apeldoorn: Garant.

Stern, D (1985) *The Interpersonal World of the Infant*. New York: Basic Books.

Vandevelde, S, Morisse, F, Došen, A, Poppe, L, Jonckheere, B, Van Hove, G, Maes, B, Van Loon, J & Claes, C (2016) The scale for emotional development-revised (SED-R) for persons with intellectual disabilities and mental health problems: Development, description, and reliability. *International Journal of Developmental Disabilities* **62** (1) 11–23.

Vignero, G (2012, 2018) *De draad tussen cliënt en begeleider De emotionele ontwikkeling als inspiratiebron in de begeleiding van personen met een verstandelijke handicap*. Antwerpen/Apeldoorn: Garant.

Vignero, G (2015, 2020) *De draad tussen ouder en kind Voor een gewone en buitengewone opvoeding*. Antwerpen/Apeldoorn: Garant.

Vignero, G (2018) *Ontwarring en ordening van de draad Verbindend werken met cliënten met probleemgedrag*. Antwerpen/Apeldoorn: Garant.

Vliegen, N (2006) *Kleine baby's, prille ouders: Samen in ontwikkeling*. Leuven: Acco.

Part IV Review

Chapter 20
Epilogue: a constructive description of emotional development

Jac de Bruijn, Jolanda Vonk, Ad van den Broek and Brian Twint

Summary

This manual focuses on the theme of emotional development in the field of care and support for people with intellectual disabilities. This theme is becoming more and more well known within this field. We are convinced that emotional development can no longer be ignored. In chapter 1 we concluded that we are dealing with a concept of emotional development that is not yet fully grown. In our view, this is related to the multidimensional image of emotional development presented in the mind map (see figure 1.1). Multiple perspectives are used and each one is relevant. Looking at emotional development from only one perspective can lead to an incoherent picture. Vonk has previously described the importance of the relationship between emotional development and social and cognitive development and developmental age (Vonk, 2014). We concluded in chapter 1 that we have to consider emotional development as a construct built up from different layers. This manual strengthens the construct of emotional development by offering readers opportunities to:

- establish common denominators between the various characterisations of the construct of emotional development, making its meaning more unambiguous
- reduce differences between ways of thinking about and acting with the construct.

This final chapter looks back on the contributions in the manual and links the 'common denominators' with the criteria that a construct must meet. We will also look at the differences in approach. We examine the extent to which the mind map provided in chapter 1 can be adjusted to the insights this manual has provided. What do these insights contribute to the meaning of the construct in light of future trends?

1 Approaches and models: what are the common denominators?

Different approaches to emotional development can be found in the contributions to this manual. In each one the authors use certain starting points for their approaches. In addition to these starting points, some authors use underlying models (explicitly mentioned or not) in which the starting points are brought together into a kind of framework. For example, in chapter 1 our own starting point was that, in caring for people with intellectual disabilities, different perspectives on emotional development may be adopted. Each of these perspectives must be justified. That is why we adopted a frame of mind, a contextual model, in which none of the perspectives was dominant. The following common principles stand out in the contributions to this manual.

Integrative approach. Almost all authors assume an integral perspective in their approach to emotional development. This means that, when dealing with the theme of emotional development, authors pay attention to the broader developmental perspective within which emotional development takes place. This offers a multidimensional framework for emotional development in which emotional development is not seen as an isolated phenomenon. This is particularly reflected in Došen's integrative dynamic development model. The personality approach is dominant in this; that is, it is assumed that emotional development cannot be understood without insight into the development of the client's entire personality. Došen's approach is taken as a starting point by many authors, both with regard to themes such as sexual development (Visser-Korevaar & Vonk, chapter 8) and with regard to research instruments such as the Scale of Emotional Development – Short (SED-S) (Sappok & Conty, chapter 12), the Scale of Emotional Development – Revised^2 (SED-R^2) (Morisse *et al.*, chapter 13) and the SED-R^2 colour profile (De Groot, chapter 14). The model also underlies the use of these scales within forensic care for people with mild intellectual disabilities (Hesper *et al.*, chapter 15), approaches to emotional development and autism (Sappok & Ronsse, chapter 7) and methodical support (Van den Broek, chapter 16). The integral perspectives are further found in the neurocognitive approach to emotional development in relation to cognitive-neurological development and context (Wijnroks, chapter 5). And last but not least, in all the chapters on support in part III we see the same integrative approach.

Coherence. In addition to the integrative approach to emotional development, in which one 'hovers above' it, as it were, a number of authors emphasise the mutual relationship between emotional development and other developmental aspects, such as cognition (Wijnroks, chapter 5), social development and adaptation (Ponsioen, chapter 4) and attachment (Sterkenburg *et al.*, chapter 6; De Belie & Vliegen, chapter 18). This implicitly reinforces the importance of emotional development, because the cohesion is seen as necessary and conditional.

(Neuro)biological basis. Of great importance is also the biological anchoring of emotional development. This is made clear in particular by Došen and Wijnroks and is affirmed by others, explicitly or otherwise, in their contributions. Most authors generally support Došen's principles. It is noteworthy that until recently neurobiological and neuropsychological knowledge and its relevance for emotional development played a far less important role. This manual brings this knowledge and its importance explicitly to the core of the discussion and thus also helps to determine the construct.

Relevance in practice. It is not surprising that the contributions seek to connect their insights to the practice of daily care. This is evident not only from the cases presented but above all from the authors' intentions: it is their intrinsic motivation to contribute theoretical and scientific knowledge to the practice of caring for people with intellectual disabilities. Emotional development has become an important and possibly indispensable theme. This may be explained by the fact that thinking about emotional development for the first time is still an eye-opener for many professionals, and it allows them to better understand what is needed to meet basic emotional needs.

Research. Further research into the uses and value of emotional development is being developed from various perspectives, and the importance of research is emphasised by many authors in this manual. At the same time, emotional development is a theme that is far from being simply a scientific research topic.

2 Where does the concept create tension?

The fact that there are similarities between the principles and models underlying the contributions does not mean that there are no differences between them. The contributions also reveal important contradictions.

Practice. In the practice of daily care the idea of emotional development appears to have found an application, especially as a way of thinking in terms of the level of emotional functioning and developmental ages. In this manual, criticisms are levelled at the use of specific levels or stages – not unjustly. There is a real danger that the stages used in diagnostic research with the SED-R², or the developmental stages of Došen's developmental model, come to be seen as static and one-dimensional. This leads to misinterpretations in assessment and support.

Emotional development is no longer seen as an integrative and dynamic construct, but as a status in itself.

Disharmony. Related to the foregoing is a scientific difference of opinion. Wijnroks and Ponsioen call for attention to be paid to the over- or underestimation of ability and capacity. In practice, the disharmony approach is sometimes used incorrectly as a static view of linear stages of development. They criticise the dichotomic approach of disharmony precisely because this does not work in an integrative manner, despite its intentions: it opposes cognition to emotion. Wijnroks explains the biological basis for an integrative approach in his contribution.

Independence. A difficult point is touched upon in relation to independence. Is it possible to speak of emotional development as an independent aspect of overall development? Following the approach of Wijnroks, Ponsioen, Sterkenburg and others, we rather talk about stress, emotion regulation and the way in which emotions work. 'Emotional development' in itself is not a relevant term for these authors. The fact that emotions are there and that they play an essential role within a given context is recognised by everyone. Considering this integrally, from the perspective of overall development, can help. The tension therefore lies in appreciating emotional development as a specific characteristic but not an independent aspect of development. In research practice, the focus is on themes such as stress, coping, empathy, affect regulation or trauma related to emotions, without going into the emotional development itself. In scientific research, emphasis is now increasingly placed on neurocognitive and neuroaffective functioning, without mentioning emotional development as an explicit aspect (see the literature referred to in chapter 5, such as Panksepp & Watt, 2011).

This is in line with the pedagogical-educational perspective that was discussed in chapter 1. Although this perspective was not further described in this manual, it is clear that the topic of this manual connects with general developmental psychology, which is a way of translating insights into emotional development into didactic tools. This means that in the pedagogical-educational context the emphasis on emotional 'functioning' and emotional 'competencies' within developmental stages is linked to developmental ages in general. The significance of emotional development in education and care is not (yet) widely accepted. However, there are certainly opportunities to connect and learn from each other. Brackett, Elbertson and Rivers (2015) provide a framework for looking at 'social and emotional learning' through theoretical approaches of systems, learning, developmental psychology and information processing. Incidentally, they emphasise that it is still difficult for theories of emotional development to link 'levels' of emotional functioning to developmental ages, an opinion that can also be found in this manual, for example in Ponsioen's and Wijnroks's chapters (Brackett *et al.*, 2015, p. 25).

3 Current situation

In the light of all the similarities and differences, the importance of clarifying the construct of emotional development should not be underestimated. Although the definitions of intellectual disability provided by the American Association on Intellectual and Developmental Disabilities, the *Diagnostic and Statistical Manual of Mental Disorders* (fifth edition) and the International Classification of Diseases (11th revision) have shifted towards each other at the level of the underlying construct ('disability'), the concept of emotional development is not yet a distinctive element in its own right. 'It is not mentioned in the definition of intellectual disability, but is relevant in understanding how it functions' (De Bruijn *et al.*, 2014, pp. 129, 134). How relevant is the construct of emotional development, and how exactly should we define this? This manual covers a wide range of approaches, both in theory and in practice, which on the one hand fit in with Došen's approach and on the other hand find ways of broadening and critically reflecting on this approach. There are scientific studies that mainly focus on neurocognitive and neuroemotional trends and information processing in which the emotional system is an important link between primary and reflex acting and executive functioning, in which cortical functioning is dominant. Integration within the personality is possible if all systems of the brain can switch well and adaptively, and can respond to what the context or social environment requires. The importance of the element of context is not to be underestimated; however, little research has been done on this area. In other words, formulating emotional development as a construct for scientific research has not yet proved that easy.

How should we make the connection between aspects from neuropsychology, emotion regulation and emotion perception, chronic dysregulation as a result of chronic stress, psychosocial development and everyday practice? And how should we do so within a field of healthcare in which attuned treatment and a humanitarian approach are so important? How do we relate to the methods and professional therapies in which it is so important to pay attention to emotional development? Support has various components, and support that is attentive to emotional development must connect with the clients (Van den Broek, chapter 11). When the above questions, similarities and differences are taken into account, the construct of emotional development can be further developed. Here we summarise the elements of the construct mentioned in chapter 1 and relate them to emotional development.

1. *The name of the construct serves to distinguish it from other constructs and is therefore specific and unambiguous*. There is no other understanding or concept that can substitute for emotional development. Perhaps we can talk about concepts such as emotional functioning and/or emotional competencies. However, these in turn depend on an underlying construct such as emotional development. Nevertheless, it must be concluded that the construct is not yet unambiguous:

first, there is sometimes a lack of clarity about the connection with level, stage and developmental age, and second, it is argued that emotional development does not take place independently but (to a greater extent) within neurocognitive processes. This element must be anchored within the definition of emotional development. There is clearly another, deeper problem here: it is about the tension between the independence of the construct of emotional development, representing a value in itself, and the autonomy of the construct, as an independent or separate development aspect. In view of the general integrated approach which is dominant in this manual, the editors conclude that emotional development is an independent but not autonomous construct.

2. *Unambiguous communication requires the unambiguous use of the construct.* Emotional development should not be confused with other constructs. Contributions to this manual show how seriously authors approach the theme of emotional development. This can be seen as an attempt to clarify and enable communication about the theme. As we have indicated, this reveals not only the differences but also the similarities between various ways of approaching this topic. We have not yet reached a state of unambiguous usage.
3. *Everyone involved in the field should be able to use the construct in the same way.* An integrative, coherent approach that includes the 'common denominators' of the construct – other development domains, the neurobiological basis and the practical relevance of emotional development – makes it possible to achieve a better alignment with content, both in theory and in practice. However, implementation in practice still requires critical reflection, as indicated above.
4. *The construct is a representation of the current state of affairs in knowledge and application.* This manual presents the state of the art in terms of the knowledge about and application of emotional development. After 30 years of development in the use of emotional development in the care of people with intellectual disabilities, the field is facing the next step. There are a number of important tasks:

- Further research is needed into the differences between various approaches and where they agree or where they offer alternatives. There is no conflict between methods, but it has become clear from the foregoing that bridges can still be built between insights into neurocognitive development and insights into developmental dynamics. Because of increasing internationalisation, this research can also be enriched from other contexts. As mentioned above in relation to context, it is necessary to pay particular attention to the organisational environment of people with intellectual disabilities. It is becoming increasingly clear that the context and all involved systems (micro, meso and macro) are relevant for the mental health of people with intellectual disabilities (Olivier-Pijpers, 2020; Knotter, 2019).

- As we have indicated, follow-up research must be carried out into the efficacy of research instruments themselves, into what the most appropriate instruments are and into effective, practice- and evidence-based methods. The desirability of follow-up research is in line with two agenda items for the future of 'social and emotional learning' (SEL). Item one: how can we strengthen the quality of evidence in the use of programmes or support systems for SEL? And item two: how can we make these evidence-based programmes accessible to as many people as possible (Weissberg et al., 2015, p. 13)? There is a wide area of possible research in emotional development and support, for instance the role of art therapy in reducing challenging stress behaviour or the role of music therapy in relation to stress in people with intellectual disabilities (Hackett et al., 2020; Witte et al., 2020).

5. *It must be possible to use the name of the construct in various circumstances, such as diagnoses, forms of support, policy and funding*. As this manual has made clear, the concept of emotional development is already widely used, albeit not in funding applications. There has been broad support for the use of this construct in care for people with intellectual disabilities. At the same time, we are now also seeing an increasing critical reflection on it. There has been criticism of existing research instruments and how they are used, and adaptations or new instruments are being developed at the same time. Research is therefore being carried out, especially within the Network of Europeans on Emotional Development (NEED) group, into the scientific reliability of the SED-S, the use of index cases for staff training and, recently, the use of the SED-S in children (Sappok, 2016, 2019, 2020 and this manual). The emotional development construct is also used in support and treatment, and this too leads to a variation in applications.
6. *When naming the construct, the 'emotional value' and/or related meanings evoked by the name must be taken into account*. The phrase 'emotional development' has no negative connotations, we believe.

In our view, the conclusion from chapter 1 has been confirmed and reinforced by the contributions to this manual: emotional development is a construct that is well on its way to meeting the stated criteria. It is an integral, conditional and distinct aspect of human development and is of added value to the practice of caring for people with intellectual disabilities. We now are able to give a possible description of the construct of emotional development:

> *Emotional development as a construct is a multidimensional composition of specific meanings, derived from the development of basic emotions themselves, that localises emotions within the development of the personality and the handling of emotions. It is possible to distinguish emotional development within developmental psychology, but not as separate from other domains, such as social, cognitive, sexual, moral or motor development.*

The emotional development construct is of great importance, but support staff (behavioural scientists and practice-oriented researchers) can be expected to remain critical of applications in practice and to be open to new developments and trends that become visible in the theory, science and practice of healthcare for people with intellectual disabilities.

4 Conclusion

It may be clear that the fact that the concept of emotional development has acquired such an important place in the care of people with intellectual disabilities over the last 30 years is mainly due to Anton Došen. Došen's model primarily focused on the mental health of people with intellectual disabilities. He has propagated his views nationally and internationally (see, for example, Došen, 1993). His model is still of great value in the treatment of problem behaviour and psychiatric disorders. This is evident from a diversity of developments in research and support methods. In the meantime, and perhaps precisely because of the foregoing, attention has also been paid to other approaches to emotional development. This has led to critical voices and to the broadening of the emotional development construct in other models and movements. In order to do justice to the title 'manual', it was necessary to weigh the merits of the construct critically and constructively and to link it to the complex, sometimes conflicting practices of other movements in order to substantiate the reports on the current state of affairs contained in the contributions to this manual.

This manual is the result of dialogue that was sometimes fierce. Extensive discussions were held within the board of editors and with various authors about chapters' titles, places within the manual and relationships to other parts. It was sometimes asked whether something should be a part of the manual at all. In this dialogue, all authors contributed to the search for connections and to an understanding of where certain contributions fitted or really made sense. In doing so they drew on how they encounter emotional development in their work as professionals in practice, but also as researchers. This was a search for what was important and why. At the end, we also took a critical look at each other: was everything covered, should there have been more attention paid to other aspects and have we done justice to the intentions? That also made it possible to look ahead at the developing construct we now see before us. To be sure, it is clear that we did not cover everything – additional aspects have already been mentioned in this epilogue. Finally, no one was in any doubt about the importance of the manual itself: something like this just had to happen. The realisation of this manual has involved an enthusiastic and pleasant effort and co-operation. In the editors' view, this manual has created a useful, multidimensional construct of emotional development as a basis for scientific research and new forms of good practice. As such this manual is an invitation for further development, discussion and research.

References

Brackett, MA, Elbertson, NA, & Rivers, SE (2015) Applying theory to the development of approaches to SEL . In: JA Durlak, CE Domitrovich, RP Weissberg & TP Gullotta (Eds) *Manual of Social and Emotional Learning Research and Practice* (pp21–32). New York/London: Guilford Press.

Bruijn, J de, Buntinx, W & Twint, B (2014) Definiëring in context revisited. In: J de Bruijn, W Buntinx & B Twint (Eds) *Verstandelijke beperking: definitie en context* (pp129–143). Amsterdam: SWP.

Došen, A (1993) *A Developmental-psychiatric Approach in the Diagnosis of Psychiatric Disorders of Persons with Mental Retardation*. Venray: Nieuw Spraeland.

Hackett, SS, Zubala, A, Aafjes-van Doorn, K, Chadwick, Y, Harrison, TL, Bourne, J, Freeston, M, Jahoda, A, Taylor, JL, Ariti, C, McNamara, R, Pennington, L, McColl, E & Kaner, E (2020) A randomised controlled feasability study of interpersonal art psychotherapy for the treatment of aggression in people with intellectual disabilities in secure care. *Pilot Feasibility Stud* **6** 180 (2020) https://doi.org/101186/s40814-020-00703-0.

Knotter, MH (2019) *The Whole is More: A contextual perspective on attitudes and reactions of staff towards aggressive behaviour of clients with ID in residential institutions*. Amsterdam: Universiteit van Amsterdam; Enschede: De Twentse Zorgcentra.

Olivier-Pijpers, V (2020) *Organisational Environment and Challenging Behaviours in Residents with Intellectual Disabilities: An ecological perspective*. Rotterdam: EUR.

Panksepp, J & Watt, D (2011) What is basic about basic emotions? Lasting lessons from affective neuroscience. *Emotion Review* **3** (4) 387–396 doi: 10.1177/1754073911410741.

Vonk, J (2014) Emotionele ontwikkeling Samenhang met sociale en cognitieve ontwikkeling en ontwikkelingsleeftijd. In: J de Bruijn, W Buntinx & B Twint (Eds) *Verstandelijke beperking: definitie en context* (pp101–112). Amsterdam: SWP.

Weissberg, RP, Durlak, JA, Domitrovich, CE & Gullotta, TP (2015) Social and emotional learning past, present, and future. In: JA Durlak, CE Domitrovich, RP Weissberg & TP Gullotta (Eds) *Manual of Social and Emotional Learning: Research and practice* (pp3–19). New York/London: Guilford Press.

Witte, M de, Lindelauf, E, Moonen, X, Stams, GJ & Hooren, S van (2020) Music therapy interventions for stress reduction in adults with mild intellectual disabilities: Perspectives from clinical practice. *Psychology* 10 December 2020 https://doi.org/10.3389/fpsyg.2020.572549.

Chapter 21 Closing statements by the advisory board

In this last chapter of the manual the floor is given to the members of the advisory board. Each member had the opportunity to make a final remark or statement or to draw some conclusions. These remarks are inspired by and relate to the closing remarks in chapter 20. Thanks to the closure statements of the advisory board members, the knowledge contained within this manual will be more widely disseminated, increasing awareness of the relevance of emotional development and the importance of research into this topic.

The collective experience of the members of the board covers a broad range of content, practice and research. Some have worked in this area for decades, on national and international levels. Their continued efforts show their commitment and determination to improve our understanding of and support for people with intellectual disabilities.

Anton Došen

Scientists have recently been paying increased attention to emotional development. Emotional development is being regarded as an essential part of personality development, responsible for physical adaptation and survival, as well as for intrapersonal and interpersonal psychological processes and social behaviour.

These findings can be considered as revolutionary because they change traditional thinking in psychiatry and psychology about cognitive supremacy in psychosocial development and psychic life. Emotions, cognition and sociability emerge at different time sequences of brain maturation and are considered as three different brain systems. In brain maturation these systems become strongly linked to each other and form a personality. However, each system may develop to a certain degree independently of the others, and may play a decisive role in the onset of personality characteristics as well as in the onset of a disturbed development and psychopathology.

By determining the level of emotional development, explanations for behaviour may be found and insight into a person's basic emotional needs may be achieved. Knowledge of the level of emotional development is an important tool in diagnostics as well as in support strategies and treatment for problem behaviour and psychopathology.

Angela Hassiotis

The editors Jac de Bruijn, Jolanda Vonk, Ad van den Broek and Brian Twint have accomplished an important task in producing this book. It is a major contribution to the understanding of the emotional development of people with intellectual and developmental disabilities, which is often omitted in other textbooks. In any other population group, emotional development is at the core of growing as an individual and improving one's prospects in adult life with regards to forming enduring, close bonds with others and reaching one's potential. Rightly, the chapters link emotional development with each of the major issues seen in clinical practice, while the introduction creates the theoretical scaffolding for the overall book. Finally, the book also devotes sections to the measurement of emotional development and treatment options. Appreciation of emotional development is an essential aspect of psychological management and possibly of treatment success. Many people with intellectual and developmental disabilities are unable to fully make use of therapy, as often they view the world as persecutory and demeaning to them. They may have suffered multiple trauma and because of their life circumstances may not have been able to establish trusting relationships. Early adverse experiences underpin and perpetuate mental ill health, which compounds the challenges that people with intellectual and developmental disabilities face.

As practising health professionals, we are all aware of the trauma, often unrecognised, that is suffered by people with intellectual and developmental disabilities across the lifespan and that may cause further impairment. Emotional regulation is central to maintaining equilibrium and to reducing anxiety or anger. Helping people with intellectual disabilities to learn strategies that facilitate appropriate expression of emotions is intrinsic to emotional well-being, better quality of life and improved health. While there is a significant amount of published research on the association between mental ill health and challenging behaviour, the latter is, in my opinion, a term that is rather reductionist and fails to fully appreciate the importance of emotional development. People with intellectual disabilities face multiple and complex challenges due to a whole host of biological and psychosocial factors. Unpacking the mechanisms that maintain what can be chronic mood states is likely to be of benefit in utilising or developing new and existing treatments to improve therapeutic outcomes. Trajectories that lead to anger and irritability are some of the emerging research areas in populations without intellectual disabilities but are nevertheless pertinent and ripe for further investigation in those with intellectual disabilities.

I welcome this book in that it articulates those issues clearly and comprehensively from multiple perspectives. It is only when we understand the underlying reasons for our patients' distress that we can begin to help them effectively.

Mark Hudson

I came to the field of emotional development in my first post-qualification role, where I worked in an inpatient unit for children with intellectual disabilities and severe challenging behaviour. Here, I was struck by the predominance of the medical model and a behavioural approach to working with these children that did not seem to capture the quality of interaction that was needed. I had previously worked in a community team for looked-after children, and recognised some similarities in their early emotional needs. While I was familiar with attachment theory, I lacked a well-validated scale to measure their stage of emotional development. Then, I found Anton Došen's Scheme for Appraisal of Emotional Development and, after joining the Network of Europeans on Emotional Development (NEED) group, have since embarked on a wonderful journey, which has provided much companionship and intellectual stimulation in my work with families.

The significance of the developmental approach lies in its focus on recognising and facilitating people's basic emotional needs, which are often missed in the routine care of people with intellectual disabilities. The cognitive differences shown by this group affect their interaction with caregivers from a very early age, often leading to situations where they feel overwhelmed, which impedes the development of social-emotional skills. It is my belief that greater education in this approach will go a long way towards improving the quality of care and mental health of people with intellectual disabilities.

Filip Morisse

Emotional development is universal and therefore not a categorical explanatory model for people with intellectual disabilities. It is fundamentally the same for every human being. There is no other 'kind' of emotional development for people with disabilities, for the simple reason that they are not a different kind of people. The benefit of this fact is that it makes it easier for us to mentalise about the emotional development and emotional needs of clients, about ourselves as professionals and about our relationships. Even in the case of certain 'extreme' behaviours, the same universal emotional needs must be met in the most humane, inclusive and normal way possible. However, practice shows that alienating, segregating, freedom-restricting and punitive measures are still applied.

We propose a two-fold paradigm shift. The first shift relates to understanding the behaviour of clients as an expression of a full and dynamic intrapsychic life. This shift should be interpreted primarily from a developmental and, in particular, from an emotional developmental perspective. The second paradigm shift, in terms of support, is one from an idea of the 'problem client' to an idea of a supportive environment that tries to align with and adapt to the client's basic emotional needs. Mental health problems and care environments for people with intellectual disabilities are complex, intricate and multilayered. Consideration of the care environment must take into account various processes in parallel (support staff, family, physical and social environment, management, policy, etc.).

Further conceptual research into the applicability of universal frameworks and models (e.g. quality of life, inclusion, the UN Convention on the Rights of Persons with Disabilities, the recovery approach, determination theory) can, in our opinion, take place in a practice-oriented way with the clients themselves, alongside their natural and professional networks. It could strengthen the theoretical basis of support and treatment and make people with intellectual disabilities less of a target group.

Strengthening the psychometric characteristics of the different scales for emotional development seems advisable, although this should be done in such a way as not to reduce emotional development to observable behaviour and not to see emotional functioning as the sum of unique and specific items (see e.g. the research of the NEED group).

With regard to improving the professional environment of these clients, researchers could consider developing or testing this process towards the family of these clients.

Another important element could be not only to attempt to strengthen the mentalisation abilities of professionals but to base these attempts on the personality and attachment styles of caregivers. While the method mainly focuses on the direct interaction of staff with clients (micro level), a similar programme could be developed at meso level (human resources policy, leadership, the culture of organisations, continuity of care) and at a macro level in society and politics. There are certainly enough challenges ahead!

Tanja Sappok

Leave no one behind is the guiding principle of the United Nations 2030 agenda that takes up the demand to consider and include persons with disabilities within global sustainability strategies in order to achieve the 17 sustainable development goals. The UN envisions 'a world with equitable and universal access to quality education at all levels, to health care and social protection, where physical, mental and social well-being are assured'. To promote physical and mental health and well-being, and to extend life expectancy for all, universal health coverage and access to quality healthcare must be achieved, and 'no one must be left behind.' Specifically, the UN commits 'to the prevention and treatment of non-communicable diseases, including behavioural, developmental and neurological disorders, which constitute a major challenge for sustainable development'.

Intellectual disability affects about 100 million people worldwide. The health problems frequently associated with intellectual disability lead to significant emotional, social and financial burdens for the patients and their social networks. The developmental approach may enrich the understanding of the prerequisites for well-being in persons with developmental delays and may further promote mental health in this highly vulnerable population. Therefore, the integration of developmental neuroscience into clinical practice and care for persons with intellectual disabilities is central to goal three of the UN 2030 agenda: 'Ensure healthy lives and promote well-being for all at all ages.'

Other titles from Pavilion Publishing

Trauma and Intellectual Disability. Acknowledgement, identification and intervention

by Nigel Beail, Pat Frankish and Allan Skelly (2021)

Frankish Assessment of the Impact of Trauma in Intellectual Disability (FAIT)

by Dr Pat Frankish (2019)

The CaPDID Training Manual. A Trauma-informed Approach to Caring for People with a Personality Disorder and an Intellectual Disability

by Jo Anderson, Dr Max Pickard, Emma Young and Toby Young (2020)

Trauma-informed Care in Intellectual Disability.

A self-study guide for health and social care support staff by Dr Pat Frankish (2019)

Nought to three – becoming me.

A guide for parents (and those who support them) by Dr Pat Frankish (2019)

Mental Health in Intellectual Disabilities (5th Edition)

by Dr Colin Hemmings (2018)

Guided Self-help for People with Intellectual Disabilities and Anxiety and Depression

by Eddie Chaplin (Ed) (2014)

Introduction to Mental Health and Mental Wellbeing for Staff Supporting Adults with Intellectual Disabilities

by Eddie Chaplin, Karina Marshall-Tate, Steve Hardy and Ruwani Ampegama (2019)

Introduction to Mental Health and Mental Wellbeing for staff supporting adults with intellectual disabilities: a training pack

by Ruwani Ampegama, Karina Marshall-Tate, Eddie Chaplin and Steve Hardy (2019)

Moss-PAS (ID), Moss-PAS ChA, Moss-PAS Diag(ID), Moss-PAS Check. Mental health assessments for adults and children with and without intellectual disabilities

by Dr Steve Moss

I Can Feel Good. DBT-informed skills training for people with intellectual disabilities and problems managing emotions 2nd Ed

by Sarah Ashworth, Natalie Brotherton, Bridget Ingamells and Catrin Morrisey (2019)

Attachment-based Practice with Adults. Understanding strategies and promoting positive change

by Clark Baim and Tony Morrison (2011)

Responsive Communication. Combining attention to sensory issues with using body language (intensive interaction) to interact with autistic adults and children

by Phoebe Caldwell et al (2019)

